Harvard Studies in Business History • 52

Published with the support of the
Harvard Business School

EDITED BY

Walter A. Friedman
*Lecturer of Business Administration*
*Director, Business History Initiative*

AND

Geoffrey Jones
*Isidor Straus Professor of Business History*
*Faculty Chair, Business History Initiative*

Harvard Business School

# RAILROADS AND THE TRANSFORMATION OF CHINA

ELISABETH KÖLL

Harvard University Press

Cambridge, Massachusetts
London, England
2019

*Library of Congress Cataloging-in-Publication Data*
Names: Köll, Elisabeth, 1965– author.
Title: Railroads and the transformation of China / Elisabeth Köll.
Other titles: Harvard studies in business history ; 52.
Description: Cambridge, Massachusetts : Harvard University Press, 2019. |
Series: Harvard studies in business history ; 52 | Includes
bibliographical references and index.
Identifiers: LCCN 2018014456 | ISBN 9780674368170 (hardcover : alk. paper)
Subjects: LCSH: Railroads—China—History. | Railroads and state—China—History. |
Infrastructure (Economics)—China.
Classification: LCC HE3288 .K65 2019 | DDC 385.0951—dc23
LC record available at https://lccn.loc.gov/2018014456

*In memoriam Michael Quirin*

# Contents

# List of Figures and Maps

## Figures

## Maps

# A Note on Measures, Romanization, and Translations

The primary and secondary sources I consulted for this book use a mix of kilometers and miles. For convenience, I converted all to American miles (1 mile = 1.6 km). All tonnage figures for freight transport are given in metric tons.

I have used the Pinyin system of romanization for Chinese terms throughout the book. The only exceptions are certain Chinese names of places or people that are more familiar to English readers in other romanizations, such as Canton (instead of Guangzhou), Chiang Kai-shek (instead of Jiang Jieshi), or Sun Yat-sen (instead of Sun Zhongshan), especially for the pre-1949 period. The different romanizations in Western-language correspondence, documents, and published sources of the names of railroad lines during the pre-1949 period can sometimes be confusing. I introduce the railroads by their conventional romanized names used at the time of their construction (for example, the Tientsin-Pukow Railroad) and thereafter use the Pinyin name (Tianjin-Pukou) to refer to the line during the remainder of the discussion.

# Railroads and the Transformation of China

# Introduction

This book is about the development of railroads as business and administrative institutions in China from the late nineteenth century to the reform period of the post-Mao years. Exploring the role of railroads as institutions with social, economic, cultural, and political functions, this study addresses the questions of how and to what extent railroads affected China's development throughout the twentieth century, and conversely, how this trajectory left an imprint on the railroad itself as a bureaucratic and economic system. Because the appearance of railroads in China coincides with the last decades of the Qing dynasty (1644–1911), the trajectory of railroad development over the last 120 years also provides a lens through which to view the transformation of Chinese society and economy in the transition from empire to the People's Republic of China (PRC). In short, this book is as much an institutionally informed history of railroad development in China as it is a focus for exploring important themes emerging in Chinese history across the twentieth century.

The Tientsin-Pukow (Tianjin-Pukou; abbreviated Jin-Pu) line provides a good example to briefly introduce the history of railroads framed by major political and socioeconomic developments in China's history. When the line opened in December 1912, Chinese were able to travel by rail from Tianjin, a major commercial city approximately eighty miles southeast of Beijing, to Shanghai for the first time. The trip took three days and two nights because of required overnight stops at Ji'nan and Xuzhou stations and time-consuming transfers across the Yellow River and the Yangzi River by boat and steam launch. However, as an excited foreign newspaper correspondent reported, through travel on this trunk line was "quicker than by sea and at the same time not any more expensive."[1] In the following years the train trip became easier with the construction of the Yellow River bridge at Lekou, the introduction of daily express service, and nighttime train service. During the time of the Republic of China (1911–1949) the line moved freight and passengers between northern China, the Shandong peninsula, and the Yangzi delta. Chinese Nationalist troops and anti-Japanese resistance fighters unsuccessfully tried to wrestle control of the line from the Japanese military occupiers during the second Sino-Japanese war (1937–1945). In the ensuing civil war (1945–1949) between Communists and Nationalists, the trunk line became a strategic cornerstone in the military encounters between both sides and in the Communist troop advance from the north to Nanjing and Shanghai, aiding in the Communists' final victory over the Nationalists in 1949.

After the 1949 revolutionary takeover of the government by the Chinese Communist Party (CCP), the Jin-Pu trunk line resumed its former function of freight and passenger transport. As the backbone of the eastern railroad corridor it linked the northern and southern railroad networks, and with new lines under construction, it brought provinces in the southern, central, and northwestern regions of China closer to the capital and the socialist agenda of the new political leadership. At the height of Maoist radicalism during the Cultural Revolution in the 1960s, the Jin-Pu line struggled to move thousands of Red Guards and revolutionary youth from all over the country to Beijing to attend mass rallies and to see Chairman Mao in Tiananmen Square. In the wake of China's opening, economic reform, and modernization policies introduced by Deng Xiaoping in 1978, railroads again began to play an important role as national infrastructure contributing to economic development and social mobility, including tourism. In fact, some readers of this book will have traveled the route of the Jin-Pu line when they took the Beijing-Shanghai high-speed train, which parallels the old train corridor and cuts the travel time between the political and commercial centers to less than five hours.

Since the beginning of the twenty-first century, China has become a leader in rail network expansion, which occupies a central role in the government's vision for the country's future economic and political leadership on the domestic and global stage. Confirming this vision, Premier Li Keqiang, in his capacity as head of the State Council, announced on June 29, 2016, an ambitious strategic plan that emphasizes the role of China's railroads as the "lifeline for the economy" and projects an expansion of high-speed tracks to 19,000 miles and conventional rail tracks to 93,000 miles by 2020. Apart from these construction plans, the government continues to experiment with railroad-sector reform to tackle the challenges facing the mammoth railroad administration with its huge workforce and the operational and organizational complexity of an expansive, asset-heavy system spanning every single province in the country.[2]

The articulation of an ambitious master plan for national railroad development by the current Chinese government has historical precedents. In 1921 Sun Yat-sen, the founder of the Chinese Republic and nominal appointee as director of National Railroad Development, proposed his master plan for the Republic's economic reconstruction in *The International Development of China*. Sun's ideas of inviting international capital for building railroads and other infrastructure projects revolved around the proposed large-scale expansion of the communications network, including 100,000 miles of new railroads, across all of the Chinese territory. His vision did not come to pass during the Republic, but the ambitious plans of the Chinese government under Xi Jinping align to a great extent with Sun Yat-sen's vision of national unification and political consolidation in tandem with economic modernization through rail expansion even beyond the nation's borders.[3]

Adding to the historical continuity of these national development plans, the strong, enduring institutional presence of railroads in contemporary China is striking and has impressed me ever since my student days as an avid train traveler during the late 1980s. The administrative challenge of serving hundreds of millions of passengers and the demands for freight transport that increase every year are just two obvious institutional characteristics of China's extensive rail system. In rail hub cities the noticeable existence of whole neighborhoods close to stations and rail yards with large work units, including apartment housing, kindergartens, schools, and hospitals, under the administrative umbrella of the local railroad bureau presents another aspect of the institutional railroad presence in China.[4] Today's workers and employees serving in the operation and administration of the railroad network still constitute a tightly knit community with strong professional and social identities.

Taking the continuing bureaucratic presence and economic significance of the railroad system for Chinese state and society in the second decade of the twenty-first century as points of departure, the goal of this historical analysis is to trace the origins of the system over time and to identify historical continuities and disruptions. This explains the rough chronological order of the topical chapters, each of which makes a different argument in relation to the railroad as an institution and its broader significance for our understanding of modern China.

## Railroads as Institutions

Considering the enduring strength and high visibility of China's rail sector today, the country's late entry into the railroad age might come as a surprise. We can trace China's first experiments with the introduction of railroad technology and construction efforts to the last decades of the nineteenth century, when in nearly every other major country railroads were already yesterday's news. The United Kingdom, the birthplace of rail transport, was some two generations ahead of China. In 1895, England and Wales boasted 14,651 miles of open tracks. With just 195 miles of rails operating before 1895, China would not match this mileage until the late 1930s (see Map 0.1).[5]

From a historian's perspective, many different methodological approaches can be used to tell the story of railroads as a technology and infrastructure in a particular national context. Considering its vast territory with its great regional and economic diversity, trying to capture the institutional evolution and socioeconomic impact of railroads in China in one book may seem to be an overly ambitious undertaking. In most national histories, railroads are considered functions of and metaphors for economic, social, and cultural modernization. As a result, a vast body of academic literature explores railroads in the West by discussing their role in relation to technological innovation and the Industrial Revolution, the rise of capitalism, and the emergence of the modern nation-state. For example, among historians working in the context of national histories in Britain, the United States, India, and Japan, railroads occupy a central role in debates about the causal relationship between infrastructure and economic growth, industrialization and financial capitalism, and the transition from empire and colonial rule to a modern nation-state. By comparison, similar studies on railroads in Chinese history are rare.[6]

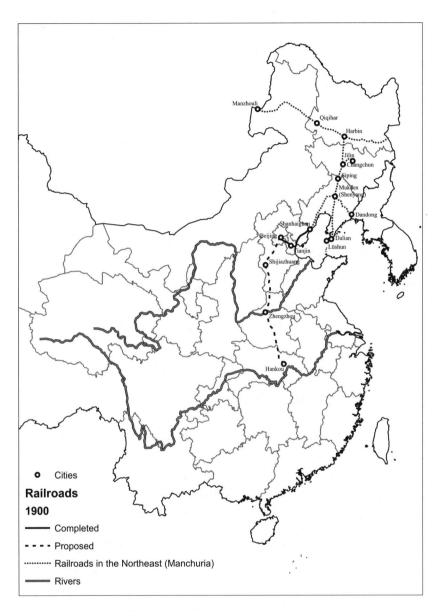

**Map 0.1** Railroads in China, 1900. Map © Elisabeth Köll (cartographic design Matthew Sisk).

The paucity of historical analyses following these established approaches has several reasons. On the one hand, China did not experience an industrial revolution or economic system with some degree of capitalist market orientation until the late twentieth century; therefore, any conceptualization of a framework for an economic analysis has to follow a broader approach outside the confines of a narrow history of capitalism. On the other hand, the origins of the railroad system in China at the end of the nineteenth century and beginning of the twentieth century occurred under semicolonial conditions. I use this term to mean that at the time China had to negotiate with several different nations trying to impose their specific financial, technological, managerial, and linguistic requirements on the process of railroad construction and management. I argue that this situation led to a patchwork of managerial structures and technical standards that converged toward centralization and became more unified only in the late Republican period under the Guomindang government in 1928. As this study shows, Chinese railroads absorbed institutional aspects of foreign management and operational practices while adapting to the political environment of fragmented central state power. My most important argument rests on the interpretation that this trajectory eventually led to an administrative hierarchy empowering railroad bureaus with a surprising degree of regional autonomy. I consider this argument especially important because it offers a historically anchored, institutional explanation for the continuing power of regional railroad bureaus within China's rail administration after 1949, even when a strong central state was in place.

As a business historian, I decided to discuss Chinese railroads as business institutions and administrative units. Before 1911, most railroads were under the financial control of foreign syndicates that evaluated the business performance of these Sino-foreign railroad ventures from the perspective of foreign bondholders and investors. After the founding of the Republic, most of the Sino-foreign railroad companies were nationalized and became part of the administration for Chinese government railroads. Although the process of nationalization restored Chinese political sovereignty over the railroads, I argue that it was not a straightforward process in terms of establishing full Chinese managerial and operational independence. Because most contractual financial agreements required the employment of foreign engineers and other professionals, Chinese railroads operated in a hybrid fashion, as part of the government railroad administration but with foreign business managers. After the 1949 revolution, all railroads were integrated into the socialist, state-controlled economy as part of the central government bureaucracy under the Ministry of Railways.[7]

In tracing the institutional evolution of railroad companies and their role in the emergence of China's modern economy and society during the twentieth century, I use the term "institution" according to Max Weber's definition of the business institution as a rational, profit-seeking economic organization with enforced regulations and a technical, operational entity divided between administrators and workers. Of course, Weber discussed the development of bureaucratic structures and institutions in the context of the emergence of the modern capitalist enterprise. In the field of business history, Alfred Chandler's *The Visible Hand* established a milestone by characterizing American railroad companies as the first modern business enterprises and as pioneers in structural and organizational innovation under managerial capitalism. However, Chandler's approach has limits as a methodological framework for our inquiry because of the absence of large-scale industrialization and managerial capitalism in the pre-1949 Chinese economy.[8]

What matters for our discussion is that institutions may arise within a culture, or they can move from one culture to another. For example, a decline of the imperial government's central power and the influence of the West led to new institutional arrangements for doing business in China in the early twentieth century. Historians have shown how the combination of different traditions influenced the evolution of the firm as an economic organization in China.[9] This raises the question of whether the evolution of railroads under semicolonial conditions led to a convergence of different traditions in their institutional organization and business practices. I argue that, especially in the first half of the twentieth century, Chinese railroad companies demonstrated institutional convergence but also substantial institutional disparities because of their application of indigenous practices in labor management and regional economic orientation while being absorbed into an increasingly centralized state bureaucracy.

Applying the institutional approach to railroad development in China allows the historian to address multiple aspects of the institution while anchoring the analysis in the evolution of the organizational management and operations as well as the physical structures and facilities. Issues related to technology transfer, labor, management, political impact, and cultural representation inform my analysis and permit a fuller discussion of the operation and reception of railroads in Chinese society. The inclusion of the important social and cultural impacts of railroads in Chinese society not only conveys with greater detail the interactions between institution and local society at the elite and nonelite levels but also allows comparisons with claims in the large scholarly literature on railroad culture in other national contexts. For example, I argue that, from the early Republic onward, Chinese writers, novelists, and poets captured the essence of the new social interactions and gender dynamics experienced by passengers on the train and in its compartments. As their works show, train culture and travel as an individual and social experience was perceived by Chinese passengers not much differently from how it was perceived by railroad travelers in the West.

Most importantly, the institutional approach enables us to follow railroad development across perceived markers, such as the transition to a socialist nation-state in 1949, because the railroads as infrastructure and their institutional apparatus remained an important part of the Chinese government bureaucracy before and after the Communist revolution. The institutional approach also allows exploration of railroads beyond the confines of specific geographical areas, such as a region or province, by comparisons among lines within the national system.

To provide regional diversity in my analysis and a comparative angle on railroad development at the national level, I selected three major railroad lines as case studies for an institutional analysis: the Tientsin-Pukow (Tianjin-Pukou) line in northern China, ultimately linking the capital to the lower Yangzi area near Nanjing; the Canton-Hankow (Guangzhou-Hankou) line in the south, connecting Canton (Guangzhou) and the Pearl River delta with core cities along the Yangzi River in central China; and the Shanghai-Hangzhou-Ningbo line, an important railroad connecting the commercial center of Shanghai with the most prosperous part of Zhejiang province. Apart from covering regional and institutional diversity, this approach also accounts for the diverse nature of sources necessary for this project and their scattered locations within China and overseas. These three lines, especially the Jin-Pu line, offer the most comprehensive body of archival resources for the pre-1949 period, allowing me to document the construction process and the interactions between foreigners and Chinese employees in managing the rail operations, land acquisition, local labor, and negotiations with Chinese officials in great detail. One of the goals of this book is to show how railroads were actually built and how the collaboration between Chinese and foreigners functioned at the construction site, in the administrative office, and at the station. Establishing these processes and dynamics supports my argument that railroad construction in the post-1949 period shows certain continuities in construction management as well as in the relationship between state and local society, even if the construction by then was conducted by the railroad construction corps of the People's Liberation Army (PLA).

Although I seek to show that the case of railroad development in China is a complex story of structural and external problems delaying large-scale expansion in the pre-1949 period, I also argue that as such it is not an extraordinary story. Here my analysis speaks to the historian Richard White's work on railroads in North America.[10] White acknowledges the transformative power of railroads, connecting the United States to world markets, but he also interprets their politics, finances, labor, and environmental consequences as near disasters, in that many railroads were powerful but unsuccessful companies in need of government subsidies for survival. Considering White's assessment of railroads and their mixed contribution to nineteenth-century American society and economy, I suggest that in comparison the initial phase of Chinese railroad development should be evaluated in a more positive light than it has been in past historical studies. As I argue, many of the structural problems in China's early railroad development emerged from its semicolonial and preindustrial environment, but they were not related to either different cultural concepts or technological prejudices. Thus, a major theme throughout this book involves the pragmatism in the embrace of railroad construction and transportation at all levels of society throughout Chinese history.

## Studies in Chinese Railroad History

With regard to the introduction of railroads as a technology and infrastructure in late imperial China, Western as well as Chinese scholars have focused on the public discourse among Chinese officials and elites about the political and economic advantages and disadvantages of railroad construction. The political and diplomatic history of railroads in the context of semicolonialism informs some studies with a focus on the transition from the late Qing to the

Republican period. Recently, new studies on various aspects of public finance and Chinese railroad investment as well as the structure of foreign financial investment in railroad ventures have contributed to our understanding of why Chinese state-funded and private investment never became a valid alternative to foreign capital investment in the late nineteenth and early twentieth centuries. The Railway Rights Recovery Movement in Sichuan province, and its impact on the trajectory of the 1911 revolution, provides another angle for studies investigating questions of nationalism and imperialism at the end of the Qing empire.[11]

A few studies center on the economic role of railroads in China. Issues of economic imperialism and the effect of railroads on market growth are at the center of Ralph Huenemann's macroeconomic analysis, which ends with the Japanese invasion in 1937. Although published more than thirty years ago, Huenemann's study remains the most recent monograph in English. Two other studies focus on the role of railroads in China's prewar agricultural economy and changing political geography. Historian Chang Jui-te wrote, in Chinese, the first history of the Peking-Hankow (Beijing-Hankou) line and its role in the economy of northern China between 1905 and 1937. Chang also produced the first study on industrial management in China's prewar railroads from the perspective of a political analysis. More recent studies focusing on socioeconomic trends in specific provinces or regions during the Republican period discuss railroads mostly in the context of social and cultural modernization rather than from an institutional or business history perspective.[12]

All these studies are valuable contributions, improving our understanding of elite public discourse, technology transfer, and macroeconomic trends in late imperial China. Many discussions, however, still deal with China as a historical case study of failure in railroad development during the late nineteenth century and of the slow and limited growth of the rail network before 1949. Most importantly, none of these studies, whether in English or Chinese, offers a comprehensive analysis of railroad development in China beyond the Japanese invasion in 1937. This book tries to fill the gap.

To that purpose my study includes new archival material produced by railroad companies operating in different parts of the country. During all of 2005 and a number of shorter periods, I visited Ji'nan, Tianjin, Beijing, Guangzhou, Shanghai, Nanjing, and Hong Kong and collected annual reports, employee records, administrative regulations, correspondence, and other documentation. I conducted field visits to railroad compounds, stations, and museums at railroad hubs and interviewed former railroad workers and engineers who in their youth had worked for various railroads, from the Japanese occupation through the civil war all the way to the post-Mao years of the PRC. Their oral testimonies as former members of railroad institutions were extremely helpful in filling in gaps in primary source information not available or accessible in written form.

This study also incorporates sources in the form of Western newspapers circulating in China during the pre- and post-1949 periods; personal diaries by engineers, businessmen, and military officials; national economic surveys; British Foreign Office records and correspondence housed at the National Archives in London; travel literature; guidebooks; and advertising materials. I also combed the statistical yearbooks on government railroads published during the Republican period until 1936 for data related to freight and passenger transportation. German engineering and diplomatic documents housed in the historical collections of Baker Library at Harvard Business School, to the best of my knowledge used here for the first time, provide important archival primary sources directly related to construction and management of the Jin-Pu Railroad.

The limited availability and access to primary sources generated by railroads as institutional units after 1949, however, present serious challenges for historical research. Regional railroad bureaus continue to have considerable clout within the central railroad bureaucracy and maintain their own archives. Because the government considers the rail sector strategically relevant to national defense, it is impossible for Western or Chinese scholars to gain access to postwar archival material held at local and regional railroad bureaus. My exhaustive lobbying finally led to a meeting at the railroad bureau in Shanghai in 2005 and a 2011 meeting at the Ministry of Railways in Beijing. Not surprisingly, both visits yielded only polite, general conversation and the gift of a public relations brochure. Because of these disappointing limitations for research, unlike the pre-1949 sections, the post-1949 section of this study must rely more on published documents and sources generated by the railroad administration, enhanced by newspaper articles and policy documents.

I purposely decided to exclude the South Manchurian Railway (SMR) from my research for this book. The SMR was part of Japan's so-called informal

empire and thus operated under fundamentally different political and economic conditions. Compared with the railroads outside Manchuria, the SMR
was a fairly homogeneous system under Japanese control, serving Japan's
broad imperialist agenda in China and East Asia. As a railroad infrastructure system with important socioeconomic functions in the development of
Manchuria, the SMR is already the subject of a large body of literature in
Japanese, English, and Chinese. One important goal of this study is to contribute new research on railroad development other than the SMR network in China's Northeast, especially because this railroad system is sometimes still treated as representative of railroad operations and development
in prewar China.[13]

## Chapter Summaries

The first part of the book covers developments in railroad history from the
last decades of the Qing empire to the first years of the Republic after the 1911
revolution. I explore the development of railroad companies in China from
the perspective of an institutionally informed business history and analyze
the emergence of railroads as a modern business institution originally adapted
from U.S. and European models. Over time, railroad companies followed a
hybrid enterprise model, combining foreign and Chinese institutional structures and practices.

Chapter 1 begins with a discussion of the issue of knowledge dissemination and technology transfer from the West to China during the late Qing
dynasty. Using the Tianjin-Pukou, Shanghai-Nanking (Shanghai-Nanjing),
and Hankou-Guangzhou lines as case studies, Chapter 1 shows how British
and German managerial, technical, and administrative expertise shaped
the evolution of these railroad companies in the early twentieth century.
Although Chinese claims to managerial and operational control were constantly challenged by foreign political and economic interests, I argue that
the Chinese embraced rail technology with great pragmatism and did not
shy away from new opportunities to further their own financial interests
(for example, during negotiations and transactions related to the purchase
of land needed for rail construction).

Chapter 2 moves the narrative past the 1911 revolution and explores how
Chinese railroad companies in the wake of nationalization experimented

with new forms of industrial management and administrative integration. As I argue, efforts to establish a highly efficient national rail bureaucracy during the first years of the Republic were jeopardized by political instability, line disruption by military campaigns of various warlords, and appointees to leadership in the rail administration chosen for purely political reasons instead of railroad expertise. This chapter introduces the railroad bureau system and argues that, aided by a weak central railroad administration, railroad bureaus were able to maintain a relatively high level of fiscal and organizational autonomy over the railroads within a bureau's regional or provincial boundaries.

Chapter 2 also introduces the formation of rail compounds in the urban context and the work hierarchies and social dynamics on the shop floors. The 1910s saw the beginnings of technical and professional education for the railroad sector, moving from company-run schools to training provided by technical colleges and universities under the control of the Chinese government. The competition between British and German engineers to dominate the language and the content of engineering education continued, but in an effort to secure supply chains for future deliveries of equipment to Chinese railroad companies.

Part 2 covers the period from the late 1910s to 1937 and explores how railroads participated in and responded to new trends in the Chinese economy and society. Chapter 3 discusses the economic role of the railroad—the logistical functions of railroads in the marketplace and their nature as business institutions operating in the market. With regard to the interactions of rail infrastructure with commercial networks, my analysis shows how Chinese railroads contributed to commercialized agriculture by giving Chinese as well as foreign companies direct access to producers of commodities such as tobacco, peanuts, and cotton and by creating new distribution channels. New railroad hubs led to a shift in the marketing of commodities. For example, grain wholesalers previously served by the Grand Canal, the only direct waterway linking Beijing to the Yangzi delta, shifted their business in north China from Tianjin to Ji'nan. There the Jin-Pu Railroad directed the commercial flows to the ports of Qingdao and Shanghai, thus improving China's access to the East Asian and global economy during the prewar period.

Chapter 3 also shows that during the Republic the limited railroad network never grew beyond the core areas of the Yangzi River, the Pearl River delta, and the Northeast and did not lead to national economic integration. Whereas my research confirms Thomas Rawski's interpretation of regional pockets of economic development in Republican China, I also make the argument that railroads contributed to the regional integration of markets by introducing new practices and regulations for freight logistics and stimulating business by outsourcing freight transport to private logistics companies.[14]

Chapter 4 introduces the economic, social, and cultural components of passenger transportation during the Republic. I argue that the lack of rail connectivity and the considerable expense of railroad travel made short-distance travel the most popular choice, with third- and fourth-class tickets generating the bulk of passenger revenue for railroad companies. For citizens with educational and professional aspirations, the railroad also brought greater mobility in terms of access to schools and employment in urban centers such as Shanghai. Furthermore, I discuss the introduction of tourism as part of the business portfolio of railroad lines and the education of passengers in matters of railroad and time discipline. Supporting the arguments concerning regional autonomy and market integration, railroad guidebooks demonstrate a continuing strong regional and provincial identity of the railroad lines without strong promotion of the nation-state during the early Republic.

Part 3 discusses the social and political changes under the Guomindang government from 1927 to 1937 and the disruptive period of the Japanese occupation during World War II. Chapter 5 explores how the national railroad administration and other parts of the government bureaucracy absorbed increasing numbers of engineering graduates from Chinese technical schools and universities who were unable to find jobs with Chinese rail lines because of the lack of network expansion during the 1920s and early 1930s. As I argue, this trend laid the foundation for the transformation of China's engineers from a technical and professional elite into a political elite who until recently also dominated the highest echelons of the CCP. Chapter 5 also explores issues of labor protests and how railroad companies excluded unskilled and potentially more strike-prone labor from the payroll. In line with the increasingly prominent Guomindang presence on rail compounds and its propaganda impact via the publication of in-house magazines, railroad journals, and social events, my discussion pays attention to the railroad visions of the government, or how railroads could serve the expansion of the political power of the Nationalist Party and its agenda.

Chapter 6 explores the disruption of railroad traffic by war and military campaigns in the wake of the Japanese occupation in World War II. On the basis of oral history interviews, I argue that Japanese management of railroads such as the Jin-Pu line actually offered more favorable working conditions to Chinese workers than the Guomindang predecessors in order to co-opt and maintain the loyalty of a highly specialized workforce. This chapter also demonstrates to what extent the strategic destruction and interruption of railroads caused economic shortages and losses during the war. At the same time, those lines operating in and close to the area of unoccupied Free China in the interior provided lifelines for refugees and new economic opportunities for the local population.

Part 4 follows the institutional development of railroads through administrative reform and network expansion from the last years of the civil war (1945–1949) to the turn of the century. Chapter 7 explores the rapid institutional integration of railroad bureaus into the work unit system under the new PRC government. As I argue, socialist values of hard work, discipline, and efficiency were easily grafted onto an institutional system with similar values previously tied to the professionalism and railroad management expertise of the Republican period. Whereas the expertise of Russian engineers helped in the reconstruction and expansion of the railroad sector in the 1950s, the construction work was performed by an arm of the PLA through the so-called railroad army corps. With a strong military identity and discipline united in dangerous construction work across the country, these railroad soldiers and their families became a strong social community representing courage and personal sacrifice in line with the party's goals for political consolidation and national defense.

Chapter 8 addresses the impact of politics through the various campaigns at the height of Maoist radicalism in the late 1950s and the 1960s. My analysis shows how much damage movements such as the Great Leap Forward and the Cultural Revolution caused the railroad system, reflected by spiking accident rates and neglect of facilities and equipment. When discipline and efficiency came under political attack during the Great Leap Forward and the Cultural Revolution, railroad bureaus and rail yards suffered not only because their workers and cadres became political targets but also because their professional expertise and values, and the managerial order necessary to run rail logistics, were portrayed as expressions of counterrevolutionary behavior.

This chapter demonstrates how the railroad network from the 1950s to the 1970s served the economic and security interests of the socialist state and the CCP. I argue that the massive post-1949 expansion of the rail network for national defense and domestic political integration created China's first true mass transportation system. After Mao's death in 1976 and under Deng Xiaoping's new economic policies, the railroad sector recovered and normalized its operations and services. In the wake of the economic reforms of the 1990s, China's railroad system continued to undergo institutional reform. The railroad bureau system still exists, but the central bureaucratic structure continues to experience substantial reorganization in order to improve efficiency and profitability and accommodate the focus on high-speed rail expansion.

In the conclusion of the book I argue that railroad companies as institutions in China were uniquely positioned to survive the twentieth century because their institutional organization under a central administrative leadership with a considerable amount of local autonomy at the railroad bureau level allowed flexibility in adapting to different political and economic regimes. Simultaneously, this study elucidates the managerial, financial, and political constraints preventing China's railroad network from reaching a substantial size during the prewar period, and it explains why the support and the political agenda of the socialist state became crucial for the development of the rail network and the concept of mass transportation after 1949.

The ability of the post-1949 state to mobilize and centralize resources for railroad construction, driven by a desire to enhance national security and bring all parts of the country under the umbrella of socialism, allowed the expansion of the Chinese railroad network. The rapid construction of a comprehensive national railroad network as an anchor of the current railroad expansion was possible only because of the institutional blueprints provided by railroad companies in the early twentieth century and the support by the central state through resource allocations and policy directives. The PRC's One Belt, One Road initiative aims to use its technical expertise and skilled, professionally managed labor force to build a Eurasian megaeconomy that connects trading blocs along the land-based Silk Road with the oceangoing Maritime Silk Road. This ambitious project will depend on the hard-won achievements of China's railroads: connecting core areas, increasing regional market integration, and linking modern rail systems with other modes of transport on both land and water.

# PART I

## COMPETING INTERESTS AND RAILROAD CONSTRUCTION

## CHAPTER ONE

# Technology and Semicolonial Ventures

n the last decade of the nineteenth century, China was reconsidering the state of its railroad development. In light of extremely slow and modest construction efforts, with a mere total of 195 miles of railroad tracks operating before 1895, Chinese officials of all ranks, intellectuals, foreign diplomats, commercial representatives, and Western missionaries participated in public debates about the advantages and disadvantages of this new technology and infrastructure for China's development. In this heated discourse two main issues emerged: foreign interference and socioeconomic progress.

Both Chinese and foreigners were among those supportive of railroad development. For example, the secretary of the Chinese legation in London, Fung Yee (Feng Yi), commented in 1890 that "once the iron network has been spread over the length and breadth of the Middle Kingdom, there will be no more halting in the march of progress, and actual retrogression, though foreigners may not realise the fact, has never taken place among my people. . . . The Chinese authorities have been especially desirous of clearly demonstrating the practicality of the system being carried out by the Chinese people themselves, independent of foreign guidance, though not altogether without practical assistance from the West."[1] Work experience in China prompted the American railroad engineer William Barclay Parsons to state in 1900 that in China "the political aspect of the situation is unique, since we see established on the soil of another country the people of six different foreign nations, with rights and privileges granted and guaranteed by the local Government, a situation which may contain the germs of future complications. . . . Some of the railway projects in China have been prompted undoubtedly much more by foreign politics than by commercial motives."[2] Fung Yee's comment expresses the pragmatically driven Chinese desire for building railroads with foreign technical assistance but without foreign political control, whereas Parsons acknowledges the complexity of constructing railroads in an environment where foreign economic interests were intertwined with political interests.

China's railroad development was anchored in a semicolonial context and framed by the political and economic motivations of foreign powers, such as Russia, Germany, France, Belgium, Great Britain, the United States, and Japan, that maintained a protected presence in the treaty port concessions after China's loss in the Opium Wars of 1842 and 1860. Offering extraterritorial rights and privileges to foreigners, treaty ports became the enclave environment where new business systems, administrative bodies, and institutions such as the Chinese Maritime Customs Service regulated and mediated the interaction and competition between Chinese interests and foreign powers as well as among the various foreign powers themselves. As Jürgen Osterhammel and other historians have shown, in order to navigate the semicolonial context in which the strategic interests of the treaty ports' powers were inseparable from Chinese industrial strategies, brokers acting on behalf of the Chinese state and the foreign powers formed a web of complex relationships, ranging from collaborative to client-patron relationships. In contrast to the historical conditions in India, where railroad development occurred under the control of one central colonial regime, the British Raj, China's situation presented a different political environment with challenges for the construction and management of a railroad system. As this chapter shows, the evolution of the management structures, practices, and business strategies of Chinese railroad companies took shape within a business and political climate of semicolonial intervention. One of the results was that Chinese railroads combined Western managerial styles with indigenous business practices in their institutional evolution.[3]

A simple diagnosis of efforts in railroad construction challenged by semicolonialism, however, does not do justice to the full complexity of railroad development in China. Although foreigners took much of the early initiative in terms of financing and building railroad lines, the Chinese were hardly passive or reluctant recipients of the new technology. Contrary to received accounts, Chinese technophobic attitudes did not prevent the slow but steady development of the first railroads in China. The general understanding of the

Chinese reaction to railroads is reflected in sources like Lloyd Eastman's classic social history textbook, where he states that "ordinary Chinese, too, were distressed that the railway tracks, the movement of the locomotives, and the stench of their engines would upset the balance of geomantic forces, with catastrophic consequences for both the living and the dead."[4] This characterization of the Chinese as hostile toward modern technology needs to be reconsidered. Although it is true that government factions feared a greater military reach of the foreign powers into China via a growing railroad network, the embrace of railroads by the local population was predominantly driven by a great deal of pragmatism. This attitude is particularly evident with respect to the issue of land sales. As this chapter shows, local Chinese were not always victims of exploitative colonial companies trying to maximize profits; rather, often they were agents who managed to become brokers in the purchasing process, and many of them proved to be shrewd negotiators of land prices by classifying their land as ancestral gravesites.

Although most of the arguments in this book can apply to all railroad projects in China proper, the evidence presented in this chapter focuses particularly on the Tianjin-Pukou Railroad, commonly known as the Jin-Pu line. The Jin-Pu line serves as an ideal case study for several reasons. The first is its age. Negotiations for the Jin-Pu line began in 1898, and its construction was completed by 1912 (see Map 1.1). Second, it rapidly became—and remains—one of the most important transportation and communication links in the country, connecting Tianjin in the north, already linked to the imperial capital of Beijing, with Nanjing and Shanghai in the commercial center of the Yangzi delta. Third, and most importantly, the construction and early administration of the Jin-Pu line epitomize the semicolonial tensions and absurdities of early Chinese railroad history. As a line built under Chinese management by two intensely competitive European powers with disparate colonial agendas—Britain and Germany—the story of the Jin-Pu line represents the story of Chinese railroads in microcosm. Although other lines operated under arrangements defined by different national syndicates, similar dynamics prevailed among many of the railroad ventures.

After a brief outline of early railroad development and knowledge transfer in late imperial China, I discuss the establishment of the Jin-Pu Railroad in terms of surveying, land acquisition, and the construction process—or more generally, how railroads really came into being in China.

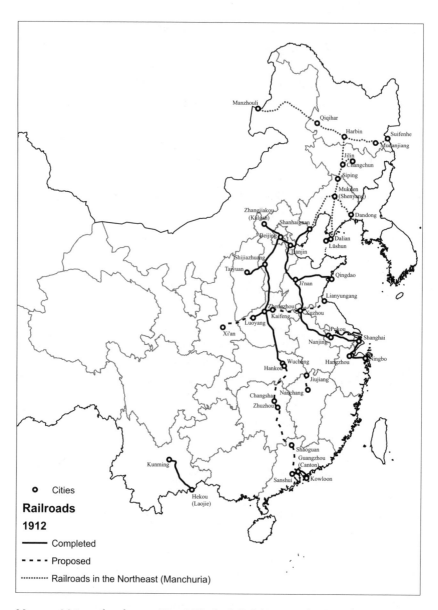

**Map 1.1**    Major railroads, 1912. Map © Elisabeth Köll (cartographic design Matthew Sisk).

## Railroad Knowledge and Knowledge Transfer

By the time that serious railroad development began in the early twentieth century, knowledge of steam locomotives and railroads had already reached China. People living near ports or navigable waterways would have been familiar with the steam engine via the steamship, and images and descriptions of railroads filtered into the Chinese cultural realm from overseas by means of a small number of publications aimed at elites, children, or the public at large. Significantly, none of these depictions expressed either hostility or fear in relation to this newfangled Western invention. Both the images and the texts assumed—and promoted—an attitude of curiosity on the part of the readers. A far greater obstacle to railroad development was the lack of in-depth knowledge of railroading and railroad engineering. The absence of an engineering establishment and a system of technological education in China delayed national railroad development far more than any supposed cultural antagonism on the part of the Chinese.

Knowledge about railroads came to China in translations from the West in the late Qing dynasty (1644–1911). The earliest images and descriptions of locomotives and railroads can be found in publications compiled and translated by scholars hired by the Translation Department of the Jiangnan Arsenal, one of several institutions sponsored by the imperial government during the Self-Strengthening Movement of the nineteenth century that sought to promote a modern Chinese military and industrial development.[5]

In keeping with the focus on applied science, the arsenal translated and published technical and scientific writing from the West. Some publications were simply textbooks: in 1872, John Fryer, head of the arsenal school, under-took with Xu Jianyin a translation of *The Engineer and Machinist's Drawing Book* (originally published in 1855), a slim illustrated volume intended to teach the basics of engineering.[6] Fryer, together with Xu Shou, was also the creator of China's first scientific journal *Gezhi huibian* (Compendium for investigating things and expanding knowledge), also known by its English title *The Chinese Scientific and Industrial Magazine*. First appearing in 1876 and mainly featuring articles on the natural sciences and technology in Europe and the United States, the journal circulated primarily in the treaty ports.[7]

Knowledge about railroad technology and the operation of lines spread via magazines such as *Gezhi huibian*.[8] Using British railroads as examples, the journal introduced Chinese readers to drawings of railroad stations; semitechnical drawings of construction blueprints for tracks, tunnels, and bridges; and panoramic views of railroads crossing open landscapes. These publications did not target a professional audience with specific interest in engineering and science but rather focused on a well-educated readership among the Chinese literati and official elite with a general interest in inventions and new technologies from the West. The illustrations and accompanying texts conveyed the technical complexity and development of the railroad, especially the transition from coach car to passenger car and adaptation and use of the steam engine.[9]

For example, a detailed essay on engines and railroads in the 1877 summer issue of *Gezhi huibian* introduced illustrations of British locomotives, passenger carriages, and railroad stations to Chinese audiences (see Figure 1.1).[10] Such drawings lay somewhere between popular prints and engineers' specifications; they revealed technical details, such as the interior of an engine, but the accompanying text did not include annotations, and some parts in English lacked translations. The framing article, partly on the basis of translations of texts supplied by the London firm Clemenson, discussed the economic advantages of building railroads and enthusiastically pointed to the positive commercial effects of improved transportation of goods for both town and countryside.

Western translation projects run by missionaries were another source of introducing railroads as tools of progress to Chinese elites. For example, the children's magazine *Xiaohai xuebao* (The child's paper), published by Western missionaries in Shanghai late in the Qing dynasty, in its June 1876 discussion of the building of the Wusong Railroad reported that the tracks between Hongkou and Jiangwan had already been completed.[11] The article described a passenger train ride in considerable detail, including the technical process, spatial dimensions, and various fare structures. Curiously, however, the railroad specifications in the text refer to an image of a much older British railroad car dating from the 1830s or the 1840s that clearly reveals the influence of the traditional horse-drawn coach in the design and appearance of the passenger car.[12] In other words, the image was already more than a

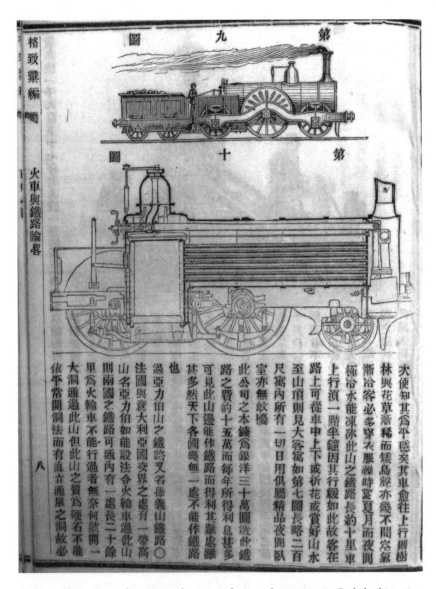

**Fig. 1.1** Illustrations of exterior and interior of a steam locomotive in *Gezhi huibian*, 1877. "Huoche yu tielu lunlüe" [Summary report on trains and railroads], *Gezhi huibian*, Summer 1877, 8A. Harvard Yenching Library, Harvard University.

generation out of date when the Chinese article was written, a time lag due to translation, publication, and commercial distribution of technological information.

The text of the missionary magazine, written from a Western perspective, offered its young readers a lesson in progress. It praised the railroad's advantages in terms of speed and commercial development and its overall benefits for the country, although not as a wonder of technological development. At the same time, the author did not fail to mention the potential dangers of thieves and bandits and the required protection of passengers by guards and soldiers, an expression of the common concerns of European rail travelers in the late nineteenth century.[13]

Inexpensive popular prints brought knowledge of railroads and locomotives to a more common Chinese audience. As historian James Flath has shown, woodblock prints created as New Year pictures (*nianhua*) in North China "carried the knowledge of industrial technology such as the railway beyond its physical limits, so that the concept of a steam engine could circulate even where the machine did not."[14] Because the two foremost printing centers for *nianhua*, Yangliuqing near Tianjin and Weixian in eastern Shandong province, were close to traditional transportation and distribution networks and also close to some of the earliest railroad lines, it is not surprising that these subjects would find their way into the print motifs.

Artists creating the Yangliuqing woodblock prints imitated images from treaty port publications. For example, *Dianshizhai huabao* (Illustrated news of the Dianshizhai lithographic studio), an illustrated weekly pictorial published in Shanghai, carried a print of the by-then defunct Wusong Railroad in 1884.[15] Again, the designs of the engines and carriages in the pictorial as well as in the woodblock prints resemble much older English models from the 1840s. Chinese woodblock prints before the 1920s depict railroads without paying much attention to cartography, technical detail, or the landscape. In fact, the vast majority of prints place the railroad in an urban context and, as James Flath confirms, use this and other foreign technology as background to illustrate changes in Chinese society in terms of class, gender, and space.[16] The most striking feature of these early woodblock prints, particularly given the technophobic stereotype of late Qing China, is the lack of hostility expressed in the representation of the railroads and their relation to the surrounding space. Railroads appear together with Chinese manual laborers and with traditional forms of transportation such as rickshaws, depicting a sphere of coexistence rather than of hostile competition for passengers.

Despite the amount of railroad information in print, railroad knowledge in late Qing China was alarmingly superficial. The Jiangnan Arsenal was responsible for some of the more detailed depictions of railroads from the 1870s through the 1890s, but its efforts to promote engineering education in China met with far less success: the demands of the imperial examination system (which continued until 1905) ensured that the Confucian classics and preparation for careers in the imperial bureaucracy retained their hold on the Chinese curriculum until the early twentieth century. It is true, as historian Benjamin Elman has shown, that the Jiangnan and other arsenals eventually developed into a significant force for the translation and spread of knowledge in the natural sciences and engineering.[17] Provincial shipyards became the cradle of engineering, in both academic teaching and applied training. For example, the Fuzhou Arsenal, established in 1866, developed a mixed-management structure of foreign technical personnel and Chinese officials under the leadership of a director general appointed by the imperial court. The arsenal introduced to China the earliest engineering training, based on a French model, in the hope of alleviating the lack of skilled laborers on whom engineers depended for successful projects. The shipyard established a separate School of Apprentices where students were taught French, arithmetic, science, and engineering, with the goal of training them to become foremen in the arsenal's workshops.[18]

In raw numbers, for many years the arsenal's influence on creating a substantial class of science and engineering graduates was minimal. Although by the 1890s twenty-nine engineering students had graduated from the shipyard's comprehensive training program, with five graduates working in railroad construction, this number was insufficient to satisfy the future demands of the emerging railroad sector.[19] Thus, when the railroads finally did arrive in China on a significant scale, they were mainly foreign ventures staffed by foreign engineers.

## The Jin-Pu Line

The semicolonial origins of China's railroads bore both similarities and differences to railroad construction in other parts of the world in the late nineteenth and early twentieth centuries. Railroad construction in India began in the 1850s under the British, and European contractors built railroads under semicolonial conditions in the independent countries of Latin America, southern Europe, and the Middle East for more than a generation. China, however, hosted not one or two but more than half a dozen imperial powers vying among themselves to dominate railroad construction. Moreover, the fragmentation of China's own central authority since the mid-nineteenth-century Taiping Rebellion (1850–1864) further complicated the politics because of rivalries among powerful provincial leaders and the European powers. Accordingly, the founding era of Chinese railroads was dominated by intraimperial rivalry at the court, provincial officials in disputes with local authorities and court factions, and tensions and misunderstandings among the colonial powers and their Chinese hosts.[20]

Overseas companies had long been eager to lay tracks in China, but official opposition kept them at bay for much of the late nineteenth century. Foreign efforts to gain railroad concessions began in 1863 when twenty-seven foreign firms petitioned Li Hongzhang, acting governor of Jiangsu province, for the right to build a line between the administrative town of Suzhou and Shanghai, the major trading port in the lower Yangzi River region. Li denied the petition and even refused to forward it to the emperor. The next attempt did not take place until 1875, when the British trading firm of Jardine Matheson, without clearing it with the authorities in advance, constructed a ten-mile track between Shanghai and Wusong. The train ran for more than a year, but in 1877 the Chinese government ultimately purchased and demolished the line, fearing that foreigners would take control of this means of transportation.[21]

Although growth in track miles was limited, official enthusiasm for railroads increased during the following decades. In December 1881 a telegraph line between Tianjin and Shanghai was opened to traffic and became the core of China's telegraph network, facilitating future railroad development.[22] In the years leading up to the 1894–1895 first Sino-Japanese War several officials with an entrepreneurial spirit, such as Li Hongzhang (whose opinions on railroads changed dramatically in the decades after 1863), Zhang Zhidong, and Liu Mingchuan, promoted the growth of railroads in memoranda to the throne. The result was the creation of the beginning of a railroad system in North China.[23] With the exception of some short tracks for mining purposes, however, government concerns about foreign control limited railroad development during most of the remaining nineteenth century. As stated earlier, by 1894 only 195 miles of track had been built in China proper.

The first Sino-Japanese War finally altered the political calculus in favor of railroad development. China's loss to Japan in 1895 not only triggered efforts to promote indigenous industrialization but also provided a new impetus to railroad construction by weakening the government's bargaining position vis-à-vis foreign companies that were seeking a foothold on the mainland.[24] Industrial development suddenly became a priority for the government, which saw this as a necessary response to compete with Japan and other nations on equal commercial terms. Officials-turned-entrepreneurs like Zhang Jian (1853–1926) became advocates of railroads, characterizing them as the "root of industry," resulting in commercial and military prosperity and, by extension, social harmony.[25]

The Jin-Pu line grew from this political moment. After the creation of a German sphere of interest (centered at the treaty port of Qingdao) in Shandong province in the late nineteenth century, Germany and Great Britain in 1898 obtained a joint concession to construct a railroad line between the city of Tianjin and the northern bank of the Yangzi River. The plan was to establish a transportation and communications artery linking Tianjin, in the north of China and easily accessible from Beijing, to Nanjing in the south via Pukou, a location for crossing the Yangzi River. The British would build and operate the part of the line within Jiangsu province, the southern section, and the Germans would be in charge of the line passing through Shandong and Zhili provinces in the northern section. In 1899 a British-German syndicate signed an agreement with the Chinese government to build the railroad.[26]

It took several years to negotiate the methods of financial control, construction, equipment, and operation for the line. First, construction was delayed by the 1900 Boxer Uprising, which brought widespread turmoil and anxiety to northern Shandong and Zhili and challenged local government control in the area. After 1910, construction of the line proceeded relatively swiftly, and both sections were completed in 1912.[27]

As with early industrial enterprises and other railroad lines in China, financing the Jin-Pu Railroad proved to be extremely difficult. Wang Maokun, a prominent retired official in Ji'nan, attempted to raise Chinese capital, but he failed to convince local investors to put their financial resources into a project that only vaguely promised profitability and steady returns.[28] As in British India, local owners of capital initially made the rational choice to invest in more familiar ventures, thus preferring investments in land resources and real estate over more risky railroad investments.[29] It was not until 1905, toward the end of the Qing dynasty, when domestic investment in industry slowly increased in a changing business environment that saw the introduction of limited liability in China's first Company Law, chambers of commerce, and the first modernization efforts in the banking sector. In 1908 the financial terms for the Jin-Pu Railroad were finally agreed upon: the first loan arrangement of the so-called Imperial Chinese Government 5 Percent Tientsin-Pukow Railway Loan consisted of a bond issue of £5 million on London's financial market, issued in two installments, with 65 percent German capital and 35 percent British capital.[30] In 1910 a supplementary loan of £3 million at 5 percent interest was issued.[31] Although the loan was oversubscribed in Europe several times (£1.89 million was raised by the Deutsch-Asiatische Bank in Germany for the 401 miles of the German section and £1.1 million was raised in London for the 235 miles of the British section), the market issue also attracted some private Chinese investors and the provincial governments of Zhili, Shandong, Jiangsu, and Anhui, which together invested £260,000.[32] Interest was to be paid from the profits of the railroad, and the loan was guaranteed by the central government and secured by the income from the *lijin* (commercial transit tax) and internal provincial revenue from the four provinces through which the line ran. In contrast to previous foreign loan arrangements, the Jin-Pu Railroad itself was not mortgaged as collateral. These new financial arrangements became known as Pukow Terms in loan negotiations between different investor groups. For the first time, construction of the line was undertaken by the foreign partners but overall managerial control, specified in painstakingly long agreements, lay in the hands of the Chinese government, at least on paper.[33]

The Jin-Pu line's financing process provides insights relevant to a broader discussion about China's ability to finance large infrastructure projects in the early twentieth century. Although there were local attempts to raise capital, in the end private Chinese investment remained extremely limited and Chinese investment funds mainly came from the state, in the case of the Jin-Pu Railroad as contributions from provincial governments connected to the rail route. The inadequate level of Chinese private investment, although perfectly rational, confirms the argument by historians that China's lack of a capital market and the imperial government's refusal to issue public debt represented a major obstacle to financing large-scale industrial projects such as rail infrastructure that required investments beyond the scope that traditional banks and private financial networks were able to provide.[34] At the same time, it is important to note how foreign investors were eager to invest their funds in Chinese rail projects. That they did so only a few years after the attacks on foreigners during the Boxer Uprising in 1900 also shows that the anti-Chinese and dismissive reports about the empire's political future in the Western press did not deter foreign investors. On the contrary, as indicated by the oversubscription of the loans, they were eager to put their money on the future of railroad development in China.[35]

The international cooperation—and tensions—within the Jin-Pu rail company became most obvious in construction and operational management. The title to the railroad remained in Chinese hands, but the Chinese side appointed experienced British and German railroad engineers as chief engineers who had to be approved by the Anglo-German syndicate.[36] The foreign engineers on the Jin-Pu line reported to the two Chinese managing directors who respectively supervised the British and German sections. Any disputes between the chief engineers and the managing directors about the hiring or dismissal of technical staff for the line were decided by the Chinese director general. In addition, the Chinese side was in charge of appointing a European chief engineer who, independently from the requirements of the syndicate, supervised the entire line after its construction.[37]

The vast fragmentation in the management of a sprawling business institution divided into sections under different national and managerial authorities led to strong, frequent, and general complaints from all parties involved. With the British and German sides competing to further their respective financial and political interests, the railroad accounting system was especially contentious. German and British railroad engineers complained constantly about irregularities. Accusations of graft and embezzlement were rife.[38] The director general was in complete control of the company's funds and could draw any amount from the loan as long as he had the signatures of the managing directors. Surprisingly, there were no foreign accountants to certify payments and to audit the books. The accounting system was only subject to irregular visits by a representative of the syndicate. In 1909 the accounts of the German section showed that 3 million taels were missing, and other incidents of graft were discovered in the accounting department.[39] Obviously, despite joint control over the accounting department by the German chief engineer and by the auditor of the syndicate, the railroad company did not apply strict accounting rules to the enterprise. In the wake of this incident, the Chinese director general and the managing directors were forced to take collective responsibility and resign; they were eventually punished, but the Germans escaped legal prosecution because of their extraterritoriality status.[40]

To further complicate the situation, the methods of traditional Chinese business accounting and Western railroad accounting were incompatible before the 1920s. Until the midteens, the Jin-Pu Railroad Company had two sets of accounts, Chinese and German, but beginning in 1909 the Chinese accounts were "translated" into German accounting methods to rein in corruption and financial irregularities. For example, the accounting systems used in China's industrial enterprises did not apply the concept of depreciation (*zhejiu*) to their machinery and buildings in a satisfactory way.[41] Depreciation rates were not related to the growth of firms' productive assets, thus creating long-term negative consequences for company finances. The lack of depreciation in the accounting system was, of course, even worse for equipment-oriented enterprises such as railroad companies. According to John Earl Baker, who became an adviser to the Ministry of Communications in 1916 and in 1923 authored a classic textbook for Chinese railroad accountants, "No accountant becomes valuable to a railway or any other business until he knows considerable [*sic*] about the technical work of that business."[42] Without prior technical knowledge about railroad construction and line operation and without the appropriate professional training, Chinese accountants faced a particularly difficult task during the early years of the railroad business.

The success of Chinese managers in building and operating the line depended on their business skills and ability to negotiate with their business partners. For example, the Chinese managing director in the British section was able to obtain construction material that previously had been purchased by foreign agents for other railroad lines, remained unused and thus cost much less.[43] Buying secondhand equipment or material originally designated for other companies was not unique to the railroad business: industrial enterprises like textile mills also relied on such affordable equipment during their initial stages.[44] The British, however, did not approve of the Chinese managing director's policy and especially criticized the outbidding of British manufacturers by American and European non-British competitors who secured contracts by supplying machines and equipment at lower prices.[45] Even on a day-to-day basis different national economic interests created a certain amount of friction between the Chinese management and the partners in the syndicate.

## Mapping Space

As studies have shown, cartographic projects during the Qing empire demonstrated its achievements in territorial expansion and imposing order on the landscape.[46] Railroad survey maps, produced mainly in the early twentieth century by railroad syndicates, reveal the combination of both cultural and scientific forms of representation and reflect the changing cultural and political environments of the time. The earliest maps of Chinese railroads were created by foreign engineers who were working for the railroad companies and were in charge of the survey and construction processes. These maps, especially the relief maps, not only documented the physical landscape but also introduced detailed geological information of economic (and thus also political) value.[47]

Because most of the first railroad companies in China were established through the foreign concessions, initial surveys were conducted by foreign engineers who brought experience from other colonial environments or from military attachments. According to the first contract with the imperial government in 1899 for the Jin-Pu line, English and German engineers could survey the land in their respective administrative sections, and they only had to inform the local authorities, who sometimes would issue permits to acknowledge the lawfulness of the surveyors' activities.[48]

On the British side of the Jin-Pu line, colonial India was important as both a resource and a model. In 1898 the Pekin Syndicate, which had obtained mining concessions in Henan and Shanxi provinces, recruited an engineering expedition consisting of six Royal Engineer officers "on loan by the government of India" under the leadership of J. G. H. Glass, chief engineer and secretary to the government's Public Works Department in Bengal.[49] The expedition's goals were to assess the value of the coal and iron ore deposits and whether the mines could be connected via railroads to waterways for transportation of the mining products. Expecting a positive outcome on the railroad issue, the engineers were also instructed to perform preliminary surveys for the railroad and to estimate construction costs. For the actual surveys, Glass hired ten Indian surveyors, trained in the Survey Department of the Government of India, who were considered subordinate staff and who had been stationed all over India.[50]

British India supplied not only personnel but also procedures for the planning of China's railroads. The survey for the Pekin Syndicate was mainly based on the "Rules for the Preparation of Railway Projects by the Government of India," which established the guidelines for data collection and their documentation, the scope of the survey, and the nature of the notes to be taken in the field.[51] Surveyors were required to make detailed notes about accommodation work (that is, the means of crossing the railroad line by level crossings and bridges, especially in the case of villages that were close to the line and owned a large amount of land on the opposite side); facilities for construction, such as the availability of building materials (stone, brick, lime, slate, and timber); skilled and unskilled labor; food and water supplies; local commodity prices and wage data; and "any local conditions likely to affect rates or methods of construction."[52] Related tasks for the expedition team included surveying important rivers for bridge building, selecting suitable sites for stations, and collecting trade information and statistics on any form of existing or future "special courses of traffic . . . such as coal or minerals, timber, pilgrims, etc."[53] Although the syndicate's mission focused on transporting coal from mines and establishing iron foundries in Shanxi province, the surveyors also assessed the commercial viability of different track projections and terminals, and they recommended Pukou on the northern bank of the Yangzi as a location with great potential for serving as a future river terminal.[54]

Regarding community relations, British procedures borrowed from experiences in colonial India. To preempt hostile reactions from the local population to insensitive behavior by foreigners, a section in the guidelines, "Relations with the Public," admonished the engineers that "every endeavour should be made to avoid interference with religious edifices, burial grounds or other objects which may be considered sacred."[55] The guidelines recommended that surveyors enter enclosed spaces only with permission and in the company of the local person in charge. As for cooperation with the civil authorities, their help was considered vital to protecting physical objects such as benchmarks or pegs left as survey data markers out in the open.[56]

The absence of maps based on Western geographical methods posed challenges for the foreign surveyors to identify villages and obtain their names. Although mapmaking was well established in China before the twentieth century, traditional Chinese maps were not useful for engineering purposes: few were constructed strictly to scale, and instead of indicating altitude by means of topographical lines, they typically included a side-view drawing of a mountain or other landmarks in roughly the correct location. From the Chinese perspective, the lack of precise maps did not constitute a problem for assessing and claiming ownership of land and property. Because China had a strong contract culture, written contracts did not specify property ownership through a visual depiction of each parcel and its measurements on paper. Instead, contracts offered detailed descriptions of the boundary lines and property locations in writing.[57]

It is important to point out, however, that Chinese local residents did not shy away from using written petitions in lieu of maps to request changes of proposed rail construction with confidence and sophistication. A case in point is the submission of a petition by two men on behalf of the city of Cangzhou to Jin-Pu management in 1904, asking that the Jin-Pu Railroad Company move the projected line away from the public cemetery south of the eastern city wall. In their letter, the petitioners welcomed the railroad construction as beneficial to the city's commercial activity and positive for the residents' mobility. As the archival records show, a Chinese assistant in the

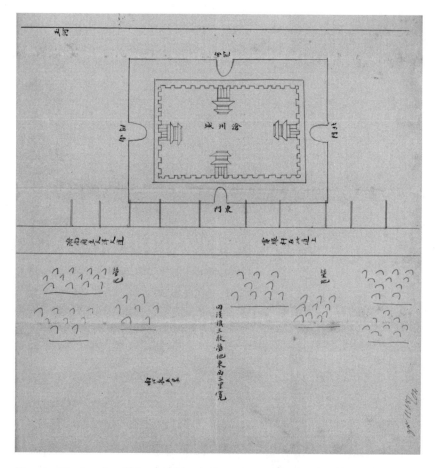

Fig. 1.2   Map based on Chinese petition indicating gravesites in Cangzhou city, 1904. Records relating to German railroad construction in China, 1898–1916, Baker Library, Harvard Business School, vol. 5, 1904, map inserted, no pagination.

railroad company's office produced a traditional hand-drawn map based on the petition with added information about the location of telegraph poles on the main road to Ji'nan outside the eastern city gate. The map demonstrates that translating written descriptions into a map was not a problem for Chinese familiar with traditional cartography. We can assume that the map conveniently provided abstract information for the Chinese management of the Jin-Pu Railroad, but was of no use to the company's foreign engineers (see Figure 1.2).[58]

For survey purposes, the railroad companies had to remedy the deficiencies of traditional Chinese cartography. Each surveyor, equipped with a list of questions in Chinese, approached a village accompanied by a local man who would write down the name of the village in Chinese. The surveyor would then write a note next to the Chinese characters and mark both with a number to place the village on the map. Afterward, the Chinese village name would be translated by the expedition interpreter.[59]

Whereas the colonial experience in India served as the model for surveying on the British half of the Jin-Pu line, the German half drew on military procedures and institutions. The first German engineers and surveyors were almost all attached to the military as part of the German colonial authorities stationed in Qingdao. They reported to the German embassy in Beijing and the German Ministry of Foreign Affairs in Berlin, and they were supervised by operations manager Heinrich Hildebrand, who, from his work for the Qingdao-Ji'nan Railroad, had experience with earlier colonial railroad projects in China.[60]

The German and British partners of the syndicate controlled different parts of the railroad and thus carried out their surveys separately. Before railroad construction could get under way, a detailed report from the German surveyors was required to decide on the course of the Jin-Pu line so as to adapt it as efficiently as possible to the landscape and to avoid the costly construction of bridges or tunnels. Within Shandong province, the Jin-Pu line paralleled an old imperial highway to minimize the need for major engineering projects, such as building trestles or blasting tunnels. The northern, or German, section was under the control of supervising engineer Julius Dorpmüller; the southern, or British, section was under the control of supervising engineer T. W. T. Tuckey. For the northern section alone, 430 maps were drawn. In 1908, the main engineering office of the northern section sent surveyors from Tianjin to the south to survey the area, redrawing older maps, and to divide the northern section into nine subsections. When the final survey was completed in 1909, the southern section was divided into three subsections. The office of the Jin-Pu Railroad in charge of land purchases then began to buy land on the basis of the maps produced from these surveys.[61]

## Land Acquisition

We know from violent reactions to railroad construction in the West that people in the countryside objected to the physical presence of tracks, telegraph equipment, and engines out of a general fear of the unknown and unfamiliar or because of religious or economic concerns.[62] Some of these issues played a part in the construction of the Jin-Pu line as well, but evidence from local history materials suggests that religious feng shui (geomancy) concerns among the local population often concealed the purely economic interests connected with land prices and fears of land devaluation or changes in ownership and tenant patterns. In fact, the Jin-Pu Railroad is a good example of how farmers in Dezhou, Jihe, and Jining counties cleverly classified their fields as gravesites and thus achieved above-average sale prices for their land because the Jin-Pu Railroad Company was eager to avoid any local dissatisfaction or unrest before the actual construction process had even started.[63]

Incidents such as the attacks on the Beijing-Baoding Railroad in late May 1900, when Boxer rebels tore up tracks and damaged stations and telegraph lines, continued to influence Western interpretations of Chinese attitudes toward railroad technology.[64] In addition to the physical damage to railroad lines and stations, five foreign railroad engineers were killed as they attempted to escape to Tianjin. One day later, the Boxers burned the Fengtai station along the Beijing-Tianjin Railroad, and in the following weeks the Boxers moved toward the capital, cutting off rail links between Beijing and Tianjin.[65] On May 16, 1900, the Boxers issued notices to the local populations in Tianjin and Zhili province warning them not to "take trains in the interest of speed, lest you meet with death on the rails" because "all railways throughout the area will be destroyed."[66] The Boxers inflicted great damage on rail-related personnel and property, resulting in fierce responses from foreign troops, such as the Russian soldiers defending the Tianjin railroad station at Laolongtou on June 18, 1900.[67]

To put things in perspective, however, we need to remember that by 1900 the network of operating railroads in North China consisted of only several short lines in Zhili province that connected Beijing with Baoding, Tianjin, the coastline at Tanggu, and the mines at Tangshan—altogether only 650 miles of track. At the time, the most extensive railroad was under Russian control in Manchuria, far away from Boxer activity. As historian Paul Cohen convincingly points out, China's engagement with the West in the nineteenth century included two different interfaces with very different reactions: imperialism as a negative force on the one hand and progress and modernity as a positive force on the other. Both served as a cause and indirect, representative target of the Boxer Uprising.[68] We should regard the Boxer attacks on Western technology in this complex context, however, as a symptomatic response to railroads as tentacles of imperialism and antiforeign sentiments in general—not as a reaction against railroad technology per se. Although a number of boatmen who had lost their jobs because of the arrival of the Beijing-Tianjin Railroad after 1896 joined the Boxer Uprising in Tianjin, they were in a minority among the large number of farmers impoverished by drought who went to the city from the surrounding countryside in early 1900 to join the movement.[69]

Apart from the activities of the Boxer rebels, other infamous incidents of Chinese opposition to rail construction and land acquisition occurred in the context of the preparations for the Ji'nan-Qingdao Railroad on the German colonial leasehold in the territory of Jiaozhou on the Shandong peninsula. This territory, which had been annexed by German naval units in November 1897, became an example of state-directed German colonialism attempting to showcase the benefits of enlightened socioeconomic policies and their execution, until the Japanese took over during World War I in late 1914.[70] Because the colonial presence in this area was guided and supported by a heavy-handed military, interactions with the local population were more politicized than those in the semicolonial area of the Jin-Pu Railroad and other railroad syndicates.

Local opposition to the building of the Ji'nan-Qingdao Railroad near the village of Gaomi appears to have been a complex response to various factors undermining socioeconomic stability of local society, including the hiring of construction workers from outside the province by the German railroad company, an uncompromising and brutal military presence along the tracks, and an unfair negotiation process for land acquisition.[71] As a direct attack on railroads representing colonialism, antirailroad protests in the German colony led to military repression, with a considerable loss of lives, mostly on the Chinese side; however, evidence of artificially low land prices is less clear, because arguments by historians are based on a single diary source from 1900 with extremely scarce and impressionistic data.[72] Therefore, we need to revisit this issue, especially because we have to consider that the overwhelming majority of Chinese railroad construction did not take place in the context of colonial leaseholds.

The prosaic process of land purchases for the Jin-Pu railroad suggests a more accommodating attitude toward the new technology on the part of the Chinese than the dramatic events connected with the Boxers. In contrast to the argument by some Chinese historians who comment on the "exploitative" nature of land acquisition by colonial railroad companies, my research shows that purchasing land from Chinese farmers along the line was not that much of a problem.[73] To avoid public protests and lengthy negotiations, the Jin-Pu Railroad Company offered a price per *mu* (0.067 hectares) much higher than the local average.[74] Railroad companies were aware of feng shui concerns among the local population and dealt with the delicate matter of moving gravesites and buying grave land by offering Chinese farmers generous remuneration. For example, in 1899 the American chief engineer in charge of surveying the railroad between Hankou and Guangzhou patronizingly stated that "a payment of about $5 per grave removes all objections."[75]

Other railroad lines reached broader compensation agreements about gravesites with the landowners along the line, independent of the actual size of the land plots. For the Imperial Chinese Eastern Railroad in the north, each resident received the sum of eight taels to atone "for the disturbance of each dead ancestor" and to compensate for moving the graves to a new burial space. From the perspective of William Barclay Parsons, the engineer whom we met at the beginning of this chapter, this lucrative compensation scheme not only resulted in removing any opposition to the railroad company's land acquisition and construction plans but also engendered new business practices related to land acquisition. Once local entrepreneurial land speculators had determined the location of a proposed new line, they would approach the owners of the ancestral gravesites on the land targeted for future construction and offer their services as middlemen. In such a capacity they would arrange for the reburial of the graves in advance of the construction process, compensate the original owners, and then claim a tariff of eight taels per grave from the railroad company. As the engineer noted, this arrangement was lucrative for both, as the railroad compensation allowed a "broker fee" for the local middleman.[76]

Gauging the general situation of land prices was among the survey tasks undertaken by the engineering corps. Along with survey categories for population figures, available labor, wage rates, the nature of the soil, and available materials for construction and transport (mules and bullocks), the so-called value-of-land category gave rough estimates of land value per major line section in the reports. For example, the Pekin Syndicate surveyors presented a wide-ranging estimate, from six to fifteen taels per *mu* to twenty to fifty taels per *mu* of land along the proposed line from Fencheng to Lushan.[77] Most of the estimates correlated population density with general soil quality; however, in their reports the engineers freely admitted the lack of detailed, precise price information, with the explanation that "it has been exceedingly difficult to obtain correct information as regards prices, as it soon became understood that it would be an advantage to the inhabitants to put the best possible price on their property, whatever it was, if marketable."[78]

It was extremely difficult for me to obtain any definite information about the price of land prospected by the railroad companies from Chinese primary sources, and surprisingly, the information in the official and unofficial documents of the syndicates is not much better. For example, in September 1899 the Pekin Syndicate surveyed the north bank of the Yangzi River near Pukou to find the best location for a terminus linking Nanjing across the river to the Hankou-Canton line. Engineer Harry Augustus Frederick Currie and two Indian surveyors considered Pukou a favorable location for the terminal because the water was 40 feet deep within 150 feet of the shore, and it was the only suitable place on the swampy north shore, even though it was located much to the east of Nanjing. In contrast to those evaluations of the more populated land along the proposed line section in Hubei, estimates for the swampy, deserted land on the shoreline averaged approximately five dollars (approximately three British pounds) per *mu,* including the cultivated and uncultivated land.[79] I was unable to assess the actual cost of the land for the company. Records containing the final estimates of the cost of construction never included the cost of the land, only the cost of track per mile, depending on the gradient per mile, the curves and their radius, and the number of tunnels, bridges, and stations.[80]

The problem of land evaluation and how to account for acquisition costs continued throughout construction of the Jin-Pu Railroad and well into the 1910s when banks and bondholders required detailed financial reports. Even the official year-end report from 1912, when the line officially opened, stated evasively that "during construction time, this office was working under continuous high pressure and was, in consequence, unable, as will be easily understood, to complete a final detailed survey of all the ground purchased as well as its demarcation by boundary stones."[81] Chief engineer Dorpmüller expressed his frustration with the situation more openly in his report of accountability (*Rechenschaftsbericht*) for the northern section of the Jin-Pu line from January 1914, which still included just one total figure for construction costs, covering land, rolling stock, stations, and all fixed assets. He considered the lack of fiscal transparency as "impossible to quantify" and blamed the Chinese side for the higher construction costs compared with costs of the German Jiao-Ji Railroad on the Shandong peninsula.[82]

The lack of information regarding land acquisition prices and expenditures might be due to engineers and surveyors being inexperienced and uninformed about property rights in China, at both the local and national levels. The 1899 survey by the Pekin Syndicate contains an appendix with the questions asked by the engineers on survey trips, including whether the government was the proprietor of all the land and about the structure of land tenure and tax collection, with very general answers provided by the local magistrate.[83] Even the reports by the German surveyors for the Jin-Pu line in Shandong produced only rough estimates of land prices in tables, with so-called *Wertklassen* (value categories) for the land based on the soil conditions as guidelines and upper price limits for the officials handling the transactions.[84] On the southern part of the Jin-Pu line, the British also adopted this metric in their approach to land values and acquisition costs.

Although lacking a detailed understanding of the local property rights arrangements, customary land prices, and local land-transfer practices, the Jin-Pu Railroad Company nevertheless was sufficiently astute to realize from the beginning that the valuation of individual land parcels and the purchase transactions would be far too complicated for the foreign management to deal with. Negotiation of fair deals and interactions with the local residents and landowners had to be outsourced. For this purpose, the Jin-Pu Railroad Company handed over responsibility for local land purchases to the Chinese joint-venture partner—the Chinese government—thus relying on local officials to handle all related transactions. These local officials became the company's de facto middlemen for negotiating the prices (within limits provided by the company) and arranging the official land transfers.[85]

Relying on local magistrates for land pricing and purchases had two major consequences. The first is the lack of documentation: few documents provide firsthand evidence related to land purchases, and those that do exist are difficult to locate in colonial records and Chinese repositories.[86] Second, this method opened the door to corruption. For example, as soon as Daotai (circuit attendant) Li Lianxi in Tianjin, in his capacity as agent for the Jin-Pu Railroad Company, learned about the proposed location of the railroad station in the Nankai district of the city, he cofounded Huaxing Real Estate Company with another official, Daotai Cao Jiaxing. The company bought the land near the station for 480,000 taels but registered it with the government as having a value of 1.3 million taels and then sold it to the Jin-Pu Railroad Company for that higher price.[87] Along with stations and warehouse districts, land close to projected bridges resulted in land speculation, which was criticized by the German construction management. Although corrupt practices discovered by the Jin-Pu German managers during an internal audit in 1909 led to some minor changes in the purchase policy, reliance on Chinese government officials continued.

Most intriguing is the question of what happened when farmers refused to sell. According to the records of the Jin-Pu line, farmers were threatened with being taken to the prefectural court, but no records documenting such legal disputes can be found.[88] We can speculate that the Jin-Pu Railroad was interested in avoiding local protests and lawsuits, and therefore it offered decent compensation and relied on the local government as the go-between in land acquisitions. It is quite certain that those officials also received a cut from the purchase process, and moreover, they could put pressure on the local landowners in their role as representatives of the imperial government.

Few documents exist that indicate serious protests by local landowners because of their dissatisfaction with the offered land price or unwillingness to sell their land along the projected Jin-Pu line. The only major exception I have encountered regarding the Jin-Pu Railroad involves the Kong family and their estate in Qufu of Tai'an county. The Kong estate is an extraordinary case, however: its owners were direct descendants of Confucius (Kongzi), and for centuries the temple and family mansion at the site had received imperial patronage. According to the original survey maps from 1900, the Jin-Pu line was supposed to run through Qufu at a point close to the western wall of Kongzi lin (Forest of Confucius), the large cemetery of the Kong lineage.[89] The original course of the railroad track would have seriously violated the feng shui of the forest of gravesites and cut through the surrounding agricultural and ceremonial land, which, for the most part, was owned by the Kong family.[90]

Kong Delin, as head of the Kong lineage, vehemently objected to this plan and in 1904 petitioned the Guangxu emperor with several memorials, claiming that the railroad would "shake the tomb of the sage" and "stop the sage's very pulse," and "the spirits of the ancestors would not be able to rest in peace" if valuable family land was sold to the Jin-Pu Railroad Company.[91] Despite this rhetoric of cultural and religious outrage, the protest perhaps also originated from more economic-driven concerns. One might speculate that the Kong family was not willing to sell part of its land in Qufu because the offered price was considered inadequate or because income derived from this land was necessary to support the estate and provide for the lineage's ceremonial sacrifices as well as its servants and dependents.[92] After being pressured by the Chinese imperial government, which historically had extended special patronage to the Kong family, the engineers of the Jin-Pu Railroad altered the planned route for the line. As a result, the railroad makes a wide curve around the cemetery forest and Kong estate, bypassing it by approximately ten miles, thus requiring visitors to the popular tourist destination to take further transportation after getting off the train at Qufu station.[93]

## Laying the Tracks

The founding and construction process of the Jin-Pu Railroad under German and British management reflected the colonial sociopolitical hierarchies as well as the almost complete absence of technical knowledge and railroad expertise among Chinese at the turn of the century. Professional training in railroad engineering did not emerge at a substantial institutionalized level in China until the late 1910s when technical institutes were established and began to produce engineers with expertise in fields such as railroad technology, geological sciences, and bridge and tunnel construction.

Employment of foreign engineers was the general solution to this problem. Reports by Westerners traveling via steamer on the Yangzi River in the early twentieth century often mention male passengers of various European nationalities on their way to work, either as employees of the Chinese Maritime Customs Service in the newly opened treaty ports or in search of jobs with railroad companies, such as the Jing-Han line at Hankou.[94] Before moving to China many of these foreigners had experience with large construction projects, such as building the Panama Canal or working for colonial railroad projects in Africa. For example, after more than a decade of successful work as chief accountant for the Belgian Compagnie Chemin de Fer in the Congo, in 1903 Joseph Loewy, uncle of the famous writer Franz Kafka, joined the Belgian railroad project on the Zhengtai line from Beijing to Hankou. As an employee of the Banque Russo-Chinoise in China he was in charge of tasks directly related to the Belgian railroad concession.[95]

In early 1910, when construction within Shandong province was proceeding at full speed, the Jin-Pu line employed thirty-eight Germans who were distributed among the four construction sections in Dezhou, Ji'nan, Tai'an, and Yanzhou. The bridge across the Yellow River (Huanghe) was a major construction project because of its concrete pillars and temporary landing bridges. For that specific purpose the German section hired sixteen employees from the German machinery producer MAN (Maschinenfabrik Augsburg-Nürnberg) Brückenanstalt Gustavsburg. Crossing the river was the greatest challenge to the line: before the German engineers completed the cast-iron bridge at the end of 1912, passengers exited the train on one side and rode ferries across the river to a second locomotive waiting on the other side (see Figures 1.3 and 1.4).[96]

Employing foreign engineers was not ideal, however. They required translators when communicating with Chinese foremen, and even then the communication problems, both linguistic and cultural, were considerable.[97] The best solution, before the local engineering institutes were up to speed, was to hire foreign-trained Chinese engineers. Thus, the railroad companies competed among one another for the few Chinese nationals who had returned to China after completing their studies in the United States or Belgium. For example, after competing vigorously with the Shanghai-Nanjing Railroad for precious human capital, in 1909 the Jin-Pu line managed to hire Albert C. Lee, an American-trained engineer, who became the first Chinese to join the company at the management level.[98] The father of the writer Han Suyin is another example. He was trained in Belgium and then worked for the railroad in Henan as a railroad inspector. According to Han Suyin's memoir, the

**Fig. 1.3**  Passengers crossing the Yellow River by boat, with the unfinished railroad bridge in the background, 1912. Records relating to German railroad construction in China, 1898–1916, Baker Library, Harvard Business School, vol. 14, 1912, p. 34.

family's lifestyle was a testament to her father's value to the company: in their travels from post to post, they lived in splendid houses provided by the railroad administration.[99]

The lack of trained specialists extended beyond expert railroad engineering knowledge. An additional problem was the lack of vocational schools to prepare Chinese employees, through basic technical and on-the-job training, for working on the railroad as conductors, engine drivers, signalers, and so forth. Because these were skilled but lower-level jobs, the German management decided to open a railroad school in Tianjin to train Chinese in these important subjects. Efforts to teach the apprentices German proved unsuccessful. In the mid-1910s, when it became clear that English had become the "railroad language" in China (see Chapter 2), the school closed and the apprentices were sent to Tangshan Engineering School, the oldest Chinese mining school.[100]

**HOANGHOBRÜCKE**
der Tientsin-Pukow-Bahn

Erbaut 1909 - 1912
von der Maschinenfabrik Augsburg - Nürnberg A. G. Werk Gustavsburg
Gesamtlänge 1255,2 Meter
Stand der Arbeiten am 2. Oktober

**Fig. 1.4** Invitation to the opening of the Jin-Pu railroad bridge across the Yellow River, 1912. Records relating to German railroad construction in China, 1898–1916, Baker Library, Harvard Business School, vol. 14, 1912, insert in "Anlage zu Bericht," No. 110, no pagination.

Because of the initial shortage of Chinese skilled laborers and clerical employees, the German engineers and directors decided to hire German nationals as foremen and lower-level managers during the early construction phase of the Jin-Pu line. However, these hires sometimes became a serious liability for the railroad company. Personnel records suggest that these foremen often had dubious backgrounds, involving legal troubles at home or unsuccessful military careers, and very little education. For them, seeking employment in China with German or international companies was an attempt to restart their careers and personal lives at much higher economic and social levels compared with employment opportunities at home.[101]

Lacking experience, cultural sensitivity, and common sense, some of these foremen committed serious offenses against the local Chinese population. The syndicates' employment of so-called low-grade Continentals with lackluster job performance was widespread among all railroad companies, and it was such a serious problem that it found its way into newspaper discussions, such as the *North-China Herald* in 1900.[102] For example, a German foreman on the Jin-Pu Railroad was prone to disorderly drunken conduct and once randomly shot at innocent local villagers, and he caused many other problems for his superiors. Fearing permanent damage to the company's reputation, chief engineer Dorpmüller and the senior management decided to fire the troublemakers and after 1909 they hired only Chinese foremen, thus de facto phasing out lower-level German managers in the company.[103]

Laborers on the Chinese railroads were largely indigenous. Construction and operation of the Jin-Pu line created nonfarm employment with cash wages for the Shandong local population living near the construction corridor. Clearing the terrain, preparing the railroad bed, and constructing the tracks were tasks undertaken solely by Chinese day laborers recruited from nearby villages. They worked in the traditional contract-labor system (*baogong*) under Chinese foremen (*gongtou*) who recruited and paid them.[104] With their considerable power over labor management on the construction site, the Chinese foremen de facto represented the lowest Chinese management level in the Jin-Pu Railroad Company. To maintain better financial control over the *gongtou,* the German railroad construction department tried to directly outsource local labor but without much success.

In the same way that some Chinese government officials carved out lucrative roles for themselves in the land acquisition process, others became brokers in the logistics process necessary for construction. For example, while being appointed an agent for the Jin-Pu line, the official Li Lianxi founded a transportation business that charged $4.50 (in silver dollars) per ton to transport material for the Jin-Pu Railroad Company. Li then passed on the order to a subcontractor who charged $1.43 per ton, leaving Li with a handsome profit. Not surprisingly, German management criticized this as a corrupt practice.[105]

The equipment and rolling stock on the Jin-Pu line consisted almost exclusively of foreign imports. In the German section, large steel companies and prominent machinery producers like MAN in Germany supplied the initial equipment, which was transported by ship to Qingdao and from there was sent via the Qingdao-Ji'nan line to the Jin-Pu headquarters.[106] According to the rolling stock inventory list for December 31, 1912, the northern section had 50 locomotives, of which 20 were for hauling goods, 20 for transporting passengers, and 10 for shunting trains between tracks. The locomotives serviced 125 passenger cars, 30 service cars such as luggage and mail cars, and 646 freight cars of different carrying capacities.[107] Although this report does not list the specific brand of the rolling stock, we can speculate that most of it had been manufactured in Germany. By comparison, the much shorter southern section required about a third less rolling stock, provided by British manufacturers.[108] The Jin-Pu Railroad and other railroad companies continued to import all rolling stock from Germany, Britain, and the United States until 1949 because the Chinese machine industry was never able to produce high-quality domestic substitutes.[109]

The standard Jin-Pu line was a single-track system with trains pulled by steam engines. Steel rails were imported from Germany but also purchased domestically from Hanyang Steelworks, China's largest steel mill at the time. In both sections each berth of steel rails rested on fourteen wooden ties imported mostly from the United States and Japan. Interlocking signals indicating a clear track at stations were available, and communications equipment in the form of wooden semaphore poles with four control cables was installed along the line.[110]

Bringing the heavy construction materials and machinery to the track construction sites was not an easy task. Water transport initially seemed the most appropriate method for heavy, bulky loads in the absence of a good road network, especially for the north–south route of the Grand Canal that passed through Shandong province and linked to the port of Shanghai where large steamships with imported equipment could dock. With these conditions in mind, the Jin-Pu engineers took a trip along the Grand Canal from Zhenjiang, where ships could enter the canal from the Yangzi River and move northward to the Shandong border. They concluded that large material transports (some carrying entire locomotives) were not feasible, probably because of the size and draft of the required ships and the silted canal bed. This situation therefore required transport via the Shandong railroad from the port of Qingdao to Ji'nan.[111]

Despite the challenges of semicolonial politics and cultural misunderstandings, construction of the line was carried out relatively swiftly, and both sections were completed in 1912. The German, northern, section of the line linked with the southern, British, section of the line using the same gauge (rail width) to eliminate costly and time-consuming transfers. Paralleling the Grand Canal, the Jin-Pu line soon competed for the transportation of goods in Hebei, Shandong, and Jiangsu provinces and also attracted a major share of the passenger traffic from Beijing and Tianjin to the lower Yangzi region. Similar to the Beijing-Hankou line, which connected northern China with the commercial center of the interior provinces along the Yangzi River, the Jin-Pu line benefited the commercial development of Shanghai, its final destination after passing through Nanjing. Thus, this railroad was a fast and convenient link between the political center and the commercial center of Republican China and between the north and the Yangzi delta. Together with the Guangzhou-Hankou Railroad and the Beijing-Hankou Railroad, the Jin-Pu Railroad became the backbone of strategic railroad development for improved passenger transport, expansion of commerce and industrial supplies, and development of the nation's communications network.

## Conclusion

Given its current status as "the postwar star" in global railroad development and ambition,[112] China was remarkably late off the starting block. Every other major country had a significant rail network by the end of the nineteenth century, whereas China had little more than a few short lines serving mining ventures. Why did the railroad come to China so late and grow so haltingly?

As this chapter shows, railroad construction in China was late and slow not because some Chinese might have been incorrigible Luddites hostile to progress but rather because of a host of structural problems having to do with the political contexts and deficiencies in certain key domestic resources, especially financing and engineering expertise. Late Qing China lacked the sort of strong central authority and economic institutional framework necessary for large infrastructure projects such as railroads. Instead, the divergent interests of the imperial government and provincial governments; different national representatives of the foreign syndicates and diplomatic missions; the provincial and local Chinese officials; and the directors, managers, and supervisors of the company on the ground had to negotiate every detail of financial and operational management through various layers of parallel but separate bureaucratic entities. This fragmentation of authority made it easier for vested interests to stall railroad construction. The case of the Jin-Pu Railroad also demonstrates, however, great tenacity on the part of foreign and

Chinese parties to move the construction along and to bring it to a successful completion.[113]

Railroad construction in late nineteenth- and early twentieth-century China presented the problem of introducing a highly complex business and administrative institution into the Chinese economic, political, and financial realm without the corresponding presence of large business institutions and a railroad bureaucratic infrastructure. Knowledge about railroads existed, but it was not yet institutionalized and incorporated into the educational system. Even with the best of intentions to foster economic and technological progress, late imperial China lacked an established tradition of engineering education necessary to mount a wholly indigenous railroad development project.

The task of bringing railroads to China was more than a matter of merely laying tracks and importing locomotives: it was also necessary to build an entire educational establishment to create the necessary engineering and managerial expertise. In contemporary terms, the introduction of railroads to China involved transferring new technology and hardware to an environment that lacked the necessary software in the form of an engineering knowledge system and technically trained human resources. Simultaneously introducing both new equipment and the associated knowledge systems to an economic and political environment was costly and involved foreign intervention at multiple levels. Chinese officials who opposed the railroad foresaw—quite accurately—that these domestic deficiencies meant that railroads in China would be an avenue for European financial and political influence.

In light of these obstacles, it should not be surprising that China's railroads developed slowly and relatively late. Moreover, the tensions and misunderstandings created by the half-dozen colonial powers building the railroads under Chinese management plagued railroad development at every stage of the process, from financing to surveying to land purchases and construction. Conflicts emerged both among fractious colonial authorities and among local sources of power, creating endless opportunities for inefficiency and corruption. As Chapter 3 will show, early Chinese railroad companies developed along a managerial path dictated by the national experience of their foreign partners and investors. At the same time, they had to accommodate dual chains of managerial control that grew from the semicolonial environment and also incorporate indigenous managerial practices, such as the contract-labor system, of local industrial companies. Examples of modern, Western-style professional management and corporate governance did not yet exist.

It is important not to expect too much of nineteenth-century corporate governance as an absolute standard in any country. Historian Steven Usselman has shown that enormous, often disruptive, challenges to U.S. railroad innovation and its regulation affected management and operations from the mid-nineteenth to the early twentieth centuries.[114] And as historian Richard White argues with great passion, even the building of the transcontinental railroads in the United States, in the context of industrialization and full-fledged capitalism, revealed railroad construction to be an inefficient and often corrupt process.[115] The managerial structures of China's railroad companies began to evolve once semicolonialism gave way to the emergence of the Chinese nation-state in the wake of the 1911 revolution. Whereas earlier conflicts mainly focused on the differing agendas of the foreign companies and the colonial interests of their governments vis-à-vis the national interests of the Chinese government, after 1911 new conflicts arose among provincial railroad companies, regional warlords, and the central government, most notably because of the adoption of a nationalization policy.

## CHAPTER TWO

# Managing Transitions in the Early Republic

T he second decade of the twentieth century was a period of volatile transitions for China as well as for its railroads. As it happened, the railroads played an indirect political role in mobilizing public sentiment against foreign loans and, by proxy, against the imperial government. The announcement to nationalize the planned Sichuan-Hankou Railroad and the Hankou-Guangzhou Railroad and to construct them with foreign loans led to an antigovernment reaction by the Chinese public in the affected regions, sparking the Railway Rights Recovery Movement in Sichuan province in May 1911. Private Chinese investors in the planned railroads, mostly merchants and gentry, protested the decision that they be compensated for two-thirds of their investment with government bonds rather than cash. Together with other provincial activists, investors presented their demands for Chinese-funded, locally run railroads in a nationalistic, antiforeign rhetoric that wildly overestimated the fiscal capability of the imperial government at the time. Unrest related to the Railway Rights Recovery Movement in Sichuan challenged the authority of the Manchu court; the resulting military power vacuum in central China allowed the rather accidental Wuchang Uprising to succeed in bringing down the Qing government in October 1911.[1]

The transition from empire to republic involved, among many other changes, substantial restructuring of governmental, economic, and social institutions so as to be appropriate for the state's new legal and political framework. The relatively small network of railroad lines at various stages of planning, construction, and completion became part of these restructuring efforts. In the broadest terms, the advent of the Chinese Republic was accompanied by the nationalization of the railroads. This process and the related public debates, however, had already begun in certain instances before 1911, such as that of the Sichuan-Hankou line, and they were not completed until many years later. As in many other reform efforts defining the new nation-state, the transition process involved resurrecting ideas and continuing changes that had originated with the post-1900 late Qing reforms.[2]

This analysis of the institutional transformation of railroads during the nationalization process must therefore encompass more than a story of linear development. It must consider the unfolding managerial and financial changes at the railroad company level that occurred over time as well as the regulatory and administrative changes at the state level that were designed to build a bureaucracy for a modern railroad. To complicate matters, the nationalization and centralization process depended also on continued involvement in and negotiations with the former joint rail ventures with foreign partners whose influence, especially in management and financial arrangements, continued well into the 1920s. As this chapter shows, although many Chinese had objected to foreign control of their railroads during the last years of the empire, it took the Republic two decades to develop sufficient managerial and administrative capacities to be able to manage its own system efficiently.

In this particular context, it is important to note that the term "nationalization" does not suggest a sudden, radical transfer of ownership and managerial control by the Chinese government expropriating all foreign rail investment. From the Chinese government's perspective, the transition toward nationalization was meant to establish the political and economic independence of a strategic sector and to secure national interests from foreign influence. In political terms, nationalization transferred full sovereignty over the railroads to the Chinese government. In financial terms, following nationalization the Chinese government continued to service the foreign loans of the former joint syndicates, and it even raised new bond issues on the public markets of London and New York.[3] In managerial terms, until the 1920s foreigners still held many senior positions in now nationalized Chinese railroad companies, whether they were fully government-owned or under Chinese managerial control, because of contractual commitments tied to the foreign loan contracts and the lack of an open labor market for Chinese engineers and highly skilled workers. For example, in 1922 approximately 25 percent of Chinese railroad lines were still owned and operated by foreigners and another 25 percent or so were under foreign influence because of loan agreements.[4] As this chapter argues, at the company level the transition toward nationalization was a slow and complicated process, producing hybrid structures that were only nominally full-fledged Chinese rail companies.[5]

The process of nationalizing Chinese railroad companies and integrating them into a bureaucratic superstructure for the benefit of the new nation-state was gradual and piecemeal. For readers familiar with the political fragmentation and volatility of the early Republic, this development will not come as a surprise. Thomas Kampen's assessment of early railroad development in the context of the 1911 revolution confirms that China's railroad nationalization came too early and did not result in substantial organizational and economic benefits.[6] The focus of this chapter, however, is not the nationalization process per se but rather the institutional evolution of the railroad companies as rational managerial, social, and financial organizations. Historians are already resigned to the fact that "the situation was different for each line," depending on its location during the political struggle for control over the young Republic.[7] This situation does not prevent us from attempting to synthesize the overall institutional process, especially as we follow the evolution of the railroad bureau system under the umbrella of the Ministry of Railways, which until 2013 remained the framework for China's rail administration.

This chapter introduces the emerging organizational structures of the national railroad administration during the early Republic and the institutional consequences of the attendant political and financial pressures. It shows how the transfer of knowledge continued and how the emerging railroad companies borrowed features from their former Western partners, such as the European departmental system of managerial organization and the American system of railroad accounts. Simultaneously, the railroad bureau system began to evolve as an administrative system that centralized the diverse railroad lines with only limited success. The discussion then moves from the management level to hierarchies and working conditions on shop floors to reveal how the railroads responded strategically to the shortage of skilled labor and engineers and how members of the workforce with different professional and social backgrounds inserted themselves into the institutional culture of the rail compounds.

## Building a National Administrative Framework

After 1911, the new government faced the huge task of bringing existing private, provincial, and government railroads into the fold of the emerging state bureaucracy and taking charge of the planning, financing, construction, and management of the railroads. As the slow and messy nationalization process moved forward, we can establish the following data points for rail lines in 1922: foreigners still owned and controlled 2,375 miles, Chinese nationalized lines with foreign-directed requirements tied to loan contracts owned 2,188 miles, Chinese nationalized lines with foreign accountants and engineering staff controlled 4,687 miles, and private local ownership held 500 miles of short provincial railroads serving mining operations.[8] With the exception of the five railroads remaining under the foreign concessions—the Chinese Eastern, the South Manchurian, Yunnan, and Shandong Railways and the British part of the Kowloon-Canton-Hankow Railroad—the Ministry of Railways supervised the 7,375 miles of government-owned or government-controlled lines as well as the private lines (see Map 2.1).[9] As discussed in later chapters, no substantial rail expansion through new trunk lines occurred throughout the Republican period, so that statistics from the end of 1934 reveal a modest increase in the track length of the national railroads; only the number of very short private industrial lines increased, bringing their track mileage to 813 miles.[10]

To be sure, government control was not a wholly new phenomenon in 1911: the central Chinese state had been involved in the nation's railroads from the beginning. From the 1880s to 1903, railroad affairs fell under the purview of the imperial Foreign Office (Zongli yamen), with a special attachment to the Bureau of Mining (Kuangwuju) beginning in 1898. When this bureau in Beijing was closed in the wake of the Boxer Rebellion of 1900, railroads and mines were moved to the newly established Ministry of Foreign Affairs (Waiwubu) until 1903. Administrative changes resulting from the late Qing reforms occurring in the early years of the twentieth century attempted to address the functional role of rail infrastructure by attaching railroad matters to the Ministry of Commerce (Shangbu) in 1903; the Ministry of Posts and Communications (Youchuanbu) assumed railroad matters from 1906 until the fall of the Qing dynasty.[11] Because different parts of the ministry were

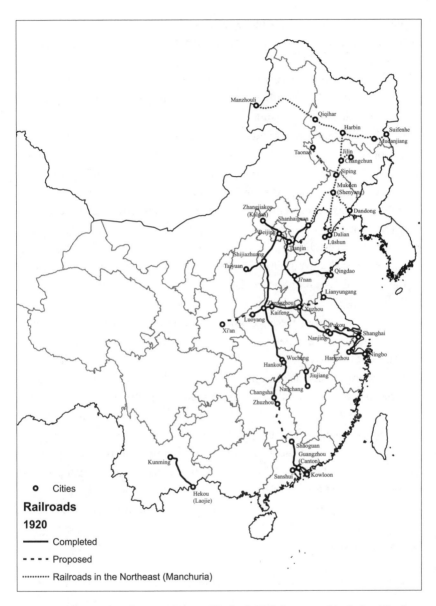

**Map 2.1**  Major railroads, 1920. Map © Elisabeth Köll (cartographic design Matthew Sisk).

responsible for different lines, bureaucratic control was defined geographically rather than according to organizational functions, thus creating inefficiencies and a lack of synergy.[12]

Under the post-1911 successor regime of the first, only provisional, government in Nanjing, the administrative structure finally shifted from a political and geographical focus to a more operational organization of rail infrastructure. Railroad affairs were handled by the Ministry of Communications and Transportation (Jiaotongbu), in charge of roads, railroads, shipping routes, postal services, telegrams, shipping transportation, and shipbuilding matters and governance of shipping crews.[13] When the Beiyang government under Yuan Shikai moved to Beijing as the Republic's first government, the ministry retained both its name and wide portfolio until the Guomindang government in 1928 established China's first Ministry of Railways (Tiedaobu) as a full-blown, specialized bureaucracy in charge of the national railroads.[14]

The railroads' changing administrative affiliations indicate a gradual shift in the official view of railroads: once seen as purely military and strategic tools, by the 1910s they were recognized as complex, multifunctional enterprises requiring specialized management in their own right. Although government officials managing China's railroad affairs since the late Qing dynasty were experienced administrators with strong political agendas, they had very little technical and managerial knowledge. In addition, the post-1911 leadership at the top of the Ministry of Communications and Transportation experienced a stunning turnover: between 1912 and 1927 the ministry was headed by no fewer than twenty-one different ministers (*zongzhang*), some of whom had repeated tenures.[15] The frequent changes at the top are not surprising against the backdrop of the fragile political landscape of shifting alliances among the split governments in both the north and the south during the early Republic, and they indicate how much the highest position continued to be a predominantly political appointment with limited practical authority.

At the departmental level of the ministry where the Bureau of Public Roads (Luzheng si) handled railroad matters through nine administrative divisions (*ke*), the executive turnover was much lower, with some multiyear appointments ensuring at least some degree of stability. By 1917 these divisions had emerged with clear responsibilities for business management, legal affairs, control, planning, supervision, hiring, negotiations, real estate, and central affairs. Apart from addressing the railroads' operational functions, the areas of real estate, legal matters, and negotiations, introduced after 1911, reflected the necessity of managing the considerable land assets of the nationalized lines and defining the legal rights and obligations of railroads as business entities and a public good.[16] This structure was to remain in place until the founding of the Ministry of Railways in 1928, which centralized railroad management and streamlined the bureaucratic apparatus down to four operational divisions: main affairs, business management, supervision, and planning.

In the midst of the frequent administrative reorganization during the early Republican period, there emerged the most important bureaucratic structure, which has become the hallmark of China's railroad system: the Railroad Management Bureau (Tielu guanliju), commonly referred to in abbreviated form as the railroad bureau (*tieluju*). Structurally, railroad bureaus grew out of the lines' former head offices (*zongju*), but during the post-1911 transition they came under the direct jurisdiction of the Ministry of Communications and Transportation.[17] It is important to the argument in this book that the railroad bureau structure has survived with great resilience into the twenty-first century (see Chapters 7 and 8). It still dominates China's rail administration today under the same name as it did some one hundred years ago.[18]

This newly formalized system divided responsibility for the Chinese national railroads according to the geographical scope covered by the major lines. Each railroad bureau became the managerial and operational headquarters of a specific trunk line and subordinate branch lines, usually headquartered in the city of the departure terminal. In the case of the Jin-Pu Railroad, for example, the railroad bureau was established in Tianjin, with a branch bureau added in 1927 in Pukou, near the new capital of Nanjing.[19] As we see in later chapters, the geographical boundaries demarcating the authority of each railroad bureau changed to some extent over time, yet the basic system remained in place.

Railroad bureaus as institutional entities have not received much attention from historians.[20] This is unfortunate because their internal records add important insights into the managerial development of railroad companies during the pre-1949 period. Considered an institutional part of the government administration serving national defense, their internal documentation is currently controlled by the Ministry of Railways and is not easily accessible.

My analysis attempts to remedy this situation by drawing on a wide variety of archival sources and internal records generated from different institutional levels during the Republican period.

It might seem ironic that the regional railroad bureau structure emerging as a formalized system encouraged a fairly high degree of autonomy during the institution-building process of the early Republic. This system, however, developed in the context of the line-specific financial arrangements and the physical damage to tracks and rolling stock due to the warlord battles, at a time when no operational synergies existed for either the larger region or the nation as such. In fact, it is misleading to discuss a connecting rail "network" in the early days of the Republic even though there was a considerable number of individual lines. The first through transport on the five largest railroads in eastern and central China became possible in April 1914, but many other lines were not interconnected until much later.[21] By the early 1920s the sixteen railroad bureaus covered the existing network of major lines, with headquarters in eleven cities throughout the country.[22] In sum, regional political fragmentation and severely limited network connectivity resulted in a regionally divided railroad system, thereby exacerbating efforts to centralize organization and administration.

The immediate post-1911 reforms are difficult to analyze from internal railroad company sources documenting the transition, but the discourse in newspapers and journals shows that the new political scenario encouraged a number of Chinese and foreign railroad experts and advisers to argue publicly on behalf of a new beginning for China's railroads. The China National Railroad Association (Zhonghua quanguo tielu xiehui), founded in Beijing in January 1912 in affiliation with the Ministry of Communications and Transportation, became the most important institutional platform for Chinese reformers. Its program involved the assembly of Chinese talent and the exchange of knowledge and expertise for the benefit of government-owned (*guo you*) and commercial (*shang you*) or private railroads. According to its founding document, the goal of the association was "1.) to assist the progress of our country's infrastructure politics, 2.) to promote the development of railroad-related industries, 3.) to protect the rights of our national railroads, and 4.) to harness the positive feelings of the people toward railroads."[23] It is no coincidence that, in a passionate speech to the association in 1912, Sun Yat-sen, then the provisional president of the Republic, promoted the use of foreign loans for new railroad construction because "the railroad issue today is really an issue of life and death for China."[24] Sun advocated a pragmatic approach to the country's infrastructure and, by extension, economic reforms to be pursued within the administration and in public discourse by the China National Railroad Association and its members.

As a combination of a governmental advisory board, a lobbying organization, a platform for professional exchanges, and a promoter of education of the public at large, the China National Railroad Association consisted of men with a wide range of professional-level engineering training, foreign education, or other railroad-related expertise. The 420 registered members in 1912 included the famous Yale-educated engineer Zhan Tianyou, at the time an assistant supervisor on the Canton-Hankou Railroad; railroad ministry officials with law degrees from Japanese universities; and stationmasters along the Jin-Pu line who had been trained in company schools.[25] Liang Shiyi, a political ally of Yuan Shikai, served as the first president of the association, with Ye Gongchuo, his political protégé, as first vice chairman. Ye's career is a perfect example of members moving back and forth between activities and posts connected to reform efforts and administrative appointments in the constantly changing political constellations of the government. After joining in the Railway Rights Recovery Movement for the Beijing-Hankou line, Ye served as the first head of the ministry's Bureau of Public Roads from 1912 to 1914 and chair of the Commission for the Unification of Railway Statistics and Accounts. When Liang Shiyi fell out of favor with Yuan Shikai, Ye resigned, but after Yuan's death he reemerged and resumed his government career as minister of Communications and Transportation in 1920–1921 and 1924–1925 and as minister of Railways in 1931–1932.[26]

Another group of Chinese experts promoting railroad reform and reorganization consisted of returning Chinese students with Western educations who, for the benefit of modernization of the infrastructure and national economic development, propagated close imitations of Western models. Among these none was more outspoken or more active in lobbying for a thorough reform than Wang Ching-chun (Wang Zhengting, 1882–1961), better known as Dr. C. C. Wang. After graduating from Yale with honors in civil engineering in 1908 and from the University of Illinois with a PhD in economics and political science in 1911, Wang returned to China, and in 1912 he was appointed vice minister of Industry and Commerce. The following year he played a crucial role on the Standing Committee of the Commission for Unification of Railway Statistics and Accounts, becoming director of the Beijing-Hankou Railroad in 1917 and serving in railroad-related positions and diplomatic and managerial roles throughout the Republican period.[27]

Whereas the China National Railroad Association focused on working through domestic political channels and its own journal, *Tielu xiehui huibao* (Journal of the Railroad Association), Wang Ching-chun used his language skills and knowledge of foreign railroad systems to promote the cause of China's railroads abroad.[28] An ardent admirer of the American political and economic systems and with strong ties to the YMCA, on the eve of the revolution Wang explained China's opposition to foreign railroad loans to an American audience in articles published in the *American Political Science Review* and the *American Journal of International Law*.[29]

In these articles Wang went to great length to argue that in principle the Chinese were not opposed to foreign loans, but they objected to the conditions tied to the loan arrangements. In many ways, Wang combined a pragmatic understanding of China's financial situation during the early Republic with a passionate nationalism that envisioned China as "a new United States." In the immediate post-1911 period of reconstruction in particular, Wang published long articles reassuring American investors of China's promising future and its desire "to do business with the United States and other foreign nations—real business, not business hopelessly mixed with international politics."[30]

Wang Ching-chun's articles supporting the economic potential of China's nationalized railroad system addressed remarks in the foreign press during the early 1910s on the less-than-stellar financial performance of certain lines, the physical damage due to the military impact, and the delay in completing planned lines. Foreign loans and involvement stipulated in the loan agreements made Westerners the de facto owners of a considerable number of railroad lines, and their governments anxiously observed whether the Chinese government would be able to repay the loans. At the same time, major new construction could be undertaken only with new foreign capital investments. Therefore, positive news about China's rail development, especially managerial and operational transparency, would help secure the interests and trust of potential investors. In these efforts, imports of Western railroad standards and regulations were useful, but as we will see later, there was not much the railroad lines could do to deflect the harm from military actions.

## Authority and Language

Establishing linguistic control over the railroad system became an equally important and complex aspect of establishing a national Chinese railroad administration after 1911. The replacement of Western languages with Chinese involved both the production of documents and interactions among foreigners and Chinese for managing railroad operations. The Chinese language was also considered instrumental for training and educating future railroad professionals and skilled workers.

As discussed earlier, the first generation of railroad-related publications in China consisted of translations of English textbooks by translators who worked for the Jiangnan Arsenal. The second generation of publications—and the first books written for the transmission of railroad knowledge—were authored either by Chinese engineers who had obtained degrees abroad or by Western engineers who had a strong interest in China due to long-term work experience in the country. For example, after graduating from Cornell University with a master's degree in civil engineering in 1905, Hu Dongchao (T. C. Hu), from Canton, wrote *Zhongguo tielu zhinan* (Guide to China's railroads), a book that combines the features of an amply illustrated engineering textbook with a general introduction to the economic and political roles of railroads.[31] In answer to the question "What is civil engineering?" Hu portrays every type of civil engineering as a contribution to the promotion of enlightenment (*wenming*) and the progress of humankind. Hu declares, "Just as enlightenment creates engineering, so does engineering create enlightenment," reflecting his educational mission as well as the intellectual and political climate of the time. During the late Qing and early Republican periods, the term *wenming* was a cornerstone in debates about the characteristics of modernization.[32] In addition to placing engineering in the context of modernity, Hu's textbook represented a departure from previous publications because he not only offered insights into the economic benefits to China due to railroad construction with foreign investments but he also explained, on the basis of his own training, the institutional organization of railroad companies and technical aspects, such as the engineering of railroad curves.[33]

That Hu Dongchao's 1906 Chinese textbook was filled with English terms for railroad-related technical and managerial concepts points to a major issue with serious implications for the development of civil engineering as an academic discipline and a professional career in China: what language should be used for knowledge transfer and the training of engineers? This was a complex issue because it involved the debate between using English or Chinese, which in turn led to fierce contestations among English, German, and French engineers in China, all of whom were competing for acknowledgment of their respective native languages as the lingua franca for engineering.

That this competition was an issue of not only academic ideologies and national pride is revealed in comments by foreign engineers who were involved in building the first railroads in cooperation with the Chinese. The choice of language for instruction and communications became an issue subject to debate, especially in relation to the Tianjin-Pukou Railroad, where the Germans were in charge of building the northern part of the line and the British the southern part. As noted earlier, the Germans had a comprehensive approach to securing their railroad interests as part of their economic and political agenda, and they were eager to train skilled workers and engineers in their own schools, where German was the language of instruction.[34] The establishment of the railroad school in Tianjin for the Jin-Pu line came under severe criticism from Chinese government officials who opposed the use of budgeted railroad funds and the use of German instead of English in the school. According to company reports from 1909, Sun Baoqi, governor of Shandong and participating director general of the Jin-Pu line, made it clear that the Tianjin-Pukou school would remain a German school only until construction of the line was completed; thereafter, the language of instruction would be English. Sun Baoqi argued that this was a general trend among existing railroads in China and that even the use of and instruction in French along the Beijing-Hankou line, a French venture, was to be gradually abolished in favor of English.[35]

From the Chinese perspective, the demand to use English had a political dimension, because it leveraged British interests vis-à-vis German interests to control the Jin-Pu line, which would rein in the dominance of the German presence in northern China that was anchored in the German lease territory on the Shandong peninsula. Another important reason was that the beginning of serious railroad construction in China and the establishment of the Ministry of Communications and Transportation promised job opportunities for those members of the Chinese elite who had trained abroad—the majority in English-speaking academic environments. Li Hongzhang, governor of Jiangsu province at the time of the discussion, was also in favor of English and suggested that the German railroad school begin to teach English because he wanted the graduates to work on the Beijing-Kalgan line, where English was the main form of communication and many of the employees were Cantonese who already had some rudimentary knowledge of English.[36]

From the German perspective, the use of German at the proposed Tianjin-Pukou Railroad School and for communication with employees furthered the securing of the railroad's future supply chain—that is, direct imports of German steel tracks, machinery, and other hardware from German industrial firms via their agents in China. The chief engineers expressed this business agenda in no uncertain terms in a 1909 report to the German consulate in Beijing, tying "the fate of future orders" directly to the use of the German language and to the promotion of German industry.[37] Of course, the broader economic and political implications of the language question were not lost on German officials, who somewhat naively hoped that German-speaking Chinese along the Jin-Pu and Jiaozhou-Ji'nan lines would be the "best defense against these English-American monopolistic desires as soon as Chinese . . . consider mastering German as a tool for professional advancement."[38]

Besides securing supply chains for national economic interests, the language issue also had implications for academic knowledge transfer. By the early 1910s, professional journals were publishing Chinese-language articles on railroad engineering that included mathematical formulas, but because the articles retained the traditional right-to-left format, it was quite difficult to read the equations.[39] Foreign engineers like Georg Baur, who taught the first engineering class in Tianjin, complained about the Chinese instructional materials and the arrangement of the mathematical proofs in the textbooks, which made teaching and comprehension of the content difficult. Despite his attachment to German interests, Baur was very much in favor of using English for instruction. He argued that because the Chinese Maritime Customs Service successfully used English in its multinational organization, it should serve as a model for all other professional sectors.[40]

The quality of Chinese textbooks improved concurrently with the growth of engineering instruction at Chinese educational institutions and the increase in the number of engineering graduates who eventually authored textbooks. The bilingual nature of the textbooks never entirely disappeared, with important technical terms usually inserted in English or added in a glossary at the end of the texts. By the 1920s, engineering textbooks and professional literature were printed with the Chinese text moving from left to right along horizontal lines, thus facilitating technical writing, including the insertion of equations and graphs.[41]

From the Chinese perspective, of course, the use of Chinese characters was a matter of national sovereignty and convenience. In the article "Railroads Should Use Chinese Characters," published in the journal of the newly formed China National Railroad Association in 1913, the author pleaded on behalf of customers who were not able to read the instructions on their tickets, freight regulations, or the timetables posted in railroad stations.[42] Even after most railroads had been nationalized, it took some time to reduce the use of English (and German and French) as vestiges of the earlier foreign influence in the Chinese public space. As the international language of railroads, however, English never fully disappeared in Republican China from the academic literature or from the railroad companies' entrance exams.[43]

## The Mess in the Books and on the Tracks

Unlike Western countries, China had almost no experience with the generation and use of modern statistical data. In Europe, military mobilization for the French Revolution and the Napoleonic Wars marked the beginning of a generalized push toward a more systematic collection of government statistics on the population and the economy.[44] A second push, beginning in about 1870 and accelerating after the turn of the century and during World War I, culminated in the emergence of a global standardized repertoire of macroeconomic statistics measuring GDP, unemployment, and inflation.[45]

The late Qing and early Republican Chinese state—including the Railway Department of the Ministry of Communications and Transportation—lacked such statistical knowledge about the institutions it was charged with administering. In the case of railroads, much of the confusion could be blamed on the railroads' semicolonial origins. In 1913, the Ministry of Communications and Transportation appointed a Commission for the Unification of Railway Statistics and Accounts, which discovered, in the words of one of its members, that "the railways were left entirely to themselves in the matter of accounts and statistics. As to finance, it seems what was then known . . . was largely a question of cash. Each railway kept its own accounts and statistics in its own way and changed its methods as it saw fit."[46]

Moreover, because China's railroads before World War I were financed by foreign loans, the lines were subject to a host of varying national interests, operating procedures, and languages. Although the bondholders were far away physically, they exerted pressure to further their own interests in several ways. The various consortia of financial and engineering companies that had negotiated the original railroad loans—the British & Chinese Corporation, the Pekin Syndicate, and the American China Development Corporation, among others—had offices in China from where they monitored administration of the railroads and lobbied Chinese officials either directly or through their diplomatic representatives. One of the largest of these, the British & Chinese Corporation—whose principal members were Jardine Matheson and the Hong Kong–Shanghai Banking Corporation—monitored railroad affairs with a remarkable level of detail, always alert to any opportunity to squeeze out more profits that would contribute to loan repayments. On occasion, the corporation's close monitoring significantly affected company decisions. In 1922, for example, the corporation's representative, S. F. Mayers, avoided paying for a shipment of new rolling stock—the popular Blue Express passenger trains—by pledging future railroad income to the manufacturer on the grounds that the practice was contrary to the original loan agreement.[47] Four years later, the cars had still not been paid for.[48]

By 1913, frustration with the incomplete and inconsistent state of railroad data outweighed Chinese bureaucrats' desire to protect their turf. The Chinese government asked the Commission for the Unification of Railway Statistics and Accounts for help in reforming the administrative apparatus. The goal of the commission was to improve statistical knowledge about the railroad in order to strengthen Chinese state interests vis-à-vis foreign financiers.

The driving force behind the commission once again was Wang Ching-chun.[49] Wang, who had written his PhD dissertation on the regulation of railroad finance in England, persuaded University of Michigan Economics Professor Henry Carter Adams (1851–1921) to spend a year in China as special adviser to the commission. During his stay in China in 1913–1914, Adams attempted to do for China's railroads what he had done for those in the United States beginning in 1887 as chief statistician of the Interstate Commerce

Commission: bring rapacious private enterprises under public control.[50] In the United States his purpose had been to impose a uniform system of accounts, thereby arming the government with information to prevent the railroad companies from charging exorbitant rates. In China, he explained in a letter home to one of his sons, he hoped to keep the "foreigners [from] sucking the lemon dry."[51] The foreign financing of China's railroads, he noted, left its managers in a difficult bind. "To preserve to the government the revenues from its railways to which it is entitled, and at the same time to preserve to the bondholders the full measure of the security for their loan, places the Chief Accountant of Chinese railways . . . in the position somewhat of serving two masters."[52] In other letters Adams expressed his irritation with the lack of financial and managerial expertise in the Railway Department of the Ministry of Communications and Transportation, mainly because it enabled shrewd foreign financiers to get the upper hand. "The difficulty here is that the gov. does not have men who know enough to stand up against the blasted foreigners, so that, if we work out a form of records for the railways, it may or may not be used intelligently."[53]

The hope was that improved railroad accounting would allow more efficient management, bringing greater profits and ultimately improving the borrowing ability of the Chinese state. Initially, Adams was unaware of the international ramifications of the commission's goals, but they became clear almost immediately after his arrival in China, when he realized that his work was "assuming an importance I never dreamed of. . . . Things are in a very bad way here, financially. . . . My work *may* prove of great assistance in giving the country credit. That is why the bankers and railroad men are so favorably impressed."[54]

Unlike many Western advisers in early Republican China, Adams appears to have had a lasting impact. He noted that there were eighteen Western advisers in Peking during his tenure, but he was "about the only one not here for ornamental purposes."[55] Nevertheless, Wang Ching-chun testified to the significance of the commission's achievements.[56] In total, the commission met more than seventy times and eventually formulated nine sets of accounting and statistical regulations to govern capital investments, operating receipts and expenditures, annual budgets, statistics on rolling stock, and other basic matters. The commission also prescribed standard procedures and formats for annual reports on railroad operations. The regulations came into force in 1915 and were implemented, with relatively few modifications, until 1937.[57]

As a result, the railroad reports became one of the few statistical bright spots in early Republican China. The Ministry of Agriculture and Commerce (Nongshangbu) issued annual reports beginning in 1914, although before the late 1920s its figures were just rough estimates. The Chinese Maritime Customs Service published trade figures based on the collection of systematic data, but the service had a foreign manager and a large corps of foreign staff. The railroads were thus the only Chinese-run state agency that compiled and regularly published quantitative data on material conditions in the nation.[58]

For most of the time, as the building of the rail administration at the government level and the restructuring of the railroad companies progressed, China was in a state of upheaval and increasing political fragmentation. The split between President Yuan Shikai, supported by the Beiyang army in the north, and the revolutionary Nationalist (Guomindang) Party in the south escalated when warlords began fighting for control over the Beiyang army after Yuan Shikai's death in 1916. The ensuing power vacuum initiated a violent and disruptive struggle between the warlords, former protégés of Yuan, and the generals with careers in provincial armies, who set up their independent spheres of military and civil control. To end China's territorial disintegration and political instability, the Nationalists and Communists joined in a temporary alliance, until Chiang Kai-shek's troops unified the country in 1928 by eliminating the warlords and purging the political left and established the Guomindang government in Nanjing.[59]

China's railroad lines were affected by these events involving the local warlord troops or the various armies in terms of damage to both their physical assets and line management, with the severity depending on their location within the war zones. This situation in turn had serious consequences for the profitability of the lines. As we will see later, many of the administrative and managerial railroad innovations of the early Republic were jeopardized by external factors beyond line management control.

Some of the most detailed descriptions of the havoc inflicted on rail equipment and track beds are derived from comments by foreign engineers and advisers who witnessed the destruction of the system that they had been charged to build. According to the diary of Thomas Johnston Bourne, a district engineer on the Jin-Pu line from 1908 to 1911, the first military damage occurred in the wake of the 1911 revolution when the infamous General Zhang Xun retreated from Nanjing, crossed the Yangzi River, and then demanded transportation for his troops from Pukou to Xuzhou. Denied service, he seized two empty ballast trains and moved his army to Xuzhou, where he took over the station and began to live in a railroad carriage "with steam always up on the locomotive so he could pull out at a moment's notice." Zhang Xun controlled and terrorized the population in the area along the line, and station platforms became a public venue for punishment and executions.[60]

During the civil war of the early 1920s, important junctions on lines with operational headquarters and railroad works became contested strategic targets. When the battle between the two major warlords in the North and Northeast, Wu Peifu and Zhang Zuolin, resumed in 1924, the city of Tangshan, as headquarters of the Peking-Kalgan line and the site of the Kailan mining operations, was drawn into the line of fire. According to the recollections of C. P. Fitzgerald, a former store manager on the line, the railroad did not take any preventive measures, although the forthcoming military campaign was public knowledge. Fitzgerald attributes this inertia to upper management still being dominated by foreigners who did not understand the political realities and naively hoped that the Beijing government would rein in the warlords.[61] Wu Peifu's efforts to move his army to the Manchurian border at Shanhaiguan affected the Peking-Mukden line by military officers' requisition of freight cars for troop transport and locomotives for unauthorized trains. Even more damaging than the seizure of hardware was the lack of understanding about how the logistics of the track system worked, bringing the line to a standstill. Similar to most railroads, the Peking-Mukden line consisted of a single track, with sidings at the stations to allow trains going in opposite directions to pass each other. Thirteen long trains soon clogged the line around Tangshan station, and the immobilized troops and their artillery and ammunition became an easy target for a surprise attack by General Feng Yuxiang's troops.[62]

The damage to the railroads during the warlord period is but one example of the military weaknesses of the warlord armies; they lacked sufficient experience and training to plan a strategic rail mobilization for campaigns that increasingly involved moving large numbers of soldiers with armaments and supplies. The warlords and their soldiers thought driving a train required "[no] more experience than the driving of a cart," and they treated the railroad staff, including the engine driver, with such cruelty that, according to eyewitness reports, all skilled and technical staff would flee the premises in anticipation of the army's arrival.[63] Captured men were forced to work to keep the trains running with "engines under steam until their grate burned out or leaky flues put out the fire."[64] And if this was not enough damage, engines would quickly fail when the troops helped themselves to all the hot water from the engine or all the cold water from the tender. During warlord Zhang Zuolin's occupation of Tianjin, John Earl Baker, adviser to the Chinese Ministry of Communications and Transportation from 1916 to 1926, witnessed the tracks at Yangcun jammed with rail cars and seven incapacitated engines obstructing the station.[65]

Even after the lines were eventually reopened, the military adversely affected traffic. Train departures were less predictable, leading to overcrowding and unhappy passengers, and military officers boldly occupied first class.[66] Less revenue from reduced freight and passenger transport and from military personnel refusing to pay for transportation severely cut into the lines' financials. In his lament about the limited expansion and quality of the railroad network at the end of the 1920s, economic historian and social critic Richard Tawney sarcastically considered the long-term effects of military-related damage to China's railroads: "A general in control of a railway is like a monkey with a watch; and, as a result of civil war, parts of it have been unusable for commercial purposes for long periods together. Rolling-stock is falling to pieces, and owing to the lack of engineering resources, cannot be put in order. Engines and coaches are detained by rebellious militarists for their private convenience. In some districts the permanent way is out of repair."[67] In the face of these chaotic disruptions, the reconfiguration of the railroad lines as business institutions and organizational structures was nothing short of a miracle.

## Line Management

With the reorganization of the national rail administration, each national line underwent managerial and structural changes under the supervision (*zhixia*) of the Ministry of Communications and Transportation. In 1914 the railroad

bureau system was formalized into a total of eleven major lines with an administration bureau (*guanliju*) for each headquarters; five additional lines
that were not yet completed at the time operated under a head office (*zong
gongsuo*) that would later become an administration bureau.[68] The foreign
lines maintained their own systems separate from the jurisdiction of the Ministry of Communications and Transportation, whereas short private and
provincial lines for mining purposes operated under supervisory offices and
sometimes ended up under the control of a branch trunk line.[69]

After 1911, a major task for Chinese railroad companies was to adapt their
institutional structure to the new control and ownership arrangements that
emerged in the wake of nationalization. As already noted, the replacement
of foreign managerial and technical staff with Chinese talent was slow and
gradual, and organizational and managerial restructuring involved adapting
foreign railroad business models to Chinese institutional structures at the
upper management and shop-floor levels. With institutional origins dating
back to the different semicolonial management styles, each railroad bureau
began with a different institutional legacy.

Most of China's railroad lines followed the model of European railroad
companies for the institutional framework of their line management. According to Alfred Chandler, who analyzed the emergence of American railroad companies as big businesses in the late nineteenth and early twentieth
centuries, "departmental" organization characterized European and British
railroads, whereas railroads in the United States preferred "divisional" organization. Chandler identified both approaches as structural innovations in
response to the challenge of managing railroads with complex procedures
of communications across spatial distances and different types of traffic,
goods, and financial accounts. Large American railroads used a decentralized line-and-staff divisional structure, which created a "direct line of
authority from the president through the general superintendent" down to
the division superintendent.[70] In contrast, the departmental structure used
by British and European railroad companies allowed a functional manager
in charge of a specific geographical division to report directly to a functional
equivalent at the head office. This centralized departmental structure, better
suiting lines with shorter track length and moderate traffic, was considered
a more "natural" form of organization.[71]

Familiar with this structural tradition, the foreign partners of the early railroad syndicates and concessions and their engineers who had been trained in the Anglo-European system introduced the departmental system in its most basic form during the initial construction period. Here the development of the organizational structure of the Jin-Pu Railroad serves as evidence of the managerial evolution in China. According to a 1909 internal memo by the managing director, the head office of the northern (German) section was to be divided into ten departments, including the secretarial office, pay, surveying, interpreting, land purchase, works, materials, telegraph, rolling stock, and supply departments.[72] Instead of an organizational flow chart—the Jin-Pu line was not yet completed at the time—the document outlines the departmental line management: engineers were to be in charge of machinery, engine shops, construction, supplies, surveying, receipt and issuance of funds, correspondence, materials, telegraphs, rolling stock, and oversight. Their deputies stationed in each section assumed responsibility for the purchase of land, correspondence, investigations, the preservation of order, interpreting, receipt and payment of funds, and work supervision. They were also in charge of the staff, such as the office servants, messengers, guards, and grooms.[73] In the hierarchical structure, the director general and the managing director, and their assistants, occupied the top managerial level without defined responsibilities, and the superintendents and assistant superintendents were in charge of judicial work, receipt and issuance of funds and supplies, interpreting, investigations, purchase of land, and managing the constables, copyists, accountants, and detectives.[74]

The first steps toward the line's restructuring are documented in a survey compiled by the China National Railroad Association in 1914: one year after the line's completion in 1912, the Jin-Pu Railroad was nationalized under full Chinese management, with eighty-nine stations along 830 miles of track between Tianjin and Pukou. The Jin-Pu Railroad management bureau supervised the mechanical works in Tianjin, the workshops in Ji'nan, and the locomotive works in Pukou. The Tianjin factory was especially well equipped, with three steam engines and an electric generator, and it employed 141 people. The workshops in Ji'nan employed 481, and those in Pukou employed 400. Considering the low level of large-scale industrial enterprises at the time and the exclusion from the survey of porters and other casual labor, the Jin-Pu

Railroad by any standard was, based on this survey, a substantial economic institution in China in terms of its work force, physical assets, and scope of offered services.[75]

The first organizational flow chart of the Jin-Pu line from 1915 shows that the managerial division into northern and southern sections, demarcating the spheres of foreign control, had been abolished.[76] The railroad bureau in Tianjin supervised the four departments of general affairs, works, traffic, and maintenance, which, in turn, were in charge of their specialized subsections. There was still no departmental structure in place. This structural change took place the next year when the works and maintenance departments split their managerial responsibilities into sections (*duan*) and subsections (*fenduan*). According to a 1916 flow chart, however, the sectional division followed the former German-British division, with Hanzhuang station at the border between Shandong and Jiangsu provinces as the demarcation. The ten subsections of the works and maintenance departments were classified by the major stations along the line.[77]

A comparison of the evolving organizational structures in the following years shows some experimentation as a result of moving the accounts office out of the general affairs office and establishing it as a separate department reporting to the railroad bureau. This step might indicate the increasing importance and standardization of railroad accounts, which were now given a greater institutional and managerial presence in the company. Other changes indicate the managerial integration of welfare institutions, such as the new hospital buildings and medical stations along the line, related to the Jin-Pu Railroad. For example, in 1917 for the first time the line's hospitals and police guards were fully incorporated into the managerial structure, each with a separate departmental status.[78]

The trend to increase the number of departments reporting directly to the Jin-Pu Railroad Bureau continued throughout the early Republican period, until the Nationalist takeover in 1927 and the reorganization of the railroad administration under the Guomindang government. From the perspective of line management, this reform effort reflected recognition of all the different operational and managerial tasks across the geographical divisions and the desire to make each part of the railroad, from locomotive shops to railroad hospitals, more efficient through centralized channels of communication and command.

Despite the departure from a basic European departmental model, the restructuring process throughout the 1910s clearly shows an increasing focus on geographical sections and an incorporation of functional divisions into spatial sections. For example, by 1918 the Jin-Pu Railroad Bureau was in charge of ten departments, including two separate work departments (based on the former northern-southern division), two separate traffic departments (one with a functional division and the other with a geographical division), and two separate accounts offices (one for central accounts and one for divisional accounts). This line of command created a huge, unwieldy organizational structure in which divisional and functional responsibilities were separated but ultimately still controlled by the railroad bureau.[79]

From a comparative railroad management perspective, it is fair to say that the centralized British and European model provided the basic framework, but the Chinese developed a hybrid model by giving the geographical sections pride of place at the departmental level. The resultant empowerment of regional and local offices and workshops with direct access to the Jin-Pu Railroad Bureau at the top left a lasting impact on the institutional nature of railroads in China because other government lines experienced a similar restructuring.[80] From a domestic perspective, one might say that the railroad reforms centralized the system at the national administrative level to some extent but indirectly enabled regionalization at the line level, empowering those in charge of local and regional offices.

Not surprisingly, the institutionalized power of the sections within the departmental system created conflict and internal fragmentation because of the lack of cooperation among section chiefs. Engineers complained about the reluctant cooperation among functional managers of sections and unclear lines of responsibility, which have to be seen in the context of coexisting departments generating excess procedures and paperwork without encouraging exchanges of information. The internal complexity of the organization also contributed to continuing differences between foreign railroad employees at the departmental upper management level and their Chinese counterparts at the divisional and sectional lower managerial levels. Disputes arose with respect to operational issues regarding the line's daily management, and as the staff correspondence shows, they could easily evolve into arguments with political or nationalistic overtones.[81]

Despite nationalization and institutional indigenization, Chinese railroads continued to hire Western managers and engineers well into the 1920s. This was partly because throughout the 1910s the pool of trained Chinese railroad engineers and managers remained relatively small and could not meet the demand of the expanding rail administration at the line level (as discussed later in this chapter). For example, the staff records of the Shanghai-Nanjing Railroad reveal that in 1920 the line still employed foreigners in the positions of engineer in chief and general manager, as well as in leading positions in the engineering, traffic, accounts, locomotive, storage, and medical departments—altogether thirty-seven people.[82]

Pressures from foreign loan consortia were another factor behind the continued employment of foreigners. Many of the original loan agreements specified that certain positions had to be filled by persons of specific nationalities. S. F. Mayers, the local representative of the British & Chinese Corporation, went to considerable length to put British subjects in positions of power on the Shanghai-Nanjing and Jin-Pu lines, particularly after March 1917, when in the political context of World War I the Chinese broke off relations with Germany and took over the German positions on the Jin-Pu line.[83] The Supplementary Loan Agreement of 1910 among Britain, Germany, and China stipulated that a European had to manage the entire line after construction was completed; yet as of 1919 this clause had not yet been honored. S. F. Mayers, after extensive correspondence with and private visits to British diplomats in China, the secretary of state in London, and the minister of Railways, succeeded in having A. R. J. Hearne appointed as the first engineer in chief of the entire Jin-Pu line.[84]

Western stakeholders seemed to have reached a consensus that having a European in charge of Chinese railroads would increase profitability and speed up the repayment of loans. This argument lacks evidence, however, and seems to express lingering sentiments of Western efficiency and trustworthiness versus Chinese organizational weakness. For example, in 1918 Mayers assisted in transferring C. L. G. Wayne from a midlevel position in the Traffic Department of the Shanghai-Nanjing Railroad to the position of director of traffic of the Tianjin-Pukou Railroad; by 1925 Wayne had risen to acting general manager of the Shanghai-Nanjing Railroad.[85] Wayne made it clear that he expected that his appointment would improve the rate of loan repayments. In one of his many letters soliciting support for his candidacy, he "point[ed] out the advantage that the British & Chinese Corporation would secure from my appointment."[86]

In the context of these managerial and institutional challenges, during the early Republican period Chinese railroads constantly changed the structure of their line management. From a purely organizational perspective, the 1911 revolution and nationalization constituted less of a radical break in terms of management and personnel than one would expect. As flow charts from internal publications and personal correspondence from managers on the ground demonstrate, the desire to restructure and make improvements was strong, but the organization became too complex and failed to tie the regionally strong and locally embedded rail interests to the national agenda pursued by the central rail administration and government. The fragmented government and administrative rail apparatus of the early Republic was in no position to effectively reach into the structure of individual railroad bureaus.[87]

Change came with China's unification under the Nationalist government in 1928 and the reorganization of the government lines, thereby undoing much of the excessive divisional process from the 1910s. For example, by 1928 the Jin-Pu line had been reorganized into six straightforward departments under the railroad bureau, and the divisional structure was relegated to the lower rungs reporting to the departments (see Appendix A).[88] In many ways, this organizational structure finally began to more closely resemble the European departmental model at the same time that Western influence in railroad management was finally beginning to wane.

## Rail Compounds and Shop Floors

Railroads emerged in the early Republican period as hybrid institutions that left a significant imprint on spheres as disparate as the urban built environment and the shop floor. The railroads transformed station towns and cities into disparate environments that grafted modern, often Western-inspired, architecture, technical facilities, and commercial infrastructure onto traditional Chinese municipalities. For example, the physical presence of the Jin-Pu Railroad had a major impact on the urban development of the provincial capital of Ji'nan.[89] Ji'nan was a major railroad junction, where the Jin-Pu line connected to the Jiao-Ji Railroad, the line crossing Shandong peninsula between Ji'nan and Qingdao. The resultant economic and urban growth of Ji'nan shifted the city's character from an administrative center to a commercial, industrial, and transportation center in the early twentieth century.[90]

The Jin-Pu line ran west of the walled city that enclosed the city space with its traditional public institutions, such as the *yamen* (magistrate's office) and temples. An earlier example of railroads operating outside and running along the city walls, where space allowed construction of larger rail yards and stations, is the Qianmen station in Beijing, as shown in Figure 2.1. Ji'nan's self-invited classification as a treaty port in 1904 led to the creation of a whole new modern city section outside the walls that also became home to railroad stations, shops, banks, a post office, and the Jin-Pu Railroad Bureau (see Figure 2.2).[91] The repair workshops, a large factory compound known as the Ji'nan Machine Works (Ji'nan jichang), complete with storage facilities and administrative buildings, occupied an entire district in the new urban settlement outside the city walls. The railroad yard at Ji'nan became

Fig. 2.1 Qianmen railroad station in Beijing, 1909. Sanshichiro, Yamamoto *Peking* (Tokyo: 1909), plate no. 4, no pagination. Reproduced from the author's collection.

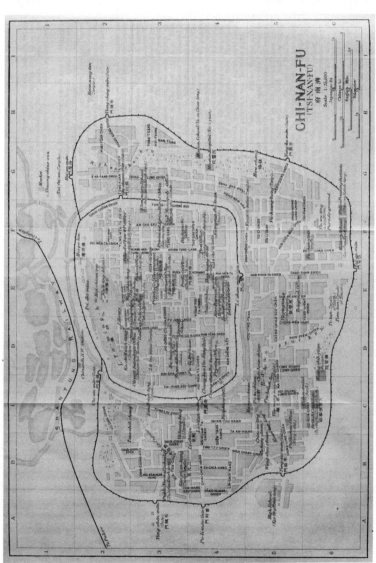

Fig. 2.2   Map of Ji'nan, capital of Shandong province, 1915. Imperial Japanese Government Railways, *An Official Guide to Eastern Asia—Trans-Continental Connections between Europe and Asia*, vol. 4, *China* (Tokyo: 1915), facing p. 104, Fairbank Collection, Fung Library, Harvard University.

the largest repair shop in Shandong province, attracting labor and administrators from all over the country.

The compound of the Jin-Pu Railroad became a major presence in the city, developing into a city within a city. The railroad as a means of transportation and large-scale business operation inspired urban planning and architecture and was reflected in the city's large number of Western-style office buildings and institutions, such as the headquarters of the Jin-Pu Railroad Company (Jin-Pu tieluju), the Jin-Pu Railroad Hotel (Jin-Pu tielu bingguan), and the Jin-Pu Railroad Hospital (Jin-Pu tielu yiyuan).[92] In contrast to the old walled city, Ji'nan's railroad district became a separate city with a modern grid of streets unimaginatively named according to a numerical system—Jingyi lu (No. 1 Street), Jing'er lu (No. 2 Street), and so on (see Figure 2.3). In the 1910s and 1920s this newer part of Ji'nan became the home of modern banks, industrial enterprises, hospitals, schools, and foreign trading companies.[93] As a representative of Western efficiency and discipline, the railroad station for the Jin-Pu line in the center of this city section was completed in December 1911 in perfect imitation of German station architecture and it was one of the first Western railroad buildings in China, complete with clock tower, waiting rooms, ticket office, and separate rooms for baggage storage.[94]

The Jin-Pu Railroad, as one of Ji'nan's major white- and blue-collar employers during the Republican period, also played a major role in shaping and modernizing the city's work culture. In 1925, the Jin-Pu Railroad listed approximately one thousand workers and employees at the Ji'nan station.[95] According to interviews I conducted with former workers on the Jin-Pu Railroad in 2005, many of them were second- and third-generation railroad workers. The term "workers" (*gongren*) here refers to highly skilled workers who underwent at least a two-year apprenticeship in the machine workshops or repair shops, and some were even sent to railroad technical colleges by Jin-Pu management to improve their skills.[96]

Many of the first-generation workers had previous work experience with machinery in arsenals, in coal mines, or as blacksmiths.[97] With skills useful in the railroad yard and repair shops, they relocated to Shandong to join the Jin-Pu Railroad in the 1910s. Their families moved to Ji'nan from Tianjin, Tangshan, and other places in Hebei province, and even today the families retain the original household residential permits (*hukou*) in their native places, outside of Shandong province. As the interviewed workers pointed out,

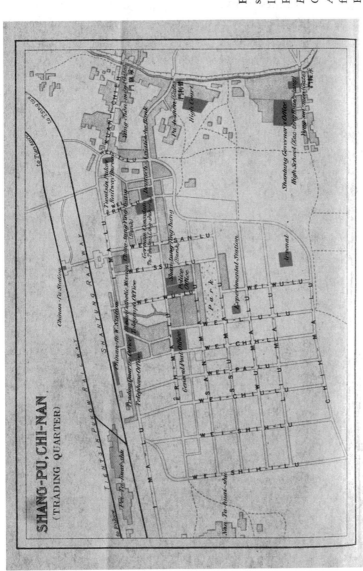

Fig. 2.3   Railroads and the foreign settlement (*shangbu*) in Ji'nan, 1915. Imperial Japanese Government Railways, *An Official Guide to Eastern Asia—Trans-continental Connections between Europe and Asia*, vol. 4, *China* (Tokyo: 1915), facing p. 110, Fairbank Collection, Fung Library, Harvard University.

career opportunities through company training, social services provided by railroad hospitals and schools, company housing, and the prestige of the Jin-Pu Railroad Company as a reliable institutional employer played an important role in attracting them as skilled workers. Similar motivations drew their colleagues in Europe and North America to work on the railroads.[98]

Training a skilled Chinese workforce for maintenance and repair work on shop floors equipped with imported and often technologically advanced tools and machinery was another challenge in building a national Chinese railroad administration. The foreign railroad companies of the pre-1911 period had achieved some degree of success in training railroad staff in China, but these endeavors tended to be small scale, short lived, and narrowly focused on the interests of the foreign companies and the nationals who ran them. The first railroad-specific technical education was offered in a class for railroad studies and was attached to the military school in Tianjin. This class was established by Georg Baur, whom we met earlier, the technical representative and consultant for all railroad-related issues and who worked for the German company Krupp in China between 1890 and 1893.[99]

The railroad class began with twenty students on November 26, 1890. The military school operated under the patronage of Governor General Li Hongzhang and included German military instructors and professionally trained railroad engineers like Georg Baur. Starting out with a class instead of an independent school seemed appropriate because a class did not require official sanction from the imperial government in Beijing. In 1893 the total number of students in two classes was twenty-eight, but of those only thirteen completed their education at the school. Ten of the graduates found employment in railroad administration, two with mining companies, and the best student stayed on to become an assistant teacher at the school.[100] Unfortunately, the school was completely destroyed during the Boxer Rebellion in 1900. In the end, it produced a total of only forty graduates. Moreover, most of the graduates were not professionally trained engineers in the strict academic sense, but they had acquired special technical and administrative skills necessary for the construction and operation of railroads.

In an attempt to bring together theoretical study and its practical application in a railroad-related setting, company-run classes exposed students to field trips and field exercises. This represented a radical departure from the traditional Chinese method of instruction. Many foreign engineers believed that technically skilled workers represented the most acute shortage in civil engineering practices, and therefore they saw the future of engineering in China to be tightly linked to training more and better skilled workers and foremen with practical experience.[101] The field became the classroom for students who were sent out to practice topographic surveying exercises in Tianjin's French settlement. To enable students to explore firsthand the technical issues of railroad construction, bridge building, and line equipment, in 1892 Georg Baur took his class of nineteen students on a study trip. For several days the group traveled from Tianjin to Luanzhou on the Chinese Eastern Railroad, with numerous stops for site visits and instruction. At Tangshan the students had an opportunity to visit railroad workshops, where they saw locomotive and railroad carriages being assembled as well as coal mines in operation.[102]

The emphasis on practical field work was a novelty in Chinese curricula and reflected the Western approach to engineering as a discipline built on scientific rationality and methodology, which could be put to test in the field and thus lead to further innovation. The first generation of Chinese students training at railroad and engineering schools was unfamiliar with this engineering mind-set. They considered themselves high-status students in pursuit of a prized modern education but an education in the tradition of the detached Chinese literati, and they did not recognize work in the laboratory or in the field as an integral part of their education as professionals. As a result, students were reluctant to perform simple but important tasks, which from an elitist perspective would have been considered beneath the social status of highly educated men. It is only fair to note that Chinese were certainly familiar with a long-established system of elaborate apprenticeship in the context of vocational training, but not in the context of formal education in a classroom setting.[103]

Despite the urgent demand for Chinese engineers and skilled labor, the absence of an accessible labor market in a modern sense created great obstacles for graduates to find appropriate employment during the early period of railroad construction. The majority of graduates from Georg Baur's railroad class found employment with the imperial Peking-Kalgan Railroad, which was under construction between Fengtai, a station near Beijing, and Zhangjia-kou (Kalgan), northwest of the capital. This railroad line was the first to be financed with Chinese funds and built under the leadership of the famous

Chinese chief engineer Zhan Tianyou (1861–1919), who had received a degree in civil engineering, with a major in railroad engineering, from Yale University in 1881 and today is often referred to as the "father of Chinese railroads."[104] Nevertheless, Zhan's success as a trailblazer for Chinese engineers and his achievements were an exception rather than the norm in the early years of railroad construction and engineering.

That graduates from in-house training classes had company-specific knowledge acquired in a Western language meant that their mobility was limited; their expertise and communication skills were not universally transferable. In addition, because of the competition among railroad companies and because foreign engineers and directors in the companies' management determined hiring strategies, Chinese engineering graduates lacked access to informal information about employment opportunities unless they enjoyed active patronage of one of the few Chinese engineers at the time.[105] Even Chinese officials in director positions for the most part had no training or experience in engineering, which often meant that they did not put the graduates' talents and skills to the best use. For example, in 1893 Zhang Shiyu, director of the Chinese Imperial Railroad, planned to place a graduate who had excellent math skills in a conductor's position, which upset both the student and his teachers.[106]

The absence of an open job market was still felt by the first graduates of Chinese universities and engineering institutions producing professionally trained engineers in the 1910s. For example, Ling Hongxun, who graduated with a degree in civil engineering from Jiaotong University in Shanghai in 1915 and later became a prominent railroad engineer and government administrator, was unable to find employment after graduation despite his prestigious degree. According to his autobiography, the lack of apprenticeships with engineering-related companies made it difficult for graduates to establish relationships with potential employers, and coming from a humble background he lacked personal connections. Thus, he opted to return to his home in Guangzhou and help with his father's small business. Jiaotong University eventually offered him a scholarship for graduate study in the United States that allowed him to complete his engineering training and pursue a successful career.[107]

Companies contributed substantially to the training of skilled labor, but more was required of the state to foster the academic education and professional training of engineers. In the months leading up to the fall of the Qing dynasty and the founding of the Republic, engineering courses at the university level were offered at only four institutions with ties to the mining, military, and arsenal sectors: the Imperial Polytechnic Institute in Shanghai, the Imperial University of Shanxi in Taiyuan, the Engineering and Mining College in Tangshan, and the Imperial Beiyang University in Tianjin.[108] As part of China's educational reforms and efforts to promote and integrate modern science and engineering into the curriculum, the government established Jiaotong University, which specialized in communications and transportation. As we will see in Chapter 5, from the early 1910s throughout the Republican period, Jiaotong University grew to be the foremost academic institution for engineering and science, as evidenced by the generous government funding from the Ministry of Railways and the substantial number of engineering graduates. Through the visible hand of the state, China's engineering education finally began to undergo a process of institution building, professionalization, and integration, which would benefit not only the railroad sector but also other aspects of the economic and social development of the Republican state.

## Conclusion

Government efforts to build a modern railroad administration during the early Republican period succeeded in creating a blueprint for a bureaucracy that structurally moved away from the railroads' political role toward functional and operational management. This key development shaped the institutional structure of China's railroad system, a structure that continued with some adjustments well into the post-1949 period. The goal of centralization and direct state control, however, was to some extent undermined by the railroad bureau system, which provided a high degree of autonomy to individual lines as a consequence of the diverse regional semicolonial legacy. Each line was exposed to different regional political and financial challenges that the central railroad administration and the government were unable to address, disrupting the lines' operations and reducing their revenue and thus their growth as business institutions. From the perspective of China's historical trajectory during the early Republic, the history of railroad development mirrors the ruptured transition of the Chinese state from empire to Republic in a nonlinear fashion. Most importantly, attempts for greater nationalization and centralization led simultaneously to greater regional autonomy in the structure of government, society, and rail infrastructure.

The 1910s were a period of experimentation with bureaucratic structures and managerial organizations during politically unstable times. As administrative institutions the railroads became a key part of the nation-building process during China's early Republican period. The emergent nature of the state had important implications for railroad development. At the macro level, the weakness of the central government led to the political turmoil and civil war of the warlord period that impeded rail operations and administrative unity. Local warlords interfered with the lines in their respective districts, requisitioning rolling stock, tearing up tracks, and in numerous other ways preventing railroad administrators from creating a coherent national rail system. As a result, railroad profits failed to meet the high expectations held both in China and overseas.

But the absence of strong central control was also an advantage. By taking a regional focus, railroad companies developed managerial structures that could overcome state weaknesses, financial inefficiencies, and the lack of engineers and skilled labor. Parallel to the administrative restructuring at the national level, railroad lines increasingly became self-contained entities that began to encapsulate a small society (*xiao shehui*) within the larger contexts of city and nation. In fact, with their housing policies, social services, and educational mission, railroad compounds began to look like a prerevolutionary version of the post-1949 socialist work unit (see Chapter 5).

As business historians Alfred Chandler and Thomas Cochran have shown for railroads in America, Chinese railroad companies developed into large-scale organizational enterprises with distinct bureaucratic features and strict hierarchical structures. Labor historian Walter Licht has emphasized that, despite the institutional characteristics of the workforce, "the work experience for the nineteenth-century American railway man remained a function of his personal relations with supervisors and foremen."[109] The experience of Chinese railroad workers in this respect was similar, derived from the specific hiring practices and informal work-time interactions based on native-place origins and identity.

The Jin-Pu Railroad contributed to nation-building during the Republican period by creating the infrastructure necessary for economic growth and social progress within specific local areas along the rail corridor. As a national railroad, the relationship between the Jin-Pu line and the central government from 1912 to 1927 was not strong. Government officials from the Ministry of Communications and Transportation interfered relatively little with either the day-to-day business of the Jin-Pu line, such as hiring practices, or the visionary planning. Nevertheless, the central government would sometimes exploit the railroad financially for public projects. For example, in 1920 the Chinese government in Beijing levied famine surtaxes on railroad fares and freight rates and used these funds to construct a highway from Weixian to Zhifu in Shandong province.[110] Once the Jin-Pu Railroad as an institution came under the administrative control of the Ministry of Railways and thus directly under the control of the Nanjing government in 1928, it would be closely supervised, regulated, and centralized by government administrators.

# PART II

# RAILROADS
# IN THE MARKET
# AND SOCIAL
# SPACE

## CHAPTER THREE

# Moving Goods in the Marketplace

D espite the interruptions of the civil war and the slow completion of surveyed lines, railroads became part of the economic and social lives of people in Republican China, offering faster, more convenient, and safer transportation of goods and passengers. In much of the world, in contrast, rail travel had already transformed economic systems both large and small. On the grandest scale, railroads contributed to a dramatic drop in transport costs over the course of the nineteenth century, setting in motion a process toward worldwide economic unification that historians have come to regard as the first era of globalization. In Europe, the Americas, and even Africa, railroads reached far into the interior, whereas in China their reach and accompanying changes did not extend much past the eastern coastal territory and the large river systems served by steamships.[1]

This chapter explores the transformative role railroads played in the local and regional economies of the early Republic. Readers should note that the aim of this chapter is not to measure and establish economic growth due to rail development but rather to analyze the institutional role of the railroad and its contributions to economic life in different regions across the nation. With a rail network of approximately 13,500 miles in place by the time of the Japanese invasion in 1937, railroads had gained a greater physical presence and become a part of an infrastructural system integrating water and motor transportation facilities. The economic contribution of railroads in China was different from that in Great Britain, for example, or the United States, where railroads became part of large-scale industrialization or resulted in the establishment of new urban settlements as major populations shifted along the lines. In contrast, the economic impact of China's railroads was most significantly felt in the agricultural sector and in the linkages they established with new regional economic hubs and coastal port cities.

At the heart of any historical debate about the socioeconomic effects of railroads is the issue of their potential contribution to growth through so-called backward linkages—increased demand for labor, coal, steel, or financial services—and forward linkages in the form of the economic effects due to lower transportation costs for agriculture and industry.[2] Considering China's regional diversity of economic conditions and different levels of railroad penetration, it would be impossible and foolish to try to offer a comprehensive analysis covering all lines and their effects on socioeconomic developments throughout the country in one chapter or a single book. Macroeconomic studies by Ernest Liang and Thomas Rawski have made convincing arguments that cities and villages along certain railroad lines profited from the increased transportation and communications options that stimulated the commercialization of agriculture during the Republican period.[3] According to such interpretations, lower transaction costs resulted in higher incomes for farmers, facilitated the integration of their products into the national market system, and even linked them to international markets. The interplay of specific local and regional economic conditions, however, limited the stimulation and created pockets of economic development rather than a national trend of economic growth tied to rail infrastructure during the Republican period.[4]

Building on these findings but reversing the methodological approach, the analysis in this chapter considers the economic impact of Chinese railroads through the institutional prism of their business operations and strategic responses, either as a catalyst for complementary businesses and adoption of new business practices or as an initiator of the strategic growth of transfer hubs. If we approach the Chinese railroad line as an institutional black box and identify its tools, practices, and mechanisms enabling the transportation of goods in a cost-saving and efficient manner, we will be better able to understand the railroad's various contributions to the local transformation of economic life and the implications for economic development (or lack thereof).

This chapter focuses on the question of how railroads as business institutions interacted with local and regional economies along the major rail corridors. The analysis begins with an examination of the development of freight businesses and their operational management and challenges along various railroad lines. When a rising supply of and demand for agricultural goods and other commodities necessitated transshipments across the nation and to overseas markets, transportation companies came into being and collaborated with railroad companies. I argue in this chapter's second section that these transportation companies became a cornerstone in the building of China's logistical transportation network because they underwrote freight insurance and facilitated the use of commercial paper—business practices and arrangements that the railroads on their own were either unable or unwilling to adopt until the 1930s.

The third section of this chapter addresses the increasing adaptation and standardization of freight business, taxation, and commercial practices into the operational management of railroads as part of the modernization process that came to characterize China's economy during the Republican period. Because the arrival of railroads in other parts of the world often led to the creation of new cities and industrial centers, the final section of this chapter examines the extent to which such a phenomenon was also at work in China. As readers will see, railroads shifted and reinforced Chinese commercial hubs, but they did not create large industrial centers unless they were directly related to the operational facilities of the railroad lines.

## Freight Transportation and Agricultural Commodities

Although railroads attracted a considerable number of passengers when lines or sections of lines opened, long-distance freight transport usually generated more revenue, especially in the case of major trunk lines such as the Tianjin-Pukou and Beijing-Hankou Railroads. Although we have only fragmentary information on the volume and revenue from freight generated by each individual railroad line in the 1910s, data collected by the Commission for the Unification of Chinese Railway Statistics and Accounts, under the aegis of the Ministry of Communications and Transportation, provide helpful insights into the capacity and economic viability of freight transportation at the time.

Statistics published as official records beginning from 1915 (see Appendix B) indicate the predominance of freight transportation to generate revenue for the major trunk lines across the north China plain and the interior. Major trunk lines, such as the Jin-Pu and Peking-Mukden lines, consistently derived more income from goods traffic than from passengers, and in the cases of the Peking-Hankou and the Qingdao-Ji'nan lines freight transportation constituted two-thirds of their revenue. As for the Jin-Pu line, its transportation revenue was 46 percent from goods and 39 percent from passengers in 1915. This ratio remained fairly stable until after 1927, when tourist services and passenger express trains increased passenger revenue. As for product types, for many years the Jin-Pu Railroad was the most agricultural commodities–oriented trunk line, with the Shanghai-Nanjing line as the extension to the Yangzi delta and the port of Shanghai (see Appendix C). Mineral freight (especially coal) accounted for an even larger proportion of the revenue in the 1930s.[5] By 1935, freight accounted for 51 percent of the total revenue generated by the national railroad system.

Shorter railroad lines with continuing competition from water-based transportation, such as the Shanghai-Nanjing and Shanghai-Hangzhou-Ningbo Railroads, derived the majority of their revenue from passenger transportation. These lines began as and remained primarily passenger lines; agricultural products and manufactured goods dominated a relatively small proportion of the freight.[6] For example, freight revenue in 1910 amounted to little more than 16 percent of the passenger revenue for the Shanghai-Nanjing Railroad. The line's weak freight business was a subject of public discussion during the early years of its existence, although its financial success as the most successful tourism-oriented passenger line in the late 1920s eventually silenced its detractors.[7]

Chinese railroads most notably offered rapid transportation for bulk agricultural commodities to new markets beyond the local and even the regional economies.[8] Freight statistics reveal the content and direction of commodity flows. The particular combination of line location, complementary infrastructure, preexisting agricultural patterns, and linkages to commercial hubs and ports conditioned the economic functioning of each railroad. Thus, none of the economic developments introduced in this chapter should be interpreted as a national trend for the entire country.

The Jin-Pu trunk line connecting the north—Tianjin and Beijing—with the seaport of Qingdao on the Shandong peninsula via Ji'nan, and Shanghai via Nanjing after crossing the Yangzi River at Pukou, created different dynamics in the production and marketing of agricultural products in Jiangsu, Shandong, and Zhili provinces. Peanuts, tobacco, cotton, and silk were among the agricultural commodities that experienced increased demand and supply because of railroad transportation. As early as 1911, the *North-China Herald* observed the effects of the railroad on peanut cultivation in Shandong province, noting that farmers were quick to realize the benefits.[9] Two decades later, a detailed investigative report for the Research Department of the South Manchurian Railway by Japanese social scientist Amano Motonosuke confirmed that the agricultural economy of Shandong had benefited substantially from the Jin-Pu Railroad and the increased commercialization of cotton and peanut production and trade along the line.[10]

Reports by Qingdao port authorities on the cargo delivered to and from the wharf by the railroads in 1931 capture the nature of the commodities and their places of origin and destination. In terms of tonnage, coal was the biggest export commodity transported from inland areas to Qingdao via the railroad, followed by peanuts, wheat bran, tobacco leaves, jujubes, and raw cotton. Coal was shipped from stations close to the mining areas in Sifang, Fangzi, Boshan, and so forth along the Jiao-Ji Railroad, and tobacco was shipped from Xindian and Ershilipu. Negligible quantities of baskets, dyes, and sundries were among the very few nonagricultural goods that made their way to the port by rail.[11] On the import side, that is, cargo forwarded from the wharf via railroads across the Shandong peninsula, coal was again the largest commodity in tonnage, but it constituted only 1.2 percent of the amount of exported coal. Construction materials, hardware, and foodstuffs dominated imports, specifically cement, iron, timber, kerosene, sugar, and flour.[12]

The rail cargo lists also reflect the flows and dynamics of trade within Shandong province. Agricultural commodities were transported to Qingdao for ongoing shipment to Shanghai, Hong Kong, and destinations throughout Asia. Bulk commodities such as tobacco and peanuts dominated this traffic, but railroads also brought smaller quantities of eggs, hides, and wool to markets. The imported goods (most arriving via Shanghai, Hong Kong, and Japan) catered to the needs of railroad workshops, mines, and business enterprises for machinery and parts. For example, foreign high-grade cement was shipped to the mines and rail workshops along the Jiao-Ji and Jin-Pu lines, as were bridge parts, sidings, timber, and oil. Cotton yarn was delivered to the spinning mills in Ji'nan and Weixian, and dyes, paints, sulfur, and material for the production of matches fulfilled the various light-industry needs in Shandong province and along the Jin-Pu corridor.[13]

For personal consumption, railroads transported larger volumes of basic goods, such as milled flour, salt, sugar, kerosene, matches, cigarettes, and fertilizer to the predominantly rural populations along the lines. According to the British Foreign Office's *South China Trade Report* for 1920, the category of "imports carried by rail" included cotton goods, such as handkerchiefs destined for Canton, and Japanese sewing cotton (thread). Indian and Japanese cotton yarn, Japanese matches, and dried and salted fish were among the major imported freight items, as was American kerosene oil.[14] Railroads also imported more luxurious items, such as dresses, furniture, foreign candles, glassware, porcelain, and tea leaves in smaller quantities to meet the needs and tastes of a small affluent population of consumers.[15] Comparing the total tonnage delivered by the Jin-Pu and Jiao-Ji Railroads to and from Qingdao, it is clear that the freight volume of exports was approximately two-thirds larger than that of imports throughout the 1920s and 1930s.[16]

The economic potential of railroads to stimulate production and trade in agricultural commodities was recognized by Chinese farmers and actively promoted by companies whose business was based on the processing of raw agricultural products. For example, the British-American Tobacco Company (BAT) introduced and promoted cultivation of American tobacco seed along the railroad lines in Shandong province. Under the direction of its capable Chinese agent, a former employee of the Jiao-Ji Railroad based in Weixian, BAT built facilities such as those for curing tobacco leaf, and imported machinery of the highest technological standards at six railroad stations. To encourage tobacco growing during the early 1910s, BAT extended lucrative offers to farmers, ranging from free tobacco seed, loans of specialized equipment, credit access, and on-the-spot cash payments for entire crops. As historian Sherman Cochran notes, these arrangements were so successful for BAT, expanding Shandong tobacco acreage from 39 acres in 1913 to 23,000 acres in 1920, that the company saw no necessity to continue the policies.[17] In addition to establishing a system of direct purchasing from tobacco growers in Weixian, in 1917 BAT opened another huge leaf-purchasing center at Xuchang, a station along the Beijing-Hankou line.[18]

Chinese railroads also actively attempted to create customers for its freight services by introducing new seeds and opportunities for commercial farming. For this purpose, in 1919 the Peking-Hankou Railroad adopted a particularly novel method for encouraging farmers to ship their goods by rail. According to Wang Ching-chun, then the line's managing director, the railroad created a special advertising rail carriage, or "seed demonstration train," which traveled up and down the line. The train contained informational exhibits and was staffed by experts who presented lectures to farmers "on new types and kinds of seeds, improved methods of agriculture, and means of placing the products on the market."[19] The Peking-Hankou line management cleverly realized that investment in education related to improved production would also increase access to new freight customers. Of course, the active role of the Peking-Hankou Railroad in public education also represented the progressive social mission of Wang Ching-chun, who fancied himself as an agriculturist. Nevertheless, the seed demonstration train was a wonderful tool for free advertising with great publicity value, especially because it also functioned as a cinema at a time when film screenings were still a scarce form of entertainment in the Chinese countryside.[20]

Silk producers were early adopters of rail transportation to carry their goods to markets, especially along the Shanghai-Nanjing line, the conduit to the silk factories in the Yangzi delta's treaty ports and the hinterland. The producers of silkworm cocoons valued the speedy delivery of their precious, time-sensitive cargo to the spinning factories in Shanghai. According to a 1910 newspaper report, the shift from water to overland rail transport dramatically reduced travel and unloading times: "An interesting feature of this traffic is the method of transportation—what may be called the change from the old to the new. Formerly these cocoons were brought to Shanghai in boats. Much time was taken up in the journey, then on arrival at Shanghai another long delay was experienced in getting the cargo unloaded, and what was formerly a matter of weeks, has now become a question of days, and, ordinarily, very few at that."[21]

In the early years the Shanghai-Nanjing Railroad, like so many other lines, encountered difficulties dealing with seasonal demands on freight transportation. For example, in the summer of 1910 an extraordinary glut of cocoons overwhelmed the railroad's ability to properly store or transport the delicate freight.[22] The reason for this was insufficient rolling stock. We lack a precise number for 1910, but the Shanghai-Nanjing line in 1915 had eleven locomotives per 62 miles (100 kilometers), which was average compared with the other Chinese lines then in operation. In the same year, however, the line had a below-average number of freight cars per 62 miles, and freight car capacity was only slightly more than that of the Jin-Pu Railroad.[23]

Coping with freight and its seasonal demands added to the existing operational and managerial rolling-stock difficulties experienced by almost all Chinese railroads. Throughout the 1910s the number of locomotives and freight cars per 62 miles and their capacity remained unchanged.[24] This dire situation led some lines to seek bank financing for major purchases of imported equipment. For example, according to a 1921 purchase agreement, the Shanghai-Hangzhou-Ningbo Railroad ordered sixteen rolling-stock underframes from Metropolitan Carriage, Wagon and Finance Company and Belgian Works represented by Jardine Matheson in Shanghai. The purchase was financed by the Railway Car Loan Chinese Banking Group, with the Hong Kong and Shanghai Banking Corporation in Beijing serving as guarantor.[25] In the same year, a much larger order was placed by the Jin-Pu Railroad Bureau, financed by the same banking group. The line purchased one hundred forty-ton-capacity steel-covered freight cars from the Belgian manufacturer Compagnie Centrale de Construction for 3.4 million Belgian francs. In this investment, Fearon Daniel Company of Shanghai represented the manufacturer and Banque Belge pour l'Etranger acted as guarantor and agent on behalf of Belgian interests.[26] With continuing civil war damage and warlord interference during the early 1920s, the Chinese government repeatedly issued ten-year treasury notes for special "railway equipment loans," backed by Belgian and British financial syndicates (see Figure 3.1).[27] Unfortunately, the state of rolling stock, equipment, and maintenance did not significantly improve until the end of the civil war and the reorganization of rail administration in the 1930s.[28]

The chronic shortage of freight cars and the problems this created for producers, merchants, and end users of agricultural products was also significant from a managerial perspective. According to a detailed report by a German inspector on an "informational journey" to gather commercial and managerial intelligence in October 1912, the lack of freight cars on the Jin-Pu line had led to an estimated revenue loss of 402,000 yuan from the export of

Fig. 3.1  Treasury note for 8 percent Belgian Railway Equipment Loan, issued 1922. Reproduced from the author's collection.

agricultural goods during the first nine months of the year.[29] The inspector complained that thousands of tons of goods were stored in the open air at stations serving as commodity centers along the lines, such as Linhuaiguan, Bengbu, and Xuzhou. To press home his point, he attached a photograph to his report showing the multilayered rows of full gunnysacks awaiting shipment on the Hanzhuang station platform (see Figure 3.2).[30] Inevitably, the vagaries of the weather spoiled a considerable amount of these goods.

The lack of freight cars also had institutional consequences that went far beyond financial losses. Here the decentralized organizational structure of the railroad lines, and the role of the stationmaster in particular, mattered greatly. As the German inspector reported, employees of the Jin-Pu Railroad took advantage of the car shortage by demanding bribes and auctioning off freight cars to the highest bidders.[31] This practice, which continued until the 1920s, was criticized by rail experts such as John F. Baker, then a railroad-accounting adviser to the Chinese government. According to his analysis, which was published in 1926, contrary to the custom in the United States, freight cars were not assigned by a central distribution office in the line's management but rather by the many dozens of individual stationmasters.[32]

Fig. 3.2    Commodity jam at Hanzhuang station on the Jin-Pu line, 1912. Records relating to German railroad construction in China, 1898–1916, Baker Library, Harvard Business School, vol. 14, 1912, p. 23.

One might interpret Baker's statement as a comment on the fairly indepen-dent and autocratic role played by stationmasters during the pre-1927 rail-road period, which led to problematic issues such as corruption. The assign-ment of freight cars based on local needs and particularistic interests without sufficient attention to planning for seasonal demands for special shipments was another negative aspect of this highly localized, stationmaster-centric organizational model.

In addition to the chronic shortage of wagons for goods, the lack of effi-cient connections between lines was yet another material constraint on freight traffic that contributed to a predominantly local orientation. The low volume of through traffic is evident in the Ministry of Railways' statistical figures for "originated" versus "carried" freight: from the 1910s until the 1930s the volume of goods that railroads transshipped from other railroad lines was remarkably small. For example, as late as 1935 only approximately 8.5 percent of the tonnage transported along the Jin-Pu line originated outside the home line. This trend, applying to all lines, points to the lack of track expansion and new construction that would have created connections among railroad lines.[33]

Another obstacle to efficient through-traffic arrangements was that different railroad lines might provide the same city with services but via different stations without any track connections, which added cost, time, and inconvenience for freight and passenger transportation. In Ji'nan, for example—served by the Tsingtao-Tsinan (Qingdao-Ji'nan) Railroad since 1904 and the Jin-Pu line since 1912—track connections did not exist between these two lines until 1924.[34] Passengers in 1911 complained about the need to change trains in Shanghai from one trunk line station to another.[35] The failure to connect the Canton-Kowloon and the Canton-Hankou lines at Canton represented another long-standing problem. For more than fifteen years, passengers and freight had to traverse the three-mile distance between the stations.[36] In a less-than-ideal compromise, negotiations between British officials in Hong Kong and Chinese officials in Canton finally led to the joint construction of a tramway loop between the two stations in 1928.[37] Passengers were certainly inconvenienced by having to change stations, but even more importantly the costs of unloading and reloading freight could make a significant difference in shipping costs.

The slow pace of construction was also responsible for many of the gaps in China's rail network. Completed sections of tracks were often opened years before the entire line was completed. The most conspicuous example of slow construction was the Canton-Hankou line. Construction began in 1902 with a thirty-one-mile extension from Canton to Sanshui, which became part of the trunk line to Shaozhou and opened for traffic in 1916. But lack of capital halted construction for the next thirteen years, not resuming until 1929–1930 with the help of a $20 million bond issue by the Ministry of Railways. Although the opened sections offered local, short-distance transportation, the entire line was not completed until 1936.[38]

## Linkages: Logistics Companies

Railroad companies as businesses stimulated commodity production in certain areas that benefited from increased freight transportation. Equally important, they indirectly initiated the evolution of an entire new group of logistics enterprises, transportation companies (*yunzhuan gongsi*). For the freight business of the Jin-Pu line, such logistics companies played an important role as partners in transshipping regional goods and fulfilled business functions that during its early stages the railroad company was unable to manage on its own.

Chief among the essential services not offered by the early railroads to their customers were freight insurance and guaranteed deliveries. Chinese railroads in the early 1910s categorically refused liability for goods shipped on their trains, forcing merchants to take the situation into their own hands, such that "when goods are shipped, the owner, or someone in his place, must buy a ticket and 'ya'—sit on—the shipment to its destination, as the railroad assumes no responsibility whatever. Every freight train consequently carries scores of passengers besides the freight."[39] Apart from the inconvenience and inefficiency, this practice could lead to serious accidents. For example, the collision of a freight train with another train on the Beijing-Hankou line caused death or injuries to many passengers traveling in the runaway cars to protect their goods.[40]

Transportation companies quickly emerged to fill this niche. By the mid-1910s, this practice was relatively standardized. In the case of the Jin-Pu Railroad, the transportation companies negotiated special agreements whereby the line gave them exclusive lower rates on freight in return for shouldering the burden of liability. A contract between the Jin-Pu Railroad and Huitong (Wai Tung) Transportation Company from 1914 exemplifies the standard agreements that extended to all railroad stations and operations along the line but not beyond the jurisdiction of the Jin-Pu Railroad Bureau. Over time, the format remained relatively unchanged, with only some adjustments to the commission rates.[41]

The contract allowed the transportation company to solicit and transport goods for the entire line. For this privilege, Huitong Transportation Company deposited a bank-guaranteed sum of 30,000 yuan with the Jin-Pu Railroad Bureau "to effect insurance on goods transported along the whole line against risk of fire, water, robberies and burglaries."[42] The railroad expressly denied any responsibility for losses, transferring potential claims and their settlement to Huitong. In the case of losses, Huitong had to pay a premium of 0.1 yuan on every 100 yuan of "goods, silver, copper and Government monies" shipped between Tianjin and Pukou, with an extra premium of 0.05

yuan on every 100 yuan of freight value crossing the Yangzi River between Pukou and Xiaguan. The risk of transporting "valuable" articles required insurance of 1 percent for every yuan of value. For goods stored in warehouses owned by the railroad or by Huitong awaiting further transport, the company was charged 0.4 yuan per 100 yuan of value of goods per year, to be paid in quarterly installments.[43]

For a railroad, the financial gains from such arrangements seem to have been substantial, because the railroad bureau ordered all its stations to collect the insurance premiums together with the freight due on the insured goods. The transportation company had to deposit 20,000 yuan with the railroad bureau in advance as a guarantee for the freight charges. Accounts were settled once a month, and Huitong was charged a 5 percent collection fee on its company account. This arrangement appears to have brought a significant, reliable, and easy-to-collect revenue stream for the Jin-Pu Railroad. The railroad also offered to place additional police on duty in freight cars that carried unspecified "super-cargoes."[44]

At first glance, this arrangement seems to have benefited only the railroad and not the transportation companies. A clause in the contractual agreement, however, granted permission to lease land and buildings at any station along the line to transportation companies for business purposes. This agreement allowed Huitong access to storage facilities and godowns, and even a connection to the station via track sidings, thus facilitating and speeding up the loading and unloading of freight. As a government-owned national railroad, the Jin-Pu line issued land leases and collected rent in advance, but it appears that the Jin-Pu Railroad Bureau did not share the revenue with the central administration at the ministry level, at least not in the 1910s, before the bureaucratic centralization and restructuring under the Ministry of Railways in 1928.[45]

Transportation companies received an annual commission from the railroad on the goods they solicited as a percentage of the total value. For example, Huitong Company received a 4 percent commission on solicited goods with a minimum value of 50,000 yuan or more, reaching 9 percent on goods valued 500,000 to 600,000 yuan, and with extra awards for values above 1 million yuan. These commission rates for Huitong were valid only on the northern section of the line, between Tianjin and Liguoyi; on the southern section, between Liguoyi and Pukou, the Jin-Pu Railroad had another arrangement with Lida (Li Dah) Transportation Company. By 1919, the commission in this agreement was 5 percent on freight values of 350,000 yuan or more, rising to 10 percent on shipments valued at greater than 500,000 yuan. Obviously, by then freight transportation on the line had generally increased, enabling the Jin-Pu Railroad to shrewdly increase the threshold for the commission fees. Not surprisingly for a nationalized railroad, transportation of government goods and materials for the needs of railroad administration were not subject to such fees.[46]

The Jin-Pu line set the terms of the agreements, with the goal of retaining as much leverage as possible over the transportation companies without damaging incentives for cooperation. The transportation companies had to supply shipping materials, such as "rattans, baskets and wrapping-cloth" and hire their own workforce for the loading and unloading of the freight trains. In return, the Jin-Pu Railroad periodically issued free passes for Huitong employees to use on the line and on the connecting ferries. Huitong also received a 20 percent discount on telegrams sent from Jin-Pu stations for business needs. The contract under discussion was valid for five years but renewable if no breach of contract or violation of railroad regulations had occurred. Here the Jin-Pu line particularly specified that no transport of dangerous goods, such as ammunition, was permitted without authorization and that the overloading of freight cars or irregularities in freight reporting would lead to punishment and termination of the contract. The Jin-Pu line also reserved the right to a potential reduction in the commission rates in future contracts.[47]

The registration of transportation companies with the Jin-Pu Railroad Bureau and the rail administration required the disclosure of company information that was similar to the registration of businesses required by the 1904 Company Law. Specifically, the transportation companies had to be Chinese owned.[48] That Chinese transportation companies in their agreements with individual railroad lines held a de facto monopoly over rail shipping business drew criticism, especially from envious foreign competitors. In 1919 the British consul in Nanjing commented on the perceived unfair treatment of foreign firms and their inability to ship directly with the railroad lines. He complained that the domestic transportation companies received "special facilities in the matter of warehouses, sidings, and so forth . . . special rebates, which are not accorded to mercantile firms or to individuals . . .

[and] preference in the matter of rolling-stock for the transportation of merchandise."[49] The latter issue was particularly important during the late 1910s and 1920s, when rolling stock was in short supply because of damage from the civil war and the expansion of freight traffic.

Many Chinese government lines paid commissions for freight transport with necessary adaptations to the requirements of the local and regional economies. The Shanghai-Nanjing line, for example, entered into contractual agreements not only with "officially recognized transportation companies," but, in contrast to the Jin-Pu Railroad, also with "private merchants and firms transporting their own goods."[50] According to a 1917 agreement, the railroad paid a commission of 5 percent on total shipped values of 15,000 yuan or more and 10 percent on total shipped values of 50,000 yuan or more. As a short-distance line providing a crucial connection between the agricultural center of the Yangzi delta (a source of cotton and silk) and the industrial center of Shanghai, the lower threshold for commission payments might indicate that, instead of relying on a few transportation companies, many merchants took over responsibility for the transportation of their own goods. In this particular local context, a clear distinction between freight and passenger traffic became necessary. Therefore, the contract specified that commission rates were limited to trains carrying only goods or to freight cars in mixed trains and excluded goods in baggage vans or kept in the brake cabins of passenger trains.[51]

To ensure greater loyalty of its logistics customers and improve the economics of a transportation business with a high volume of smaller freight, the Shanghai-Nanjing Railroad sternly reminded merchants that commissions would be paid only if the required minimum value of shipped goods was reached within the fiscal year. Merchants could also apply for special commission rates when they shipped large quantities of specified special commodities. Silk cocoons are a primary example of a special agricultural commodity transported according to special rates and excluded from any commissions. To keep additional middlemen from potentially abusing the commission system, individual merchants and firms functioned as both the consignor and the consignee of the goods to qualify for a commission. Companies transporting goods on behalf of unofficial transportation companies (i.e., not registered with the Shanghai-Nanjing Railroad) were able to obtain a maximum commission of only 5 percent on shipped freight valuing 15,000 yuan per year.[52]

A comparison of the contracts provided by the Jin-Pu and the Shanghai-Nanjing Railroads shows that the latter organized a much simpler commission system to serve a large clientele of mainly smaller individual merchant businesses. Commission rates were integrated into the line's freight tariff system without additional obligations for insurance or risk management of the logistical operations. From the perspective of railroad management, requiring consignors also to be the consignees, either as an individual or from the same firm, mitigated the risks of irregularities to some extent. The absence of time-limited contracts and renewal requirements reduced administrative paperwork for the railroad and allowed the merchants relative flexibility in their transportation choices. They benefited from the commission rates as long as they abided by the rules dictated by the accounting for the fiscal year. The Shanghai-Nanjing agreements also imply the continuing existence of alternative water transport options in the Yangzi delta. Without affecting the long-term relationship between the railroad and its customers, the commission contracts indirectly encouraged merchants to move seasonal traffic, such as silk cocoons, to waterways when the freight capacity of the line was stretched to the limit.

The contractual agreements between major trunk lines and their official transportation companies did not provide the clients with the same flexibility. Because they were required to register (*zhuce*) with the Ministry of Communications and Transportation and to renew the agreement every five years, the transportation companies at times felt at a disadvantage in terms of negotiating contractual conditions. As a result, companies occasionally would join forces. For example, in January 1918 the Tianjin General Chamber of Commerce petitioned the Jin-Pu Railroad Bureau on behalf of ten transportation companies, all located in the city of Tianjin, to protest the announcement that the companies would lose their registration with the ministry and their commission privileges.[53] The companies complained that in the previous year military transport had received priority using train cars, which, in turn, had considerably reduced their business capacity.

The detailed petition not only illustrates the complex business relationship between the transportation companies and the Jin-Pu Railroad but also reveals how these private logistics firms framed the conflict as an issue of government (*guan*) versus private or merchant (*shang*) enterprise.[54] Transportation companies considered the commission on solicited freight business to be fair compensation for their assuming responsibility for the risk or loss of equipment on behalf of the line—a situation different from the other lines. In their opinion, the Jin-Pu Railroad Bureau had solicited the establishment of the companies in 1912 for its own benefit because its warehouses and other freight facilities were insufficient. Subsequently, as the companies charged in their complaint, the railroad had enjoyed the profits of the freight business with few of the liabilities. The railroads provided the freight cars, but the companies were in charge of every other step in the capital-intensive transportation process. When the railroad bureau reduced the commissions upon renewing the contract, the companies protested, citing pressures from "daily increasing responsibility and capital expenditures." As a result, some transportation companies folded. The ten companies that remained registered challenged the Jin-Pu line, and by extension the railroad administration, for an agreement perceived as unfair.[55]

In addition to the burdens of anticipated higher costs and payment of transportation fees, the companies complained about shouldering the risks of rain, dampness, rot, and mold, which were high, especially for agricultural commodities: "How can our companies who cover the risk with such huge financial responsibility depend on such trivial commissions as compensation?"[56] The petitioners, pleading in the name of the mutual dependency of the railroad bureau, the consignors, and the transportation companies, argued that insufficient commissions would automatically harm the other two participants in this interactional triangle. In fact, as the companies argued, they would have to pass the loss of revenue on to their customers, the consignors.[57]

The significance of the negotiations between the transportation companies and the Jin-Pu Railroad Bureau is that the bureau, as part of the national railroad administration and a government entity, had control over the fate of transportation companies by controlling their registration and commission rates. On the one hand, their investments were tied to the line and were thus not easy to recoup. On the other hand, the transportation companies also realized their own role in the functioning of freight traffic and the financial impact on the railroad and the regional economy if freight traffic were to suffer. They argued that the high fees and the amount of paperwork would drive freight transportation to water channels when possible and to the Japanese-managed Jiao-Ji Railroad on the Shandong peninsula but not to other national railroads.[58]

The insufficient number of freight cars and the relative power of railroad employees and stationmasters also influenced the business practices of the transportation companies. They were subject to paying bribes and inflated fees and passed on these costs to the consignors and the producers of the shipped goods who were in a relatively weak position to negotiate the prices if they wanted to move their freight, especially in the case of seasonal, perishable commodities. Consignors complained to the railroad administration when sixteen companies operating on the southern part of the Jin-Pu Railroad between Xuzhou and Pukou inflated prices in 1912, whereas the companies complained to the bureau about the railroad employees whose practices caused the price inflation—with neither side achieving much success.[59]

Another reason for complaints about transportation companies as middlemen in the transshipment process was their habit of collecting extra fees from their consignors at the stations. For example, in 1919 a Mr. Tweedy tried to ship a load of tobacco from Pukou. He "experienced the greatest difficulty in finding anyone to book the goods, and, when this was eventually done, in obtaining an account [there was apparently an extra charge, which he decided was 'squeeze,' and therefore made it very difficult for him]."[60] Mr. Tweedy's experience emphasizes the transportation companies' control over freight shipments, which allowed them to liberally dictate their own terms. At the same time, it was no secret that the railroad administration discouraged direct dealings with the railroad lines and deliberately steered any business toward the transportation companies. Contemporaries suspected that many high-level Chinese officials in the railroad and line administrations were investors in the transportation companies; even without any direct proof, this seems to be a convincing explanation.[61]

The fee problems between consignors and transportation companies continued throughout the Republican period, but over time the methods of overcharging became more sophisticated and institutionalized. As 1937 correspondence from the Chinese Maritime Customs Service shows, transportation companies demanded a substantial fee from customers whose merchandise had been detained for customs inspection in Hankou. The fee was charged under the pretext of bribing the customs inspector to release the consignor's goods. What might have been an accepted nuisance and an unspecified business expense in previous years now became an official and legal issue because the consignors had recorded the fee in their account books as a charge to bribe customs officers. Such account records led, for example, to an official investigation of Hsien Kee (Xianji) Transportation Company in Hankou, which had approached several companies for fees allegedly used to bribe customs officers.[62]

Despite the complaints, even a typically critical foreign observer acknowledged the essential services provided by the transportation companies in insuring the goods that traveled under their supervision. In 1919, the British consul in Nanjing forwarded one of his countrymen's grievances to the ambassador in Peking, but he also noted that by providing financial services for local producers, Chinese transportation companies facilitated trade that otherwise would not have taken place: "It must not be overlooked that they have been largely instrumental in developing the export trade of the districts through which the line passes. They act as bankers as well as carriers; they advance money to the farmers and others on their consignments and take full responsibility therefore, and thus enable many to market their produce who would otherwise find it impossible to do so. It must be added that they charge an extortionate price for their services, nevertheless they meet a real need."[63]

In view of the great demand for these profitable services, why did Chinese railroad lines not operate these services on their own, as vertically integrated companies, especially considering their nature as government institutions? From a financial perspective, one explanation for the outsourcing of services to independent transportation companies is at least partly related to the continuing difficulties of sending through shipments across different lines where goods had to be unloaded and reloaded onto new freight cars. As a commercial handbook from 1920 informs us, charges for transferring freight for so-called through business by transportation companies at railroad junctions were often cheaper than the per diem charges for freight cars in use for changes between slow lines.[64] Transportation companies offered competitive rates because they were able to draw on a large pool of cheap unskilled manual laborers to load and unload at junctions, such as Xuzhou, Pukou, or Shanghai. From a managerial perspective, Chinese railroad companies must have considered it an advantage not to be engaged in the management of a large, mostly unskilled, and volatile workforce outside their administrative and workshop compounds, which were organized according to the traditional contract-labor system supervised by local foremen.[65]

Considering the constraints on available rolling stock in all Chinese railroad companies in the 1910s and early 1920s, transportation companies fulfilled an additional important role by quickly freeing up freight cars and shortening their turnaround time. Until the late 1920s Chinese railroads were plagued by a constant shortage of freight cars and engines because of military requisitions. According to a 1920 report on rolling stock, Chinese railroads had approximately 0.2 locomotives, 0.4 passenger cars, and fewer than 3.3 freight cars per mile of line in operation, a much lower average than that of foreign railroads with similar earnings or traffic volume.[66] Heavy seasonal demand for the transport of commodities exacerbated the already strained situation for rolling stock. For example, in 1920 the Jin-Pu line was unable to cope with the heavy demand for cargo transportation, so "native produce was piled at every station awaiting its turn and much of it was spoilt."[67] According to an official estimate, November to January were the busiest months for transshipment deliveries at Pukou, with approximately seven freight trains arriving per day carrying 1,600 tons of coal and 3,500 tons of produce. The rest of the year total daily freight deliveries at the river junction were approximately 25 percent lower.[68]

If we consider transportation companies as forward linkages resulting from the freight business opportunities created by Chinese railroads, the establishment of new steam-powered launch companies represented forward linkages resulting from the need for additional passenger transportation services. For example, soon after completion of the Shanghai-Hangzhou Railroad a new launch company named Dexin formed a business cooperation with the line to facilitate passenger transport. According to their agreement, both companies sold through tickets for journeys that combined launch and rail travel from Suzhou to Hangzhou, including free through-baggage service. The Dexin launch took passengers on the six-and-a-half-hour boat trip via the Grand Canal from Suzhou to Jiaxing, where they could catch the fast train from Shanghai at 3 p.m. and arrive two hours later in Hangzhou.[69] Commercial launch services also ferried railroad passengers across major rivers lacking bridges. For example, in October 1910 steam launches carried passengers across the Yellow River north of Ji'nan to resume their train journey.[70]

Launch services to railroad terminals could be such a lucrative business that they occasionally led to price wars between competing launch companies. After the southern section of the Canton-Hankou Railroad reached the North River (Beijiang) in 1911, passengers continued their trip via steam launches to Yingde and from there via a "shallow draught stern-wheeler" to Shaozhou, thus reducing the travel time from fourteen days to only two days. Two rival companies competed for passengers between Yingde and the railroad head in Guangzhou, leading to a price war and even a fist fight between the two launch crews.[71]

On occasion steam launches and railroads were competitive rather than complementary means of transportation. In Shanghai, for example, the Shanghai-Hangzhou Railroad attracted disapproval in 1911 for locating its terminal too far from the center of trade and the Huangpu River. As a result, the steam launch companies retained their edge and, on the basis of their low prices, were still a competitor to the railroad line in 1918.[72] Throughout the 1910s and the 1920s new launches and ferry services that arose as complementary transportation businesses brought passengers to railroad stations along sparse trunk line systems, often far from passenger and freight final destinations.[73]

Well into the Republican period even some mining districts had to rely on steam launch services rather than on railroads to transport their products. For example, in 1919 large steam barges transported coal from the mines in Leping and Yugan counties in Jiangxi province across Poyang Lake to Jiujiang, where the waterway connected with the Yangzi River. Although these coal-rich areas were close to the line of a surveyed railroad from Nanchang to Wuhu, it was not until the late 1930s that a line was completed to connect to the Guangzhou-Hankou line for through transport to the coast.[74]

## Business Regulations and Taxation

As modern business institutions evolved in the early twentieth century, railroads influenced the formulation and practice of regulations governing the operation of a highly complex infrastructure system and its interactions with the economic environments at the local, regional, and national levels. Throughout the Republican era railroads as institutional entities focused on standardization and best practices in the operational management of the lines and the professional conduct of the workforce. Best practices and regulations were also established to educate passengers, travelers, and the general public in safety and discipline. Best practices and regulations for freight transportation grew with the increasing volume and variety of goods shipments and began to address related issues, such as insurance, safety, taxation, and financial services, thus facilitating the flow of goods and internal methods of accounting and currency exchange.

Passengers brought goods in ever-increasing volume on board, and soon sets of rules began to specify the luggage and goods allowances for individual travelers in the passenger carriages. By the late 1910s guidebooks and railroad publications listed the permissible categories of products and transportation fees for goods assigned to freight car transportation. Detailed lists ranked the safety level and the fee structure per unit, ranging from grain and textiles to industrial and mining products. Special sections also stated the transport fees for vehicles and livestock, including rickshaws, bicycles, and coffins, with reduced fees for empty coffins.[75]

Perishable freight was another category that saw gradual but steady increases in regulation during the Republican period. In the early years of the Jin-Pu, Jiao-Ji, and Long-Hai Railroads, the transportation of fresh goods was limited to the scope of the respective lines, and the only way for merchants to transport these goods was to make their own arrangements and to send an escort. Under German management from 1904 to 1914, the Jiao-Ji Railroad on the Shandong peninsula had three double-axle refrigeration cars, but shipments of fresh fish were still negligible. After the line was transferred from Japanese to Chinese ownership in 1923, efforts were made to protect perishable freight. The line acquired a series of refrigeration cars that were coupled with the passenger trains to ensure faster shipment. The annual fresh freight, much of it eggs destined for the Japanese market, amounted to approximately one thousand tons.[76] The Jin-Pu and Long-Hai Railroads, which mainly served inland areas, transported far less perishable freight. The Jin-Pu Railroad had only one refrigeration car in the 1920s, and the Long-Hai line had none. When the Japanese occupied the Shandong peninsula in the wake of its invasion of China and took control over the Jiao-Ji Railroad in 1938, an "express goods train" (*jixing huowu lieche*) was introduced, with refrigerated cars to provide stations along the line from Qingdao with fresh fish, an important part of the Japanese diet.[77]

Whereas each railroad line developed its own set of freight regulations during the early Republican period, after 1927 the Ministry of Railways standardized the regulations across the line network. The Station Management Methods (*zhanchang guanli banfa*), announced in 1932, gave certain key stations authority to regulate freight transportation. For example, the Ji'nan and Xuzhou stations along the Jin-Pu line and the Xuzhou and Tongshan stations along the Long-Hai Railroad were authorized to issue permits for freight shipments and shipping lists for goods entering and leaving the stations. Although these standards did not remove authority from key rail junctions and their personnel, the new regulatory system improved standardization by categorizing the freight districts and freight units by serial numbers to be provided to the inspectors controlling the freight.[78]

These regulations also addressed the shipment of dangerous goods, such as kerosene and matches, that previously had been handled by each line in different ways. Like many others, the Jin-Pu and Long-Hai lines had left arrangements and responsibility for safety to the owners of the goods. Not until after 1932 did railroads assume direct responsibility for the shipment of such "normal goods," whereas responsibility for explosives, arms and ammunition, toxic chemicals, and so forth still rested with the owners.[79] The issuance of insurance for railroad property across the national administrative apparatus was introduced relatively late. It was not until June 1936 that the Ministry of Railways ordered the railroad bureau of every government line to take out fire insurance.[80]

Chinese railroads operated within a taxation system with roots in the late Qing period. Instability and territorial fragmentation under different warlord regimes during the early Republican period severely challenged the authority and ability of the central government to collect taxes from the evolving nation-state, especially before 1927. As a result, the government's two main revenue streams consisted of the custom taxes and the salt taxes, which were administered through the Chinese Maritime Customs Service and the Sino-Foreign Salt Inspectorate but were then directly channeled to the central government.[81] Far more robust was the collection of the *lijin*, or transit tax, which was the primary source of provincial revenue until its gradual abolition during the Nanjing decade (1927–1937) as part of the Guomindang government's efforts for fiscal reform.[82]

Every railroad line faced the problem of the ad valorem transit tax, which had been collected for goods since the late nineteenth century, most commonly at 2 percent, along the transit routes and sometimes also as a production tax, similar to a sales tax, at the point of origin or at the final destination.[83] In the early years of railroad construction, the *lijin* was often blamed for the relatively low utilization of railroads for freight transport because merchants favored transport by other means to avoid the taxation. A complaint by Alexander Pope, general manager of the Shanghai-Nanjing line in the early 1910s, exemplifies many comments by line managers during this time. In his view, railroads lost out on business because merchants using the line had to pay the "legitimate" *lijin* at the full amount, but they paid only 30 percent of the authorized figure when sending their goods by water. Naturally, railroads tended to lose business to rival boat traffic.[84]

Located in the dense river and canal network of the lower Yangzi region, the Shanghai-Hangzhou line faced similar challenges. According to a 1911 *North-China Herald* report, "The railway does not, as yet, serve to any extent as a vehicle of trade between Shanghai and Hangchow, because of the likin [*lijin*] duties levied at Fengching, where the line crosses the boundary of Chekiang and Kiangsu." The Chinese merchant, the article concluded, "finds it still to his advantage to ship his goods by water under the aegis of the Imperial Customs."[85] The transit tax issue was widely discussed, and its abolition was prematurely announced several times, including in 1911, 1912, 1920, and 1927.[86] The power of the provincial authorities, however, was such that the *lijin* was only gradually abolished in 1930 and was replaced by excise taxes on products such as cigarettes and cotton yarn under a new consolidated Tax Administration.[87]

In light of high shipping costs, including taxation, smuggling activities along the railroad lines increased. Smuggling activities were not only actions orchestrated to transport "illegal goods" but one of the foremost methods of tax avoidance integrated into the operational structure of the railroad lines and their workforce. For example, railroad workers carried goods on their own—"pidgin cargo" in the English-language newspapers—so as to avoid the taxes and freight charges. On the Jin-Pu Railroad, this form of smuggling included opium; the geographical center was situated at Pukou and Puzhen, where many railroad workers lived close to the locomotive workshops and bought their contraband to take up north.[88]

The government supported efforts to reduce the extraneous costs on merchants shipping goods via rail by convening the Peking Railroad Conference "to restore the sadly abused but very great earning power of the Chinese Railways" a few months before the Nationalists came to power in 1928.[89] This move reflected the railroad administration's desire to restore state control over freight traffic and its revenue but also to run the railroad lines more like for-profit business entities so as "to bring back that public confidence and economy of management which the Government Railways used to enjoy only a few years ago both at home and abroad."[90] Apart from simplifying the transit taxes, the railroad conference also demanded the eradication of military interference with railroad funds and operations. Interruption of rail traffic by troop transports and war damage had again become a significant problem during the civil war of 1926–1927, when Chiang Kai-shek's Northern Expedition armies defeated the warlords in southern and central China.

Demands for more transparent transit taxes came not only from the railroad companies but also from the chambers of commerce, both Chinese and foreign, operating in major commercial hubs such as Beijing or Tianjin. Their complaints did not question the taxation system as such but blamed the stationmasters for their corrupt habits of levying excessive charges. The debates during the 1927 railroad conference were amply publicized in the newspapers and gave voice to the chambers' outrage about existing unfair charges: "It was shown that the total transportation cost for a ton of wool from Paotow [Baotou] to Tientsin [Tianjin] including all the taxes and other illegal charges is six times more than the freight between Tientsin and New York! A certain Chamber of Commerce informs the conference that a station master makes a profitable business by demanding extra charges for the use of cars according to a well-made tariff schedule of his own—$32 for a 20-ton car, $88 for a 30-ton car, etc. Such valuable information will be placed before the conference of department chiefs of the different lines for reference in the formulation of definite and detailed measures for enforcing the conference decisions."[91]

Even if we consider the reported charges with caution, these complaints demonstrate the power invested in the stationmasters at the most local levels of each railroad line, in terms of both institutional hierarchy and geographical location. We also have to interpret the complaints in the context of the decentralized railroad bureau system, as discussed in Chapter 2. The administrative and managerial structure of Chinese government railroads enabled a high degree of regionalization at the line level that continued to empower those in charge of local offices, none more so than the stationmasters. It is not surprising that the localized structure led to abuses of power, especially as the transit taxation system represented the hand of the central government in the commercial realm.

Because of the many internal and external obstacles to through traffic during the 1920s, its facilitation became an important item on the agenda of the railroad administration.[92] To that end, a committee of technical experts tackled standardization issues related to technology, such as signaling, and representatives from the largest government railroad lines met at annual conferences to negotiate through-traffic conditions. The success of these conferences was limited. Resumption of through-traffic facilities was still on the list of necessary reforms at the 1927 railroad conference in Beijing. The program included a discussion of the necessary steps "to exchange rolling stock at junction stations with temporary limitations, to settle all through traffic balances with cash payments, to investigate and to promote movement of through freight by seeking co-operation of shippers," and to "control junction station reports."[93] This agenda demonstrates that the traffic system continued to suffer from operational issues related to the methods of borrowing rolling stock, payments, collaboration with transportation companies, and control over local rail stations. Creating greater transparency, centralization, and standardization in all aspects of the operational and fiscal management of the railroad lines after 1927 therefore became a central reform issue for the Nationalist government to tackle during the Nanjing decade.

Finally, the great variety of local currencies—and constant change in relative values—appears to have been a persistent problem for railroad operations. For example, according to a report from 1911, passengers traveling along the Jin-Pu line were greatly inconvenienced by different stations requiring different types of currency to buy train tickets. In fact, the journey from Tai'an on the trunk line to Qingdao via the Jiao-Ji line across the Shandong peninsula required four different kinds of currency.[94] On the Canton-Kowloon Railroad, Hong Kong currency was accepted only on the British portion of the line; both Hong Kong dollars and Chinese currency were accepted at the Chinese end, which changed the value of the fares depending on where the tickets were purchased.[95]

## Commercial Hubs and Global Connections

The arrival and expansion of the railroad in China did not bring a wave of new industrial cities springing up along the trunk lines. In fact, unlike the railroads in the United States, for example, Chinese railroads led to the creation of very few new hub cities (with the exception of the South Manchurian Railway under Japanese control in the Northeast).[96] Chinese railroads before 1949 did not expand into the country's sparsely populated and underdeveloped "wild west" but rather ran through the most densely populated and cultivated areas of the eastern coastal corridor, central China, the Pearl River delta, the Yangzi delta, and the Beijing-Tianjin hub in the north. As in the case of the north–south trunk lines between Beijing and Shanghai, rail lines often ran parallel to old canals and roads that supplied complementary and sometimes competitive services.

Railroads did contribute to changes in urbanization by shifting economic trends. In key junctions such as Ji'nan or Xuzhou, the cities had been significant urban centers as, respectively, the provincial capital in Shandong and the prefectural seat in northern Jiangsu many centuries before the arrival of the railroad. The railroad changed the cities' previous characteristics from being predominantly seats of government administration to a more commercial orientation. Cities such as Tianjin and Shanghai that had become treaty ports in the late nineteenth century embraced the commercial potential of the railroad with enthusiasm. The terminal stations and railroad bureaus were often located in or close to the foreign settlements, which led to the growth of commercial districts with warehouses, trading companies, and financial institutions.[97]

Ji'nan's transformation began even before completion of the Jin-Pu Railroad because of its transformation into a treaty port in 1904.[98] Seven years later, the *North-China Herald* noted the electrification of the main streets and public buildings and the considerable work on the roads. The changes were particularly noticeable in the foreign settlement, which was "well laid out with beautiful macadamized streets lined with trees. Fine, well-built buildings in European style are numerous and one can easily imagine oneself in Shanghai or Tientsin."[99]

The physical presence of the Jin-Pu Railroad had a considerable impact on urban development in the provincial capital of Ji'nan.[100] After Ji'nan's self-initiated promotion to a treaty port and the opening of the Jin-Pu line, urbanization, especially in the foreign concession, accelerated and helped the city develop into a commercial, industrial, and transportation center. Located near the Qingdao-Ji'nan railroad station, the Jin-Pu railroad station facilitated transportation of agricultural commodities from southern Shandong and northern China and the increasing commercial traffic into eastern Shandong and long-distance shipping from the port of Qingdao. The resultant economic and urban growth of Ji'nan in the early twentieth century shifted the city's character from an administrative center to a commercial, industrial, and transportation center. The railroad station of the Jin-Pu line attracted commercial establishments, shops, and warehouses to the neighborhood.[101] I do not argue that railroads caused urban growth, but with their stations and operational facilities they certainly contributed to urban expansion, especially of commercial districts.

The modernity of the railroad, as a means of transportation and a large-scale business operation that inspired urban planning and architecture, was reflected in the many Western-style office buildings, warehouses, and commercial institutions connected to the railroads.[102] Again, the Jin-Pu Railroad compound, with its workshops, housing, and social services, constituted a modern "city within the city," which was architecturally and structurally similar to railroad compounds in the West. In similar fashion, huge, modern brick warehouses and storage yards surrounded Tianjin's railroad station close to the foreign settlement (see Figure 3.3). Station buildings in such hub cities were built as architectural representations of Western efficiency and discipline. Outside the modern, urban environments of the foreign settlements, however, station buildings tended to display a more pronounced Chinese architectural influence. For example, the station building at Qufu incorporated a stone wall resembling a city wall, with an entrance on each side, into the German architecture (see Figure 3.4). The Ji'nan East station for the German-owned Jiao-Ji line featured traditional Chinese tile roofs with decorative figurines and chimneys.[103]

The most important result of the new business district surrounding the Jin-Pu line was the relocation of merchants and businesses away from the old city and the canals feeding the Grand Canal to this new section of Ji'nan. As maps

**Fig. 3.3**   Railroad tracks at the Hotung yard in Tianjin, 1923. G. Warren Swire. University of Bristol—Historical Photographs of China, reference number Sw06-034. George Warren Swire photographic collection. Courtesy of John Swire & Sons Ltd.

**Fig. 3.4**   Qufu railroad station on the Jin-Pu line, 1912. Records relating to German railroad construction in China, 1898–1916, Baker Library, Harvard Business School, vol. 14, "Anlage zu Bericht," No. 110, 1912, no pagination.

from the early Republican period and city business directories show, grain stores opened on Jingyi Road opposite the station, where grain could be easily transported and loaded onto the trains.[104] After 1912, the convenience and opportunity to access new markets faster than via ships led to most grain being transported by rail to Shanghai instead of being sent to Tianjin as had previously been the case.[105]

Expanding trade and commercial activities at the Ji'nan station required increasing the number of porters (*jiaofu*) who were organized in various groups (*bang*) and who fought over the right to load and unload trains. Competition among the groups became so fierce that the Jin-Pu Railroad police who controlled and regulated the business district in the 1910s and early 1920s were forced to intervene. They established a system that ensured order at the station by distributing the loading tasks more evenly among the different porter groups.[106]

Cities like Xuzhou gained new significance by becoming junctions for east–west and north–south trunk lines, thus according them strategic military and economic importance. The negative side effect of this general logistical advantage was that these junctions became major targets during military campaigns and suffered from track congestion and military occupation of the station buildings and railroad facilities. For example, warlord Zhang Xun chose Xuzhou as his general headquarters during the civil war of the early Republic, and he ran his campaign from inside the station. For similar strategic reasons, Xuzhou became the "northern supply station" during the 1927 war between Chiang Kai-shek's troops and the armies of warlord Sun Chuanfang.[107]

Although railroads in China generally had a greater impact on agricultural development than on industrial development, Shijiazhuang in the northern province of Hebei, a town without previous industrial production, experienced substantial industrial growth in the wake of its connection to the Beijing-Wuhan line. Shijiazhuang developed from a backwater into a rail hub attracting textile companies because of its location close to the agricultural production area of cotton and the farmers who used the industrially produced cotton yarn to weave cotton cloth in household production. Apart from the availability of cheaper raw material and labor, the fast commercialization of textile products via rail encouraged some cotton mill entrepreneurs in Wuhan to establish branches in Shijiazhuang during the 1920s.[108]

Because Chinese railroads contributed to the commercialization of agriculture more than to the establishment of new industries, the rail effect on urbanization was most significant in smaller areas that became important either as collection centers for specific agricultural products or for providing forward linkages in the agriculture-related processing industries. For instance, places such as Bengbu in northern Anhui province had been fairly insignificant until the Jin-Pu Railroad made it a major agricultural hub specializing in beans, wheat, and *gaoliang* (sorghum).[109] Because of its connection with the Huai River and the canal system in Anhui province, Bengbu also became an important agricultural trading center by integrating water transportation with the railroad, which attracted financial institutions and stimulated new financial practices. For example, in 1934 the prominent economist Ma Yinchu used Bengbu as a case study to demonstrate the circulation of new paper instruments such as promissory notes in commercial transactions involving agricultural commodities and rail transportation companies for which short-term financing was particularly important to the consigning merchants.[110] Close by, Linhuaiguan underwent a similar experience, growing from a backwater into a railroad transportation hub for salt shipped from the interior. The modest appearance of the Jin-Pu station in Linhuaiguan belied its commercial significance; built opposite a canal landing, the station's location allowed porters to move sacks of salt directly from boats onto freight cars for transport to Ji'nan and the coastal port cities (see Figure 3.5).

The growth of physical assets related to the business of railroads contributed to the status and pride of place of rural areas and even to their urban aspirations and modernization. As one example among many small towns in the 1920s, Zhumajian along the Long-Hai line in Henan province was transformed from a nondescript mountain town to a place with "sheds for rolling-stock and railway material, water-tanks and residences of officials connected with the railway" near the station. In short, the expanded physical presence of the railroad literally put these places on the map and into the guidebooks of the time.[111]

The few new settlements directly related to the railroads in prewar China were there to meet specific needs of the railroad lines; their emergence was not due to external commercial or industrial growth. Pukou and Puzhen serve as examples of these rather exceptional cases. Pukou, on the northern side of the Yangzi River opposite Nanjing to the northwest, was a swampy,

Fig. 3.5   Loading salt onto freight cars on the Jin-Pu line at Linhuaiguan, 1912. Records relating to German railroad construction in China, 1898–1916, Baker Library, Harvard Business School, vol. 14, 1912, p. 16.

undeveloped patch of land before 1912. It gained in significance only because, lacking a bridge, passengers and freight had to be ferried across the river to the terminal at Xiaguan.

As early as 1912, possibilities for Pukou's future were explored. In this first year of operation of the Jin-Pu line, the potential of this port with its surrounding waterways was obvious to the public: "At the present time one of the points of the greatest interest in commercial circles is the future in store for Pukow [Pukou]. . . . Whilst passenger traffic amongst the Chinese continues all the time, the greatest proportion of the earnings comes from produce brought to the railway from down the Huai River. With so large a traffic at this early stage of its history the railway may anticipate a terminus of considerable wealth at Pukow. Here the natural course of events would be for sea-going shipping to call, taking and bringing cargo direct."[112]

Obviously, the possibility that Pukou could also serve commercial ocean shipping via Shanghai and the Yangzi delta moved the trading opportunities to a higher level of global interconnections. Originally, however, Pukou was not a treaty port, which elicited strong debates among the foreign powers and the Chinese government. The options were either to make Pukou into a treaty port because it was vital to bring foreign shipping to the port or to include it in the treaty port district of Nanjing on the other side of the river.[113]

Pukou became a treaty port in 1912, and in the following years it underwent a fundamental transformation. Beginning with a messy station area that looked like a village with an accidental railroad track (see Figure 3.6), Pukou grew into a substantial industrialized and commercialized settlement. The engineering section of Jardine Matheson equipped the wharf with electric cranes capable of lifting 120 tons. To service the engines and railcars, the Jin-Pu Railroad erected workshops in nearby Puzhen, which housed its workers and engineers in a modern rail compound. To supply the necessary electricity for the machinery at Puzhen, the Jin-Pu line ordered that a powerhouse be built close to the workshops.[114] The significance of both places rose and fell

**Fig. 3.6**   Pukou station on the northern bank of the Yangzi River, 1912. Records relating to German railroad construction in China, 1898–1916, Baker Library, Harvard Business School, vol. 14, 1912, p. 12.

solely with the demand for rail transshipments. As soon as a double-decker road-rail bridge was built between the Pukou district and Nanjing in 1968, Pukou's importance as a commercial hub quickly declined.[115]

Of course, winners and losers in the competition for freight and passengers also included places that had initially tied their economic fates to requests for a rail link to a trunk line but then had been left untouched by the rail construction plans. For example, throughout the 1910s the local chamber of commerce in Zhifu clamored for a railroad. "Chefoo [Zhifu] will never hold its own unless the railway is constructed," the *North-China Herald* complained in 1919, noting that several silk filatures had left the town for Andong in the coastal Northeast, where transport facilities were better.[116] The rise of Qingdao as the commercial center of the Shandong Railroad, with all its infrastructure investments during the years of German control, was interpreted as an immediate disadvantage for the development of Zhifu.[117] The strength of Qingdao, however, was certainly not a convincing argument for building a branch line to Zhifu to improve the commercial opportunities for a group of local Chinese businessmen.[118]

Another category of places losing to the railroad were trading centers that had benefited from trade along the Grand Canal before its decline. Zhenjiang at the mouth of the lower Yangzi delta serves as a striking example. For centuries, Zhenjiang had been a distribution point for goods (and passengers) carried by junks on the Grand Canal, but after Grand Canal shipments were diverted to the railroad, Zhenjiang lost its commercial significance.[119] According to a somber description from January 1929, the Grand Canal was impassable because of "the silting up of the channel, the uneven rainfall, and the unregulated use of water in the rice fields bordering the canal," particularly in the winter months. At the time, the canal as "the cheapest transportation to the outside markets," meaning northern Jiangsu province, was blocked by boats that ran aground north of Gaoyu. Although motorbus lines carried passengers to at least some destinations in good weather, they did not provide freight services to relieve the situation.[120]

On the northern end of the Grand Canal, Tongzhou was a city that lost importance because of the arrival of the railroad. As soon as the city was connected with Beijing in 1902 via a short line that provided a rail connection to Tianjin and as shipments along the Grand Canal declined, Tongzhou was no longer a great distribution hub for goods arriving from the south destined for the capital and Northeast.[121] Some places, however, lost their importance along the waterway in exchange for a new rail hub identity. With the opening of the Jin-Pu Railroad, the city of Dezhou in northern Shandong province shifted its economic identity from an important shipment station along the Grand Canal to a major rail station for shipments of products from Shandong.[122]

## Conclusion

In 1932 economist Richard Tawney provided a harsh assessment of China's infrastructure, stating that with "no through communication from north to south, or from east to west, the effect of railways is still local, rather than national" and that "except for certain limited areas, railway and motor traffic are insignificant, and as far as the mass of peasants are concerned, might as well not exist."[123] He went on to point out that only the six provinces of Jiangsu, Liaoning, Hebei, Guangdong, Shandong, and Hubei, hosting roughly 36 percent of the nation's population, were home to 53 percent of the nation's railroads and 42 percent of the motor roads at the time.[124] Throughout the Republican period, Chinese-owned rail infrastructure remained concentrated in the eastern and central parts of the country, reaching the middle Yangzi River at Hankou and linking the Yangzi and Pearl River deltas with important seaports on the eastern and southern coasts. At the time, the railroads did not open China's massive interior and border territories to the West.

Scholars have generally acknowledged the limitations of rail infrastructure as a "national" network in prewar China, but some have also documented the significance of railroads to the development of local and regional economies. In a detailed macroeconomic study, Ernest Liang demonstrates that railroad construction stimulated growth in agricultural output and led to important gains in farm incomes.[125] Thomas Rawski argues that the expanded market integration was due to the growth of the banking sector in tandem with the improved transportation and communication networks, especially in the rural areas.[126] Focusing on Shandong province, Zhuang Weimin documents the changing flow of merchant capital into the treaty ports and commercial centers with the arrival of the new infrastructure.[127] Finally,

Kenneth Pomeranz enhances our understanding of the dynamics of the prewar rural economy in Shandong and Hebei provinces by moving the state back into the center of the discussion. According to his interpretation, the interactions between the modern and traditional sectors of the economy in North China were political as well as economic, and they were strongly influenced by "state strategies" in different forms.[128]

The evidence presented in this chapter to some extent confirms these interpretations and extends the argument further by focusing on Chinese railroads as emerging business entities and as the institutional arm of the Chinese state interacting with the local and regional economies. Although the majority of China's railroads were nationalized during the early Republican period, they retained a strong regional emphasis in their organizational structures, their disjointed track networks, and the markets they served. A close reading of the institutional evolution of the major trunk lines shows that their decentralized structure encouraged economic activities and interactions within regionally defined boundaries, which were often driven by local incentives and were not aligned with the operational and managerial efficiencies expected from Chinese "national" railroads under the central government.

As we have seen, railroads such as the Jin-Pu or Shanghai-Nanjing lines contributed to economic growth by stimulating agricultural production and commercialization, increasing trade flows to old and new markets, and attracting a financial infrastructure necessary to facilitate the payments for such activities. By outsourcing the freight business to a complex system of transportation companies, railroad bureaus created business opportunities for regional firms. Although this arrangement empowered these firms as the sole providers of transportation services and the necessary financial and insurance guarantees, their operations were at the mercy of the stationmasters at the bottom and the rail administration at the top. The term-limited contractual agreements gave the state-owned lines great organizational flexibility but rendered the firms completely dependent on the conditions and strategies established by the railroad bureaus. To put the discussion in the context of the relationship between state and business, the transportation companies felt the demanding reach of the state channeled through the regional railroad bureaus because their businesses could not be easily moved due to the exclusive nature of the contracts and their heavy investment in fixed assets such as warehouses or land attached to a specific railroad line.

Chinese railroads experimented with and constantly changed the structure of their line management throughout the early Republican period. The desire to restructure and improve at the national administrative level was strong, but despite ardent railroad reformers and much public debate, the rail administration failed to tie the strong regionally and locally embedded rail interests to a cohesive national agenda supported by a strong central bureaucracy. The various railroad bureaus handled the challenges they faced according to regional economic and political preferences and incentives. Major institutional change occurred only in the wake of unification under the Nationalists and the centralized reorganization of the government lines in 1928.

## CHAPTER FOUR

# Moving People, Transmitting Ideas

P assenger transportation and train travel are excellent prisms through which to explore the social history of Republican China. As numerous studies by historians demonstrate, the transition from late imperial China to the post-1911 Republic resulted in new social and gender identities, consumption practices, cultural expressions, and a changing relationship between citizen and state.[1] All these developments had their origins in nineteenth-century late imperial China, underwent political and social adaptations during the early Republic, and were solidified in yet another adaptation under the state-centered Nationalist government during the Nanjing decade (1927–1937) (see Map 4.1). In many ways, the operation, management, and public representation of Chinese rail transportation relate to all these issues. Despite the temptation of the rich textual and visual documentation available for the study of train travel in the early twentieth century, the institutional focus of Chinese railroad companies remains the center of this investigation. How did the companies experience and shape the passenger business, and how did the results spill over into the public realm of the Republic?

Although freight traffic was always the primary source of operating revenue for Chinese railroads, this chapter argues that passenger traffic was also a significant part of their business portfolio during the Republican period— more significant, in fact, than in other national systems that historically depended even more heavily on goods shipments, such as the United States or the Soviet Union. Furthermore, with regard to individual lines, several shorter lines in the Yangzi and Pearl River deltas derived the majority of their revenue

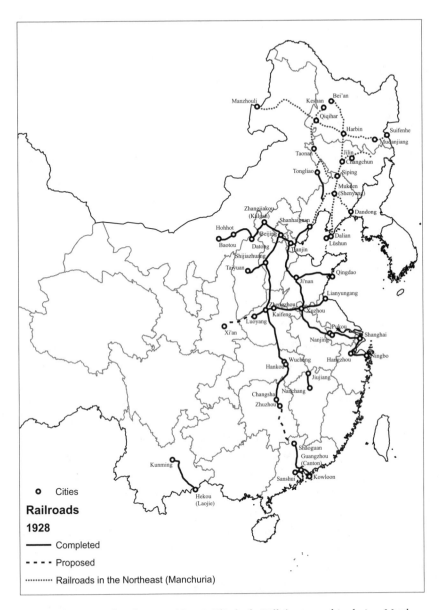

**Map 4.1**    Major railroads, 1928. Map © Elisabeth Köll (cartographic design Matthew Sisk).

from passenger ticket sales. Throughout the system, the passenger business was, although seldom primary, always significant.

It is relatively easy to show that passenger travel was important to China's railroads, but it is more difficult to show how passenger travel was significant for China. One of the more striking features of the passenger traffic emerging from the annual statistical reports of the Ministry of Railways is the short length of the average journey. The main trunk roads were very long—the Tianjin-Pukou line was 631 miles, the Beijing-Hankou line 817 miles—but between 1915 and 1935 passengers never traveled on average more than 60 miles at one time.[2] Moreover, despite these short distances a large proportion of the nation never even set foot on a train. In comparison to Britain in the 1910s and 1920s when rail traffic was so extensive that each person took on average thirty-five train journeys per year, the (entirely hypothetical) average citizen of Republican China took one journey every ten to fifteen years.[3]

As historians have shown in numerous other geographical and historical contexts, part of the novelty of rail travel was due to the strict practices and social norms it imposed on the traveling public. China was no exception. To complete a journey by rail, passengers had to master bodily and behavioral practices that were unfamiliar to the majority of the population: the uncompromising discipline of timetables and trains that wait for no one, segregation of travelers by ticket class but not by gender, obedience to the authority of impersonal rules and regulations, and even mundane practices such as queuing patiently at ticket counters and platforms.

As symbols and geographical links, railroads became part of the national education system aimed at transforming the Chinese population from imperial subjects to citizens of the Republic. Historians have established the crucial contributions of railroads to state-making efforts in several national contexts.[4] I argue here that railroads in the early Republican period were unable to foster a strong sense of national belonging by enabling large numbers of Chinese to view the vast expanses of the country and its cultural landmarks, and thus come to think of themselves as members of a nation; passengers were too few and the average journey was too short. Instead, the railroad as a business and administrative enterprise constituted a host of institutions that sought to inculcate new disciplines and desires, from schools and factories to financial institutions and regulatory systems, in Republican China. One of the historical accidents of Chinese railroads is that they emerged in tandem with the modern nation-state rather than building on a preexisting scaffolding of systems and institutions, as they had in most Western nations. More so than in many other historical contexts, railroads in China became closely associated with the transformation of the Chinese people—gradual but still incomplete by the time of the Japanese invasion in 1937—from members of a traditional society to citizens of a modern administrative state.

This chapter begins with an overview of the business related to passenger travel on Chinese railroads before 1937. Two features of the passenger business stand out from the body of statistics published annually by the railroad administration: first, the public's overwhelming tendency to use the rail system for short-distance travel, and second, the high cost of rail tickets relative to the purchasing power of ordinary Chinese people. These two features reinforced the local and regional impact of railroad freight business, as previously discussed. The second section of this chapter shows how China's railroads applied "modern," Western-influenced standards of efficiency and discipline, in terms of timekeeping, personal behavior and bodily functions, gender interactions, and public health. Travelers' guidebooks and materials aimed at schoolchildren make it clear that communicating these norms and practices to would-be travelers was a conscious project. Passenger traffic led to the growth of a small but flourishing independent tourism industry in the 1920s and 1930s, as shown in the third section. The final section explores Chinese railroads' influence on culture in the realm of public discourse, literary production, and the visual arts. By the late 1920s, rail travel represented a cultural ideal that was not only disciplined but also aspirational. The railroads offered a transformational experience that allowed people to assume different roles and identities within the new social space of railroad facilities and railroad compartments.

## Passenger Transportation

In contrast to the detailed portrait of freight traffic that emerges from official statistics, newspapers, commercial publications, port authority and consular reports, sources documenting rail passenger traffic are relatively scarce. Whereas many commercial sources tell us the exact amount of freight and its origins, destinations, and transport routes, passenger data published by individual railroad companies or the Ministry of Railways provide very few annual figures on passenger numbers per line per class, aggregate revenue numbers, and the average length of journeys. There is no way to tell where passengers began their journeys or where they alighted. Did passengers typically use the railroads to access major cities, or did they travel between two points in the hinterland? Were they more often urban dwellers or rural folk? For the most part, the sources do not answer these questions. Nor is there any indication as to whether the millions of annual passenger journeys were completed by a small number of regular travelers or by a large number of passengers who traveled infrequently. The purpose of most travel, whether for business, family affairs, or leisure, remains almost wholly opaque. Still, existing sources do offer some clues about the characteristics of passenger travel and how it was used.

Passenger ticket sales were an important source of revenue for all the nation's railroad lines. In each year between 1915 and 1935, passenger traffic accounted for 32 to 41 percent of revenue for Chinese government railroads. As Chapter 3 points out, major trunk railroads tended to have stronger freight businesses. But even though long-distance lines, such as the Peking-Hankou and the Peking-Mukden lines, derived most of their revenue from freight transportation, they still transported a considerable number of passengers. For example, 70 percent of the revenue of the Peking-Hankou line in 1935 came from freight; yet in the same year the railroad also transported a total of more than 3.4 million passengers (see Appendices B and D).[5]

For some lines, passenger traffic was the major source of revenue. Short lines in the Yangzi and Pearl River deltas—the Canton-Kowloon, Shanghai-Nanjing, and Shanghai-Hangzhou-Ningbo lines—connected passengers from the densely populated hinterlands to the commercial centers of Hong Kong or Shanghai.[6] The status of the cities as national and international transportation hubs, via steamship on domestic rivers or on coastal routes, was a major force behind the dominance of passenger traffic on these rail routes. Water transport, with its comparatively cheaper rates, continued to move commodities on the waterways throughout the 1920s and 1930s, especially along the two major river delta systems. From early on, however, passengers seem to have valued speed and convenience. In 1918, the Shanghai-Nanjing Railroad derived 71 percent of its revenue from passenger traffic; this figure decreased slightly to 64 percent in 1923, rose to 72 percent in 1930, and then declined to 66 percent in 1935, the last year of available data.[7] The Shanghai-Hangzhou-Ningbo Railroad followed a similar pattern, with approximately 65 percent of its revenue originating from passenger traffic; passenger-related revenue on the Canton-Kowloon line remained almost constant at 85 percent throughout the 1920s and 1930s.

System-wide, passenger traffic underwent a substantial and steady increase in volume on all national lines during the Republican era, although it fluctuated considerably from year to year in response to adverse economic conditions and political upheavals. According to data extrapolated from the annual statistics collected by the Ministry of Communications, there was a total of 12.6 million passenger journeys on Chinese national railroads in 1915, the first year of recorded data. This number quickly doubled to 24.6 million in 1918 and then rose to almost 40 million in 1923. During the crucial civil war years from 1926 to 1928, the statistics include information only on revenue figures, not on the volume of passengers. This hiatus might be explained by railroad companies during those years being forced to transport military personnel and soldiers without compensation. With the consolidation of political control under the Nanjing government after 1927, passenger travel quickly recovered. In 1932, there were 34 million passenger journeys in total, and this number increased to almost 44 million in 1935, just before the 1937 Japanese invasion and occupation interrupted the railroad system as well as data collection for several years (see Appendix D).[8]

Passenger experiences on Chinese trains do not appear to have differed qualitatively from those on European or American trains. Railroads in China followed Western practices and offered services in three, or sometimes four, classes. Although this pattern of social division does not appear to have occasioned significant comments from among the Chinese public or in the press at the time (perhaps due to the semicolonial origins of early railroads), it marked a significant departure from the socially informal and relaxed etiquette of existing modes of travel by boat or cart.

In contrast to other realms of Chinese public and private life where it was common to divide groups along gender lines, railroads introduced new patterns of gender interactions. Most railroad lines did not provide gender-specific carriages; female and male passengers shared the same public space, the cultural ramifications of which I discuss later in this chapter. Nevertheless, lines like the Shanghai-Hangzhou-Ningbo Railroad that focused primarily on tourism and passenger transportation paid particular attention to the needs of female customers. For their convenience, the third class offered a separate carriage with exclusive seating for women and children. Despite the short distance, the train also had a sleeping car with two berths per compartment, which could be reserved in advance for female passengers. Obviously, female tourists counted for a considerable number of passengers, so the railroad company considered these accommodating arrangements to be economically profitable.[9]

Many of the most detailed descriptions of passenger accommodations in early twentieth-century China come from foreigners. Despite their often uncomplimentary conclusions, foreigners were keen observers because they were interested in a comparison with the state of railroads in their home countries. Missionaries, businessmen, diplomats, scientific explorers, and adventure seekers tended to note aspects of rail travel that domestic passengers might have taken for granted. Unsurprisingly, they offer a wealth of information about first-class travel but comparatively little in the way of firsthand descriptions of third- or fourth-class travel.

The inventories of rolling stock listed in the annual statistical reports of the Ministry of Railways suggest that, on most of the Chinese government lines, first-class travelers traveled in coaches separate from other classes.[10] From the beginning, the first- and second-class cars featured brightly colored paint on the outside to distinguish them from the cheaper carriages. Photographs also indicate that many lines were painted with large Roman numerals on the side of the carriage, indicating the class.[11] Descriptions of first-class train interiors mention well-sprung leather seats, polished teak paneling, lace curtains, venetian blinds, carpeted floors, advanced heating and ventilation systems, and fine-mesh window screens to keep out mosquitoes and cinder from the engine.[12] On some lines, the lavatory was reserved for use by only first-class passengers.[13] No mention is made of how other travelers relieved themselves.

Unlike the separation into different travel classes on the basis of ticket price, train travel in China was unencumbered by racial segregation into Chinese-only and foreigner-only classes and carriages. In fact, white British travelers in China, many of whom were familiar with the segregated seating on the British colonial railroads in India or Africa, often complained that the first-class carriages were not set aside exclusively for foreigners.[14]

Not all lines in China had sufficient first-class traffic to justify separate carriages, leading to first-, second-, and even third-class passengers all being accommodated in the same railroad car. An account of the conditions on the French-run Yunnan Railroad in 1925 notes that first-class passengers were limited to one small compartment containing only two leather seats. The second-class passengers were seated in two similar compartments, "slightly less regally upholstered," and the third-class travelers sat on benches in the same carriage separated only by a swinging door. The train's second passenger carriage was devoted entirely to fourth-class travelers, indicating the most popular ticket category in terms of passenger volume.[15]

Conditions for third- and fourth-class travel were spartan and sometimes outright shabby, in contrast to travel in second-class cars, which were often equipped with "serviceable wooden seats" instead of upholstery.[16] From the late 1890s through the early 1910s, we find numerous references to passengers packed into open gondola cars, with neither seats nor protection from the weather—traveling literally just as if they were freight.[17] Although we associate wartime conditions with military troops and refugees resorting to this type of transportation, the image in Figure 4.1 reveals that open gondola cars were a normal practice, in this instance transporting civilians with baggage and individual soldiers along the Peking-Suiyuan line in 1925.

The distinction between third class and fourth class appears to have varied across lines and over time. Most lines provided only three classes. A fourth class was labeled "coolie class" in the official annual reports of the Ministry of Railways until 1919.[18] Fourth class was offered only on the Jin-Pu and Jiao-Ji Railroads in Shandong and on the tourist lines in the Yangzi River delta for much of the Republican period.[19] The category of fourth-class travel, which cost roughly half that of third-class travel per mile, not only referred to the physical accommodations but also indicated the length of the journey. Annual statistics show that, generally, the shorter the journey, the lower the class of the ticket. First-class passengers traveled farther than second-class passengers, who in turn traveled farther than those in third class. For example, in the case of the Jin-Pu line in 1923, passenger travel distance averaged 445 miles in first class, 257 in second, and 81 in third (see Appendix E).[20]

We encounter an exception to this pattern for the Jin-Pu line. In 1923, fourth-class travelers traveled an average of 209 miles, more than twice the distance of the average third-class traveler. The reason for this unusually high figure was

Fig. 4.1   Traveling third class on the Peking-Suiyuan line, ca. 1925. John Freeman Collection. Photograph album documenting expeditions in China and the Philippines, 1924–1925, seq. 54, photo 373, Harvard-Yenching Library, Harvard University.

the extensive labor migration from Shandong and other northern provinces to Manchuria (Dongbei, or the Northeast) in the 1920s and early 1930s. Cheap fourth-class transportation on the Jin-Pu line allowed prospective migrants to reach the Shandong peninsula and then take boats from ports, such as Yantai or Qingdao, across the Yellow Sea to the Liaodong peninsula. After arriving in port cities such as Lüshun or Yingkou, migrants would travel via the Russian-controlled Chinese Eastern Railroad and the South Manchurian Railway into the interior in search of work and livelihoods in the 1920s and 1930s.[21]

It appears that by 1919 most third- and fourth-class passengers could expect to have a roof over their heads, although seating could not be taken for granted.[22] When third- and fourth-class travelers did have seating, it typically consisted of four long benches that ran the length of the car, pairs of benches facing each other rather than being crosswise with a center aisle, as in the better classes of service.[23] As several observers noted, this type of longitudinal seating arrangement, whose primary advantage was its ability to pack in more passengers, was characteristic of railroads in British India but it was not used on European lines.[24] The orientation of the benches, particularly after they had been polished by years of seated travelers, resulted in passengers sliding into one another when the trains accelerated or stopped suddenly. The windows were often unglazed, so on particularly crowded trains, as one European traveler in South China reported, passengers sat with their legs dangling out the windows.[25]

In many cases, it took some time for the railroad companies to get full passenger service up and running. With railroad construction often months or years behind schedule, the lines began offering third-class travel as soon and as far as track was laid, with the passengers usually riding with the freight. A correspondent for the *North-China Herald* noted in 1911 that, on a section of an unfinished line in Hubei, "the passenger traffic is a bye-product [sic] of the railway for which no provision is made. Each passenger must . . . ride perched on the tops of the ironstone if he is going riverwards, or squatting in the cotton with his goods and chattels if going inland."[26] From the perspective of the railroad companies, which were not liable for any safety issues, the opening of sections ensured at least some revenue for the line and increased support and expectations among the local population.

The Jin-Pu Railroad provides another example of lines opening before all operations were in place. A newspaper report from December 1912 documents the travel experience of a correspondent, testing the still-rough inaugural services on the line from Tianjin to Shanghai several months after it had opened.[27] The first leg of the trip from Tianjin to Ji'nan took twelve hours in a passenger railcar that combined first and second classes. Meals were prepared in an attached freight car rather than in a proper dining car, and passengers had to spend the night in a hotel in Ji'nan, bringing their luggage with them because the station at the time had no facilities to keep the luggage safe overnight. The next day's journey, from Ji'nan to Xuzhou, took another twelve hours, which the reporter criticized for the lack of first-class seats, a crowded carriage, mediocre food, and lackluster sanitary conditions. In Xuzhou, where German line management passed into British hands, the sleeping and dining cars were attached to the train. Passengers were thus able to spend the night on the train with their luggage, even though, as a general safety measure, the train did not travel at night. Once the train reached Pukou after another nine hours of travel on the third day, passengers crossed the Yangzi on a steam launch arranged by the railroad company and then continued on their journey from Nanjing on a night train, arriving in Shanghai the following morning.[28]

Although revenue from passenger transportation on most lines, especially the major trunk lines, was secondary to revenue from freight, its distribution among the different categories of passengers is quite surprising. Annual statistics indicate that ticket sales for third- and fourth-class services were by far the most important revenue stream for the passenger business of the railroad companies.[29] For example, in 1915 the Jin-Pu line derived 76 percent of its passenger revenue from third-class tickets, 12 percent from fourth-class tickets, and only 8 percent and 4 percent from first- and second-class tickets, respectively. This revenue distribution among the different classes continued over time. In 1923 third-class tickets provided 82 percent of the passenger income on the Jin-Pu line, fourth-class tickets 4 percent, and first- and second-class tickets approximately 7 percent each.[30] Even after the Jin-Pu Railroad had grown into the major north–south trunk line of the nation in the 1930s, with daily express and through trains between Nanjing and Beijing, the pattern of passenger traffic did not change substantially. In 1935, 88 percent of passenger revenue still came from third-class tickets, 7 percent from second-class tickets, and only 5 percent from first-class tickets. This pattern applied to traffic on other long-distance trunk lines as well, such as the Beijing-Hankou Railroad. Fourth-class travel was no longer offered after 1932, with the exception of two short lines connecting Shanghai with the capital in Nanjing and Hangzhou on West Lake, and Ji'nan with Qingdao. In these cases, fourth-class travel was the preferred choice for regional commuters traveling in the lower Yangzi region (see Appendix D).

With the move of the capital from Beijing to Nanjing after 1927, the number of first-class tickets increased as government officials and businessmen began commuting back and forth between the two hubs. Even so, first-class travel was never financially or numerically significant. The statistics make it clear that a long train journey from terminal to terminal was a first-class affair for only a limited number of passengers who had disposable income, and it never became a major revenue source for the Chinese railroads.

But how affordable was train travel for ordinary Chinese? Comparisons to the standard-of-living and price indexes of the 1920s suggest that the cost of train travel represented a major purchase for Chinese on most rungs of the economic ladder. In 1923, a one-way trip of 911 miles from Beijing to

Shanghai had to be broken into five segments using three different lines (from Beijing to Tianjin on the Jing-Feng line; from Tianjin to Ji'nan, Ji'nan to Xuzhou, and Xuzhou to Pukou on the Jin-Pu line; and then from Nanjing to Shanghai on the Shanghai-Nanjing line), at a total cost of 52.45 yuan in first class, 33.25 yuan in second class, and 16.75 yuan in third class.[31] In the urban centers of Beijing and Shanghai, monthly food expenses for a working-class family of four or five came to approximately 11 yuan, but the poverty line for households was set at approximately 10 yuan of family income per month.[32] The expenses of well-off families for housing, food, and transportation in Beijing amounted to approximately 80 yuan per month, whereas a female household servant would receive a monthly wage of only 3 yuan in addition to room and board.[33] Of course, these urban income levels do not reflect the cheaper prices for food and accommodations along the railroad lines in the rural areas far away from the political centers and commercial cities.

Regardless, the impressionistic standard-of-living data leave no doubt that a train ticket was not a casual expense. A one-way first-class ticket from Beijing to Shanghai amounted to approximately two-thirds of typical monthly household expenses for a middle-class urban family. Traveling by second class amounted to almost half a monthly household budget, whereas a member of an affluent family in Shanghai with a monthly family income of approximately 200 yuan did not have any difficulty traveling by first class.[34] Train travel was an even more considerable expense for people from lower-income groups. For example, in the early 1930s the relatively short 42-mile journey from Xuzhou to Lincheng in Shandong province on the Jin-Pu line cost 1.3 yuan in third class. Thus, the cheapest train fare still amounted to about one-third of the monthly cash income of an urban laborer at the time.

In sum, there were two prominent features of rail travel on Chinese government lines during the Republican period. First, travel overwhelmingly consisted of passengers of modest means who traveled by third or fourth class and generated the bulk of revenue for the railroad companies. Although first- and second-class rail travel was more visible and thus arguably more significant culturally in terms of tourism and leisure consumption by an emerging urban middle class with disposable income, third-class passengers were the most important customers because of their mass mobility and revenue generation.[35] The second significant feature of the passenger market is that the majority of the traveling public used the network primarily for short distances. As a result, the passenger business reinforced the regionalizing effects of freight traffic, with its powerful stationmasters and line-based logistics companies. As part of the business portfolios of Chinese railroad companies, passenger services thus contributed to the regional rather than the nationwide orientation of transportation infrastructure during the Republican era.

## Railroad Time and Discipline

Railroads introduced a new form of time discipline affecting the social behavior of passengers and employees. Western-style time discipline was imposed as an essential organizational aspect of the railroads' operational management. This evolved into an accepted practice in the early Republic, particularly in the urban areas. Similar to the role of the railroad in the formation of nation-states, such as in Japan, modern forms of timekeeping and time discipline became part of the educational mission envisioned by the Chinese state.[36] In China, the regionally fragmented networks and lack of central-government control across vast spatial stretches of the country created additional challenges to implementing time standards and discipline for those who traveled and worked on Chinese railroads.

Timetables as tools of information for passengers evolved over time. Train schedules published in city guidebooks or in general travel guides of the late 1910s and the early 1920s gave priority to each station's price information for distance and class.[37] For example, a 1927 guidebook to Tianjin painstakingly listed information on the exact distance (in *gongli*, or kilometers) between the city's terminal and each stop along the feeder Beijing-Mukden and Jin-Pu lines. Detailed information on luggage restrictions reinforced the impression that information on travel from local stations to the city with carry-on goods was more important to the visitors than such information for long-distance trains.[38] This focus shifted after 1928 when trunk lines, such as the Jin-Pu Railroad, were able to operate express trains without interruption and could expand their business, linking the former capital with the new capital in Nanjing and the commercial center of Shanghai. As timetables from 1933 indicate, departure and arrival times were then noted in a Western twenty-four-hour style and offered information on specific services, such as express, ordinary, or mixed passenger and freight trains and their train numbers. Information on ticket prices was secondary and was provided only for the thirty major stations between Pukou and Beijing. Obviously, travelers using these long-distance trains were less price-sensitive and more time-sensitive and wanted to know exact travel times and information on sleeping and dining cars instead of information on luggage restrictions.[39]

Train timetables in the early Republic did not convey any information on the spatial order of the rail line and its stops. Timetables from 1907 and 1910 were arranged in an encyclopedic style, divided into upper and lower sections per page and written from right to left using Chinese numerals.[40] Whereas educated Chinese were familiar with this traditional style of entry, which was also used in gazetteers and dictionaries, and would have been able to easily look up data points, less-educated passengers and those who could not read Chinese would have had great difficulty. Most importantly, such records conveyed no visual abstraction of the information as part of the line's physical and data organization.

Chinese timetables over time became more abstract, similar to what Edward Tufte calls "envisioning information," by establishing the appropriate visual relationships among the different layers of information according to their relevance.[41] By the 1930s timetables consisted of large single-page tables with information on times using Arabic numerals and on places using Chinese characters in both directions of the line, and displaying their spatial and temporal relationships to the terminals with great clarity. Because this was still a new way of envisioning and absorbing information, inserted remarks and arrows advised the traveler regarding the table's different reading directions (*dufa*) for mining different layers of information.[42] In this respect, the evolution of the abstract, modern rail timetable had some similarities to the introduction of the modern Western calendar to China after 1911, when the combined use of the solar and lunar calendars according to purpose turned calendars into "a series of layers."[43]

Large clocks and clock towers naturally became new symbols of the time discipline at Chinese railroad stations throughout the country, with time discipline constituting a universal characteristic of railroad culture around the globe.[44] As early as 1880, woodblock prints featured a Western-style clock situated prominently above the entrance to the Shanghai station of China's first railroad to Wusong, with the departure times imprinted above the building.[45] The question of whether the departure times were real is less important: both the timekeeping instrument and the data points stressed modernity in the form of the time discipline introduced by the technology and services of the railroads. Photographs taken by inspectors of stations along the Jin-Pu line in 1912 reveal that clock towers were often the first architectural features to be completed at a construction site, long before the station buildings or the yards had been completed. As Figure 4.2 demonstrates, the lonely presence of a clock at the unfinished Ji'nan station was a harbinger of the future order and modernity to be imposed by the railroad's services, while probably also serving as a constant reminder of time and labor discipline for the construction workers.[46]

It is difficult to assess the extent to which railroad time discipline was internalized by passengers and employees. On the outside, the impressive public display of time discipline via clocks and posted timetables coincided with and

**Fig. 4.2**   Construction site of Jin-Pu line station in Ji'nan, with clock, 1912. Records relating to German railroad construction in China, 1898–1916, Baker Library, Harvard Business School, vol. 14, 1912, p. 32.

was facilitated by new industrialization and modernization projects that had been under way since the last decade of the nineteenth century: paternalistic factory owners built clock towers on compounds as part of their new industrial regimes, and the reform efforts by local elites promoted clock towers as aspirational signs of urban modernity throughout the country.[47] At the Bank of China, paternalistic senior executives regimented the lives of their junior employees by imposing moral and time discipline through living arrangements in the bank's communal compounds and rigid scheduling of collective activity.[48] By contrast, the personal embrace of time discipline by passengers and railroad employees was more ambiguous. Here the historian must rely on documents such as newspaper reports, diaries, and other forms of literary production that reflect attitudes toward the time concepts of Chinese elites but not of ordinary, short-distance passengers who made up the bulk of travelers.

The punctuality of the trains and their conformity with actual timetables were major issues, especially in the early Republic. Not surprisingly, English-language newspapers, such as the *North-China Herald,* were full of articles complaining about late trains. These journalists were predominantly Western commentators who, in their complaints, took on an air of superiority and often equated the tardiness of Chinese trains with the lack of modern development.[49] One of the worst cases reported occurred on the Peking-Hankou Railroad in 1910, when the managers of the line had given up entirely on any sort of a schedule, trains arrived and departed as they became available, and stations made no pretense of posting a timetable.[50] However, a few lines earned considerable praise from Westerners, including the Jin-Pu line which was commended for its punctuality and polite staff.[51] The Shanghai-Nanjing Railroad was considered, by all accounts, China's safest and most punctual railway during the Republican period. This line was also the first to employ electric train dispatching methods, as used in the United States and Europe at the time, with forty-nine way station telephones under the control of one train dispatcher operating in Shanghai.[52]

Exact departure and arrival times, or at least the promise thereof, was a novelty for Chinese writers documenting their journeys and travel experiences. For example, the new time discipline found its way into the literary diaries of travelers such as that of Wang Tongling, who not only noted the dates when he arrived or departed from certain cities and the sightseeing venues along the long train journey but also the exact timing of the stops. The train's punctuality and performance according to a fixed schedule seemed to heighten Wang's travel experience as he carefully recorded every step along the journey as a spatial and temporal experience.[53]

The question arises whether travelers were able to check the time with devices other than station or public clocks before wrist and pocket watches became common. In urban settings, travelers depended on clocks that announced the hour for information on when to leave for the station.[54] Ordinary passengers making their way from the countryside to rural stations, however, must have experienced the specific departure times more as general concepts, such as morning or afternoon, because they had no clocks to rely on. Very much like Chinese industrial workers in rural settings who often arrived at their factory compounds long before their shifts were to begin, rural passengers spent considerable time at the stations waiting for the arrival of their trains.[55]

For the railroad companies, the creation of timetables presented operational challenges as well as problems in adapting railroad time to the more traditional time concepts that were in place along the railroad lines. In the case of the Jin-Pu Railroad, the Chinese traffic managers put together a timetable that was plagued by insufficient coordination of the trains to the platforms, often resulting in chaos. For example, on one day five trains tried to enter the Yanzhou three-platform station simultaneously.[56] Another, although external, factor influencing timetable management was the closing time of the city gates near the larger stations. In 1912 the first train service from Ji'nan to Tianjin for first- and second-class passengers was scheduled to depart at five o'clock in the morning and to arrive near midnight, after the city gates were locked, so the passengers had to spend the night at the station in the new railroad district outside the city walls.[57]

Experimentation with time schedules and local adaptations in the first years of the twentieth century were signs of inexperienced Chinese railroad management and a still-truncated rail network. The lack of an efficient central railroad bureaucracy synchronizing the timetables of the various lines and the absence of network connectivity that required cooperation among the different lines meant that until 1928 individual lines were fairly independent in establishing their own timetables. Operational issues and local conditions determined the individual line schedules without regard for a transportation network on a national scale, which at that time was yet to be created. In fact, even the introduction of standard time zones in China did not interfere with the regional autonomy of the various rail systems in the north, south, and eastern parts of the country.

Throughout the world, railroads were instrumental in bringing about the concept of standard time, with the United States as the most prominent example.[58] As complex institutions, railroads required the standardization of time across space to efficiently manage their services and operations and to facilitate integration into the economy. Recent historical studies emphasize that, despite the market forces unleashed by the new technology, government and other institutional forces also played a crucial role in introducing standard time and global twenty-four-hour time zones.[59] Within East Asia, the adoption of standard time as a tool to introduce homogeneity and discipline by the Japanese colonial regime controlling Taiwan after 1895 is a case in point. Time zones expanded and contracted in sync with the Japanese colonial and wartime empire until the end of World War II and came to include Taiwan, Korea, and the South Sea Islands.[60]

Without a strong central government or imposition of governmentality by a single specific colonial power during the early Republic, standard time and time zones did not automatically evolve during China's railroad development. One of the first steps by the new Republican government in 1912 was to abolish the lunar calendar and adopt the Western solar calendar so as to facilitate international trade and foreign relations. Together with the new calendar and the six-day work week, the concept of clock time (without specifying precise standardized operating hours) was introduced into urban and rural schools. Although many schools did not rush to acquire desk clocks, by 1917 the Educational Promotion Bureau in charge of inspecting primary schools reported on those that lacked horologic equipment.[61]

Although there had been discussions about a standard time zone in the treaty ports along the China coast during the late Qing dynasty, no action was taken until 1918, when the Chinese Central Observatory, the institution that produced the official state calendar, proposed dividing the territory of the Republic into five standard time zones: Zhong-Yuan as the central standard time zone for central and coastal China; Long-Shu for the midwestern regions, including Gansu and Sichuan provinces; Hui-Zang for Xinjiang and Tibet; Kun-Lun for the mountain ranges in the far west; and Chang-Bai for the Northeast.[62] The Zhong-Yuan standard time zone was eight hours ahead of Greenwich Mean Time and included fourteen provinces, stretching from the northern border with Mongolia to the Pearl River delta and Hainan Island in the south. The proposal was made official through publication in the 1919 edition of the *Almanac of the Republic,* but acceptance of the new time regime was slow, especially in the absence of widespread radio communications.[63] If we consider the unenthusiastic response to the introduction of the solar calendar by people from all walks of life and the government's inability to eradicate the lunar calendar, the issue of standard time was an even less pressing issue for the citizens of the Republic. After the Nationalist Party (Guomindang) came to power in 1928, it continued the time-zone policy in its general push to spread scientific practices throughout society and culture, and it declared that the new capital of Nanjing would be the reference for the central standard time zone along longitude 120° east.

That the Zhong-Yuan standard time zone covered such a vast territory, including the most populated and commercially developed regions in China, explains why time zones did not pose a problem for the railroads during the Republican period. From the first appearance of the lines to the largest expansion of the rail network on the eve of the Japanese invasion, all lines were within the borders of the Zhong-Yuan time zone under central standard time. Not until the 1950s did new rail lines reach the midwestern and southwestern provinces. Although the Zhong-Yuan zone was only one of five regional Chinese time zones, it functioned as a national time zone because of the overlap of its economic and political strength within the body of the Chinese Republic. Transportation and communications networks, such as shipping, railroads, and telegraph and postal services, operating within its borders reinforced the standard time concept through their operations and institutional presence at telegraph and postal offices, railroad stations, bureaus, docks, and custom houses. Local time regimes, however, continued in the regions outside the Zhong-Yuan time zone until the Communist government of the PRC in 1949 established a single time zone throughout the country, based on so-called Beijing standard time (see Chapter 7).[64]

Although time discipline changed the passengers' expectations and behavior at the stations, other forms of discipline became necessary because of the breakdown of established hierarchies and the creation of unconventional hierarchies during train travel. For one, male and female passengers mixed freely in the carriages. In the third- and fourth-class carriages in particular there were no separate carriages reserved for female passengers.[65] This situation, considered by more conservative Chinese as improper, led to the incorporation of rules for appropriate gender behavior by railroad companies such as the Jin-Pu line.[66]

Over time, issues of railroad-specific discipline began to enter the public realm via textbooks and newspaper discussions, especially after 1927 when the virtues of punctuality and order became an important part of the centralizing agenda of the Guomindang state (see Chapter 5). Textbooks for first-year primary-school students published in 1932 featured several illustrated lessons on the use of clocks and watches, and the benefits of personal time management. They even included a separate lesson on how to properly behave at railroad stations.[67] The textbooks admonished the students that train arrivals and departures follow "firm times" (*yiding shijian*) and "are not the slightest bit late." Texts and images focused on the orderly queue of passengers in front of ticket windows and at the entrances to station platforms. Instructions such as "people who arrive later queue behind those who arrive first" and "in due sequence [*shunzi*] enter the platform" addressed queue-jumping as one of the most difficult public-order issues at railroad stations—in Republican as well as in contemporary China.[68] Although the texts explained the physical components of the train, their main aim was to demonstrate the different flows of passengers and baggage in the process of embarkation and disembarkation and how orderly behavior allowed the individual to effortlessly fit into that process.[69]

As institutions, Chinese railroads had a crucial impact on the development of Chinese society by promoting and imposing a culture that transformed ordinary citizens into passengers with rights and obligations to certain expectations on the trains. The railroads' amalgamation of railroad-related time and body discipline with other Western "civilizing" aspects of social engineering aimed at broader concepts, such as courtesy or hygienic awareness in public space. This was an important contribution to the evolving Republic and in line with the social agenda of the state. The railroads' transformative social and cultural impact was aided by the explosive surge in print publications beginning in the 1910s, which allowed the spread of information and education and the entertainment of passengers through a wide range of publications that also served advertising and marketing purposes. As a result,

Chinese railroad companies were transformed into business institutions with a more pronounced customer orientation, and their passengers became consumers of travel.

## Linkages: Travel Services

What the freight transportation of the railroads achieved with forward linkages in the form of logistics companies was mirrored with forward linkages of passenger transportation in the form of travel business. Railroads became the catalyst for a modern tourism industry in China, both as an instrument of transportation and as the provider of travel-related services from guidebooks to hotels. Although we see its early beginnings in the 1910s, rail tourism took off in both scale and scope once the major railroad corridors were completed and the network was free of civil war–induced military disruptions. The Nanjing decade, from 1927 to 1937, provided military peace along the existing line network, a growing urban population with disposable income, and a ubiquitous print culture advertising travel as an aspirational activity. Chinese railroads, especially those passing cultural and scenic destinations along the eastern corridor, dealt not only with passengers but increasingly with tourists as well.

Tourism was, of course, not a new phenomenon in Chinese society. For centuries Chinese had been touring sites with religious, cultural, and historical significance all over the country, and they had documented their experiences in poetry, diaries, and literature. In premodern times, merchants engaged in long-distance trade, and the duties of officials included travel throughout the imperial realm. At the time, travel involved a high level of personal danger, risk, and inconvenience, which people tried to ameliorate by consulting almanacs for auspicious travel days and by presenting offerings to the road gods. Nevertheless, a positive evaluation of travel and sightseeing began to appear in literary works as early as the fourth century.[70]

Religious pilgrimages in particular offered common people, especially women, a rare chance to travel outside the confines of their households and communities and to escape male supervision.[71] As early as the Song dynasty, pilgrimages involved tour groups, commercial travel arrangements, and tour guides.[72] In 1877, when the short-lived Wusong Railroad was still in operation, the *North-China Herald* reported that throngs of people from nearby villages and Shanghai came by train to attend the religious festival at the Kin Liu temples near Shanghai.[73] In late imperial China, the increasing commercialization of the economy combined with the flourishing of a print culture in urban centers led to the publication of commercial city guide-books. They provided visitors to the capital and other important cities with information ranging from sightseeing to shopping for local merchandise and food to entertainment at restaurants and brothels.[74]

When the first railroads, especially the major trunk lines, began offering passenger transportation in the early Republic, passenger travel was driven not by leisure but by obligations related to work, education, or family affairs. Passengers began to travel by train to conduct business outside their home regions and provinces, to attend new institutions of higher learning, or to take jobs related to the country's new administration and institutional reforms. Of course, railroad travel also facilitated returning to one's native place for a wedding or funeral. Railroads were considered a safe and status-appropriate mode of transportation so that even important dignitaries traveled by train from the very beginning of passenger services. For example, after visiting the famous Lama monastery at Wutaishan in Shanxi province, the Dalai Lama followed up on an invitation from the imperial court for an audience with the emperor and the empress dowager in 1908. Traveling by train, he arrived in Peking from Henan province via the Long-Hai Railroad for his audience on September 28, 1908.[75] After 1927, when the new Nationalist government moved the Chinese capital from Beijing to Nanjing, the Beijing-Shanghai rail corridor became the main commute for government officials, businessmen, and professionals between the old and new centers of political power. The Blue Express, a direct express train between Tianjin and Pukou, catered to this new group of affluent passengers.[76]

Male and female students traveled by train to reach the new institutions of higher learning in the cities, Chinese academies and universities, and middle schools and training colleges. Furthermore, it should not be under-estimated how much the option of rail travel, which was considered relatively safe, improved women's access to education. Universities even collaborated with railroad lines in arranging price reductions for student travel. For ex-ample, in 1926 the president of Ji'nan University petitioned the Jiao-Ji Railroad

Bureau to reduce ticket prices for his students traveling back home for the summer break.[77]

By the late 1910s and the 1920s, railroads increasingly explored business opportunities related to transportation of and services for tourists. Designing travel packages and organizing destination vacations for passengers with their host of logistical details was a challenge for railroad companies and did not right away become a popular business model. Although individual railroad companies made some efforts to promote leisure travel—by 1919 the Shanghai-Nanjing and Shanghai-Hangzhou-Ningbo lines facilitated travel to the Mogan Mountains in Zhejiang province, erecting a hotel and selling passes for journeys that included rail and water transport—China's first travel agency dedicated to Chinese travelers actually emerged from the financial, not the railroad, sector. Thomas Cook, American Express, Compagnie Internationale des Wagons-Lits, and other Western firms had established travel agencies in some of the larger treaty ports around the turn of the nineteenth century, but these institutions seldom regarded Chinese as potential customers. In 1923, an enterprising banker, Chen Guangfu, established a small travel agency as part of his Shanghai Commercial and Savings Bank (Shanghai shangye chuxu yinhang). China Travel Service (Zhongguo lüxingshe), as he called it, did little more than break even during the first decade of its existence, but Chen regarded it as a way to raise the profile of his bank, which was struggling to compete with the large international financial institutions in treaty-port China. It suffered some setbacks during the warlord period, but by the time war erupted with Japan in 1937 China Travel Service boasted some sixty branches, guesthouses, and other facilities throughout the nation.[78]

In terms of forward linkages, a lodging industry had to develop in order to meet the accommodation demands of China's emerging tourism. Similar to the origins of the travel agencies, foreign establishments were far ahead of Chinese efforts. Since the middle of the nineteenth century a limited infrastructure for the hotel needs of inbound, or foreign, travelers in China had evolved. Until the 1920s, however, these hotels, guesthouses, and restaurants did not extend past colonial and semicolonial spaces: foreigners controlled much of the industry and were the major customers.[79] China's first Western-style hotel was Richards' Hotel and Restaurant, founded in 1846 by a chandler who had abandoned ship in Shanghai. Shortly thereafter it was renamed

Astor House Hotel; by the 1910s, it had expanded to more than 350 rooms and was, by one estimation, "where all business in Shanghai is done."[80] At the same time, there were European-style hotels in nearly all the treaty ports and major cities. The 1924 revised edition of the Japanese Government Railways' *Guide to China*, by far the most complete guidebook in English, listed more than fifty European-style lodging establishments in China, ranging from the modest accommodations of the YMCA in Hangzhou at 2 yuan per night to the grandest suites at Shanghai's Astor House Hotel at 25 yuan per night. Shanghai boasted more than 800 European-style rooms, although many were rented on a monthly basis to nontourist visitors. The guide listed a similar number of Japanese-style inns, clustered along the South Manchurian Railway and in northern cities such as Tianjin and Qingdao as well as in Hankou and Guangzhou. The Japanese hotels averaged 3 to 6 yuan per night, compared with 6 to 10 yuan per night for Western-style lodging. According to the guidebook, the "better" Chinese inns averaged 0.5 yuan to 1 yuan per night.[81]

A modern Chinese hotel industry was slow to emerge, in part because lodging outside the major cities in local inns was traditionally patronized only by those who had no other options for accommodations. The 1924 Japanese Government Railways guide advised its readers against seeking lodgings in inns that did not specifically cater to foreign clientele. "The upper class Chinese . . . when traveling in the interior, take with them bedding, washbasins, and other daily requisites, being accompanied by several servants; and they try to obtain lodging in a government house or in the house of a friend."[82] In the southern coastal cities of Xiamen and Fuzhou, for example, the guide noted that Chinese inns were numerous, but virtually all were part of emigration agencies primarily engaged in soliciting indentured laborers for transportation to the British West Indies or similarly distant colonial labor markets.[83]

The lack of appropriate hotel accommodations along the newly opened Chinese lines was such a serious problem during the early period of rail operations that railroad companies became quite inventive in seeking solutions. For example, although Xuzhou in northern Jiangsu province was a major hub and a prefectural seat, in 1913 it lacked appropriate hotel accommodations for passengers on the Jin-Pu line. Therefore, the management of the Jin-Pu line placed a furnished sleeping car at the Xuzhou station for first- and second-class passengers so they could rest for the night—an important service that was widely advertised in print.[84] Food was usually available in dining cars serving passengers in first and second class, and travelers in the less-privileged classes would rely on food sold by vendors on the platform during stops at railroad stations (see Figures 4.3 and 4.4).

China's own hotel boom, like its first travel agency, dates from the mid-1920s.[85] Notably, the larger establishments were not established and financed by Chinese private investors but rather by government initiatives underwritten by leading figures in railroad company management. The combination of a line director with a position in the Ministry of Communications and Transportation was particularly useful for promoting forward linkages in the form of hotels. For example, in 1920 Xu Shizang, then vice minister of Communications and Transportation and director of the Jin-Pu Railroad, promoted the idea of building two hotels close to Qufu and Tai'an as exclusive tourist accommodations. According to a news report, the railroad

Fig. 4.3   Food vendors and passengers at a station along the Peking-Hankou line, early 1930s. "Along the Pinhan R. R.," Rev. Claude L. Pickens Jr., part of the Rev. Claude L. Pickens Jr. collection on Muslims in China, Harvard-Yenching Library, Harvard University.

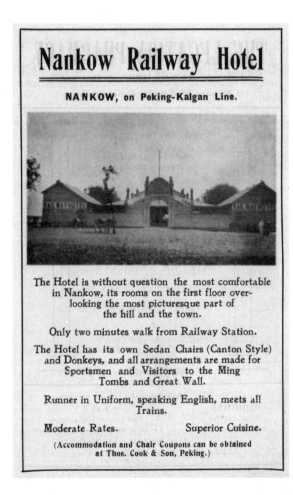

# Nankow Railway Hotel

**NANKOW, on Peking-Kalgan Line.**

The Hotel is without question the most comfortable in Nankow, its rooms on the first floor overlooking the most picturesque part of the hill and the town.

Only two minutes walk from Railway Station.

The Hotel has its own Sedan Chairs (Canton Style) and Donkeys, and all arrangements are made for Sportsmen and Visitors to the Ming Tombs and Great Wall.

Runner in Uniform, speaking English, meets all Trains.

Moderate Rates.            Superior Cuisine.

(Accommodation and Chair Coupons can be obtained at Thos. Cook & Son, Peking.)

Fig. 4.4  Advertisement for Nankow Railway Hotel, 1917. *Peking and the Overland Route* (London: Thomas Cook & Son, 1917), advertising section, p. xi, Widener Library, Harvard University.

administration also considered "a poultry and dairy farm to be attached to these hotels so as to ensure proper food and milk."[86]

In 1921 the Ministry of Communications and Transportation announced plans to establish twenty-one modern railroad hotels, similar to the business model of the Japanese-run Yamato inns along the South Manchurian Railway. All major trunk lines were to benefit from this plan, including the Peking-Hankou, Jin-Pu, and Shanghai-Nanjing lines.[87] Upheaval during the period of civil war, however, slowed and at times even reversed expansion of the hospitality business: there were three hotels in Tanggu in 1924; by 1928 they had all folded.[88]

Although hotel accommodations and travel agencies for Chinese customers were not readily available in the early Republic, Chinese railroad companies began to promote and advertise leisure travel and leisure activities connected to travel as an important part of their business operations. By 1922 the concept of group travel (*tuanti lüxing*) had already become a separate business category, with specific operational requirements for assessing passenger capacity in each class and for booking entire train carriages.[89]

The publication of railroad guidebooks became another method of marketing tourist-oriented train travel. Depending on the line's proximity to famous cities or cultural sites, various railroads published elaborate guidebooks in multiple editions throughout the Republican period. These guidebooks were modeled on the familiar traditional format of the local gazetteer (*difangzhi*), presenting the rail route as a linear cultural experience of time and space.[90] Over time, however, the publication of line guidebooks became increasingly oriented toward travel-related consumption of hospitality services, travel equipment, and local merchandise. As strategic marketing tools, these guidebooks reveal information about the targeted reader-passenger clientele as well as about the integration of tourism into the urban economies of the central stops along the lines.[91]

Railroad guides also presented a perfect medium for educating passengers about proper train use, fare and freight regulations, and behavioral discipline according to the practices of individual railroad lines, and therefore, were mainly in-house publications by line management offices (*guanliju*). For example, the 1922 Canton-Kowloon Railroad Travel Guide (*Guang-Jiu tielu lüxing zhinan*) provided detailed information on departure and arrival times along the short routes, slow trains, through trains, and so forth, followed by more than one hundred regulations for passengers and freight.[92] Numerous regulations covered how to purchase tickets at the stations and how to use them on the train. Passengers were reminded that large stations would stop selling tickets after the first ring of the bell five minutes before the train's departure, whereas small stations would continue selling tickets until the train reached the platform. In painstaking detail, regulations explained controls over platform tickets for those seeing off passengers and over seat tickets on the train. For example, the Canton-Kowloon Railroad used a color-coded system for the different classes of trains: red for first class, white for second class, and blue for third class, with yellow, green, and brown for through-tickets beyond the line. Children under the age of four traveled for free and those up to the age of twelve traveled at half price, indicating that family travel had become a normal part of passenger travel. Other regulations repeatedly addressed personal safety issues, such as prohibitions against bringing flammable materials onto the carriage. Whether the requirement that people suffering from infectious diseases or mental illnesses obtain special permission from the head of the operations office before boarding the train was observed in reality is rather doubtful.[93]

The blurring of lines between what counted as luggage and what counted as freight was a major concern for railroad companies. Elaborate regulations on luggage limits indicate not only the desire but probably the necessity to set limits on the things people were allowed (or probably tried) to take on board. Heavy items such as chairs, tables, bedroom furniture, bicycles, motor bikes, tricycles, and anything weighing more than 330 pounds were classified as "not luggage" and thus subject to special transportation surcharges. In the same context, surcharges for live chickens, ducks, and so forth were listed in the passenger section, along with the requirements for proper containers and restraints.[94]

As examples of organizational control and discipline, these complex regulations were not exceptional for railroads as service-oriented institutions with complex levels of operational management. More importantly, they confirmed a lacuna in the passenger business of Chinese railroads—namely, the legal insecurities with regard to insurance and liability. Railroad companies went to extreme lengths to absolve themselves from any legal responsibility (*fu zeren*) for the safety of the passengers and for their accompanying luggage and freight. At the time, Chinese railroad companies were not insured, and so they offered reimbursement only for lost or damaged personal luggage that had been separately registered and insured in advance, up to a limit of 200 yuan.[95] In addition, items on a long list of "valuables," ranging from hard currency and paper bills to jewelry, watches, medicine, scientific instruments, and art objects, were automatically excluded from the railroad's responsibility in case of loss.[96] Individual coverage through travel or accident insurance did not yet exist as a concept in China, where even life insurance policies did not become a familiar practice until the 1930s.[97]

## Train Travel in Fact and Fiction

"Fast, safe, inexpensive"—railroad companies focusing on passenger transport along major trunk and tourist lines used these attributes to promote their services in 1928.[98] Publication of rail travel services and customer experiences in newspapers, magazines, and professional journals was a crucial part of the companies' efforts to increase domestic passenger traffic and to reach the urban, educated middle classes as a new customer segment. The boom in print culture and literary production for mass consumption and elites during the Republican period assisted and magnified those efforts. In the most extreme cases, tourist-oriented lines like the Shanghai-Hangzhou Railroad actively sought collaboration with famous writers of the time to produce rail guidebooks. For example, in 1933 the head of the train division from Hangzhou in Zhejiang province to Yushan in neighboring Jiangxi province, one of the most scenic parts of the line, invited the famous writer Yu Dafu (1896–1945) to take a train trip and produce a Baedeker-style travel guide for the line.[99]

Published travel literature in the form of travel diaries or reports, short stories, and poems over the course of the 1920s and 1930s reveal a transition from presenting external travel observations to individual travel experiences and interpretations. For example, the *Xin youji huikan* (Series of new travel reports) was published in 1921 and contained detailed travelogues on specific provinces, famous cultural sites, and scenic spots.[100] Individual authors composed each entry in essay form, and the narratives commented on travel as a mix of cultural and individual experiences. The publication lacked any form of commercial advertising but it contained decorative vignettes with images of trains, carriages, and so forth.

Chinese railroad guides documented every railroad stop or station and listed characteristics of the place in terms of its history, culture, and commercial significance. By the late 1910s, rail guidebooks increasingly supplemented such descriptive entries with black-and-white photographs of important sightseeing venues.[101] Following this descriptive approach, the traveler experienced the railroad line as a transportation corridor linking important cultural markers in the surrounding landscape. At the same time, the format of the guidebooks resembled the structure of the local gazetteers, the standard

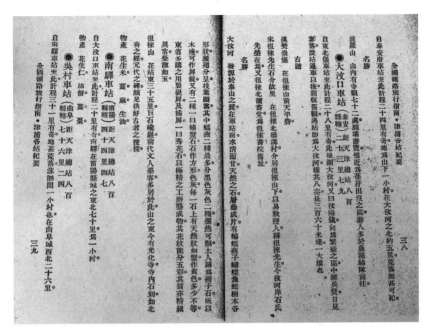

**Fig. 4.5** Descriptions of each station along the Jin-Pu line in Guangyi shuju bianji, comp., *Quanguo tielu lüxing zhinan* (National railroad travel guide). (Shanghai: Guangyi shuju, 1921), 60–61. Shanghai Library.

written record of local histories in China, and would have appeared very familiar to educated travelers. The page from the 1921 railroad guide on the Jin-Pu line in Figure 4.5 exemplifies the gazetteer style. Reading from right to left, the black circles indicate the train stations, the name of the county in parentheses plus the distance from Tianjin as the station of the train's origin. Depending on the size and prominence of the place, the guidebook identifies the categories of general information, places of historical significance, famous sightseeing spots, and local products. The category of local products may appear odd at first, but I speculate that it was included because local products, especially food famous from the place or region, would be offered by vendors on the platform of the railroad stations.[102]

Compared with Japanese railroad travel guides published about the same time for Japanese audiences, Chinese railroad guides lacked the interactive component of pictorial maps that added a spatial experience to the visual component of train travel.[103] The differences of spatial representation and experience of train travel between Chinese and Japanese maps and guide-books are considerable. Train guides published in Japan by the Ministry of Railways in the early 1920s were particularly impressive in their organized information because numerous isometric or bird's-eye-view maps of rail-road lines allowed passengers not only to locate their position along the route and in relation to their final destination but also to the country as a whole.[104] They appear almost as interactive maps, visually and virtually drawing the reader into the map.

Certainly, the Japanese had a superior set of railroad maps, not only because rail technology made its appearance earlier in the late nineteenth century but also because of the strong documentation of the Gokaido road network as a strategic concern of the Tokugawa regime (1600–1868). With that motiva-tion, the shogunate commissioned a set of ninety-one volumes of detailed proportional linear maps of the road network, individual highways and their checking stations, religious sites, and population figures at postal stations in 1806.[105] Travelers in pre-1900 China without a doubt were also able to draw on a vast source of printed sources in the form of gazetteers, local maps, guides, and travel accounts for geographical information, with a strong em-phasis on the expression and description of spatial experience through text.[106] This textual approach continued to inform the design of railroad guides during the Republican period; the publications were much less map-oriented and instead situated the readers as spectators inside the railroad carriage rather than drawing them actively into the experience of the landscape and the famous sites outside the window.[107] In addition, rail line guidebooks did not feature any personal travel experiences to showcase railroad travel as a metaphor for experiencing the Chinese nation.

Not surprisingly, a much stronger incorporation of maps in guidebook publications developed after centralization of political control under Chiang Kai-shek's Nanjing government in 1927. Because of the Guomindang govern-ment's emphasis on the national unity and cultural strength of the Republic, Chinese railroads became not only a central part of the newly reorganized bureaucracy but also physical symbols linking localities and regions into a national body, as perceived by the party-state. Bringing different regions of the national landscape closer to the center of administrative and political power was, of course, very much in the interests of the Nationalist govern-ment. Not surprisingly, the production of comprehensive railroad maps and guidebooks for the entire country became part of the government's nation-building efforts in the 1930s and, by extension, part of the role of the central railroad administration.[108]

As railroads increasingly symbolized spatial and political convergence for the public, new social dynamics developing with respect to other passengers in a carriage or a compartment became a significant topic influencing literary production during the Republican period. In the most basic form, textbooks took on a vital role in educating children about socialization on the train. For example, textbooks published in 1932 aimed at transforming children into responsible citizens in the public space through brief topical descriptions and illustrations drawn by the famous artist and writer Feng Zikai.[109] Texts and illustrations invited children to "play train" (*zuo huoche*) as a group, imitating the movements and sounds of the train. Children read advice on appropriate behavior and were encouraged not only to become better-disciplined citizens but also to be better team players in the environment of communal mass transportation.[110]

In the realm of literary fiction during the 1920s and 1930s, the Chinese railroad compartment became a new focus and canvas for describing emotional personal encounters or reflecting on the outside world as seen through the window of the train. Train travel created spatial scenarios for individual passengers and their experiences because of the "drama in the compartment," a phrase coined by cultural historian Wolfgang Schivelbusch.[111] In his interpretation of train-travel experience in the West, one major change involved the transition from the communal seating arrangements of the traditional coach to sitting in separate compartments under the control of a conductor who maintained law and order almost like a prison guard.[112] Train travel as a new individual experience of time and place while being immersed in a randomly assembled group of strangers was not lost on Chinese writers like Feng Zikai. He discusses his individual observations of travel experiences and the human drama unfolding during rail travel in his essay "Rail Carriage Society" (Chexiang shehui) as early as 1935.[113]

Communications among strangers in isolated compartments required new forms of social behavior as well as institutionalized control of Chinese train passengers, especially for interactions between male and female passengers. The theme of interactions—voluntary or involuntary—between the sexes in a secluded space within a public train carried over into famous popular novels such as Zhang Henshui's *Ping-Hu tongche* (*Shanghai Express*), published in 1935. The novel's narrative revolves around the exciting and adventurous relationships that develop between male and female strangers from different social and passenger classes who spend three days together on a train ride from Tianjin to Shanghai.[114] These encounters outside the perceived norm for gender-specific behavior fueled the imagination of many writers, exemplified by Sun Fuyuan's chapter "The Woman on the Tianjin-Pukou Train" (Jin-Pu cheshang de nüren) in his travel essays.[115] Sun's encounter with an independent woman traveling by herself leads him to contemplate his own unhappy, arranged marriage and the advantages of personal freedom, independence, and the option of divorce in society at large. Famous poets, such as Xu Zhimo, also commented on the experience of isolation and alienation during travel and the dramatic social dynamics of the compartment in their avant-garde poems of the 1920s and 1930s.[116]

The train and its class structure in many ways became a miniature representation of the increasing social and professional mobility emerging across society during the Republican period. As the novels and short stories based on the train environment demonstrate, young, poor, ambitious professionals might set out in third class to pursue their dreams of a career and a better life only to return to their hometowns via first class after having achieved success in the city. In a similar vein, rich speculators and self-important political figures might display their economic and social power through first-class travel, but after failed careers and loss of social status in the city, they might return home in misery on third-class hard benches.[117]

## Conclusion

The significance of rail travel in Republican China lies less in the size, scope, and nature of the business than in the ways it contributed to the transformation of individual practices and social interactions in the public space associated with the railroad. This chapter argues that passenger services on railroads involved a new and decidedly modern mode of engaging with the social world, one that promoted values and behavior radically different from those cultivated by the traditional social order. This is not to say that the railroads dramatically changed Chinese mobility. For one thing, Chinese had long made use of water transport along canals, rivers, and coastal routes as well as of road transport on foot, horses, bullock carts, and other vehicles. The high cost of rail travel relative to purchasing power, the short average length of a rail journey, and the relatively small proportion of the population riding the rails suggest that the advent of railroads did not significantly shift existing mobility paradigms and practices. Following the pattern set by freight transport, railroads assumed a new and significant socioeconomic role for passengers via their integration into the already existing or the newly evolving networks of transportation.

As institutions, railroad companies responded to the challenges of developing a business that depended on transforming people into passengers and consumers. Historians, such as Karl Gerth, argue for "the importance of material culture in defining and sustaining nationalism" in the context of consumption in Republican China.[118] The cultural production associated with railroad travel generated individual and social experiences similar to developments in other railroad cultures, but they were not very much geared toward a national experience before 1928. During the Nanjing decade rail travel acquired a certain glamor in print publications that portrayed the consumption of leisure rail travel as an integral part of the emerging urban consumer culture: images of train passengers and travelers were used to sell mass-produced commodities ranging from cigarettes to powdered milk.[119] At the same time, railroads imposed disciplinary standards to increase operating efficiency—orderly boarding and exiting practices meant decreased wait times and faster turnaround of trains—and sanitary regulations supported the government's agenda of stricter social control and improved public health. Participation in rail travel came to represent participation in the bureaucratic, well-ordered, and above all modern urban life that the Chinese Republic sought to create in the years before 1937. In sum, the power of the railroads as an aspirational symbol of modernization and efficiency was out of proportion to their actual territorial expansion and their significance for rural passengers traveling short distances in Republican China.

# PART III

# THE MAKING
# AND THE UNMAKING
# OF THE STATE

## CHAPTER FIVE

# Professionalizing and Politicizing
# the Railroads

I n the eyes of the Chinese general public and foreign observers, after Chiang Kai-shek's Northern Expedition and the civil war in 1926–1927, China's railroads were in poor shape, both operationally and financially. Chiang's Nationalist troops had fought warlord armies and political enemies in military campaigns with a strategic focus and reckless use of railroads, resulting in immense damage on the lines in central and north China. The Tianjin-Pukou Railroad is said to have suffered material damage estimated at 18.6 million yuan, including the destruction of 83 locomotives, 315 passenger cars, and 1,058 trucks.[1] On other lines, armies used railroad cars for troop barracks, often ruining them for further service.[2] The detention of rolling stock and the complete interruption of train service between Pukou and Tianjin even led to questioning in the House of Commons, indicating that British bondholders were gravely concerned about the returns on their financial investments.[3]

The ten years between the Nationalist government's ascension to and consolidation of central power and the Japanese invasion in 1937 was a period of an institutional and visionary quest for modernization. Under Chiang Kai-shek's leadership, the government experimented with models of predominantly urban reforms that sought to create a modern centralized state through state-led investment and social engineering. Apart from concerted efforts intended to transform the urban and rural populations into modern citizens with Western practices and attitudes, new institutions, from ministries to professional organizations, were charged with providing the institutional framework for a modernizing society. Railroads, as institutional entities with administrative and managerial hierarchies, were no exception. As this chapter shows, during this period the national railroad system made astonishing strides in managerial and administrative organization and efficiency despite the physical and operational damage to the network. Railroad companies benefited from major improvements in the higher-education system, especially in the training of engineers who became a new professional and social elite and whose influence went far beyond the railroad compound and office.

Historians of Republican China have devoted numerous studies to evaluations of the state-building efforts of the Nationalist government.[4] To this day, the debates still focus on whether the efforts to centralize and to be consistent with the Nationalist vision led to a stronger or weaker state and what role institutions played in this process. Some scholars have adopted the political science model of the developmental state to explain the strong visible hand of the state to marshal resources for economic and industrial growth during the Nanjing decade.[5] The modernization of large administrative bodies, such as the Sino-Foreign Salt Inspectorate or the Customs Administration, has led to interpretations that the Republican state came to lack central power able to permeate all levels of administration, especially in the rural areas. At the same time, the state managed to generate some strong institutions that served the Nationalist modernization agenda but remained primarily confined to urban China under Nationalist control. Other institutions, such as the Ministry of Finance, gained in strength and were able to serve the Nationalist modernization agenda with some success.[6]

In many ways, this chapter shows the simultaneous strengths and weaknesses of railroads as institutions during the Nanjing decade. Without a doubt, the expansion of China's railroad bureaucracy during the late 1920s and 1930s is evidence of strong government-led reorganization and financial investment, even if there was very little new track building until the mid-1930s (see Map 5.1). The analysis in this chapter, however, also demonstrates that the reorganization and professionalization of railroad companies was not a straightforward story of institution-building and progressive development directed solely by the state. As I argue, the training and professionalization of railroad employees and workers continued efforts that dated back to the 1910s. Most importantly, railroads were forced to respond to changing labor

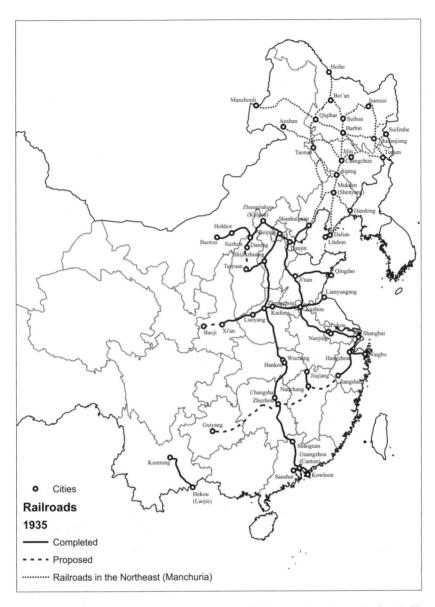

**Map 5.1**  Major railroads, 1935. Map © Elisabeth Köll (cartographic design Matthew Sisk).

market demands, which were sometimes countercyclical and outside the control of the government. As individual career paths show, graduates of engineering and technical schools frequently moved among railroad companies, private firms, and even educational institutions before signing on with the central railroad bureaucracy.

As administrative institutions, railroads did contribute to state building via the professionalization and politicization of their employees. In addition to offering political and moral education in support of the government's general desire to build an efficient, technocratic political economy, railroad companies became the bastions of the Nationalist Party, with special party branches targeting administrative and engineering elites in all railroad bureaus and headquarters. Another aspect of this institutionalization and professionalization that has been neglected in previous discussions is the incorporation of unskilled workers into the workforce through training and social inclusion. The efforts by railroad companies and the central administration to reduce illiteracy rates, and the establishment of night schools combined with social services and cultural activities created workers with improved skills and higher efficiency but also with greater loyalty to the railroad as a professional, social, and political institution. From a long-term historical perspective, this development created the preconditions for the survival of the railroad bureau system and the administrative organization of railroad compounds as socialist work units after the 1949 revolution.

To illustrate the impact of the state-led educational and bureaucratic reforms on the railroad companies as institutions, I first discuss the changing workforce as cohorts of engineers and employees graduated from the new Chinese technical schools and universities. At the same time, academic standardization of engineering education and the increasing social prestige of the profession resulted in the formation of important social and knowledge networks. The second section of this chapter explores how employees, by underwriting the ethical obligations of the engineering profession that were tied to individual and national interests, developed a strong identity with their employers and a closer affinity to the Nationalist Party. How training and education of workers created parallel institutional loyalties and a reluctance to embrace radical labor activism is discussed in the third section. The final part of this chapter explores the Nationalist Party's vision for rail development during the prewar period, before the Japanese invasion cut short any plans for network consolidation and expansion.

## Technical Education and Bureaucratic Careers

Early engineering education in China was fragmented and oriented toward specific national or company interests, but the founding of the Republic in 1912 and the broader educational mission of the new nation-state led to more organized knowledge transfer in state-sponsored institutions. During the months leading up to the fall of the Qing empire and the founding of the Republic, engineering courses at the university level were offered by four institutions with ties to the mining, military, and arsenal sectors: Imperial Polytechnic Institute in Shanghai, Imperial University of Shanxi in Taiyuan, Engineering and Mining College in Tangshan, and Imperial Beiyang University in Tianjin.[7]

As part of China's educational reforms and efforts to promote and integrate modern science and engineering into the curriculum, in 1921 the government established Jiaotong University, also known as the University for Communications and Transportation, by merging the three colleges in Tangshan, Tianjin, and Shanghai, which were pioneers in industrial and technical education. The Shanghai campus of Jiaotong University was situated on the campus of the former Nanyang College, which was established in 1896 but, like the other two campuses, had come under the control of the Ministry of Communications and Transportation in 1906. By the late 1920s, Shanghai Jiaotong University was the most prestigious campus among the three, with strong departments in electrical engineering, mechanical engineering, and railroad administration. Symbolizing the close links between the government and the university, Minister of Communications Wang Peichun served as president of the university.[8]

Beginning from the early 1910s and throughout the Republican period, Jiaotong University developed into the premier academic institution for engineering and science, as evidenced by the generous government funding from the Ministry of Railways and the substantial number of graduates. By 1935 the Shanghai campus of Jiaotong University consisted of five colleges: science

(77 students), management (171 students), construction engineering (150 students), mechanical engineering (122 students), and electrical engineering (140 students).[9] The campus in Beijing (Beiping at the time), called Railroad Management College (Tiedao guanli xueyuan), was dedicated exclusively to railroad-related studies, with 170 students enrolled during the 1932–1933 academic year. The Tangshan campus was the smallest among the Jiaotong schools, with only 158 students attending a general engineering college. The Ministry of Railways matched its funding to the respective size of each campus; therefore, Shanghai Jiaotong University received twice as much funding per student as the Beijing campus.[10] The Ministry of Railways might have opted to focus on the flagship campus in Shanghai as the supplier of engineering talent for the future needs of the government in Nanjing because teaching railroad management required less investment in expensive equipment and laboratories compared with that required by the Shanghai engineering colleges.

The most significant part of the Ministry of Railway's collaboration with Jiaotong University was an arrangement whereby almost 80 percent of the graduates from the engineering colleges were systematically assigned apprenticeships (shixi) with the thirteen major railroad lines throughout the country.[11] As discussed in Chapters 1 and 2, graduates faced difficulties securing employment in the early years of the twentieth century due to the company-specific language-training requirements in English, German, or French; the lack of academic and on-the-job training; and the absence of an open labor market. The apprenticeships assigned by the Ministry of Railways gave graduates the requisite practical experience in addition to academic training and thus prepared them for entry into the labor market. According to the ministry's statistics, among Jiaotong's graduating class of 228 students in 1933, 182 were placed with railroad lines; of these, twenty-two students each went to the Jin-Pu and the Beijing-Hankou lines, twenty students to the Kaifeng-Luoyang line, fourteen to the Guangzhou-Hankou line, and thirty to the Nanjing-Shanghai-Hangzhou line. Graduates from Shanghai Jiaotong University tended to be strongly represented on the southern railroad lines, whereas graduates from the schools in Beijing and Tangshan dominated the apprenticeships with railroads in central and northern China.[12]

As Chinese graduate students apprenticing with Chinese railroad lines increased, the number of Jiaotong University students studying overseas, with full or partial funding from the Ministry of Railways, decreased. By 1933, only twenty-three students were studying abroad, eight in the United States, six each in England and Germany, two in France, and one in Belgium.[13] It is likely that the improved quality of instruction and career options at home no longer necessitated that Chinese students go abroad to receive a good engineering education, especially at the undergraduate level.

Compared with engineering graduates in the 1910s and early 1920s, graduates during the Nanjing decade had better opportunities for employment and were finally able to penetrate the upper stratum of chief engineers and managers in Chinese railroad companies. For example, the personnel structure of the Shanghai-Nanjing Railroad in 1920 employed foreigners in positions of engineer-in-chief and general manager and in leading positions in the engineering, traffic, accounts, locomotive, storage, and medical departments— a total of thirty-seven people.[14] With the exception of one managing director, the Chinese staff of forty-five people mainly filled the assistant and deputy positions in the engineering, traffic, and locomotive departments or served as inspectors for various operational functions. The only department where Chinese clearly dominated the workforce was the police force—a necessity because the police interacted with the public and the Chinese authorities had to demonstrate the political autonomy of railroads under full Chinese sovereignty.[15] In a major shift, by the late 1920s and early 1930s Chinese engineers and employees began to fill the overwhelming majority of upper and middle management positions on the Shanghai-Nanjing line, the Tianjin-Pukou line, and other major railroad lines.[16] Chinese railroads were finally managed by Chinese, and the total number of full-time salaried employees in the operational and managerial parts of the railroad administration had risen from 60,000 in 1916 to 130,000 in 1935 (see Table. 5.1).

The strong demand for graduates with railroad-related technical expertise was reflected in frequent, almost desperate, advertisements issued by the Ministry of Communications and Transportation in Beijing in the early 1920s. These job ads appeared in engineering journals seeking Chinese students trained either at universities and higher technical schools in China or at foreign institutions for every conceivable position, from traffic management to accounting and bridge design in the ministry's Railway Department. The application process required submission of diplomas and any published work, along with an application to the ministry's director of the Railway

Table 5.1  Employees of Chinese government railroads, 1916–1935

| Year | Employees | Employees per mile |
|------|-----------|--------------------|
| 1916 | 59,857 | 14.2 |
| 1917 | 60,447 | 17.8 |
| 1918 | 63,795 | 18.7 |
| 1919 | 63,795 | 19.8 |
| 1920 | 77,622 | 20.8 |
| 1921 | 89,043 | 23.5 |
| 1922 | 91,356 | 23.3 |
| 1923 | 107,376 | 25.6 |
| 1924 | 113,091 | 30.0 |
| 1925 | 119,434 | 27.5 |
| — | — | — |
| 1931 | 132,273 | 27.2 |
| 1932 | 121,718 | 28.3 |
| 1933 | 127,151 | 28.5 |
| 1934 | 128,392 | 29.0 |
| 1935 | 129,164 | 29.0 |

Source: Ministry of Communications (subsequently the Ministry of Railways), *Statistics of Government Railways* [Zhongguo tielu tongji] (Peking (subsequently Nanking): Tiedaobu tongjichu, 1915–1936). The series covers the railroads' fiscal years until 1935 / 1936. Because of the impact of the civil war years on railroad operations, reports were published with long delays. The volume with 1925 data was published in 1929, and the volume with 1928 appeared in 1933. From 1926 onward each volume contained English and Chinese versions. Beginning in 1930 the name of the series changed slightly to *Statistics of Chinese National Railways* [Zhonghua guoyou tielu kuaiji tongi huibian].

Note: The reports contain no employee data for 1926–1930. Only full-time salaried employees are included.

Department. Applicants not residing in Beijing were explicitly told that they did not need to file their applications in person. The publication of advertisements in professional journals with both domestic and international readerships indicates the ministry's recognition that China's national railroad network had to draw talent from the widest possible pool of talent.[17]

Ironically, the growing number of engineering graduates also generated problems because the graduates of the 1920s were ahead of the substantial expansion and construction of new lines in the railroad network that only came about in the early 1930s. For example, Harold Stringer, an adviser to the Chinese railroad administration, complained in the *North-China Herald* in April 1929 that "all departments have been compelled to return an increasing number of returned students, for whom there was no adequate employment. For sixteen years there has been no railway expansion. Railway men rust in routine."[18]

In light of this asynchronous development, employment in the government bureaucracy, which expanded after the Nationalists' rise to power in 1928, became an even more important career choice and alternative for engineering graduates. The state's role as a promoter of institutionally legitimized knowledge through its sponsorship of Jiaotong University has already been discussed. With limited engineering demand from railroad line operations and private firms, the government, more specifically the Ministry of Railways, became a major employer of engineering graduates. This integration of engineering graduates into bureaucratic service as technocrats can be compared to the absorption of Chinese graduates from the new law schools by the central government's judicial departments.[19] One might also assume that, as an employer of last resort, the central government and by extension its political agenda enjoyed a high degree of loyalty and support.

As the 1929 employment records of the Ministry of Railways reveal, graduates from Chinese colleges and professional schools worked in equal numbers side by side with Chinese graduates with degrees from foreign universities in departments with managerial, operational, administrative, and financial responsibilities.[20] For example, in the Operations Department (*gongwusi*) the most senior employees (ages forty and older) all had engineering degrees from American institutions, such as Columbia University or the University of Michigan. This situation makes perfect sense because these men had begun their studies between 1900 and 1905 when comparable engineering institutes in China did not yet exist. Not surprisingly, employment records list younger employees, in their twenties and early thirties, with degrees in engineering or the sciences from institutions such as Jiaotong University, Tangshan College, Peking University, and various provincial schools teaching commercial and industrial sciences.[21]

Career information in the Ministry of Railway's employment records also indicates other important changes in the Chinese engineering profession: in contrast to the first generation of employees with degrees in law, commercial science, or economics from Japanese universities and who were working for the Ministry of Communications in 1911, only one of the fifty-two employees in the Operations Department in 1929 had a degree in railroad science from a Japanese institution.[22] The reasons for this change are most likely related to nationalism and labor-market conditions. The increasingly complicated political relationship between China and Japan after World War I and Nationalist reactions to Japanese imperialism, especially by China's educated youth, likely influenced a considerable number of Chinese students to forgo study at Japanese institutions.[23] I argue that, in addition, the market-driven nature of the engineering profession encouraged students to seek all or part of their education in the West. The railroad sector played a much larger role in the economies of North America and Europe compared with that of Japan, and the demand for human capital to supply rail companies and related industries created excellent opportunities for advanced academic study, research, and practical training for both domestic and foreign students.

In fact, as the engineering career paths recorded in 1929 reveal, many employees who had first received an engineering degree in China went on to obtain an advanced engineering degree in the United States (several also received degrees in England, France, and Germany). To round out their educations, these young engineers then went on to gain work experience in junior positions with American engineering firms and railroad companies before returning to China to work for the national railroads, either in company management or government service. With their valuable academic training and overseas work experience, a considerable number of these returnees joined Chinese engineering schools as faculty for several years before moving into the Ministry of Railways' bureaucracy.[24]

The professional development of Wu Puchu, a twenty-eight-year-old graduate from She county in southern Anhui province, employed as an assistant technician by the Ministry of Railways in 1929, is a typical example of the career trajectory of an aspiring engineer during the Republican period. After graduating from St. John's University in Shanghai with a bachelor's degree in science, Wu obtained a bachelor's degree in railroad engineering from the University of Illinois in the United States and then completed his formal education with a master's degree in civil engineering from Cornell University. Adding on-the-job experience to his academic credentials, Wu worked as an engineering employee in the Telegraph Department of the Susquehanna Railroad in the American Northeast and as a controller in New York Central Railroad's Engineering Department before returning to

China, where he entered the private sector by joining Ruifuchang Machinery Company (Ruifuchang jiqi gongsi) as an engineer. Rounding out his career with teaching experience, he became a professor in the Railroad Engineering Department at Ji'nan National University in Shanghai before joining the Ministry of Railways in the capital.[25]

The impressive mobility of many Chinese engineers in the course of their academic and practical training to some extent reflects a strategy to compensate for the institutional deficiencies in engineering education, especially at the postgraduate level, and the lack of company-based professional training in the much less industrialized economy of early Republican China. The extensive career mobility and so many returnees moving to the teaching track for at least some time during their careers also had the effect that these graduates became active agents of knowledge transfer. This transfer benefited the formation of engineering as a profession in two ways: first, it allowed the speedy incorporation of up-to-date engineering research and related teaching into the domestic engineering curricula, and second, their work experience flowed back into the operations and management of Chinese railroads and businesses in the commercial and industrial sectors. As an additional benefit, academic involvement bestowed on engineers the traditional Confucian high social status given to teachers and allowed them to share their academic and professional knowledge, as well as their overseas experience, with the next generation of students.

## Engineering Professionalization

With these formative educational experiences and often substantial overseas training, engineers formed strong networks among not only their Chinese peers but also among foreign colleagues working on projects in China or teaching abroad. Professional associations began to mushroom in the late 1920s and the early 1930s when Chinese graduates in professional occupations began to organize. In 1931 the Chinese Engineering Society and the Engineers' Society of Beiping (established in 1912) were amalgamated into the Chinese Institute of Engineers. With the expansion of the profession and the nationwide academic training, its number of members increased dramatically. Engineering degrees became the new currency of professional success and social status. According to a "Who's Who" register of Chinese engineers, compiled in 1940 under the National Resources Commission (Ziyuan weiyuanhui), more than 20,000 Chinese had graduated as engineers and were working in China at the time.[26] Reflecting this trend, membership in the Chinese Institute of Engineers grew from 2,500 in 1934 to 8,292 in 1944—more than 40 percent of all civil engineers in the country.[27]

The Association of Chinese and American Engineers (ZhongMei gongchengshi xiehui) became the most important cross-cultural organization. Headquartered in Beijing, in 1920 it founded its own journal to serve as a forum for Chinese and foreign engineers working in China to discuss ongoing civil engineering projects and to facilitate knowledge exchange. The association's stated aim was "the advancing of engineering knowledge and practice, the maintaining of high professional standards, and the fostering of [a] spirit of co-operation and fellowship among engineers."[28]

Membership of the association was dominated by engineers and experts working in the railroad sector or for the Chinese government and government-sponsored projects. In 1920, K. Y. Wong, the general superintendent of mechanical works and consulting engineer on the Peking-Suiyuan Railroad, served as president. Murray Sullivan, acting chief engineer of the Zhuzhou-Jinzhou and the Zhoujiakou-Xinyang Railroads was vice president. The board of directors consisted of a mix of railroad directors, representatives of American engineering companies in China, and several technical experts working for the Chinese government. Judging from the names of the engineers serving as officers (which, of course, varied from year to year), the association clearly intended to have equal representation of Chinese and Americans. In 1920 the board of directors consisted of nine Chinese and nine American engineers.[29]

With their meetings, lectures, social events, and publications, engineering associations became a forum for knowledge exchange and technical discussions, especially with regard to standardization. This issue was the main topic in many articles published in the association's journal during the 1920s. In his article comparing American and European bridge standards in China, P. H. Chen approached the topic with a clear statement of how engineering could help overcome the technical challenges presented by different multinational technical standards and specific national preferences:

As engineers, we are most fortunate to be in China, because here we can see examples of railroad practices of the whole world. We find here not only bridges designed by the Chinese, American, British, German, French and Belgian engineers, but also locomotives and track supplies manufactured by these countries according to their different specifications and their different practices. But here also we find the difficulty of choosing just what are the best makes and designs for China. For railroad supplies from different countries often do not fit well together, and costly mistakes are not uncommon. Therefore it is up to the engineers to investigate fully the reasons for the wide differences. *Engineers are practical scientists. They must not copy things without thorough investigation and their judgement should not be biased by solicitors.*[30]

Chen's article, which he presented at the association's fall convention in 1922, offers a strong endorsement of the engineer as an independent arbiter of technical standards, irrespective of political interests or economic motivations. Chen did not consider the presence of multinational standards as an obstacle for China's railroad development but rather as an opportunity to observe different standards in practice and to select the best options suitable for China. In practical terms, he recommended reducing the unnecessary weight in the driving wheels of American and British locomotives, allowing them to safely cross bridges of German or French design, and Chinese railroad companies to freely place orders with suppliers with different national standards. In many ways, Chen's statement is an elegant expression of the desired scientific autonomy that would lead to political and economic autonomy in the interest of the nation.[31]

It should be noted that the transfer of expertise was not one way, from West to East. For example, to close a breach in the embankment of the Yellow River in 1936, Chinese engineers used "sausages" made out of willow branches, hemp rope, and *gaoliang* (sorghum) stalks. In the same year, this ingenious method was published in a detailed article in the association's journal, noting that foreign engineers would have found this task difficult because of their thinking in terms of machine labor rather than manual labor.[32] Thus, discussions of engineering problems under different socioeconomic conditions in the field—more labor but less machinery in the Chinese case—with unconventional yet successful solutions led to a reverse, outbound knowledge transfer, introducing to foreign engineers different but efficient methods of approaching engineering problems.

In addition to the exchange of professional expertise, engineering associations also offered a platform to shape a perception of the engineer as a citizen working for social progress and modernity. For example, the Association of Chinese and American Engineers became actively involved in philanthropic missions, in particular during the drought and famine crises in North China in 1920–1921. Foreign engineers active in the association, for instance, O. J. Todd, complained that "generally speaking, engineers were not called in to advise on this subject [to set up public works for labor to receive long-term famine relief] and rationally discuss 'engineering overhead.'"[33] Although the resistance of relief organizers probably reflected more traditional, charity-driven attitudes toward famine relief, the association formed an action group during its annual meeting in Tianjin in 1920, proposing to the Beiyang government a combination of a public works program with famine relief. As a result, with the permission of the Ministry of Communications two stretches of railroad embankment and approximately five hundred miles of county highways in Shandong were built by some seventy thousand workers, whose relief in the form of grain, and sometimes cash, supported them and their five hundred thousand dependents.[34]

The engineering societies' engagement in philanthropic and educational projects during the Republican period helped establish a vision for members of the profession that went beyond the mere achievement of technological progress. It introduced a moral vision of the role of the engineer. Similar to journalists, geographers, and academic professionals, engineers were expected to make a positive contribution to society and the nation as a whole.[35] As professionals, engineers became core members of the project advancing the technological, economic, and educational modernization of society while operating with a moral and patriotic mind-set framed by the government's agenda. Of course, this vision of a professional ethos was not specific to engineering in China; there was ample precedent in the European and American contexts. For example, the Association of German Engineers was established in 1856 with the goal of merging "the putative synthesis of industry and science with other aspirations for middle-class emancipation into a progressive, patriotic-idealistic vision of the future."[36] In Germany, as in China, the shared identity among members of professional engineering associations, through their experiences in institutionalized education and formalized training, was reinforced by an enthusiastic vision of the future of industrial technology creating a new nation and a new world.

Such a vision was put forward most boldly in the "Precepts for Chinese Engineers" (*Zhongguo gongchengshi xintiao*), which were articulated by the Chinese Engineering Institute (Zhongguo gongchengshi xuehui) at its annual meeting in Wuhan in 1932. In terms of style and content, the six precepts read like articles of faith, requiring that engineers

1. not forsake their responsibilities or neglect their duties;
2. not accept excessive remuneration;
3. not deviate from conduct expected of people in their profession;
4. neither directly nor indirectly damage the reputation of the profession and its duties;
5. not compete with inferior methods for business or positions; and
6. not make false claims about the profession or engage in conduct harmful to the dignity of the profession.[37]

These guidelines set the highest expectations for proper professional conduct by engineers and for their conscientious, honest, and respectful moral behavior; yet at the same time, they conveyed a general sense of pride by equating the profession with "dignity." In reaction to China's wartime situation caused by the Japanese invasion, the Society of Chinese Engineers rephrased and expanded the guidelines at its annual meeting held in Chengdu in 1941. In a spirit of patriotism and sacrifice for the greater good, engineers were also encouraged to put "their professional plans at the core of the strategy of the shared ideal of national reconstruction" and to pursue "the objectives of industrialization and modernization for the rescue of the nation."[38] The guidelines still demanded impeccable moral conduct and high professional standards, but they then also emphasized a political dimension by mandating that engineers assist the nation in its current crisis and align their professional goals and identity with the reconstruction efforts for postwar China.

Academic journals, professional associations, and standardized rules of conduct helped aspiring Chinese engineers internalize a professional identity as transmitters of technical knowledge for the benefit of society and even the nation, and the flourishing print culture of the Republican period and events such as engineering exhibitions allowed the social status of engineers to be displayed in public. For example, Jiaotong University held an Engineering and Railway Exhibition under the auspices of the Ministry of Railways in April 1933 on its Shanghai campus. Designed "to bring before the Chinese public, particularly the people engaged in business and education, the latest developments in engineering, industrial, and scientific products," the ten-day event was admission-free and open to the public, who were entertained by lectures, sports events, and concerts on the spacious exhibition grounds.[39] The university was especially proud to show off its new Engineering Hall, a building of 21,000 square feet that housed state-of-the-art classrooms, laboratories, testing facilities, and projection rooms that served the high-quality, modern education of its graduates.[40]

Even in the popular realm of commercial advertising, the image of the engineer as a well-educated, progressive white-collar professional made its way into newspapers. For example, a 1936 story-length advertisement for Dr. Williams' Pink Pills for Pale People, a nostrum of iron oxide and magnesium sulfate, featured a civil engineer.[41] The drug company regularly used the personal experiences of professionals, such as lawyers or teachers, to demonstrate how the product improved their health and productivity and thus contributed to national growth. In this particular case, a much-praised civil engineer, Wang Yinhuai, was able to perform the difficult task of road construction in Jiangxi province because of the beneficial health effects of the drug. Without trying to push the interpretation too far, it seems appropriate to consider this advertisement as an indication that by the mid-1930s engineers as professionals had joined the ranks of China's small but growing urban middle class in terms of socioeconomic status and social prestige.

## Labor Organization and Relations

The state played a significant role in fostering the education and professionalization of railroad engineers, ultimately transforming them into the bureaucratic and social elite of the Republic. But bringing the workforce on the shop floors and along the railroad lines under state control was a much more complicated matter. We need to remember that the term "worker" used in the context of the railroads during the Republican period refers to highly skilled employees who first served as apprentices for at least two years in machine workshops and repair shops. As in the case of the Jin-Pu Railroad, some of the most talented workers were even sent by management to railroad technical colleges to improve their skills and technical expertise.[42] Unskilled workers, for unloading freight, cleaning equipment, or moving coal, did not fall into this category of "worker" and were not considered part of the regular workforce of the railroad bureaus.

As in the West, engine drivers occupied the top of the work hierarchy in terms of wages and prestige. According to 1931 wage data from the Jin-Pu Railroad, engine drivers (*siji*) earned almost four times as much as firemen (*silu*) and three times as much as foremen in charge of train services. Usually engine drivers started out as firemen in the locomotive cab where they manually moved coal from the floor into the furnace, a backbreaking and sometimes dangerous job. After several months of apprenticeship under the engine driver, firemen could apply for a promotion. An experienced engine driver was usually allocated a specific engine that became "his" engine, symbolizing professional expertise and pride.[43]

The Jin-Pu Railroad's difference in wages was similar to that in other Chinese railroad companies: on the Guangzhou-Hankou Railroad the monthly wage of an unskilled worker washing engines (*cache*) amounted to 12 yuan in the early 1940s, whereas a fireman as a skilled worker earned 45 yuan. The advanced professional skill and responsibility earned engine drivers a higher monthly wage. According to the railroad's employee records, an engine driver starting out earned 55 yuan, but after three years of experience he earned 61.5 yuan, and with overtime and on-the-road expenses he could earn as much as 100 yuan per month.[44]

In terms of labor and social organization, native-place origins and local networks largely determined how skilled workers bonded with one another on shop floors. For example, many workers in the Ji'nan workshops of the Jin-Pu Railroad traced their origins to outside of Shandong province. With so many workers originally hailing from places such as Tianjin, Tangshan, or Dagu in Hebei province, the Hebei gang (*bang*) began to dominate the shop floor, reaffirming a social group identity via shared dialects, customs, and the consciousness of being different from the local workforce. The absence, or the small number, of skilled workers and employees from Shandong province on the shop floors of the Jin-Pu line is surprising. For example, according to an employee record published in 1937, the materials workshop in the Jin-Pu compound had thirty workers on the payroll, among whom nine were from Zhejiang, six from Hebei, four from Guangdong, and not a single one from Shandong province. The situation in the machine shop was similar.[45]

Interviews with former workers reveal that not all social organizations unfolded along native-place origins. They could also develop in specific workshops or for tasks in the railroad compound. For example, workers in charge of operations in a particular workshop reported the emergence of a special vernacular on the shop floor as a substitute for dealing with railroad technical terms. Workers developed idioms (*shuyu*) to use on their shop floors to explain signals (*xinhao*) and their required order. During my interviews at the Ji'nan Railroad Machine Works in 2005, a retired worker impulsively recited a skit that he and his coworkers had performed in the train shed to remind them of the step-by-step signaling and safety procedures necessary for lining up and driving the engines into the station.[46] On the basis of experiences and daily routines in the familiar shop-floor setting, workers translated abstract terminology and processes into a vernacular with pragmatic instructions, thus giving them an additional, work-related identity beyond that of their place of origin.

In addition to native-place groups, ritual-based brotherhoods also played a powerful role in workforce dynamics. In interviews, former Jin-Pu Railroad workers referred to these associations as part of the "underworld society" (*hei shehui*), terminology used in the official post-1949 narrative of the Communist Party.[47] The leaders of these brotherhoods ruled with absolute power over their sections in the railroad yards and acted as mediators and negotiators in job-related disputes and at social functions. Workers had to pay respect to them and present gifts to them on occasions such as the New Year's celebration. Personnel files in the Guangzhou Archives of the Yue-Han Railroad show that this phenomenon was not limited to the north or to the Jin-Pu Railroad. For example, in 1948 newly hired members of the Yue-Han Railroad's police force had to sign a formal document accepting the requirement that they not join a gang association (*banghui*).[48]

The power of native-place affiliations and brotherhoods among railroad workers became significant in the organization of Chinese labor, antagonizing politicization attempts following the rise of the Communist movement. In contrast to many other nations where the railroad was a cradle of radical labor politics, Chinese railroad workers were notably slow to organize. Evidence suggests that serious politicization of Jin-Pu Railroad workers did not take place until after 1945. During the pre-1937 period, 1,800 unskilled dock workers at the Pukou crossing on the northern bank of the Yangzi River constituted the largest number of railroad-affiliated union (*gonghui*) members. This far exceeded the number of Jin-Pu Railroad union employees and workers working directly on the line.[49] As day laborers, these workers were not part of the railroad bureau's regular workforce; rather, they were outsourced through a contract-labor system that supplied many Chinese industrial operations with unskilled workers during the early twentieth century.[50]

Articles in professional railroad magazines, such as *Tielu zhigong zhoubao* (Railroad employee weekly), suggest that unionization on other railroad lines in China was also slow. The strong party presence of the Guomindang (GMD), with branch offices in each railroad bureau and rail compound, and the high number of GMD party members among the engineers and management might partly explain why labor unions had a hard time finding an audience among the labor aristocracy in the environment of the railroad workshops. Apart from party activities and special political events, the GMD spent substantial funds on publishing line-specific newspapers and journals that content-wise were geared toward professional education and the improvement of technical railroad knowledge but also contained poems and stories aimed at entertaining employees with a railroad-work background.[51] Of course, in terms of political discussions of domestic and international politics, these publications followed the GMD party line. Importantly, however, the intense presence of the GMD in physical offices, party organizations, social events, and control over the in-house print media, aligning work with political agendas created a specific political dynamic in the offices and on the shop floors of railroad companies that influenced labor-management relations during the Japanese occupation and after the end of the war (see Chapters 6 and 7). With regard to the broader significance of railroads in the history of labor activism, the situation in the railroad bureaus was very different from the labor activism on the shop floors of large industrial enterprises in Shanghai. There the skilled workers became much more heavily involved in labor protests and Communist organizations than did the unskilled workers during the 1920s and 1930s.[52]

China experienced two major railroad strikes during the early Republic. The opposite outcomes of the two strikes point to how specific regional politics combined with specific geographical locations affected different outcomes from labor activism. The first railroad strike occurred in 1922 at the Anyuan mines, where the first generation of dedicated Communist activists succeeded in building an impressive infrastructure for educating and engaging the workers politically. Elizabeth Perry, a scholar of Chinese politics and history, argues that the strike was successful in Anyuan "thanks to its relatively remote mountainous location and the forbearance of the local elite, [and it] was spared the devastation that befell other hotbeds of labor organizing at this time."[53] In Perry's interpretation, the local warlord and the commander of the military garrison did not suppress the workers' protests and protect the company's interests because Communists were not yet a real political concern at the time. Even more importantly, both the local warlord and the military garrison saw the activities of the Anyuan workers' club as stabilizing, not destabilizing, the social and political fabric of society.[54] This strike's success, due to the support of the workers by local elites and the military, presents a rather exceptional case and contrasts with industrial labor protest in urban environments, where workers on strike were considered to be harming the social, political, and economic equilibrium of the elites and the military forces.

As a counterexample, the strike of 1923 along the Beijing-Hankou (Jing-Han) line represented a complete loss for Communist organizers and railroad workers. Their protests at Changxindian, one of the major workshop and repair operations, and at a number of other stations were brutally put down by the warlord Wu Peifu, who did not tolerate any social activism. His violent approach to quelling labor protests was a warning to new and potential labor organizations along the rail network. No other labor protests occurred along the Jing-Han line, and the labor union at the Jin-Pu Railroad, founded in March of 1921, shut down for good in the aftermath of the suppression of the Jing-Han railroad strike, as did the labor union at the Jiao-Ji Railroad in Shandong.[55] Former workers of the Jin-Pu Railroad confirmed in interviews that the number of Communist members working in the repair shops and maintenance yards in Ji'nan was extremely small throughout the Republican period. When asked whether they had known, or guessed, the political affiliations of coworkers, all interviewees reported that they became aware of their Communist colleagues only after 1937, when the beginning of the Japanese occupation added greater urgency to the Communist cause and united the shop floor in patriotic, anti-Japanese sentiments.[56]

## Railroad Visions

After the establishment of the Nationalist government under Chiang Kai-shek's leadership in 1928, railroad management and affairs were decoupled from the Ministry of Communications (which continued to oversee roads, air traffic, and telegraphs) and became a separate administrative unit, the Ministry of Railways. Sun Ke, Sun Yat-sen's son, served as its first minister from 1928 to 1931, followed by Gu Mengyu from 1932 to 1934 and Chang Kia-Ngau from 1935 to 1938. After the turbulent years of constant structural and personnel changes in the institutional framework, the railroad administration finally settled into an organizational hierarchy with prominent public and political figures at the helm.

The railroad vision of the Nanjing government was broadly based on Sun Yat-sen's vision of national reconstruction through infrastructure development. Sun's proposal, published in English in 1922 for the first time, presented railroad expansion as the most efficient approach to defending China's frontiers, opening the interior for improved labor migration and commercial flows between the richer eastern coastal regions and the poorer central and western provinces, and integrating the Republic into the international economy. His suggestions addressed the role of railroads in alleviating pressing domestic political concerns and socioeconomic problems, but Sun Yat-sen also had a bold vision of China's future railroad development where "our projected railways will command the most dominating position of world importance. It [the rail system] will form a part of the trunk line of the Eurasian system which will connect the two populous centers, Europe and China, together. It will be the shortest line from the Pacific Coast to Europe. Its branch from Ili will connect with the future Indo-European line, and through Bagdad, Damascus and Cairo, will link up also with the future African system. Then there will be a through route from our projected port to Capetown. There is no existing railway commanding such a world important position as this."[57] Of course, Sun Yat-sen's grand plans of linking China via rail to Europe and Africa did not materialize during the Republican period, but seem to have provided a blueprint for China's railroad ambitions in the early twenty-first century.[58]

Chiang Kai-shek did not share Sun Yat-sen's bold global vision but agreed that railroad development was necessary to access natural resources in the interior and facilitate industrialization on a larger scale.[59] In 1936, Chiang authorized a five-year construction plan with the intention to build 5,300 miles of new rail lines extending into the provinces of the northwest, southwest, and southeast, but the Japanese invasion in 1937 prevented the realization of this expansion.[60] Instead, the creation of a centralized railroad administration, new institutions for scientific and technical education, and ongoing efforts to introduce international standardization to the rail system expressed the Nationalist government's vision of the railroads, especially their economic mission.

It is important to note that the government benefited from the railroads financially; they de facto subsidized the government throughout the Republican period. According to economic geographer Chi-Keung Leung, between 1918 and 1935 the government owed the railroads an annuual sum of several million yuan for rendered services in military or political operations. In his estimate, outstanding payments equaled between 11 and 40 percent of the rail network's total annual revenue if the government had paid its debt.[61] Thus, the Nationalist government's vision and treatment of railroads as economic entities contrasted with that of railroad experts like Wang Ching-chun who had proposed to separate railroads from politics and "to administer the railways as a business enterprise" in the early Republic.[62] In a similar vein, Ling Hongxun, a prominent railroad engineer and administrator, pleaded for running China's railroads like commercial, profit-oriented enterprises (*qiyehua*) and reducing the role of state financial interests.[63]

Apart from utilizing the railroads financially, the government increasingly recognized the benefits of using railroads for political propaganda, especially during the Nanjing decade. As the consolidated rail network gained greater visibility in public space, trains, travel agendas, and the railroads' printed publications became conveyors of symbols and ideas representative of the Chinese nation as perceived by the Nationalist government. In southern China, where the GMD had a stronger political foothold than in the north, the GMD special party branches (*tebie dangbu*) at the railroad bureaus published magazines, such as *Yuelu dangsheng* (The party's voice of the Yue-Han Railroad), addressing topics of primarily political and professional interest. Other journals published by the railroads' GMD special party branches began to display maps of their regional networks on the magazine cover in the Guomindang's party colors of blue and white, prominently framed by the Guomindang party emblem. These maps can be interpreted as the government's confirmation of the regional role of the railroads and the GMD's visual claim to territorial and political authority over the national network.[64]

Railroad bureaus and compounds became home to GMD party branches and activities, but the GMD also began to incorporate the physical facilities of trains and stations into its propaganda work. Railroad stations were transformed into venues for highly publicized visits of political dignitaries and even ritual events confirming the legitimacy of the Guomindang party-state. One of the most notable displays of railroads in the context of state ritual was the funeral train that transported Sun Yat-sen's coffin from Beijing on the Jin-Pu line for reburial in a newly constructed mausoleum at Purple Mountain in Nanjing in 1929. The use of the train as part of a state ritual was modeled after Western precedents, such as the funeral train carrying Abraham Lincoln's coffin. The visibility of this special train and its incorporation into the ritual celebration before arrival in Nanjing was highly publicized and commemorated. At the former Pukou railroad station a sculpture still marks the resting place of Sun Yat-sen's coffin before its transfer across the Yangzi River to Nanjing (see Figure 5.1).[65] In the early 1930s, the GMD used trains as propaganda tools and direct political advertisements to promote patriotic nationalism as the political legacy of Sun Yat-sen by displaying his stylized portrait on the side of carriages (see Figure 5.2).

As part of the government's national vision, railroads were instrumental in bringing the citizens of the Republic to sites connected to the political heritage of the Guomindang Party. Organized visits to places celebrating and commemorating Sun Yat-sen as the founder of the Republic, and by extension the Nationalist government, became an important part of educational and leisure activities promoted by the government railroads, their published guidebooks, and government-sponsored textbooks. For example, the 1932 Chinese textbook *Guoyu keben,* produced by Kaiming Company, devoted one chapter to a class visit to Sun Yat-sen's mausoleum in Nanjing. According to the

Fig. 5.1   Sculpture marking the previous resting place of Sun Yat-sen's coffin at the former Pukou railroad station before its transfer across the river to Nanjing in 1929. Photograph © Elisabeth Köll.

textbook, the students were impressed by the stone steps, buildings, and the statue of Sun Yat-sen, whose eyes greeted them "with serious determination and kind affection."[66]

During the Nanjing decade, train travel, taking place under the administrative and political control of the state's railroad administration, became the conduit for citizens to experience a cultural nationalism that served the political agenda of the Nationalist Party. Apart from promoting visits to commemorate the sites and figures representing the political legacy and by extension the legitimacy of the Guomindang Party, railroads also engaged in promoting travel destinations to study the cultural foundations and characteristics of Chinese culture, as interpreted by the Nationalist government. For example, the Tianjin-Pukou Railroad promoted Qufu, the ancestral home of the Kong lineage, with the Confucius temple (*Kong miao*) and the forest of Confucius (*Kong lin*) as a major tourist destination in Shandong province. Nearby Mount Tai was another cultural tourist destination pro-

**Fig. 5.2**   Nationalist propaganda train with Sun Yat-sen's image, 1931. (A Chinese propaganda train with drawings and ideograms on its side, 1931) Central Press / Stringer / Getty Images, 3088533.

moted by the railroads. Visitors were impressed not only by majestic Mount Tai but also by the view from its peak of the historic Shandong landscape, with the Yellow River in the distance, taking in with pride the perceived origins of the ancient Chinese traditions. Here the railroad created the physical link between China's past and present, between the cultural markers of Chinese history and the citizens of the Chinese nation-state whose government championed those values associated with ancient Chinese culture and tradition.[67]

From the Nationalist government's perspective, the celebration of ancient Chinese culture and history supported its plans to socially engineer Chinese society, especially urban society, throughout the 1930s. Chiang Kai-shek's New Life Movement of 1934 promoted hygienic and behavioral reforms in society for the purpose of revitalizing the nation and "achiev[ing] the most fundamental goals of the Chinese revolution without sacrificing native traditions."[68] As institutions whose professional standards demanded efficiency, punctuality, and discipline, the railroads fit well with the movement's agenda and values. New Life Movement regulations and instructions were publicized at railroads stations and on trains, and the call for punctuality and disciplined bodily behavior was perfectly aligned with the discipline railroads expected from their workforce and passengers. According to a 1936 report, standard time clocks were set up to promote punctuality, but I have not found evidence that this effort had any impact on the railroad system or improved time management at railroad stations in the rural areas.[69]

## Conclusion

The role of the state features prominently in the story of the formation of engineering as a discipline and profession in Republican China, and it also provides us with insights into the development of a highly educated workforce to be employed in the railroad bureaus and the central rail administration. Training engineers not only transferred knowledge and created educational institutions but also built a labor market of considerable size and with national economic significance. As I have argued, in the early twentieth century the Chinese labor market offered many positions in the emerging railroad sector for a very limited number of suitable graduates who had relevant engineering expertise. Chinese job seekers found that access to these positions was difficult due to imperfect information. By the 1920s, however, engineering graduates were numerous and well-trained, but the growth of the railroad sector had not kept pace with job creation, hence many graduates were absorbed into other branches of the government bureaucracy. To some extent, the government was the source of this problem because it did not invest enough in the construction of new rail lines. Therefore, the Nationalist government offered a solution by recruiting engineering graduates into the civil service and into strategic institutions, such as the Bank of China, the Ministry of Finance, and the National Resources Commission.[70]

In many ways, the emergence of the engineering profession in China was directly affected by market-driven forces related to infrastructure construction and expansion. The development of railroad engineering in terms of professional and academic practices reflects some of the trends that historian James Reardon-Anderson identifies for the field of chemical research in Republican China. Whereas "China had no laboratory research of any kind" in 1920, during the Nanjing decade productive research was undertaken at major Chinese universities and research institutes attached to the newly founded National Central Research Academy (Academia Sinica) in 1928.[71]

This chapter has emphasized the important contributions of the railroad sector to modern education in China. The evolution of engineering as a legitimate profession based on a defined academic discipline, career trajectory, and social status became possible, however, only after the Guomindang government took control of, and was able to support, an institutional framework for nationwide engineering education, fieldwork, and training. Elite institutions such as Jiaotong University in Shanghai trained engineers and future railroad administration civil servants who developed strong professional networks by joining engineering societies with large national and international memberships. Simultaneously, the engineering profession gained social status and prestige through state sponsorship and its integration into the bureaucratic apparatus. As part of the state's railroad vision, the declaration of June 6 as "Engineers' Day" and a national holiday in Republican China allowed the Guomindang government to publicly celebrate the contributions of engineers to the development of the nation and also to celebrate itself as the institutional home and workplace of so many engineers.[72]

The relatively unsuccessful trajectory of railroad unions and labor activism in Republican China might come as a surprise. The collusion of warlord military power and local government in the absence of a strong central government resulted in brutal suppression of the strike on the Beijing-Hankou line, which occurred just around the time when the first labor organizations appeared at the railroad yards of Jin-Pu and other railroads in the early 1920s. Railroads were instrumental in shaping the politics of class struggle in the United States during the last quarter of the nineteenth century, at a time when the country was the most unionized and strike prone in the world.[73] In Japan, the first significant strike took place in 1899 at the Japanese Railway Company, where engineers and skilled workers, in a language of respect and status rather than natural rights, protested the existing job-classification system and the humiliating requirement that they had to kneel before assistant stationmasters.[74]

Despite the lack of successful union organization in prewar China, the railroads contributed significantly to the social welfare of the workforce by improving literacy and workers' education. We need to remember that even with many skilled workers in the railroad yards, the percentage of illiterate or barely literate workers was substantial. According to a 1930 survey of educational levels among the Jin-Pu Railroad and Jiao-Ji Railroad work-force, 55 percent of the Jin-Pu and Jiao-Ji rail workers were illiterate or some-what literate. Only 0.3 percent of the Jin-Pu workers and 1.5 percent of the Jiao-Ji workers had educations above the junior-middle-school level.[75] In order to improve educational levels, the railroad bureaus of all major lines established literacy schools. For example, by 1932 the Jin-Pu rail administra-tion ran sixty literacy classes, with thirty-seven teachers in Puzhen, Bengbu, Xuzhou, Lincheng, and Ji'nan—all of which were stations with large num-bers of freight transportation workers.

It is difficult to evaluate the improvement of literacy standards at individual railroad bureaus over time due to a lack of data. Of course, the railroad ad-ministration under the Nationalist government promoted workers' educa-tion not only as a means of social reform but also as a necessary step toward improving the workers' livelihood and job satisfaction, and ultimately as a way to avoid strikes.[76] Whereas night classes and workers' education programs organized by Communist labor activists at Anyuan were aimed at empow-ering the workers politically, the educational opportunities offered by the railroad bureaus during the Nanjing decade sought to professionally and materially empower workers so as to avoid labor activism on the shop floors as well as political challenges to the Guomindang government.

## CHAPTER SIX

# Crisis Management

**W**ar wrought tremendous damage on China's railroad network. After cautious beginnings during the first two decades of the twentieth century, China's railroad system finally began to expand again in the early and mid-1930s. The Japanese invasion in the summer of 1937 and the following occupation of large swaths of territory in eastern China meant the loss of many railroads and, by extension, any connectivity they had provided between eastern and central China. According to statistics produced by Chiang Kai-shek's wartime government in Chongqing, by 1939 China had suffered a loss of sixteen railroad lines, either by enemy seizure or from dismantling for military purposes. The government declared these "in liquidation," but it also established a committee to plan for the "rehabilitation and improvement of the respective railways as soon as they are recovered" after the end of the war.[1] In 1943, only 2,200 miles of the 16,800 miles of prewar railroad tracks were operating in Free China, outside of the Japanese occupation zone. Furthermore, the record of damage does not include destroyed bridges, stations, and other construction sites that had to be rebuilt to resume railroad traffic. The years after the end of the war in 1945 saw initial rebuilding efforts, but they were once again undone by damage to the track system in the civil war between the Guomindang (GMD) and Communist armies. It took massive reconstruction efforts by the new PRC government, aided by militarized railroad construction teams (*tiedaobing*) and Soviet engineering support, to rebuild the network to approximately 15,000 miles by 1952.[2]

This chapter explores the impact of war on the Chinese railroad system from the beginning of the second Sino-Japanese war in 1937 to the end of the civil war in 1949. The Tianjin-Pukou Railroad provides an excellent lens for examining how Chinese railroads responded to the challenges of war, both as transport and administrative operations managing crises and as institutions embedded in local society. Although the Jin-Pu line went through Jiangsu, Shandong, and Hebei provinces, this chapter focuses on developments along the Shandong corridor, which was the heartland of the Japanese military presence as a strategic core region connecting the north, the Shandong peninsula, and the Yangzi basin. The Jin-Pu Railroad did not come under direct Japanese influence until late 1937, but as part of the provincial and national railroad network, it was affected by the changing political and military authorities in the area and their respective demands on the infrastructure.

The first section of this chapter explores the physical damage to the Chinese railroad system in the wake of the war from a military and strategic perspective. I argue that the damage was due to strategic decisions on both sides of the conflict: The Japanese military used the railroads to advance troops and expand the occupied territory, and it also targeted the destruction of strategically selected tracks and lines. Special units of the GMD caused a considerable amount of track and equipment destruction to prevent the Japanese from advancing farther into the interior. This argument challenges the conventional interpretation of rural Communist guerrilla forces as the main saboteurs, and it establishes a close link between special GMD army units in charge of destruction and railroad engineers who supervised the technical aspects of army operations.

My discussion then turns to the managerial and political dynamics developing within railroad compounds under Japanese management in occupied China. Testimony from oral history interviews shows that most social dynamics, including hiring practices and shop-floor hierarchies, did not change under Japanese management, which focused on maximizing efficiency and creating a cooperative, and even collaborative, workforce. The occupation did change relationships among the regional worker groups, which for the first time were united in their resentment of the Japanese as a common enemy. The third section reveals that despite the operational challenges, railroads remained important economic lifelines for the Chinese population in the occupied territory. Railroads transported not only refugees but also food and other vital supplies. I argue that as physical tools of transportation and as markers of territorial currency circulation and commercial flows, railroad lines continued to designate and carve out pockets of economic activities that in some instances almost managed to escape Japanese control, especially in the rural areas.

The final section of the chapter addresses the flow of people at the end of the Sino-Japanese war and during the civil war period when former refugees returned to the coast from the interior. At the same time, Communist troops and supporters began to build up their influence by taking over the former Japanese rail corridors in the Northeast and moving toward central China. Equally significant, many middle- and upper-management employees who had fled with the GMD to Chongqing and Free China during the war years successfully demanded reinstatement into their previous positions in the railroad compounds and administrative bureaus. I argue that this dynamic alienated many skilled workers and employees, who were subject to the disappearance of any advances that they had achieved during the war years. That these returnees were primarily Nationalist Party members who had avoided "patriotic resistance," waiting out the war in the interior, opened the door to Communist activism and to increasing anti-Nationalist sentiments among the workforce. The ensuing politicization of labor in favor of the Chinese Communist Party (CCP) helped organize the Communist advance via the railroads during the civil war and prepare for the CCP's institutional takeover after liberation in 1949.

## War and Strategic Damage

From the beginning of the Sino-Japanese war, railroads were important in establishing and expanding military control. Controlling the railroad lines not only provided access to communications and transportation but also achieved a critical objective of military and political significance. Depending on the specific strategic role of a railroad line, junction, or section in their overall military campaign, the Japanese selected different approaches—either destruction or defense of the line or a mix of both. Sometimes, as in the case of the early 1938 Xuzhou campaign in Shandong, the opposing sides controlled different sections of the same railroad line. At the time, Chinese Nationalist troops controlled the Xuzhou railroad hub that connected the Jin-Pu line with the Ping-Han line, allowing them to order reinforcements and obtain supplies via the Ping-Han line from Wuhan. The Japanese, however, were in control of the terminals at both ends of the Jin-Pu line, in Pukou-Nanjing in the south and in Tianjin-Beijing in the north, which made it impossible for the Chinese to permanently hold on to Xuzhou.[3]

Destruction of railroads and infrastructure vital to military operations in the wake of the Japanese invasion is a well-known part of China's wartime history. For example, Japanese planes destroyed most of the bridges on the Nanjing-Shanghai Railroad during the battle of Shanghai in November 1937. After the occupation of Shanghai and Nanjing, the Japanese moved on to Wuhan in the Yangzi valley and then on to the city of Nanchang, which had gained strategic value as the center of the anti-Japanese war of resistance. Jiangxi was a semioccupied province, with regular and guerrilla GMD forces controlling a large part of the province away from the large cities and the railroad lines. Beginning with the battle of Wuhan, the Japanese army used the southern banks of the Yangzi River as a main route in its campaign, resulting in the decision by the Nationalist government to position its troops along the Nanchang-Jiujiang Railroad in northern Jiangxi province to defend Wuhan. This proved to be a fruitless move. In February 1939, the Japanese succeeded in occupying Nanchang. Planning to extend the occupation deeper into Jiangxi, the Japanese army also sought to cut the Zhejiang-Jiangxi Railroad to put additional pressure on the Nationalist government.[4]

As historian Peter Merker notes, the Zhejiang-Jiangxi Railroad was of strategic importance because many Chinese air force bases were situated along the line. In response to the first U.S. bombing raids on Tokyo in April 1942, the Japanese launched the battles of Zhejiang and Jiangxi by systematically moving their troops to occupy the entire length of the Zhejiang-Jiangxi Railroad and subsequently to destroy airports, railroad tracks, and other infrastructure along the line. The destruction of rolling stock led to the gradual closure of the Zhejiang-Jiangxi Railroad, extending to the west from Nanchang toward the border of Hunan province. In desperation, the Chinese abandoned the railroad and destroyed many of its facilities so that they would be unusable for the Japanese occupiers. By 1944 only 53 miles of the previous 620 miles of the line were still operating (see Map 6.1).[5]

The strategic occupation of railroad hubs and seaports by the Japanese resulted in water transport along rivers and canals becoming a crucial substitute for commodity, passenger, and troop transport, especially in southern

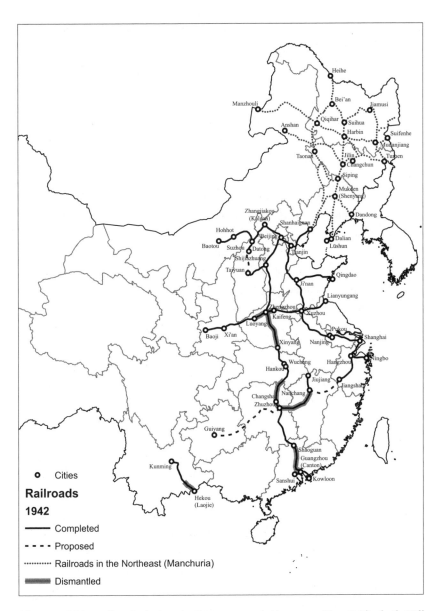

**Map 6.1** Major railroads during the Japanese occupation, 1942. Map © Elisabeth Köll (cartographic design Matthew Sisk). Map following data in United States, Office of Coordinator of Information, Geographic Division, *Land Communications of China* (Provisional ed.) (Washington, DC: OSS Repro. Section, 1942).

China. In the words of historian Micah Muscolino, "waterways, railroads, and warfare intertwined."[6] One of the most infamous incidents was the 1938 blowing up of the Yellow River dikes near the city of Zhengzhou by GMD armies to slow the oncoming invading Japanese troops. Destruction of the dikes produced catastrophic floods and unspeakable tragedies for the local population attempting to flee the "ecological cataclysm."[7] The interruption and destruction of rail transportation links in certain areas revived water transport alternatives, which had suffered from rail competition before the war, and created new temporary economic markets and hubs.[8]

In contrast, lines in China's interior, such as the Long-Hai Railroad and the Yue-Han line from southern Guangzhou to Hankou, were bombed by the Japanese to prevent the advance of the GMD troops. As much as Chinese railroads contributed to troop transport and the movement of refugees into the interior and the south on a national scale, between 1938 and 1949 the railroads were overwhelmed in terms of equipment use, passenger and freight capacities, and physical destruction.

In 1937 the Japanese invasion of China and the ensuing occupation of Shandong province presented additional challenges to the Jin-Pu Railroad and its management. In 1938 the Japanese assumed active control of the Jin-Pu and the Qingdao-Ji'nan Railroads and established Japanese military authority in the railroad stations along the lines. Because there were still 116 stations along the entire line in 1945, we can assume that this considerable physical network was conveniently used as checkpoints to exert Japanese military control in Shandong.[9] The Jin-Pu Railroad was of extreme strategic importance to the Japanese war effort because it provided the Japanese army with the fastest and most efficient way to transport troops, equipment, and administrative personnel between northern China and the Yangzi area.

The Japanese controlled not only management of railroad traffic but also the land adjacent to the railroad tracks, and they enforced law and order within these rural communities in a heavy-handed manner. In response to the oppressive Japanese military presence, anti-Japanese resistance fighters sabotaged supply trains for Japanese troops by repeatedly destroying tracks and important bridges in the flat countryside south of Ji'nan. Pamphlets with titles such as *Zenme pohuai tielu* (How to destroy the railroads) explained the technical aspects of damaging tracks and engines with minimum effort and equipment.[10] The intended audience of these technical pamphlets published by a special unit of the Nationalist military administration was not the guerrillas, most of whom were illiterate.[11] Rather, the instructions were addressed to military personnel, requesting their collaboration with engineers and technical staff from the railroad companies, who could provide the necessary expertise with explosives and hence the most efficient damage to tracks and railroad beds.[12] Therefore, rural resistance fighters under the guidance of the CCP did not have a monopoly over the strategy of sabotaging Japanese rail control.

From post-1949 party-sponsored oral history projects we know that some of the guerrilla activists were CCP-affiliated workers who had basic railroad skills. Instead of gaining their experience in the Jin-Pu Railroad workshops, these guerrillas had been trained in the nearby coal mines in Boshan and other traditional mining areas on the Shandong peninsula.[13] These railroad guerrilla squads (*tiedao youjidui*) were organized in seven different branches, each with a membership ranging from between twenty-three and three hundred people, operating as the "Jin-Pu Workers' Destruction Squad," the "Lieshan Mining Guerrilla Squad," and so forth.[14]

In 1938 and 1939, the guerrilla squads' success in destroying tracks, attacking Japanese supply trains, and robbing them of goods and useful freight— weapons, explosives, and in some cases even the payrolls—was particularly noticeable. As one would expect, the Japanese military authorities tried to prevent further attacks with punitive expeditions into the surrounding countryside and with strict but relatively ineffective regulations. For example, public decrees issued by the Japanese military authorities in Ji'nan in 1940 limited the height of crops grown along the tracks and the major roads so as to minimize the danger of ambush by guerrilla fighters hiding in the fields and waiting to attack Japanese soldiers.[15] I have no evidence that Shandong farmers did not pay attention to these demands, but I doubt that they would have obeyed such regulations, which suggest a considerable level of fear and lack of control among the Japanese occupation forces.

The popularity of these guerrilla squads has been heavily exploited in the postwar CCP narrative about Communists being the only truly patriotic force fighting the war of resistance in Shandong with strong support from all levels of local society. For example, the extremely popular novel *Tiedao youjidui*

(The railroad guerrilla squad) by Zhi Xia, who supposedly had firsthand experience with Shandong's guerrilla fighters, was published in 1954 and later turned into a popular propaganda film.[16]

In reality, however, the guerrilla squads mainly consisted of mining workers, approximately five thousand of whom were stationed in all of Shandong in 1940, whereas the number of railroad workers in the squads associated with the Jin-Pu Railroad Company—sixty or so—was relatively small.[17] The company's highly skilled workforce enjoyed much better working conditions than miners and workers in other industrial enterprises. Therefore, CCP activists found it more difficult to infiltrate the workforce and to convince the skilled workers to sabotage their own work in the name of the anti-Japanese resistance.

Building fortifications was another Japanese strategy to prevent saboteurs from cutting off supply lines for the Japanese troops. After 1941, in particular, the Japanese army was intent on wiping out the Communist troops of the Eighth Route Army in North China through "large-scale 'mop-up' and encirclement campaigns."[18] For example, the 110th Division of the Japanese occupation army, stationed in central Hebei, attempted to cut all connections between the bases of the Eighth Route Army and the occupied zones with construction projects: "We have built a blockade line which stretches several hundred kilometers, to the west of the Beijing-Hankou Railway. This line consists of stone walls and blockhouses. The walls are two meters high and one meter thick at the base. This line is to cut off the supply lines [for the Eighth Route Army] to western and central Hebei. It took 70 days and 100,000 laborers to build the line."[19]

Similar to Chinese railroad companies building their lines early in the twentieth century, the Japanese recruited laborers from the local villages along the railroad tracks, but, of course, they were forced labor and not paid. Conscription of local farmers for construction work even during the busy agricultural season seriously reduced the level and quality of agricultural production throughout northern China in the early 1940s.[20]

Diana Lary and other historians show that the Japanese occupation in North China took on very different forms outside of the major urban areas. Although the Japanese controlled the cities and the surrounding areas as well as the zones along the railroad lines and the major roads, they did not control the countryside. Thus, in many provinces north of the Yangzi River that had fallen under Japanese occupation in 1937–1938 (Hebei, Chahar, Henan, Shandong, northern Anhui, and northern Jiangsu), guerrillas carried out armed resistance either in formal army units or as autonomous forces. Establishing power over the triangle consisting of the Jin-Pu–Ping-Han–Long-Hai lines translated into dominance over the North China plain—not in terms of actual command over every square inch of the territory but rather over the economic and social resources of the area. The Jin-Pu Railroad represented an important part of this struggle for control of the countryside in northern China.[21]

Fear of guerrilla attacks led the Japanese to take extreme security measures along the tracks that proved to be costly because they slowed passenger and freight traffic and required special, expensive military equipment, such as armored tanks (see Figure 6.1) and even draisines. These light auxiliary rail vehicles could usually move ahead of Japanese train convoys, testing the rails and security in the environment and moving along the tracks in both directions.[22] For example, an eyewitness described the situation along the Ping-Han Railroad in 1939:

Trains are now running twice a day during day time, but only as far as Siao Chi Cheng [Xiaoyizhen], south of Changteh [Zhangde], beyond which the territory is under the control of the Central Government [GMD] troops. It is really comical to see that each train is made up with an additional locomotive at the rear, so that it may go backwards immediately, once its forward movement is interrupted. An armored car and a special railway tank car are installed in front of the locomotive, and in addition each train is heavily guarded by over 100 Japanese soldiers. One can imagine the difficulties of operating passenger and freight trains under such circumstances.[23]

The overwhelming majority of guerrilla activities occurred in the rural areas, and they rarely spilled over into the big cities. One of the few exceptions was the May 1941 activities of the fascist Blue Shirts organization in Shanghai in response to the increase in pro-Communist guerrilla activities close to the city, especially along the Shanghai-Ningbo Railroad. According to historian

**Fig. 6.1** Japanese armored rail car, 1938. Papers of Ruth Cowan Nash, ca. 1905–1990, MC 417, folder #592. Schlesinger Library, Radcliffe Institute, Harvard University.

Frederic Wakeman, railroads became an easy target for "day-to-day terrorism," sponsored by the GMD exile government in Chongqing and organized by the Blue Shirts. For example, in July 1941 a huge time bomb blew up parts of the tracks on the Shanghai-Nanjing Railroad, destroying fifteen sleeping cars.[24]

Remarkably, even with all the interruptions due to the war, the Jin-Pu Railroad transported 4.2 million passengers in 1940. Although resistance from the local population who cooperated or sympathized with the guerrilla fighters predictably and repeatedly generated cruel countermeasures by the Japanese military authorities, the Japanese took a different approach in their management of the workforce on the Jin-Pu Railroad.

## Shop Floors under Japanese Occupation

When the Sino-Japanese war broke out in the summer of 1937, railroads were the largest employers of both blue- and white-collar workers in Republican China. In the wake of the Japanese occupation, from 1938 to 1940 the Ministry of Railways fell under the Nanjing transitional government as part of the renamed Ministry of Communications and Transportation, and then under the collaborationist Wang Jingwei regime until January 1943, when the Ministry of Communications and Transportation was combined with the Water Resources Commission (Shuili weiyuanhui) to form the Ministry of Construction (Jianshebu). But the Ministry of Railways continued as a bureaucratic entity during the Wang Jingwei regime in 1940–1941.[25] After the end of the war in 1945, the Nationalist government reorganized its structure and railroads once again, and until the end of the civil war in 1949 railroads came under the control of the Ministry of Communications and Transportation.[26]

The Japanese managers and engineers realized the need to operate the Jin-Pu Railroad as smoothly as possible to provide uninterrupted military supplies for the occupation army troops in Shandong, Hebei, and North China in general. They were aware of their dependence on cooperation from the highly skilled Chinese workers in the railroad yards, and thus they tried to co-opt rather than alienate the workforce by improving working conditions on the shop floors.

Some of the improvements were substantial. As former Jin-Pu Railroad workers revealed in interviews, beginning in 1938 when they worked under Japanese management, they received free lunches, they were still given free train tickets to return to their native places during the lunar New Year, and their working hours were more regulated than they had been during the pre-1937 period.[27] For example, skilled workers employed in the Jin-Pu maintenance workshop in the early 1940s worked twenty-one days a month, with ten-hour shifts each day. The importance of this schedule is not so much the rest and recreation time during the free days but the time it allowed for black-market activities. The workers used the free train tickets to which they were entitled as employees of the Jin-Pu Railroad and joined the wartime black-market economy as small traders (*zuo xiao maimai*).[28]

For example, some workers took the train from Ji'nan to Qingdao on the coast of the Shandong peninsula, which enjoyed better food supplies than central Shandong during the wartime period, to purchase food, in particular grain and fresh fish, and then they resold these goods for a large profit margin on the black market in Ji'nan.[29] That the workers belonged to the workforce of the Jin-Pu Railroad made them, as well as their baggage, less suspicious to the Japanese railroad guards patrolling the stations and the trains.

Reminiscences about working conditions under Japanese management related in interviews with retired skilled workers in a variety of jobs in the Ji'nan rail compound reveal both different and sometimes common individual experiences. All the workers employed with the Jin-Pu Railroad after the beginning of the Japanese occupation complained about the difficult working conditions. They had all received their positions through the mediation of a relative or a native-place acquaintance who already worked for the Jin-Pu Railroad. Universally, for those in their early teens, becoming an apprentice in the Jin-Pu workshops was a considerable step up from previous employment and brought higher, and much desired, cash wages to support their families. For example, thirteen-year-old Yao Hongsheng performed backbreaking labor at the Kailan mines in Hebei province, unloading coal from wagons coming out of the mining pits, until his uncle, an engine driver at the machine shop in Ji'nan, was able to secure work for him in 1942. According to Yao's testimony, this was not an easy decision for his uncle, who hated both the Japanese occupiers and the Jin-Pu management.[30]

The shop-floor hierarchies and native-place networks under occupation resembled those in the 1910s and 1920s, when there were large contingents of workers from Hebei province and Tianjin city. The Japanese managers did not change the hiring practices for unskilled and skilled workers, which continued via the Chinese labor-contract system. If anything, Japanese management introduced new terms to define different employment categories, such as hired laborers (*yongyuan* and *guyuan*), employees-in-training (*zhun zhiyuan*), and full employees (*zhiyuan*).[31] The significance of these new categories is that they all use the term *yuan*, indicating salaried work, instead of *gong*, indicating wage labor or work in general.[32] Japanese management must have been aware of its general unpopularity and perhaps wanted to avoid the attraction of the workforce to labor unions and the rise of a worker identity tied to possible Communist infiltration. However, there is no evidence that this change in job titles actually changed the political inclinations of any Chinese workers or employees.

From former workers' testimonies, I conclude that the Japanese management of the Jin-Pu Railroad was more successful in attracting good workers and creating, if not company loyalty, at least some form of cooperation among the workforce by offering incentives related to job training and benefits. Apprentices (*xuexisheng*) underwent rigorous four-year training, spending every morning in the classroom with Chinese and Japanese teachers to study subjects such as Japanese language, moral education, mechanics, metallurgy, and math. Every afternoon they studied the use of work tools and techniques. In their second year, apprentices spent their afternoons engaged in practical training on the shop floors, rotating each month among the different workshops. Most importantly, Japanese management also sent them to railroad training institutes in Shanxi and Hebei provinces where they received free specialized professional training. Once they completed their training, the graduates were distributed among the various workshops and were assigned tasks according to their abilities and skills.[33]

Japanese management invested considerable resources in the training of railroad workers with technical expertise that was crucial to the Japanese war effort—that is, operation and management of the railroad network in occupied China. Recollections I heard by former workers lead me to believe that they were not subjected to the same level of harassment and exploitation as the unskilled workers in the confiscated commercial industrial enterprises, such as the cotton mills and silk filatures under Japanese management.[34] To avoid alienating important strategic human resources in war-related enterprises, Japanese managerial discipline kept the Chinese railroad workers under control without causing extreme alienation or provoking serious sabotage.

For example, from the perspective of Japanese management, identity checks were crucial for security reasons, but at the same time they were a sensitive issue for the Chinese workforce. According to recollections by former workers, every morning apprentices had to sign in, but if they missed work, their colleagues would use their chops to sign in on their behalf. After graduation, workers received identifying work badges to wear in the compound. Japanese guards and Chinese police enforced strict discipline to control the badges when Chinese workers entered the compound, and when they left the compound they also performed body searches looking for stolen articles in the workers' clothing.[35]

As several interviewed workers confirmed, relations between the Chinese workforce and the Chinese police guards were fairly positive during the Japanese occupation, which had not always been the case during the pre-1937 years. The presence of Japanese management led to a new surge of patriotic sentiments and a general bonding among regional groups of workers who were differentiated by the dialects of their places of origin and by their different social status in the compound. In rare occurrences, resentment against the Japanese enemy, especially Japanese guards, united "outsiders" (waidi ren) and "locals" (bendi ren) and reportedly even prevented fights between workers from Shandong and those from outside places during the occupation.[36]

## Railroads as Economic Lifelines

Railroads were lifelines in the most literal sense because the civilian population used them to flee the advancing enemy troops and to escape from the occupied territory into the area of Free China. Some of the most haunting photographs of the war period picture distraught Chinese civilians and soldiers camping out at railroad stations or trying to board overcrowded trains with their meager belongings.[37]

The negative impact of the war on China's economy became manifest in the destruction or hostile takeovers of manufacturing facilities, warehouses, and transport channels, as well as in the new import-export policies dictated by the Japanese authorities. An indirect result of the decline in Chinese economic sovereignty and the destruction of economic structures and institutions was a fragmented, chaotic currency situation throughout the country, compounding the already difficult interregional flow of goods, especially between Free and occupied China. Arthur Young, an economic adviser to the Nationalist government, quantified the war's hindrance to collection and transportation of vital export goods, such as tung oil, antimony, and tea, from the interior to the southern coast as early as December 1937 on the Kowloon-Canton-Hankou Railroad (see Appendix F).[38]

A May 1939 statement by former Minister of Finance Song Ziwen (T. V. Soong, 1894–1971) of the Republic of China highlights the Nationalist government's difficulties in maintaining foreign trade for the purpose of obtaining foreign exchange and moving goods from the unoccupied areas in the interior to the coast. Song complained,

> Since the beginning of hostilities, the Government, in order to meet its requirement for foreign exchange, has been compelled to institute the system of Export Control by purchasing through the Foreign Trade Commission proceeds of exports at the official rates of exchange. The system operated quite successfully as long as goods were able to move freely and speedily along the Canton-Hankow Railway Lines. However, the situation has changed completely during the past six months. With the interruption of means of communications, the cost of shipping has increased prohibitively, and the result has been a precipitous decline in the amount of foreign exchange available from exports. . . . At the same time, the wide spread between the official rates and the open market rates of exchange has greatly encouraged smuggling and other forms of circumventing the control. It is reported that there are very large accumulations of exportable goods in various regions of Hupei, Hunan and Sichuan, which are not being moved by merchants simply because of transport difficulties and of the unremunerative level of prices artificially maintained by the system of control. If this situation should be permitted to continue, it is bound to affect seriously not only production in the interior but our export markets as well.[39]

Song Ziwen's comments address a number of issues resulting from the Japanese occupation that affected China at the macro- and microeconomic levels. First, the interruption of rail freight transportation, in this case the Canton-Hankou line, led to a dramatic decline in the flow of exports that produced foreign exchange as well as to dramatic price increases for alternative means of transportation. Owing to insufficient highways and their security risks, motor transportation was neither a viable nor an economical option for long-distance transportation of goods at the time; freight shipping via commercial vessels of varying sizes was viable but much slower and also carried the risk of destruction by Japanese bombing raids along major waterways or by hostile requisition.[40]

A second major impact of the war was on currency circulation and competition between good and bad money, an issue that was closely linked to the railroad network. According to internal reports by the Bank of China, by mid-1939 the unstable and chaotic currency situation in the interior provinces resulted in legal tender notes—banknotes issued exclusively by the Bank of China (Zhongguo yinhang) and the Bank of Communications (Jiaotong yinhang) in Tianjin—gaining the same high exchange status as that of silver currency. The Bank of China noted this trend with great concern because it led the local population to hoard these banknotes. Hoarding was problematic because paper money could be easily destroyed if not kept properly; supposedly, as a consequence many farmers suffered considerable losses.[41] As a bank report stated,

> The authorities in the interior adopted an unusual policy of absorbing legal tender notes [only those issued by the two previously mentioned banks] by issuing in exchange what is called the "Frontier Bank Notes." Partly by coercion and partly by persuasion, their effort has met with considerable success. To start with, shops were unconditionally supplied with a certain amount of "Frontier Bank Notes," against which they were requested to hand back a similar amount of legal tender notes at a later date. This policy has now spread to and [is] being enforced in quite a number of districts along the Ping-Han and Tsinpu [Jin-Pu] Railway Lines, but it cannot be ascertained how much legal tender notes have actually [been] exchanged. Nor is it possible to estimate the amount which may be exchanged in the future. According to reports, however, the number of the "Frontier Bank Notes" already issued has run up to seven digits.[42]

According to Chinese government authorities, this local currency policy and the intervention were justified because it protected farmers from the risk of their legal tender notes being confiscated by the Japanese occupation authorities or by the collaborationist Wang Jingwei regime residing in Nanjing. Because legal tender notes had actual exchange value, they were wanted by the Japanese, who would not accept the Frontier Bank Notes that carried no exchange value beyond the local area marked by the course of the railroad lines. Therefore, Chinese local authorities considered it safer for the farmers to keep the latter notes. Of course, it is difficult to determine whether farmers trusted their own local government authorities and willingly handed over the legal tender notes. The local authorities must also have met a certain amount of resistance because the Bank of China reported that it made repeated announcements that this currency intervention had been approved by the central government in Chongqing and that the legal tender notes collected through the exchange would be properly kept and eventually handed over to the central government.[43]

Railroad hubs and stations became centers of vibrant exchange activities during the war period, especially in areas with competing currency regimes. For example, bank notes issued by the Hebei Provincial Bank were supported by the government authorities, but they were also accepted by the Japanese and the collaborationist puppet regime. In the interior provinces, however, these Hebei Provincial Bank notes were not treated in the same way as legal tender notes, which led to the emergence of flourishing exchange markets around the railroad stations. An eyewitness described with admirable logic the decision by local residents to change currencies for profit in order to obtain the daily necessities required for survival:

> Daily necessities, such as salt, kerosene, flour, etc., have to be purchased from cities along the railway lines. Before making their purchases, the farmers mostly bring "Hopei [Hebei] Provincial Notes" to the neighborhood of railway stations where they are changed into "Reserve Bank Notes" in order to make a profit on exchange. (Though more profit could be obtained if they change their legal tender notes, no one is willing to do so.) There is no danger of possible shortage in the supply of "Hopei Provincial Notes" in the interior; on the other hand, articles such as salt and kerosene are essentials which must be procured. As a result, places within 3 to 5 *li* [1 *li* = 0.3 mile] from the railway lines have virtually become exchange centers for paper money. The latest rates quoted are: $1030 F.R.B. [Frontier Bank Notes] = $1000 H.P.B. [Hebei Provincial Bank Notes]; $1040 H.P.B. Notes = $1000 Legal Tender Notes.[44]

According to these ratios, local Chinese were able to exchange about $1,070 of Frontier Bank Notes for $1,000 of legal tender notes. In other words, in 1939 legal tender notes were, in terms of Frontier Bank Notes, worth approximately

5 percent more in the interior than in Tianjin, which explains the continual smuggling of legal tender notes into the interior during the war.

Although the railroad zones and the interior came under different political control, communication between them was still possible. People entering the interior from the railroad zones, however, were subject to thorough searches and strict examinations, and unless they were local residents or could be identified by some local friends, their movements would be under constant surveillance by a cautious local community. Anyone found possessing Japanese banknotes ran the risk of endangering his or her own life by being (rightly or wrongly) identified as a collaborator or sympathizer with the Japanese occupation regime. Farmers entering the railroad zones from the interior encountered a similar type of inconvenience in the form of body and luggage searches and interrogations, although to a less severe extent. The coexistence of the two zones, occupied and unoccupied, and relations among the Japanese, Communist, and Nationalist troops along the railroad corridor, as a mutually respected demarcation line, are obvious in this 1939 description:

At the present time, the influence of Japanese troops does not extend beyond four or five *li*s from the Ping-Han Railway line, while forces of the Red Army and the Provincial government often penetrate through the Railway Zone. The Japanese are able only to maintain a few strategic communication points, and except at railway stations military preparations and Japanese soldiers are not in evidence elsewhere. In fact, Japanese troops dare not to venture beyond the relatively safe railway zones. Efforts of authorities in the interior are at present mainly directed toward the consolidation of their political organizations and intensive training of the peasants, and there is left for them really no opportunity to engage in other forms of activities against the enemy. Thus, there exists an atmosphere of mutual non-interference between the two camps.[45]

Smuggling was another important economic activity closely related to the operation of rail infrastructure. Smuggling in peacetime might be defined as trade conducted by professionals for profit in clear violation of official regulations and policies.[46] Under occupation and during wartime, however, smuggling very often carried the character of informal trade in a rather gray area, especially if the smuggling involved the supply and transportation of food and instrumental goods for basic survival. As one might expect, smuggling activities on and along the railroad lines included people who worked for the railroads as well as individual or organized traveling smugglers.[47]

The smuggling of food between the countryside and the urban areas by Chinese with privileged access to food and transportation, such as the Jin-Pu Railroad workers engaging in the black-market economy, was a logical response to scarce food supplies, increased demand, and inflated prices that promised handsome gains. Smuggling along the railroad had been a familiar phenomenon since the early Republican period, and it often involved intricate collaboration among the smugglers, train staff, and station personnel. For example, opium and currency smuggling by postal train escorts collaborating with the train staff was a frequent occurrence that caused considerable problems for the administrators of the Jin-Pu Railroad in the late 1910s.[48]

Once the Jin-Pu Railroad came under Japanese management during the war, Japanese soldiers automatically became part of the smuggling networks, both because they were easily able to offer the necessary protection and because the smuggling provided them with additional personal income. Like any other commodity, the supply of drugs was affected by the war, which led to a shortage of opiates for the Shanghai narcotics market. Filling a lucrative market niche as middlemen, Japanese soldiers smuggled opium via the Jin-Pu Railroad from North China and then sold it to the Hongji shantang, a cartel posing as a pharmaceutical company. As Frederic Wakeman notes, this opium supply chain to Shanghai was disrupted when the central part of the Tianjin-Pukou Railroad in Shandong province became a frequent target of guerrilla activities. Opium prices rose and thus the influx of fake and doctored drugs increased, with serious health implications for the city's drug addicts.[49]

Smuggling via railroads continued during the civil war. It was particularly rampant along the Yue-Han Railroad, concentrated around the railroad stations of Guangzhou and Hong Kong and turning them into hubs for black-market trade in penicillin, opium, gold, and currency in southern China between 1945 and 1949. Arrest files from the Yue-Han Railroad Police Department in Guangzhou from 1946 to 1949 provide copious evidence of the smugglers' identities, organization, and criminal tactics.[50] As one might expect, the smuggler groups worked in strict hierarchical networks involving men and women from the train staff and hired hands for carrying the goods into the station and onto the train cars and making the handover after the train's arrival. As police interviews with arrested smugglers at the Guang-zhou train station document, most of the smugglers were ordinary people without criminal backgrounds. Poverty and displacement because of the war drew them to this line of work, which required only the ability to follow instructions, and it carried the incentive of being paid in cash through middlemen without ever knowing the head of the smuggling operation.[51] Throughout the occupation and civil war, Chinese railroads played a vital role in supporting both the formal and informal economies by connecting suppliers, middlemen, and consumers in trading networks with new participants, all of whom benefited but also suffered from the ongoing political crisis. Railroads in China maintained their vital role in the informal economy for suppliers as well as for consumers until the early 1950s, when private economic activities, both legal and illegal, were increasingly marginalized before being (at least officially) phased out by the new PRC regime.

## War Mobility: Refugees and Returnees

Considering the damage and disruptions to the Chinese railroad network from 1937 to 1949, it is remarkable how much mobility the network was able to provide to those seeking to depart for Free China and destinations beyond, to those whose lives and work continued in the occupied territory, and to those who returned from the interior after the end of World War II. As the war continued, it became increasingly difficult for railroad lines to cope with all the demands for passenger, freight, and troop transport. To improve military-related logistics, the Japanese military authorities set up a railroad headquarters (*tiedao silingbu*), with a regional headquarters for each line and an office at each station under its direct command for better coordination.[52] Treating each line as a separate institutional entity of the network, the Japanese authorities recognized the different local operational challenges and attempted to embed their own administrative and military reach as close to the tracks as possible.

The plight of refugees from the eastern provinces of Jiangsu and Zhejiang, particularly from cities such as Shanghai and Nanjing where the Japanese invasion had been particularly brutal in the treatment of the civilian population, is documented from several perspectives. During the early years of the war, Western observers and reporters commented on the appalling treatment of Chinese civilians in foreign publications and newspapers, some of which were also published in Shanghai's International Settlement, which remained out of Japan's reach because of the legal status of the concession until 1942.[53] Chinese war correspondents added their voices to the interpretation of the unfolding war and constantly moving military front. As historian Parks Coble shows, however, many of the journalists regarded their work as a patriotic mission to keep up public morale in the fight against the Japanese and therefore underplayed the defeat of Chinese troops, Japanese atrocities, and the plight of civilians, including refugees.[54] Focusing on the fate of refugees from Zhejiang province and their individual journeys into the interior, historian Keith Schoppa's moving account provides us with a better understanding of the refugee experience in the domestic context and how it changed people's identities.[55]

In most cases, the refugees' journeys into the interior involved a number of transportation methods, including trains, buses, boats, wheelbarrows, and, of course, their own feet. Accommodating damaged or interrupted track sections, many railroads still offered at least partial services on the lines, but timetables became increasingly unreliable. Waiting at railroad stations, often for days on end, for trains that might appear at short notice, consumed much of the time that refugees spent on their journeys. Refugees from all social backgrounds had to deal with the lack of basic accommodations, food shortages, unhygienic conditions, illness, and fatigue, as well as deprivation of any material comforts. For example, the famous architectural historians Liang Sicheng and Lin Huiyin left their home in Beijing in September 1937, taking the train to Tianjin, from there taking a boat to Qingdao on the Shandong peninsula, and then connecting via train to Ji'nan with the hope of reaching a safe destination. "Wherever we can reach after five changes— preferable Changsha—with as few air raids as possible in between," was their hope.[56] The family reached Changsha by "zigzagging" its way via Hankou on the Yangzi River to Hunan province, but frequent air raids prompted them to resume their journey to Kunming in Yunnan province, which at the time was beyond the reach of Japanese planes. Despite bus breakdowns, gasoline shortages, illness, and dangerous stretches when they had to walk in the dark with young children, the family reached its destination through resilience and good luck.[57]

Although it was almost impossible for refugees to plan their itineraries in advance because of the constantly changing availability of transportation, even in wartime railroads were relatively fast and safe compared with buses, boats, and journeys on foot. Lines with a strategic value to the Japanese, however, were more dangerous because the Japanese military could easily identify railroad stations, and even trains, as targets during their shelling and bombing campaigns. The blacking out of stations and passenger trains did not make movements of the trains at night any safer. On the Long-Hai line train accidents occurred regularly owing to Japanese attacks, which meant long waiting times for passengers because traveling cranes had to be requisitioned to move the damaged engines so that the tracks could be repaired and the journeys could continue.[58]

The problem of refugees attempting to escape Japanese occupation and the unavoidable chaos along the railroad lines have been treated in the literature, not only providing heart-wrenching descriptions of frightened, uprooted people with the will to survive but also sometimes offering satirical reflections on human behavior in existential crises. There is no shortage of descriptions of the refugees' travel experiences throughout the country.[59] For example, writer Xiao Hong (1911–1942) begins her short story "Tao nan" (Flight from Danger) with the protagonist asking himself, "How's a person expected to get on that train?" In this fictional treatment, the protagonist and his family miss the train several times or are unable to board it because they cannot decide what to take on the journey and whether to burden themselves with heavy suitcases and household items. After much frustration and debates between husband and wife, the family finally manages to board a train, only to lose their belongings in the rush to get on. Xiao Hong herself fled from Shanghai to Hong Kong via the interior and must have encountered similar stampedes at the railroad stations. The image of the family's scattered personal items on the railroad ties and on the platform presents a powerful metaphor for the uprootedness of Chinese refugees and the futile attempt of trying to hang on to one's dignity and identity through material possessions in time of war.[60]

The most riveting literary treatment of the chaos on trains transporting Chinese refugees into the interior is the play *Luanshi nannü* (*Men and Women in Wild Times*) by writer Chen Baichen (1908–1994), published in 1939. At the Nanjing railroad station a diverse cast of characters, including a member of the resistance on leave, an official and successful businessman, a night-club entertainer, an editor, and a writer, are leaving the city on an over-crowded train in November 1937, just weeks before the brutal Japanese attack and takeover of the capital. During the long train ride to Hankou in the interior, the play's characters, all of whom are affluent urbanites or intellectuals, reveal their political and social pretensions, selfish interests and sole concern for their own well-being, and total disregard for the plight of the refugees hanging on for dear life on the roof of the train. Chen Baichen not only vividly captures the fight for scarce resources (good seats, food, and drink) and develops a narrative from the dynamics in the compartment but he also presents a critical picture of economic and intellectual elites who pay lip service to progressive ideas but lack a true commitment to the war of resistance and to the social welfare of their less fortunate fellow travelers and society at large. Chen himself moved to Sichuan province after the outbreak of the war, which must have offered him ample opportunities to observe human behavior under the pressure of a national crisis. War and displacement added a whole new layer of existential and moral dilemmas to the already familiar "drama of the compartment."[61]

How did those who decided to remain or to return to occupied China after years on the road continue to use the railroads as part of their daily lives? In my interviews with residents in Shanghai and Nanjing about their war experiences, the story of Chen Xinsheng from Nanjing reveals why people decided to return and how they adapted to life under occupation in all its forms.[62] A native of Nanjing with seven siblings, Chen rode the railroad for the first time when his father gathered the whole family to evacuate Nanjing in late November 1937, just in time to escape the Japanese attack on the city. The family first traveled on foot and then by boat to reach Hankou in early 1938. They then boarded trains, first to Changsha and then farther south to Guangzhou. When Chen arrived in Guangzhou, the railroad station there had been bombed by the Japanese and was seriously damaged. The railroad staff had no offices, and they were forced to sell tickets out of little suit-cases on the premises. This can-do attitude complemented there no longer being any difference between first-, second-, and third-class tickets because the trains were hopelessly overcrowded and the train schedules irregular.[63]

From Guangzhou the family took a boat to Hong Kong, where they stayed for a while. With so many refugees there, however, it was too expensive for the entire family to remain, and they returned to Shanghai on a ship under the British flag where, in late 1938, they found quarters in the International Settlement. When, after the horrific slaughter of civilians by the Japanese military in Nanjing, the situation had somewhat calmed down, the male family members decided to return to Nanjing to explore the fate of their hardware store and family home. While his mother and sisters stayed in the safe zone of Shanghai's foreign concession, Chen, his father, and his brothers took the Shanghai-Nanjing Railroad, which by that time had been renamed the Central China Railroad (Hua-Zhong tiedao) by the Japanese authorities in charge of operations.[64]

It might come as a surprise that in interviews Chen Xinsheng pointed out the positive aspects of the railroad managed by the Japanese—an unpopular perspective missing from the official narratives and oral histories intent on demonstrating patriotic resistance. In Chen's opinion, the Japanese managed the station and the trains with efficiency, punctuality, and order. Chen also recalled his fear when he saw Japanese soldiers at the entrance to the station spraying passengers with disinfectant to prevent the spread of disease. After the train crossed the border between the International Settlement and the Japanese concession, all passengers were searched by Japanese soldiers at the checkpoint.[65]

Chen's recollections remind us that during the occupation Japanese soldiers, Japanese employees, and Chinese railroad workers were all employed by the Hua-Zhong Railroad. Inside the trains, Japanese soldiers controlled the tickets and made regular rounds through the carriages searching for "dangerous" goods, such as weapons, material for military use, and contraband. Those working on the Shanghai-Nanjing train, including the engine driver, were Chinese and were referred to as *hei maozi* (black hats) because of their black uniforms and caps; however, the train manager was Japanese.[66]

Throughout the war years, the railroad between Shanghai and Nanjing saw much black-market activity. For example, people carried bags of grain from the countryside on the train to Shanghai where they could pocket high profits. The mobility afforded by the railroad line was crucial for these small black-market traders, called *pao dan bang*, The name, literally translated as "the walking group of one," refers to the traders moving back and forth between city and countryside as individual persons instead of carrying out their business in organized smuggling gangs.[67] The black-market traders were also known for their close cooperation with the Chinese train staff who would let them bring bags of produce onto the carriage in exchange for a bribe.[68]

Finally, Chen Xinsheng's recollections reinforce the impression that during the occupation the class system of different ticket categories was much less prevalent than during the prewar period. On the one hand, first-class and second-class rail cars were often unavailable or their condition was so compromised that the additional expense did not warrant the higher price. On the other hand, Japanese military and administrative officials, as well as Japanese merchants, traveled in first or second class, so the Chinese passengers, even if they were well-off like Chen Xinsheng and his family, had to or preferred to travel in third class. Whether in first or third class, passengers had to have much patience for travel that often took twice the scheduled time, even under good track conditions. The reason for the massive delays was that transportation of military troops had priority, requiring passenger trains to move to a side track to let them pass before they could resume their journey.[69]

Chen Xinsheng's experiences as a refugee and returnee under occupation are fairly representative for a large number of mostly urban Chinese with sufficient means for train travel. His case also indicates that even during the war railroads continued to provide a level of limited mobility, allowing people to travel for work or personal reasons within relatively short distances. Although the Japanese military became part of China's rail infrastructure in occupied China, for pragmatic reasons people continued to travel under enemy management. Whether service by the Japanese was better or worse than that offered by the Chinese is difficult to judge because the impact of war and politics was too immediate and disruptive. It seems that operationally Japanese train management was quite successful in providing services, with a diverse workforce consisting of Japanese soldiers and Chinese and Japanese civilians distributed along a large station network and in urban rail compounds. After the end of the war in 1945 and the departure of the defeated Japanese military, the railroad system did not have much time to recover and reorganize before it had to deal with a new wave of returnees from the war capitals in Chongqing and Kunming, who were heading to the eastern coast, and displaced civilians from throughout the country returning home.

## Conclusion

Chinese railroads became militarized between 1937 and 1949 and served as a strategic tool in the battles between the Japanese, GMD, and Communist armies. An examination of the strategic assaults on the Jin-Pu line confirms Diana Lary's argument that the strategic use of railroads during the anti-Japanese war replicated tactics formerly employed by the warlords during the early Republican period.[70] From the perspective of the railroad lines, the military and strategic impact did not align with the business or administrative interests of the institution. Chinese railroads during the war featured great regional disparities in terms of destruction of rail tracks and train equipment, some experiencing disastrous effects, whereas the railroad compounds under Japanese occupation operated without substantial physical damage.

Most existing studies of railroad development in Chinese history end in 1937.[71] A closer look at the Sino-Japanese war and the civil war periods and the political dynamics developing between the railroad workforce and the managerial aspects of wartime shop floors in the occupied territories is helpful for understanding the rapid post-1949 recovery of the railroad network and its bureaucratic system under the Communists. Once the Jin-Pu line came under Japanese control in 1937 as an important lifeline for the supply of Japanese troops in the north, Japanese management employed a mixed strategy of repression and concession to co-opt the skilled Chinese workforce. Oral history interviews with former workers under Japanese occupation uncover relatively good working conditions for skilled workers on the Jin-Pu line after 1937 due to their importance for the Japanese war effort to maintain a strategically vital infrastructure. As I argue, railroad workers did not necessarily fare worse under Japanese management compared with the former management under railroad administrators affiliated with the GMD.

As I have stated before, national railroad lines in Republican China faced specific challenges created by the unique local political patterns and specific local economic conditions—all these issues were magnified by the challenges of the war period from 1937 to 1945, with certain regional variations. The railroads' major strategic significance for the Japanese war effort, including sustaining the occupation economically, meant that the railroads' civilian function of passenger and goods transport was subject to the military agenda and under constant threat of imminent physical destruction. Unfortunately, during the civil war, large parts of the tracks and facilities, which had been repaired after 1945, were again destroyed, rendering impossible a quick reconstruction or expansion of the Chinese national railroad network in the immediate postwar period.

Effective railroad development as an integral part of nation-building efforts in China was successful only after 1949, when the state aggressively expanded railroad networks into the western, southern, and central regions of the country. Without competing political and economic agendas, railroad construction and management came under the complete control of the socialist government in a highly centralized and militarized system driven by a political program of national security and economic development. Expanding the railroad network in post-1949 China became synonymous with establishing and cementing the physical and ideological presence of the newly established socialist nation-state and finally providing mass transportation for the Chinese people—goals that had been impossible to realize during the war.

PART IV

ON TRACK
TO SOCIALISM

## CHAPTER SEVEN

# Postwar Reorganization and Expansion

I n the decade following World War II, the world's railroad networks fell on either side of a distinct and growing gulf. Railroads were a mature or even declining technology in nations with democratic political systems and relatively free market economies. Western Europe did not see significant additions to track mileage after the war. The U.S. rail network actually shrank by an average of 600 miles per year between 1945 and 1954. In contrast, railroads flourished in countries under Communist leadership. The USSR added an average of 534 miles per year in the decade after World War II, and post-revolutionary Cuba boasted more railroad tracks per square mile in the 1960s than any other country in the world.[1] Throughout the Cold War era, railroads thrived in socialist states with centralized economic planning. With its marked rail-network expansion after the 1949 revolution, China became a prime example of this trend.

· To achieve the goal of network expansion, after the surrender of the Japanese in 1945, as a priority China's rail administration had to undergo a major overhaul. First, the end of the occupation meant that railroads in all parts of China, including the former Manchukuo in the Northeast (the Japanese-controlled puppet state in Manchuria from 1932 to 1945) and Taiwan (under Japanese colonial rule from 1895 to 1945), had to be reunited and reorganized into one administrative system. Although Japanese-run lines in Manchuria, such as the South Manchurian Railway, purposely are not included in this study, their post-1945 integration became an important and difficult part of institution building during the civil war. With the complicated political and territorial situations due to the Soviet presence in the Northeast until 1946 and the normal level of chaos characteristic of any immediate postwar period, this centralization effort was an enormous task. That the Guomindang (GMD) government proposed a regional management approach to the reconstruction of railroads demonstrates how little the central government was able to support the rail system with financial and human resources.

A second key factor in the postwar institutional development concerned the rebuilding of rail compounds and line operations as tensions between the GMD and the Communists increased. Beginning in 1946, Communist activists increasingly inserted themselves into labor and social politics in the rail compounds, but they had to do so clandestinely. In fact, we see a rather gradual Communist infiltration that was possible only because labor unions provided their organizations with a secret platform supporting the party's agenda.

In many ways, this chapter adds to recent historical interpretations claiming that the year of the Communist revolutionary takeover in 1949 was not as much of a watershed as one might expect. Despite the setting up of Communist party branches and Communist activism before 1949, it took some railroad bureaus until 1950, a year after the founding of the People's Republic of China (PRC), to organize their party structure. On a national scale, the railroad administration did not begin to operate as a centralized body until the early 1950s. This interpretation is consistent with the assessment of historians who have worked on the transformation of Chinese society from the late Republic to the early PRC.[2] But my analysis also emphasizes the continuation of prewar aspects of line operations and construction management with familiar practices and approaches that then became framed through the ideological lens of the Chinese Communist Party (CCP).

This chapter begins with a discussion of the reconfiguration of the railroad system immediately after 1945 and the related difficulties in uniting institutional units and administrations that had different political pasts. Fewer skilled laborers and technicians in the Chinese workforce led to different approaches to the repatriation of Japanese technical personnel in the Northeast and central China. The second part of this chapter explores how the central government's political and economic goals shaped the role of railroads and directed their reorganization and expansion throughout the 1950s. We encounter the formation of railroad bureaus as administrative entities under strong party leadership and supported by skilled workers who benefited from relatively high salaries and good social services. Under the sponsorship of the party and driven by the needs of the First Five-Year Plan to advance China's industrialization through rapid acquisition of technical knowledge, railroad engineers studied in the Soviet Union, and Soviet engineers and technicians in China offered their technical and managerial expertise in factories and offices. Such assistance was particularly important to the reorganization of the railroad lines in the North and Northeast, whereas railroad operations along the southern lines needed it less.

After demonstrating the institutional integration of the party and the politically acceptable foreign expertise into the rail compounds, the discussion moves to the external expansion and construction of new railroad lines with the help of the army. The railroad corps, established as a unit under the leadership of the People's Liberation Army (PLA), enabled the decisive construction of railroads in China's interior by mobilizing human and material resources on a grand scale. As I argue, the presence and representation of the state through the integration of the army into local society built on practices familiar from the construction process during the Republic. Finally, the last part of the chapter discusses the use of railroads in propaganda and in forms of cultural production promoted by the state. Railroad images in films, books, songs, and propaganda posters elevated the significance of this transportation system to serve as an engine for socialist state building. My analysis shows that railroads assisted the interests of the state at unprecedented levels but also that railroads as operational and managerial institutions skillfully managed to transform "railroad values," such as the punctuality and efficiency from the pre-1949 period, into "socialist values" of the New China.

## Administrative Consolidation and Party Integration

After the founding of the People's Republic of China on October 1, 1949, the administrative organization and management of the railroad system were integrated into a core part of the new government's political and economic agendas. As physical entities and means of transportation, all existing railroad lines became part of the people's railroad (*renmin tielu*) system. Not surprisingly, the system's institutional reforms and innovations were based on the framework provided by the Nationalists in their attempts to rebuild and consolidate the railroad system between the end of the second Sino-Japanese war and the Communist victory.[3]

The new PRC government inherited a rail network saddled with both old and new physical problems. Military campaigns and battles between GMD and Communist troops during the civil war caused considerable damage to the network, undoing some of the repairs that had been under way as part of the Nationalist government's "postwar rehabilitation" program.[4] According to the GMD's own interpretation, by 1947 approximately 4,000 miles of tracks had been "destroyed or seized by communist rebels,"[5] particularly in the Northeast and North China. For example, in their attempt to establish control from their base areas in the north, Communist troops blew up the Beijing-Baoding section of the Beijing-Hankou Railroad on six occasions. The Nationalists responded to the "continued Communist sabotage"[6] by changing the roadbed of this strategically important line on five occasions, still without being able to completely restore traffic. In the case of the Tianjin-Pukou line, approximately 270 miles of its trunk and branch sections in Shandong province, one of the main battlegrounds during the civil war, were destroyed in 1948. Because repairs and repair attempts were undone by swift Communist counterattacks, the Nationalist government's rehabilitation program was successful only south of the Yangzi River, a region without a Communist military presence at the time, where rehabilitation restoring lines damaged by the Japanese could take place without any external interference.[7]

Taking control of rail routes became an important factor in the PLA's strategic development "from mobile guerrilla warfare to sustained maneuver warfare" under a united command, which became a major turning point in the Communists' military efforts to defeat the Nationalist armies.[8] For example, during the Liaoxi-Shenyang campaign in the Northeast in the fall of 1948, the PLA seized the main rail lines and roads to Shenyang city and Jilin province, thus rendering retreat or reinforcements impossible for the Nationalist troops.[9] This strategy contributed to the Communist victory in the North and anchored China's most industrialized region under PLA control. Even more pronounced, the Jin-Pu and Long-Hai lines and their rail hubs became strategic markers during the Huaihai campaign when the PLA defeated the Nationalists and thus secured control over Shanghai, Nanjing, and the lower Yangzi region.[10] Nationalist troops retreating from the advancing PLA and refugees on the move or stranded at stations added fur-

Fig. 7.1   Chinese Nationalist troops retreat to the Yangzi River, 1949. Photo by Jack Birns / The LIFE Picture Collection / Getty Images, 92936543.

ther strains to the operation of the rail network on the eve of the revolution (see Figures 7.1 and 7.2).[11]

In March 1946 the Nationalists announced an official regional management system for improving efficiency and economic performance. A closer look, however, reveals that this division of the railroads into fourteen regions (*qu*) was really not much different from the prewar railroad bureau divisions focusing on established trunk lines, with the exception that they were renamed regions.[12] As administrative units, the regional trunk lines were to control both small and branch lines. For example, the Jin-Pu region (Jin-Pu *qu*) still maintained its headquarters in Ji'nan and administered the trunk line between Tianjin and Pukou, the former Shandong Railroad from Qingdao to Ji'nan, the short Shijiazhuang to Hengshui section, and the Bengbu to Shuijiahu branch line. The only significant change in the divisional order was the inclusion of a new Taiwan region. As part of the administration by the provincial government, the regional railroad management committee was in charge of reorganizing the railroads built by the Japanese during colonial rule (1895–1945) on the island.[13]

Fig. 7.2   Refugee family
at Pukou railroad station,
1949. Photo by Jack
Birns / The LIFE Picture
Collection / Getty Images,
50517110.

    With these steps toward operational order and administrative centraliza-
tion well under way, 1949 was in many ways less of a watershed for the reorganization of China's rail system than generally assumed. One of the first
and most pressing issues for the new government was the establishment of a
CCP presence and structural organization within the individual railroad
bureaus, in the rail compounds, and on the shop floors of the major lines. In
compounds and factories of former Japanese-run lines in the Northeast,
where Soviet influence had filled the power vacuum after Japan's surrender
until May 1946 when the Chinese Communists began their military campaign, party organization began fairly early. For example, the large machine
shops in Dalian, serving the former headquarters of the South Manchurian Railway, saw the establishment of a Communist party branch (Dalian
tielu gongchang dangzhibu) with a secret party structure as early as No-

vember 1945.[14] Owing to the initial unstable political situation, the party branch and its secretaries had to operate in cooperation with and under the cover of union committees and activities before they could openly celebrate party organization in the factories in April 1949, five months before the Communist takeover.[15]

In many large-scale rail compounds of the North and Northeast, the years of transition from a clandestine to a full-blown party organization allowed the CCP to become involved in many important political and social matters concerning the railroad factories and their workforce, thus enhancing its political status and legitimacy. For example, in March 1946 the CCP party branch successfully directed union negotiations for a wage increase and, together with the Dalian factory management, it organized the relocation of more than two hundred Chinese families into housing compounds vacated by the repatriated Japanese.[16] Many railroad workers and employees thus experienced tangible economic and social benefits during a time of continued material hardships and political insecurity in postwar China, thereby lending credibility to the CCP in the railroad compounds throughout the country as a political force with a pragmatic and strong social agenda.

With similar pragmatism, the GMD, Soviets, and even the Chinese Communists permitted the employment of Japanese engineers and technicians in the immediate postwar period to secure continued and efficient work in specific strategic industries, including railroads. Because of Japan's imperialist control over Manchukuo from 1932 to 1945 and the import of Japanese employees to operate the South Manchurian Railway, the lack of Chinese skilled labor in the Northeast before and after 1945 was particularly pronounced. For that reason, during Soviet control over the former Manchukuo between August 1945 and May 1946, there was no official, direct repatriation of Japanese citizens from Manchukuo to Japan. According to historian Rowena Ward, some of the hired Japanese technicians continued their specific work assignments as before, whereas others were assigned the task of training local Chinese workers and preparing them to take over rail operations in the future. Even with relatively high salaries and GMD-sponsored regulations for employment of the Japanese technicians, sooner or later they all left China during the waves of organized repatriation beginning in December 1946.[17]

Of course, railroad compounds outside Manchuria did not experience the same issues. As we saw in Chapter 6, even those railroad lines that had been under Japanese management during the occupation functioned with a high percentage of skilled Chinese labor and Chinese engineers under a small contingent of Japanese managers and military personnel. After the end of the war against Japan in 1945, these railroad bureaus and rail line compounds in previously occupied China experienced not only the departure of Japanese personnel and military staff but also the return of former employees who had left with the Nationalist government in 1938, waiting out the war in the interior, unoccupied territory. In the case of the Jin-Pu Railroad, the GMD retook the facilities and operations in the fall of 1945 and reorganized the line by establishing two railroad bureaus, one in Ji'nan and one in Xuzhou, with geographically based administrative jurisdictions.[18] Aside from the Ji'nan workshops, the Ji'nan Railroad Bureau also assumed responsibility for the workshops in Qingdao. The workers who had remained in Ji'nan during the war and had put up with Japanese management and military occupation harbored resentment for the new factory management. According to recollections by former workers in the Ji'nan workshops, they referred to the returned GMD members who were back in their former positions by two derisive terms—upper-level technicians and managers who had flown in from the wartime capitals of Chongqing and Kunming were called *fei,* or "fliers," and newly recruited employees with GMD affiliations who arrived by car from nearby provinces, such as Hebei, were called *pa,* or "crawlers."[19]

In existing discussions of China's postwar transition and Communist successes during the civil war, the attitudes of workers and employees toward the returnees from the interior have not received adequate attention. From the workers' perspective, the slight was perceived at several levels. On the one hand, many of them shaped and even advanced their careers under Japanese management because their skills were important to railroad operations and added a valuable human resource during the war years. On the other hand, they also endured the insults of working and living under Japanese occupation, while the technicians and managers who had relocated to the interior enjoyed relative freedom and security in unoccupied China. In the recollections of former workers, those employees who upon return assumed their former, or even higher, positions were envied and resented for both personal and economic reasons. In the course of the civil war, however, union leaders and Communist organizers were able to transform the workers' personal feelings into ideological sentiments by blaming the GMD and its members for any professional or personal restrictions.[20]

Another reason for the growing dissatisfaction in railroad compounds, such as the Ji'nan workshops, was the hyperinflation of the *fabi*, the currency introduced by the GMD in 1935, which affected workers and employees at all levels of the work hierarchy.[21] Wages were paid once a month at the Ji'nan compound. Beginning in 1946, the devaluation of the *fabi* led to such rampant inflation that workers had to bring sacks to pick up their cash wages. Eventually, the windows in the cashier's office through which the cash was passed to the workers waiting outside had to be enlarged to hand over the bulky bundles of notes.[22]

Dissatisfaction with inflation on real wages, increasing unemployment, and the inability of the GMD government to contain the inflation resulted in local worker unrest and strikes within various sectors of the Chinese economy, including the railroad bureaus. For example, from February to March 1946 in the railroad machine shops of Ji'nan more than 1,000 workers who had lost their jobs went on strike demanding reemployment.[23] Eventually, 110 of the dismissed workers were reinstated. Compounding the problem of an already precarious economic situation, long-term line interruptions due to troop movements and military actions intensified worker unrest because the resultant loss of freight and passenger revenue ultimately led to wage reductions and job losses. After the disruption of the Jin-Pu line in the summer of 1947, approximately 3,000 railroad workers in Ji'nan staged a protest against personnel and salary reductions that eventually turned violent, injuring the leader of the railroad bureau.[24] Rough balance-sheet figures in an internal publication of the Jin-Pu Railroad Bureau administration from November 1947 confirm the precarious financial situation of the line. In that month, the Jin-Pu Railroad section suffered a substantial loss—only 88.4 billion yuan in revenue and 110.4 billion yuan in expenditures.[25] Wages alone came to almost 50 percent of monthly expenditures, thus explaining why the railroad bureau had to resort to workforce reductions.

Considering the scale of these examples of labor protest, one might assume a strong union presence on the shop floors of the railroad compounds. After the readmission of union organizations in the winter of 1945 (unions had been illegal during the Japanese occupation), however, the overwhelming majority of union members and leaders were GMD members from outside the railroad compounds who were not interested in representing the interests of railroad workers. According to the recollections of former workers, union leaders even actively tried to prevent factory workers from participating in the 1947 strike for higher wages by locking them in their workshop.[26] Not surprisingly, the lack of support and solidarity offered by a union controlled by the GMD desperate to maintain political power, plus frustrations with the failing GMD economic policies, made workers inclined to consider a political alternative in the form of Communist labor organization and politics. At the same time, as representatives of middle and upper management, GMD members became easy targets for Communist labor organizers who rejected them on grounds of party membership and class ideology.

Although one must be cautious when evaluating workers' recollections of individual experiences in oral history projects and of information in CCP-sponsored publications celebrating China's labor movement, the deep politicization of railroad workers during the civil war period is nevertheless striking. During one of my interviews in 2005, a former worker broke into a song that almost sixty years earlier had circulated among his colleagues on the Ji'nan machine shop floor: "Even without skills they [the GMD] are able to rise to the top [of the factory management] . . . workers with dirty hands have such a tough time, while those with clean hands treat us worse than they treat even dogs."[27] The song expresses deep contempt for the white-collar management of the factory, which by then had become synonymous with GMD members. When the city of Ji'nan was taken over by Communist troops in 1948, many skilled workers, and especially salaried employees, left the Jin-Pu Railroad and either accompanied the GMD retreat to Taiwan or went abroad.

After the Communist victory in 1949, reorganization of the railroad sector involved a return to the former classification and terminology of bureaus (*ju*) instead of regions (*qu*).[28] Representative of the centrally directed reorganization at the time, the Ji'nan Railroad Bureau, as the administrative headquarters of the Jin-Pu line, established the CCP's presence and institutional integration by creating a parallel party structure copying the line's operational organization. Ji'nan became the seat of the line's party committee, supplemented by separate party committees for the branch bureaus in Qingdao, Xuzhou, and Bengbu. By 1951, the Ji'nan Railroad Bureau was absorbed into the Shandong Railroad Bureau, under direct supervision by the central party committee of the Ministry of Railways.[29]

Numerous administrative changes occurred during the following years, ever deepening the reach of the party into each administrative and operational level of the railroad line; in 1957 the party committee of the Ji'nan Railroad Bureau oversaw 18 general party branches (*dangzong zhibu*) with 118 party branches (*dang zhibu*), compared to a total of only 37 party branches in late 1949. To further illustrate this development, on the eve of the Great Leap Forward in 1957, the existence of 614 branches (76 general branches and 538 party branches) ensured CCP control over the Ji'nan Railroad Bureau system, the Jin-Pu line, and other Shandong lines under its jurisdiction. Indicating even greater centralization of the economic and managerial aspects of the railroad bureau system, four separate party committees directly oversaw the administrative body of the four branches of the railroad bureau in Ji'nan, Xuzhou, Qingdao, and Bengbu, with a separate party committee in charge of the railroad bureau's managerial organization.[30]

### Economic Recovery and Technical Aid

Like every other administrative institution and production unit in the country, railroad bureaus not only had to adapt their overall strategies for passenger and freight transportation but, by extension, for their management and mission to fulfill the new political directives. Railroads had to respond both to the new demands originating from China's domestic economic development goals and to the external political challenges emerging during the early Cold War years.

On the domestic front, in the First Five-Year Plan (1953–1957) railroads were designated to support industrial development. Although the drafting of the plan had begun in 1951, several revisions and adjustments delayed its official completion until 1955, when the plan had already been in operation for two years.[31] Industrial construction was at the center of the plan, receiving 56 percent of total capital investments for economic construction and cultural and educational development during the five years. Departments in charge of transport, postal services, and telecommunications received only 19 percent of the investment funds, compared with 58 percent for the industrial departments.[32] According to the plan, "Capital investment in transport in our First Five-Year Plan is also not large, but it can, in the main, satisfy the needs of the First Five-Year Plan period and the initial stage of the Second Five-Year Plan."[33] Whereas the expansion and renewal of the railroad network was not an explicit focus, the plan projected 2,500 miles of new railroad tracks as well as rail reconstruction work, including modifying some single-track lines to become double tracks. By the end of the First Five-Year Plan, total operating mileage had increased by approximately 2,400 miles, of which 500 miles consisted of new double- or multitrack sections.[34] Electrification of the Chinese rail system did not take place until 1962, with a meager 60 miles of electrified lines. This situation did not improve significantly until the beginning of the economic reforms in 1978.[35]

For industrial construction, there were great hopes that new plants and mines would be built with the help of Soviet technology. In a spirit of economic autonomy and self-reliance, output from the integrated and reconstructed Anshan Iron and Steel Works was expected to finally enable the domestic production of locomotives, motor vehicles, and rails.[36] The need for new rolling stock to replace the equipment that had been damaged or destroyed during the anti-Japanese and civil wars was particularly pressing. At the end of 1945, modest funding made available by the United Nations Relief and Rehabilitation Administration allowed urgent railroad repairs and support for 240 new engines, 3,500 rail carriages, and more than 80,000 tons of tracks. The new equipment almost exclusively benefited railroads in the south under GMD control, such as the Yue-Han and the Guangzhou-Kowloon lines, where there was no Communist military presence at the time.[37]

The great financial and material needs of China's railroad sector and the potential for future business opportunities were not lost on foreign manufacturers and rail industry associations that in great detail assessed the new export opportunities from China's postwar economic reconstruction. For example, H. J. von Lochow, an "Erstwhile Adviser to the Chinese Ministry of Communications and First Councillor of German State Railways," wrote a treatise that laid out China's railroad development during the war and its ongoing postwar reorganization for an international audience of railroad professionals.[38] Focusing directly on future business opportunities, John Earl Baker, rail expert and also former adviser to the Chinese rail administration, addressed American industry associations with estimates of equipment, tracks, and ties in need of replacement and the costs for Chinese buyers.[39] Interestingly, similar to the early Republican period, debates again emerged about whether to use specific technical standards to secure future supply chains and limit competition in the Chinese market. This view was vehemently defended by the former commercial attaché in China, Julean Arnold, who believed that British and European competition would outbid American firms for new equipment. He argued, "By selling China our outmoded equipment, suitable for China's needs for some time to come, we can establish our [American] standards."[40]

The First Five-Year Plan also identified four new railroad projects of massive scale and scope with respect to track mileage and construction challenges that would integrate the interior provinces or remote regions without existing rail links into the national railroad grid and thus help consolidate central state power. Line construction from Lanzhou in Gansu province to Urumqi in Xinjiang province, from Baoji in Shaanxi province to Chengdu in Sichuan province, and from Yingtan in Jiangxi province to Xiamen in Fujian province was completed in the late 1950s and early 1960s (see Map 7.1). Line construction to Erenhot at the northern border with the People's Republic of Mongolia was promoted to provide a future link between China and the rail system of the Soviet Union.[41] Not all these lines were totally new initiatives, however. The First Five-Year Plan also revived certain rail projects that the GMD government had already considered to be of great economic and strategic importance. For example, in 1936 Minister of Railways Chang Kia-Ngau had sought financing from a Belgian syndicate for the construction of the Baoji to Chengdu line, which would provide a link to the Long-Hai Railroad, facilitate troop movements, and "help develop the resources of China's great Northwest."[42] He was able to negotiate a loan, but with the beginning of the Japanese invasion in the following year, construction of the line never materialized.[43]

Facing the tremendous challenges of China's postwar economic recovery and knowing that progress would be slow or delayed because of the lack of technical expertise and industrial implementation, Mao Zedong turned to Stalin for help. Mao admired the Soviet industrialization model and obtained Stalin's agreement that beginning in 1948 Soviet advisers, experts, and teachers would be sent to China to help rebuild the economy and to restore enthusiasm and social support. These Soviet experts followed the model of High Stalinism, characteristic of the Soviet Union's own economic recovery after World War II, which emphasized strong party leadership in government and all realms of life.[44]

The contrast between China's and the Soviet Union's development and condition of their respective railroad systems could not have been greater.

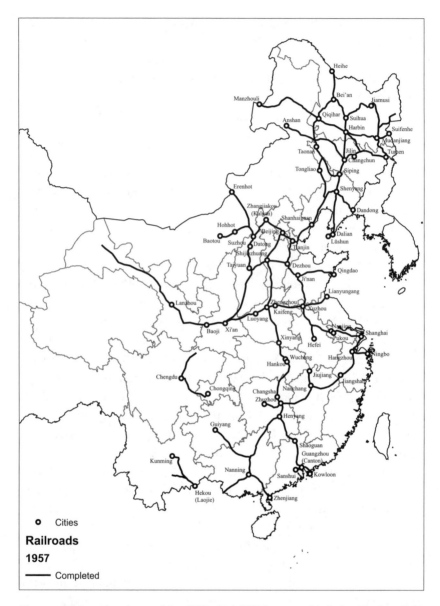

**Map 7.1**   Major railroads, 1957. Map © Elisabeth Köll (cartographic design Matthew Sisk).

From the very first years of Lenin's rule, the Bolsheviks had made the railroad system a major part of their economic planning. Unlike the American experience, however, which resulted in a quickly built but relatively lightly used network, the Soviets focused on intensifying productivity without a corresponding increase in investment. Between 1913 and 1956, railroad freight traffic increased 16 times and passenger traffic increased 5.5 times—yet the relative shares of total investment in transport declined from an average of 23.8 percent between 1918 and 1928 to a low of 10.7 percent in 1933, rising to 20.4 percent during the Soviet Union's Third Five-Year Plan period. Despite the limited resources, railroads absorbed large freight increases, rising from 58,000 million tons per mile in 1928 to 751,000 million tons per mile in 1957—more than the U.S. system transported in 1957.[45] Soviet economists were prone to boast of the superior productivity of their system. "Our country, having a railway network almost ten times less than the remainder of the world, already achieves a freight turnover equal to almost three-quarters of the freight turnover of the remaining world's railways."[46]

To understand Soviet approaches to rail transport, comparisons with the American system are helpful. For one, the productivity of the Soviet system did not extend to labor productivity. In the USSR, wrote one contemporary analyst, "the aim is to get as much use as possible out of equipment, even if this entails a lavish use of labor."[47] In 1955, each Soviet railroad worker produced an average of 97,500 freight tons per mile, whereas his American counterpart produced 352,000 freight tons per mile, more than three times as much. In the same year, the Soviet rail system employed an estimated 4 million workers, at a time when the population was little more than 200 million. The United States, with a population of approximately 165 million, employed just over 1 million railroad workers.[48]

By early 1950, a joint declaration by the Chinese and Soviet governments outlined details for the employment of Soviet experts, including salaries, housing, food, and other subsidies to be paid by the Chinese government.[49] Among the very first Soviet experts in China were approximately 400 engineers and technicians working for the railroads in the Northeast during the transition from Soviet to Chinese control. The nature of the advisers' roles quickly shifted from economic and technical assistance to military concerns when approximately 1,600 Soviet military advisers with navy and air force backgrounds went to China in 1950 at the beginning of the Korean War.[50]

Once the government shifted its focus to economic reconstruction and development during the Chinese First Five-Year Plan, the demand for expertise in electrification, steel production, machine manufacturing, shipbuilding, rail rolling-stock production, and construction projects clearly exceeded the available Soviet assistance. For example, the model Anshan Iron and Steel Works had only 150 experts on site from 1950 to the end of 1952.[51]

Soviet advisers became involved in every aspect of rail transportation, from logistics to repair shops to material supplies. Although charged with specific tasks within the Chinese enterprises, the Soviet experts had limited knowledge about the Chinese political situation on the ground and about local conditions. According to the interviews by comparative historical sociologist Deborah Kaple with former Soviet experts, the latter were impressed by the diligence, accuracy, and dedication of Chinese workers, especially their hard physical labor in the absence of machinery and tools. In particular, they observed that their Chinese coworkers wanted to learn and to apply the results to their tasks as quickly as possible, putting in extremely long workdays.[52] The combined efforts of a dedicated workforce guided by new technical approaches under Soviet expert management led to many productivity records along the railroad lines. For example, in 1951 labor productivity on the Changchun Railroad increased by 28 percent over the previous year, and train dispatches at the Shenyang station rose by more than 60 percent.[53] Some Soviet experts were introduced to new methods of managerial control, such as that by the head of the Changchun Railroad's administrative bureau. He became famous for convening a meeting every morning at ten and scheduling an evening phone-in consultation at nine to check on the dispatch of trains and the logistics work of all branch bureaus.[54] Even if one approaches these data and examples with a healthy dose of skepticism, the Soviet advisers' expertise and the can-do attitude of the Chinese workforce during the early 1950s brought positive improvements to productivity, cost savings, and management of railroad operations.

Within the political framework of Sino-Soviet friendship, as complicated and rocky as it was, the number of technical experts (*jishu zhuanjia*) and advisers (*guwen*) increased steadily, peaking at about 3,500 in late 1956 and early 1957.[55] In the railroad sector, 1957 marked a milestone with the completion and opening of the railroad bridge across the Yangzi River at Wuhan. The public celebration of the bridge, which for the first time allowed rail and road traffic to cross the middle reaches of the river, also included praise and thanks to the Soviet engineers involved in the project.[56] This praise came to a halt when relations between China and the Soviet Union began to deteriorate owing to Khrushchev's denunciation of Stalin in 1956. In addition, radical Chinese political campaigns, such as the Great Leap Forward and irrational demands for ever-faster production, undermined the advisers' technical expertise and instructions and made their work difficult if not impossible. By 1959 only five Soviet advisers were left in China. In 1960 all the remaining technical experts (1,160) were recalled to the Soviet Union.[57]

As tightly structured operational and administrative organizations with an enormous workforce under party control, railroad bureaus across the country in the 1950s developed into large, almost self-sufficient, work units (*danwei*). From the perspective of former workers on the Jin-Pu Railroad, this decade was a golden age for China's railroad reconstruction, which was accompanied by restoration of the professional and social prestige of railroad work. During the 1950s, China's banks, postal services, and railroads were celebrated work units because of their stable work environments and favorable working conditions.[58] Compared with workers in other work units, railroad workers received comparatively high wages and sufficient grain rations, and every year they were entitled to a number of free train tickets. The workers either used the tickets to visit relatives or privately exchanged them for other goods and services.[59] Railroad workers were also able to send their children to the free primary and middle schools attached to the railroad bureaus and to use the medical services of the railroad hospitals that were part of every large rail compound.

Former workers fondly remember the return of order and regularity (*zhengchang*) to the shop floors and to railroad operations in general, reviving their professional pride as skilled workers with job stability (*wending*) and security (*anquan*).[60] Nevertheless, like all other work units, the Jin-Pu Railroad Bureau and its workforce were drawn into the political developments of the time. Because of the significance of railroads for military logistics, railroad workers, particularly from railroad trunk lines in the North and Northeast, were encouraged to sign up for service in the Korean War, which began to unfold in the summer of 1950. Party-directed propaganda extolled the virtues of Chinese participation on the side of North Korea in the war against U.S. imperialism and praised the superhuman efforts by railroad workers at all hierarchical and managerial levels in support of the war effort. In November 1950 *Renmin ribao* (*People's Daily*) published elaborate descriptions of such efforts under the headline "Railroad Workers in Battle at the Frontline of National Defense," citing the example of an office worker who never left her office so as to answer every telephone call and to distribute information.[61] The paper commented patronizingly that "she understands that the telephone is the central nerve [*shenjing*] of railroads and plays an important part in fulfilling logistical tasks."[62] The virtues of the railroad, such as the workers' economical use of materials, speed, and efficiency, were directly linked to the success of the war effort, or in the brutal words of party propaganda, "every piece of saved coal kills another invading American soldier."[63]

Considering these party and patriotic pressures, it is not surprising that 48 percent of the 15,918 workers at the Ji'nan Railroad Bureau registered as volunteers for deployment on the Korean front, and approximately 3,000 workers were actually recruited in October 1950.[64] Not much later, as part of the wider rectification campaign, the CCP began to introduce class identification within the Ji'nan Railroad Bureau through its party representatives to create categories for the future class struggle. By April 1951, approximately 2,500 workers and employees were classified as "counterrevolutionaries" (*fan geming fenzi*). It seems plausible that the bureau's many so-called counterrevolutionaries reflected the large share of skilled workers and engineers with professional training and expertise that had been acquired during the Nationalist regime.[65] Of course, the prestige of the skilled railroad workers and technical employees began to seriously deteriorate when the radical campaigns of the Anti-Rightist Movement and the Great Leap Forward changed the party's political attitudes toward expertise and knowledge in 1957 (see Chapter 8).

## The Arm of the Army

As a major aspect of the post-1949 reorganization, the national railroad administration underwent a militarization that supported military defense, increased political education, and extended its representation throughout the network. Aside from their economic functions, railroads were considered strategic tools for national defense and political stabilization by offering improved passenger and freight services and directly extending the power of the CCP and the government into the most far-flung parts of the nation.

Executing huge, ambitious rail construction projects in remote areas of the country required a large, disciplined, and dedicated workforce willing to operate under often inhospitable and even dangerous conditions. Throughout the 1950s the railroad system had become home for PLA members demobilized after World War II and the Korean War. To expedite strategic rail infrastructure projects, in 1953 the central army committee decided to establish the railroad army corps (*tiedaobing*) as a centralized military vanguard for constructing new railroad lines in south, central, and western China.[66] The organizational origins of the *tiedaobing* can be found in the "railroad columns" (*tiedao zongdui*) of soldiers. The PLA mobilized these soldiers to repair sections of damaged railroad tracks in the Northeast that were of strategic importance to the advance of the Communist troops in 1948.[67] Renamed the railroad corps (*tiedao bingtuan*) after the end of the civil war in 1949, they continued to repair and construct railroads until they were officially integrated into the PLA as Zhongguo renmin jiefangjun tiedaobing (Chinese People's Liberation Army railroad soldiers).[68]

By combining centrally directed construction and a military presence, this strategic approach enabled the building of ambitious railroad projects in difficult terrains, such as the 1,200-mile-long line from Lanzhou to Urumqi, built between 1952 and 1962, and the 705-mile-long Chengdu-Kunming Railroad completed in 1970.[69] Both construction projects carried strategic significance for the military because for the first time they created rail links to sensitive border areas in Xinjiang province connecting to the Soviet Union, Afghanistan, Pakistan, and India and in Yunnan province connecting to Vietnam, Laos, and Burma. The railroad construction projects also addressed current and future political hotspots during the Cold War: in the south, the line to the coast of Fujian province was to support plans to invade Taiwan, and the line to the border with Vietnam was built to provide bulk supplies to Ho Chi Minh in his struggle against the French colonial government and later on against the South Vietnamese government (see Map 7.1).[70]

Railroad construction enabled and executed by the railroad army corps brought the politics and culture of the new socialist nation-state to the interior and to the borders. To illustrate the modus operandi of the railroad army corps in its interactions with local society during the construction process and the professional background of its members, I describe a case study focusing on Yang Baoqing, a retired *tiedaobing*.[71] His life and career are representative of men who joined the railroad army corps after 1949 and who maintained a lifelong identification with the organization. Yang was born in 1931 in Anhui province, the son of a farmer, and had five siblings. He attended a privately organized primary school for two years, followed by one and a half years in a government-run primary school. When he was eighteen years old, he became a soldier and, with the blessing of his father who supported the CCP, he joined the Communist guerrillas (*youjidui*) in the mountains of Anhui to fight the GMD during the civil war from 1947 to 1948. After the 1949 revolution, he became a regular member of the PLA and in early 1952 he served in the Korean War. Fortunately, he worked in the army's accounts office issuing pay for soldiers in yuan and won and he did not see military action at the front. Following demobilization, in 1954–1955 he worked as a *tiedaobing* in Henan province where, because of his educational background, he managed the account books and financial records for construction projects.

Yang Baoqing's career path reminds us that many of the soldiers, especially those from rural guerrilla backgrounds, were illiterate or barely literate. Therefore, the army considered even a modest level of education to be a valuable human resource for assuming managerial responsibilities. As a PLA soldier, Yang was required to spend three months of every year at the railroad construction site engaged in some form of manual labor. After completing work in Hebei, until his retirement Yang and his family were relocated to work on construction projects for new lines in Shanxi, Guangxi, Fujian, Hebei, Jiangxi, and Sichuan provinces.[72]

According to Yang Baoqing, engineers on projects for new lines were dispatched centrally by the Ministry of Railways. Many of the younger Chinese engineers of the 1950s and 1960s had been trained at newly reorganized railroad academies (*tielu xueyuan*), such as the institutes in Tangshan and Shijiazhuang. In the 1950s, the monthly pay for an ordinary soldier (*zhanshi*) in the railroad army corps was 5 to 6 yuan; a military or party cadre earned a monthly wage of approximately 50 yuan. For actual construction work, such as digging the road bed, the army employed many local, temporary workers (*difang mingong*). Although their pay was low, cash income was an attractive offer to local farmers in remote areas.[73] In fact, because locals competed for jobs that offered cash wages, cadres acting on behalf of the local government would select workers from the poorest local families and recommend that they be hired by the railroad corps. On occasion, temporary workers would also come from outside the county where the construction was taking place.[74]

The PLA maintained a contractual arrangement with the Ministry of Railways regarding overall construction management, with the ministry assigning railroad soldiers to oversee project management of each new line. Accommodations were paid for by the army, but they consisted of what was available locally, which often meant simple shacks or dilapidated houses. *Tiedaobing* families had to buy their own food, but hospital visits were free; if they encountered financial troubles due to illness or other family obligations, they could ask the army administration for financial assistance.[75]

Railroad army soldiers would move together with the construction projects, thus housing and living arrangements were not permanent. When Yang had to move his family to Chengde in Hebei province to build the Jing-Tong Railroad, the entire family and their few belongings were transported in an open cattle carriage to Chengde, where they lived close to the army unit in a rough shed outside the city. According to Yang Baoqing, the lack of adequate schooling was the most serious problem for military families because army children had to make do with (and pay for) whatever education was available locally. The PLA did not provide schools for railroad soldiers because the families were always on the move and the construction projects had limited time horizons. The army provided a kindergarten for the children while the families worked in construction.[76]

Yang Baoqing's work took place in administrative offices as well as on construction sites, which allowed him to experience many different aspects of the projects. Railroad soldiers performed hard, back-breaking daily work because, in the absence of even the most basic mechanical tools and machinery, almost every step in the construction process had to be performed manually. For example, jackhammers were not used until the 1970s, when Japanese tools made their way to the construction sites. Concrete was not used to build tracks until the late 1970s. Before the introduction of concrete, the wooden ties had to be replaced every three or four years, depending on the dryness of the local climate and the quality of the wood. Most of the wood was shipped to the construction sites from forests in the Northeast; the steel for the tracks mainly came from the Anshan Iron and Steel Works. Until their withdrawal in 1960, Soviet advisers worked together with the railroad corps.[77]

Although the work was dangerous and accidents frequently occurred during construction, workers had very little equipment to protect their health and safety. Safety hats were made out of reed, shoes were made out of cloth, and their army uniforms also served as work clothes. During the required three months of labor at the construction site, Yang Baoqing often worked as a supervisor or acted as a liaison among several different construction sections. Coordinating and streamlining complex work processes and the appropriate use of the equipment were crucial not only for efficiency but also for safety, especially when explosives were used to blast tunnels. In addition to work accidents, railroad soldiers and workers were also afflicted with diseases, such as malaria and Dengue fever, which were prevalent in the inhospitable tropical climates. Those *tiedaobing* who died during their work assignments were posthumously referred to as "heroes" and their families were subsequently cared for by the army administration. When locally hired workers died during construction-site work, their families would receive compensation from the PLA. If they survived an accident but became disabled, they received compensation according to the seriousness of their injuries, which the army divided into four categories.[78]

Relations between the railroad soldiers and the local laborers and the general population were not problematic in Yang Baoqing's experience. If workers at construction sites used local dialects, local cadres would help out with the translations. Work on the sites continued nonstop in three shifts, starting with a first shift at 8 a.m. Railroad soldiers worked seven days a week, with no vacation time except for national holidays. Meals were delivered to the site, and at night electric lighting was provided by a generator. The harsh discipline was intended to accelerate the construction work, based on the motto "Explore, design, and build."[79]

During construction, railroad soldiers exerted considerable cultural influence on local society. Most local people at the remote construction sites, such as the mountains of Fujian province, had never before seen a locomotive or traveled by train. For them, contacts with the railroad army corps and observation of the progress on the construction sites brought excitement to their lives. For example, when the locals heard the whistling of the train, people explained it as "the locomotive is hungry and wants to eat." In the spirit of maintaining good community relations, railroad soldiers sometimes gave the local people free train rides on finished track sections before the entire line was opened.[80]

The PLA sent its cultural departments to the railroad army corps at construction sites all over the country where they would perform songs, dramas, and so forth to support the soldiers and also to educate and mobilize the local rural populations.[81] The presence of *tiedaobing* brought films for the first time to many villages in the remote countryside. The films reflected the political friendships between China and various foreign allies, and many were originally from Vietnam, North Korea, Albania, and Romania. According to Yang Baoqing, once a week a movie would be shown outdoors for the general entertainment of the villagers.[82]

The most visible interaction between local society and the government occurred at the opening ceremony (*kaigong*) of new line projects, complete with red paper decorations, banners, and other festivities.[83] As highly orchestrated celebrations, these ceremonies incorporated various aspects of traditional village rituals with new, state-sponsored rituals that affirmed the role of the party and the state. The highest-ranking party cadre was given the ceremonial spade for breaking ground. The new political ideology did not permit the selection of auspicious dates based on local or religious traditions for beginning construction work; dates with approved revolutionary or political meaning, such as International Labor Day on May 1, were chosen to begin the construction work. The ceremony after completion of a railroad line was even more elaborate. The act of connecting the final two rails (*tongche*) from the opposing directions was accompanied by celebrations evocative of marriage rituals. After the tracks were united, the locomotive would undertake its maiden voyage, festively decorated in red and often adorned with portraits of Mao Zedong and other party leaders on the front of the engine.[84]

Any new railroad line had a substantial trial period. Quality control was a constant concern for the railroad army corps. Once the construction of a line was officially completed, the *tiedaobing* left the site and handed the tracks over to the new railroad line administrative office, which managed the transition during the test period. Yang Baoqing remembers that a concrete bridge had to be blown up because it was not sufficiently stable. After one to two years (sometimes even longer) of testing, the administrative office handed the line back to the Ministry of Railways, which then began management.[85]

As an accountant, Yang Baoqing helped manage the budget for building the railroads and during our interviews he recalled the cost structure of the process. Constructing the road bed was the most expensive part of the project. If there were houses in the way of a projected railroad line, the owners received cash payments in exchange for their relocation. It is interesting that the PLA used a very careful approach when dealing with gravesites that occupied land marked for railroad construction. As a general rule, farmers received compensation for the gravesite land, but most importantly, the railroad administration also helped with the removal of the graves to other sites. If there were local concerns about the feng shui of a proposed line, the leaders of the railroad corps tried to engage the local people in conversation in order to dispel any fears. However, as Yang admitted, feng shui concerns remained strong in rural China in the 1950s. The PLA railroad corps had no qualms about destroying small, insignificant temples if they stood in the way of construction, but larger and more important temples were bypassed by track lines. According to Yang Baoqing's recollections, even the hardened *tiedaobing* were anxious when dealing with important temple structures, and they feared that accidents would occur in retribution for the demolition.[86]

The harsh living conditions, local isolation, and frequent forced mobility created a strong group identity and tight personal networks among the *tiedaobing* and their families. In fact, to this day former members of the railroad corps and their relatives are organized in associations, complete with reunions, commemorative trips, songs, pictures, and narratives shared via their websites and publications.[87] The strong attachment of the railroad soldiers to their work experience and their pride and dedication were framed by their distinct military identity. Yang Baoqing told me that he was a soldier (*junren*) first and a railroad accountant second. For example, when his children went to meet him on a return home, he would not hug them because this was considered improper behavior for men wearing military uniforms.[88]

Adherence to military discipline under all circumstances—geographical, environmental, cultural, or political—was characteristic of the railroad soldiers' approach to work. During their work, no matter where they were, they observed strict military discipline. To some extent, the overall discipline at work carried over into their personal lives, as loyalty, friendship, and mutual support among soldiers provided the stability and normalcy that was often missing from their working and living conditions. This strong bond of camaraderie did not lead to many intermarriages among families from the railroad corps, however. The next generation of sons and daughters perceived the frequent moves as a hardship, and they were eager to find stable work in an urban environment.[89] With the majority of the high-stakes railroad construction projects either under way or completed by the mid-1980s, the railroad army corps was officially disbanded as part of the PLA in 1984. The civilian construction tasks of the corps were merged with the Ministry of Railways, and beginning in 1990 they were handled by the newly established China Railway Construction Corporation under the supervision of the ministry.[90]

### The Engine That Could: Railroads as Socialist Metaphors

Fulfilling much-needed construction tasks and, as a by-product, offering political education for the local population, the presence of the railroad army corps ensured the reach of the party and state into the countryside and peripheral areas. At the same time, the image of the railroad, or its abstract metaphor, underwent unprecedented levels of representation in the books, propaganda posters, films, theater, and even music of the 1950s and 1960s. Engines, tracks, and the railroad workforce evolved into perfect metaphors to visualize the virtues and goals associated with the building of a new socialist society in China: the railroads represented the speed, economic efficiency, punctuality, discipline, technological advances, professionalism, dedication, and heroism necessary to promote the ideals of the party and the government at large.[91]

Celebration of heroes in railroad construction was generally deserved because so many of the new construction projects in the 1950s and early 1960s required exhausting physical labor in inhospitable environments with considerable danger to the lives and well-being of the workers and engineers. Explosions when digging tunnels, accidents involving heavy equipment, falling rocks and mudslides, and illnesses at high altitudes or in tropical climates were only a few of the causes of death among a considerable number of railroad workers and army soldiers. Their ultimate sacrifice for construction of the new railroads was commemorated with monuments erected along the lines, declaring them to be "revolutionary martyrs" (*geming lieshi*). Many of these monuments lie along the Chengdu-Kunming Railroad in the southwestern border region, where a particularly challenging terrain, with mountain cliffs, many tunnel excavations, and an inhospitable climate, caused frequent accidents.[92] The martyr monuments carry statements such as "died for the people" (*wei renmin er si*) and they list the names of those who gave their lives. For example, the text on one stone monument commends the bravery of the PLA railroad soldiers who died during a violent flash flood and mudslide as they attempted to save the lives of other workers at the site.[93]

The martyr monuments describe the railroad workers' revolutionary spirit as "fearing neither hardship nor death" (*bu pa ku, bu pa si*) and frame their sacrifice as service for the greater good of the country and its socialist reconstruction.[94] The public commemorations and elevation of the reputation of the workers through stone monuments were not an invention of the Communist Party; rather, they had much earlier precedents. During the Eastern Han period (AD 25–220), stele inscriptions commemorated famous officials who had arranged and supervised road construction and thus improved the livelihood of the local population.[95] Of course, at that time conscript laborers performed the actual road work for projects initiated by local officials or by imperial orders. After their death, these local officials often became gods and objects of local cults.[96] Although monuments to railroad martyrs have not developed cultlike status in local society, the official elevation of accidental deaths to a heroic "dying for the people is weightier than Mount Tai" implies a sort of revolutionary apotheosis.[97] Contemporary descendants of former railroad soldiers are attempting to document their family histories through visits to these monuments and often complain on websites that the monuments should be better preserved in accordance with the heroism of their forebears.

Metaphorically and practically, railroads also became crucial transmitters of the new time standard introduced after the founding of the People's Republic. Before 1949 (see Chapter 4) China had been divided into five time zones, but because the existing railroad network hardly extended beyond the coastal eastern zone, time differences did not affect train schedules. According to Guo Qingsheng, the term "Beijing time" (*Beijing shijian*) was used for the first time by the People's Broadcasting Station in Xi'an on October 7, 1949.[98] In the following weeks, provincial capitals in the interior, such as Chengdu in Sichuan province, announced the official use of Beijing time, and by early 1950 all provinces in China, with the exception of Xinjiang and Tibet, used Beijing time as a nationwide, unified time standard. Tibet adopted Beijing time in 1960, whereas Xinjiang used Beijing time only for the operation of government offices, railroads, and the postal system, and it was only allowed to use Urumqi time (two hours behind Beijing time) informally.[99]

The use of a unified standard time was important for rebuilding the expanding national railroad system. As early as November 1949 railroad bureaus began to add comments to their train schedules informing passengers about any discrepancy between local time and Beijing time and the newly adopted standard.[100] From an operational perspective, use of one time zone instead of working with five different time zones facilitated freight and passenger transportation schedules, especially as the rail network expanded into the northwestern and southwestern interior regions.

Punctuality as part of railroad time discipline became an important aspect of the metaphorical role of railroads, signaling professionalism, respect for operational and managerial standards, and dedication to providing quality services. For example, issues related to punctuality and time management appeared prominently in the 1951 film *Nü siji* (Female engine driver), whose story focuses on a group of women undergoing training to become engine drivers on trains in China's Northeast. The women, especially the protagonist, dedicate themselves to their careers through "education by the Communist Party and assistance from the Soviet Union," as personified by a younger Soviet engineer with technical expertise and a skilled Chinese railroad worker with thirty years of experience.[101]

The film is a tool of propaganda in that it demonstrates the ambitious plans of the party to improve the skills and technical knowledge of the railroad workforce, which, in turn, would contribute to building the new socialist society and China's economic progress. At the same time, the film introduces the multilayered world of railroad work, as performed on shop floors and in locomotives, classrooms, and offices, with its own code of behavior and work ethic. The focus on punctuality and time management is striking. When the women have to pass the practical part of their exam by driving an engine on their own and on time, concerned telephone time checks from the station headquarters remind the audience of the seriousness of the exam. The story climaxes when the protagonist, after saving the lives of two farmers and their donkey stuck on the tracks by applying the brakes in time, arrives at the train's final destination on time by driving the engine at full speed. The virtue of time discipline thus ideally serves the technical operations without compromising service to the people.[102]

On a practical note, railroads also required tools for timekeeping. Large clocks were displayed at both old and new railroad stations to convey the time. But away from the stations, how did the workforce keep track of time? Wrist watches were still a luxury in 1951 and not affordable for most Chinese workers. Films and posters depict skilled workers using pocket watches on the job, and wrist watches were suitable for the elevated social status of engineers and technicians, both Soviet and Chinese.[103] The film *Tekuai lieche* (Express train) from 1965 addresses time discipline from a passenger perspective. The train attendants and conductors not only heroically save the life of an injured PLA soldier by delivering him to a hospital but they also treat passengers from all walks of life both courteously and professionally. Asked by an old farmer about the train's arrival time and onward connections at a particular station, the young, inexperienced train attendant, lacking intricate knowledge of the various timetables, is able to offer information only in vague terms. When the senior train manager gently corrects her, she earnestly promises the passengers "to guarantee not to use the words 'at about' [*cha bu duo*] and 'roughly' [*dagai*] in the future."[104]

In terms of new gender roles and equal employment opportunities, China's railroad sector early on introduced new workplace role models who represented the political and social aspirations of the new government. Before 1949 very few women worked for the Chinese railroad lines. But a small number of women found employment as kindergarten teachers or nurses in the schools and hospitals attached to the railroad compounds, and a few women had jobs as secretaries or accountants in the railroad administrative departments.[105] The composition of the workforce changed dramatically in the 1950s. For example, Li Shi, the first female engine driver apprentice, graduated to full engine driver status with much fanfare on National Day in 1951.[106] In the following year, railroad work units across the country began to employ women in all aspects of railroad-related work, especially in the service sector as train conductors, station personnel, ticket sellers, and administrators.

As a visual representation of its goals, the Ministry of Communications and Transportation introduced an official emblem to represent China's national railroad administration in January 1950. The red sign consists of an abstract locomotive formed by the Chinese character indicating a person (*ren*) embracing a steel rail, symbolizing the people's embrace of its national railroad system in a clever and meaningful way (see Figure 7.3).[107] The emblem developed into one of the most ubiquitous symbols in China's public space, identifying anything related to the government's rail transportation and administration, including railroad bureaus and offices, related enterprises, train and station signage, uniforms, and publications.

Trains and speed, symbolizing revolutionary fervor, also inspired popular songs, such as "Huoche xiangzhe Shaoshan pao" (The train to Shaoshan), celebrating Mao Zedong's birthplace in Hunan province. This extremely popular song from 1967 at the beginning of the Cultural Revolution translated speed and train movements into music and also presented the train

**Fig. 7.3** Signage for Shanghai Railroad Bureau subdivisions, displaying national railroad symbol, 2017. Photograph © Elisabeth Köll.

journey as a multiethnic experience, bringing passengers into contact with minority groups and their cultures.[108] The song captured the desire for freedom and adventure in the spirit of the revolution at a time when young Red Guards were traveling throughout the country and were experiencing for the first time exposure to different ethnic groups and minority regions.

## Conclusion

The 1950s were an important decade in the reorganization of China's railroad sector and its adaptation to the economic and political demands of the new PRC government and the Communist Party. The transition from the last years of the civil war to the early 1950s demonstrates that centralization and consolidation of railroad lines into one national network was a highly complex task because of the different political experiences of the railroad bureaus and their workforce during the war. As I have shown, the decision of Chinese railroad workers to support the Communist cause was not always an ideologically motivated decision; rather, it could also be influenced by economic hardship and the desire for a political alternative. This presents a significant aspect of my argument: in the broader context of Chinese postwar history, the reorganization of rail administration and railroad companies was not a straightforward story of GMD failure and Communist takeover followed by institutional adaptation for the realization of CCP goals.

Economic reconstruction and the government's plan to introduce industrialization as rapidly as possible presented major challenges but also great opportunities for China's railroads. On the one hand, much hard manual work was required to repair the war-damaged network because of scarce machinery and little modern technical and managerial expertise. The assistance of Soviet experts helped improve the productivity of logistics operations and efficiency in equipment maintenance, but the departure of the Soviets did not lead to a decline in the rail sector. On the other hand, the desire of the party and the government to compensate for the lack of appropriate capital investments by focusing on the mass mobilization of workers and any available resources meant that new railroad construction was undertaken. Certainly, railroad expansion served the goals of the First Five-Year Plan to accelerate industrialization and was aligned with PRC interests regarding national defense. The "outsourcing" of railroad construction to the PLA in many ways was a brilliant move because it allowed a riskier approach for the construction of new lines, while also providing the benefits of the disciplined work ethic of railroad soldiers and the mobility of the military. At the same time, the experiences of former *tiedaobing* on construction sites also demonstrated that certain issues related to railroad construction, such as negotiating land acquisitions, hiring local labor, and interacting with the local population, were not fundamentally different from the practices employed during the Republican period. Railroad soldiers brought economic and social change to the local communities indirectly via rail construction, but they also came to be seen as state protectors and mediators, without their own entrenched interests in railroad development.

Finally, the decade of reconstruction also reframed the identity of railroads as administrative and managerial institutions and aligned them with the new socialist vision of the Chinese state. Values such as discipline, managerial efficiency, punctuality, and so forth, which during the Republican period were interpreted as virtues of Western modernity and technological progress, were now reinterpreted as values representing the goals of revolutionary socialism. This reinterpretation and transfer of values from Western to socialist modernity conformed with the economic goals established in the First Five-Year Plan, but it also helped create an identity for railroad workers based on expertise, skills, and professional dedication to their work. Chapter 8 explores how railroad workers and rail operations reacted when their technocratic orientation came under attack by the destructive influence of the political radicalism on China's railroad network during the Great Leap Forward and the Cultural Revolution.

## CHAPTER EIGHT

# Permanent Revolution and Continuous Reform

As an important part of China's economic and social reconstruction, railroads did not escape the reach of the mass political campaigns of the late 1950s and 1960s. Rendering services to achieve the economic and political goals of the Great Leap Forward (1958–1961) and the Cultural Revolution (1966–1976), railroads simultaneously became both agents and victims of these destructive campaigns. During the Great Leap Forward, the misguided policies of mass mobilization to jump-start high-growth industrial production and rural collectivization to guarantee food self-sufficiency resulted in disastrous costs: millions of farmers in the countryside died from starvation.[1] This utopian experiment promoted by Mao Zedong so severely reduced economic productivity that it took until 1965 for grain and industrial output to return to their 1956 yields.[2] The economic stagnation of the early Cultural Revolution years was due to the disruption of transportation networks and the lag in industrial production in urban factories because of the focus on nonstop revolutionary activism. Although industrial-growth rates were back on target by 1969, a total politicization of society, in combination with a shortage of talent due to the closure of the university system, produced long-lasting effects on China's economic development.[3]

As seen in Chapter 7, the bureaucratic reorganization of the rail network after 1949 was swift, and it successfully integrated Chinese Communist Party (CCP) branches into the local levels of the railroad bureaus. The First Five-Year Plan (1953–1957), based on the Soviet model, generated a highly centralized planning system, with production and financial goals for the regional railroad bureaus set by the Ministry of Railways, which was also the recipient of all their revenue. Use of the construction corps of the People's Liberation Army (PLA) to realize ambitious track expansion and intensive cultivation of railroad workers' public image as the revolutionary vanguard contributed to creating a top-down centralized rail administration that had a strong institutional and professional identity. The regional railroad bureaus did not have any financial autonomy, but the local leaders and the branch offices and stations along the lines were able to incorporate some local concerns into their operational tasks and services.

This chapter addresses the Chinese government's experimentation to undo and then reestablish central authority over the railroad system. In keeping with the institutional focus of this study, I discuss how the Great Leap Forward and the Cultural Revolution forced changes on China's railroads in terms of their bureaucratic organization, capacity for goods and passenger transportation, operational efficiencies, and maintenance of physical assets. I argue that China's rail administration served the political campaigns as an instrumental tool for human and economic mass mobilization. At the same time, the railroad system, like all other state economic institutions, suffered greatly from structural changes and from demands motivated purely by political goals without consideration for efficiency or economic balance.

The forced embrace of these campaigns' political strategies by the railroads is not surprising, but the nature of the highly skilled and professional railroad workforce added further complexity to the process. As discussed in the first two sections of this chapter, professional expertise and specialization were considered counterrevolutionary, and because managerial and operational changes reflected such attitudes, there was a higher accident rate as well as dangerous inefficiencies during the Great Leap Forward. This pattern carried over to the Cultural Revolution when millions of Red Guards enjoyed free train travel to bring the permanent revolution to every part of the nation. Former rail workers whom I interviewed reported they were horrified by the abuse of the rolling stock without regard for technical maintenance and economic capacity. In addition, as professionals and expert technicians they hated being under the command of cocky teenage Red Guards who commandeered the train schedules.

The officially sanctioned use of trains as a revolutionary device offers us an opportunity to explore the travel experiences of the Red Guards and other passengers at the time. As I show, train travel became a metaphor for youthful awakening and adventure combined with dutiful exploration of the motherland, especially its more remote areas. During the 1960s, cross-country train travel, as a novel experience, brought engagement with the frontier areas and the ethnic minorities into the consciousness of the young travelers. In fact, national ethnic harmony mediated by the rail infrastructure became part of the political ideology of the Cultural Revolution. The trips by urban youths sent down to the countryside of far-flung provinces, such as Guangxi, Sichuan, or Heilongjiang, always began with train travel. In such cases, the train also often symbolized a cultural outpost for despondent students who were not permitted to leave their rural work assignments at will. Many had to wait for years after 1976 to return to their families in the cities, and some were never allowed to return.

The last two sections of this chapter move the narrative to the period of reform following Mao Zedong's death in 1976. Charged with the huge task of normalizing economic and political developments, Deng Xiaoping immediately recognized the importance of a well-functioning rail sector for economic growth. Section 3 discusses how normalization of rail transportation became a cornerstone of Deng's reform policy at both a pragmatic and an ideological level. Recentralized as a government body under the State Council in 1978, the Chinese railroad administration was transformed into a massive bureaucracy with more than three million employees; institutionally, it resembled a state within the state. Supported by a comprehensive system of social services, from hospitals to educational institutions, the railroad administration was also in charge of its own police force, courts, and prisons. As a socialist work unit with explicit judicial and executive functions, China's railroad sector, with bureaus at the local and regional levels under the Ministry of Railways, became a hugely self-sufficient and insular economic and administrative monopoly. The resultant lack of transparency and institutional inertia created challenges with which the rail sector in China today is still coping.

The final section of this chapter completes the book's narrative by briefly addressing the more recent reform efforts in China's rail sector, including growth of the high-speed rail network and ongoing attempts to introduce economic incentives for greater private investment. Because both private and foreign investment depend on reform of the state-owned enterprise model, railroads have now entered a phase of permanent reform. To that end, the

2013 elimination of the Ministry of Railways appears to be a major change. In its stead, the China Railway Corporation is now charged with running the national railroad system, and the administrative functions of the former Ministry of Railways are under the Ministry of Transport. Despite these institutional changes, very little private investment has occurred, and the government's tight grip over the sector has not been relaxed. The integration of the railroad network into the One Belt, One Road initiative under President Xi Jinping's leadership in 2015, designed to connect China with the economies in Asia, Europe, and even Africa, is confirmation of this trend. Finally, from a historical perspective, the similarities with earlier visions of China's economic and political reach through rail expansion during the Republican period are striking and allow for historical comparisons beyond the twentieth century.

## Mobility and the Great Leap Forward

After China's intervention in the Korean War and with its increasing tensions with the Soviet Union following Stalin's death in 1953, Mao Zedong began to steer China's political direction toward a new domestic goal of self-sufficiency. Mao's Great Leap Forward policy attempted to maximize agricultural production in the countryside through large-scale farm collectivization and the establishment of "people's communes" (*renmin gongshe*). China's industrial self-sufficiency was to be achieved via small but ultimately inefficient furnaces to produce steel. Railroads, as the most important means of transportation, were an integral part of both of these programs because of their assigned tasks of moving the projected massive grain surplus from the countryside to the cities.[4]

Before analyzing the socioeconomic effects of the Great Leap Forward on rail transportation, we will review mobility in the early 1950s. It is important to note that in contrast to the draconian control of mobility between rural and urban areas during the Great Leap Forward, movement of the population was not officially restricted during the first years of Communist rule. Railroads provided a high level of individual mobility between rural and urban areas during the first years of the PRC's reconstruction, particularly along the northern and northeastern corridors where the railroad network was well developed and damage from the war was repaired fairly rapidly. In fact, in the early 1950s both workers and the unemployed traveled to Beijing and other large cities in search of employment or improved opportunities.[5] A major reason for this high level of mobility was that, contrary to later developments, the *hukou* system, or household registration, in those years was designed to alleviate food shortages and to "ensure public security, not to restrict movement between city and countryside."[6]

Railroads provided the transportation for this unbridled mobility that enabled people to escape hardship and to move to the cities. So many moved to the large cities that in the early 1950s refugees from the countryside presented a major problem for the new PRC government. War refugees had received money for transportation and food to enable them to return to their home villages in the Northeast in early 1949.[7] The dire circumstances in the countryside due to recent droughts and floods, however, only a few months later sent new rural economic refugees to the cities. Tianjin's city government tried to solve the situation through resettlement programs in the interior along the border with Inner Mongolia, offering land to a mix of refugees, unemployed factory workers, and peddlers, to reduce urban pressures.[8] Railroads played a crucial role for the new settlers by providing transportation paid for by the government.

As transportation providers, however, railroads indirectly exacerbated the problems, because they enabled entrepreneurial farmers and unemployed migrants from surrounding counties, and even neighboring provinces, to move to the cities for the sole purpose of taking advantage of the resettlement perks. At the Tianjin train station, some migrants sold their free train tickets home, whereas others actually lived off the practice by moving back and forth between the countryside and the large cities in northern China, claiming travel funds and food for each trip.[9]

The parameters of rural-urban mobility began to change dramatically when, in late 1953, the government established a grain monopoly, thereby forcing farmers to sell their surplus grain to the state at artificially low prices. Designed to ensure provisions for the growing urban populations, this policy caused panic purchasing by residents in the cities and grain hoarding by farmers in the countryside.[10] The grain situation in the cities ultimately stabilized at the expense of declining grain consumption in the villages. Facing increasing food shortages, many farmers decided to live with relatives in the cities, where they hoped to make a living. Another farmer response involved individual (and illegal) transportation of the grain in the cities back to the countryside. The Tianjin train station became a departure hub for farmers who bought large amounts of cornmeal from city residents to take home to their villages to alleviate the food shortages.[11] In response to these violations of grain management that threatened political stability in the cities and food security in the countryside, in July 1955 the central government introduced a new policy that imposed mobility control through the household registration system. By only allowing residents registered in urban households to qualify for urban food rations, the government finally established strict control over mobility between the cities and the countryside.[12]

During the transition leading up to the Great Leap Forward, railroads deported rural migrants from the cities back to their home villages. Despite the restrictive policies, people with a rural *hukou* continued to seek urban refuge from the natural disasters, desperation, and black-market activities in the countryside. During the night, large numbers of migrants would take shelter at the train stations, causing considerable problems for both the city and the railroad administration. City officials appointed to carry out the deportations worked together with the railroad police. For example, in 1957 they arranged trains to deport the 2,700 migrants living at the Tianjin station and to immediately send home any new arrivals.[13] As historian Jeremy Brown notes, some rural migrants tried to escape the watchful eyes of the inspectors at the train stations, posing as legitimate travelers by wearing new clothing and claiming bogus family visits. The massive relocation and on-site population controls at the train stations were generally successful, however, and they even became a model for rounding up and deporting rural migrants and refugees elsewhere in the cities.[14]

State control over rural-urban mobility via grain policies linking food distribution to household registration was, of course, a vital part of the mass collectivization envisioned for the Great Leap Forward in 1958. Whereas Mao saw the Great Leap Forward as a revolutionary movement to make the transition to socialism, economic reformers hoped that the large-scale collectives would yield higher agricultural output to sustain industrialization in the cities. The disastrous economic and social consequences of the Great Leap Forward have been widely discussed in the literature.[15] As is well known, radical collectivization, utopian policies, and misguided production methods resulted in millions of famine victims in the countryside and reduced food supplies in the cities.

Evidence regarding the impact of the Great Leap Forward and the Cultural Revolution on railroad operations is scarce in sources published by the Ministry of Railways and the railroad bureaus.[16] Yearbooks and administrative histories limit entries about these years to only a few lines, with general remarks about operational constraints and the ongoing expansion of the track network. Published railroad sources unsurprisingly fail to mention any operational and managerial effects from these mass campaigns. Such comments would reveal the desperate actions by the impoverished farmers and the ineffective and coerced reactions by government officials, and thus would jeopardize the government's political legitimacy. Several publications geared toward a purely technical readership, however, are surprisingly frank in their assessments and provide some insights into the challenges of rail operations at the time.

According to official railroad statistics, at the end of the First Five-Year Plan in 1957, freight and passenger transport showed impressive figures, indicating the success of the postwar recovery of the network as well as of the general economy during the 1950s. Compared with 1949, the volume of freight transported on Chinese railroads increased approximately fivefold, that of passengers threefold.[17] The government's Second Five-Year Plan, beginning in 1958, prescribed constructing 4,400 to 5,000 miles of new lines and extending them to 44,000 miles within fifteen years, which, according to rail professionals assessing the situation during the post-Mao period, "was obviously a directive impossible to put into practice."[18] The Great Leap Forward targets for all-out steel production put even greater strains on the capacity of rail transportation owing to the insufficient number of locomotives and freight cars. After consultations with the State Council and national meetings for leading cadres in the railroad administration, the Ministry of Railways attempted to address the shortage of rolling stock by reducing the turnaround times for freight and train cars, with different targets to be met by the national network, the railroad bureaus, and the railroad stations. Other solutions included mandating higher speeds for freight trains and increasing the weight of freight. To be able to transport more coal for industrial production, carriages were remodeled and replaced by wooden boxcars. Despite all these improvements, rail-transportation capacity remained strained, especially when compared with the high targets set by the government.[19]

By 1959 the government had to revise downward its monthly quotas for steel, reflecting the low grade of steel production. To support the government's production targets, the railroad administration mobilized party leaders and workers, via numerous emergency meetings, phone conferences, and broadcasts, to respond to party appeals to adopt "coal transportation as the core" (*meiyun wei gang*). Similar to other parts of the government bureaucracy, by 1960 the Ministry of Railways was fully galvanized as an institution embracing mass mobilization under "one party, one people, one line" (*quandang, quanmin, quanlu*) and had its own slogans touting "bumper harvests" (*fengshou*) with regard to transportation productivity and safety records.[20]

In addition to adjusting transport operations because of government pressure to meet the Great Leap Forward targets, the rail system also had to make institutional changes to accommodate central and local initiatives. For example, in June 1958 the previously separate railroad administrative bureaus and engineering bureaus were consolidated into one railroad bureau, with two sets of party leaders representing the central ministry and the local administration. This move can be seen not only as an effort to politically unite administrators and workers but also as a bold attempt to extend the reach of the central government directly into the local railroad bureaus and stations. As a result, every province had its own railroad bureau, increasing the number from seventeen to twenty-nine, and the former branch railroad bureaus were demoted to offices of the railroad bureaus. From the perspective of railroad professionals, these changes weakened the organization of the entire rail system and compromised its centralized dispatch system. In fact, the flow of regular traffic throughout the rail network saw massive transport blockages.[21]

During the Great Leap Forward, regionalism (*diquxing*) in railroad administration became even more pronounced when the central authorities decided to establish transportation command centers (*yunshu zhihuibu*), which were charged with coordinating local resources for mass transportation projects and for building railroads. In the pragmatic spirit of the Great Leap Forward mass mobilization, these joint projects united tens of thousands of locals and soldiers to load and unload rail cars, repair railroad tracks, and so forth. Thereafter, the Ministry of Railways would hold huge mass rallies, together with its administrative collaborators and local command centers, to celebrate the experiences at the work sites and the spirit of struggle and endurance in support of the socialist goals. The authors of a 1994 railroad transportation gazetteer dryly note, however, that "mass mobilization could not solve every problem."[22]

Throughout the years of the Great Leap Forward, the railroad system suffered significantly from the vilification of technical expertise, scientific management, and principles of economic returns, which were deemed "capitalist" and "rightist."[23] This ideological interpretation found further confirmation in the 1958 slogan "destroy restrictions and taboos," which evolved into a campaign targeting complex technical and managerial instructions and guidelines in work units and replacing them with simpler procedures guided by the can-do spirit of the masses and revolutionary dedication.[24]

With respect to the operation of China's railroad system, this campaign led to disastrous consequences. At the top, the Ministry of Railways undertook a revision of the system's guidelines, eliminating a third of its regulatory guidelines, or approximately 1,200 pages of paper.[25] At the lower levels, mechanical workshops and stations adopted the same approach, canceling approximately 90 percent of their written work and safety-procedure regulations. For example, in the spirit of all-out socialist cooperation, the Anshan railroad station in charge of transport arrangements for the massive Anshan Iron and Steel Works in Liaoning province, a core industrial enterprise of the Great Leap Forward, went so far as to eliminate most of the regulatory guidelines ensuring the safety, quality, and economic rationale of its transportation services.[26] As a consequence, there was widespread cutting of corners in the repair of equipment, a decline in the quality of construction and product manufacturing, and neglect of necessary economic planning and vital safety measures. In hindsight, as railroad professionals assessed the precarious situation, "there were no guidelines to be followed, and if there were, they were ignored."[27]

The ideological war on regulations and safety measures turned out to be particularly damaging for the railroad system, because the lack of safety affected not only the workforce on the shop floors but also the passengers on the trains. Official accident statistics from 1950 to 1990 reveal a steady decline in the rate of national rail accidents during the First Five-Year Plan, followed by a steady increase in the rate beginning in 1957 and a dramatic spike in 1960. The accident rate increased by more than 70 percent between 1957 and 1960, with more than six hundred heavy rail accidents (resulting in deaths, injuries, and serious damage) throughout the country.[28] Once the ideological policies that restricted guidelines and safety measures were rescinded in the latter half of the Great Leap Forward, accident rates declined steadily until the chaos of the Cultural Revolution produced a new rise in railroad accidents.

The greatest impact of the Great Leap Forward on China's railroad system did not stem from the government's transport demands in support of industrialization and supply of the urban economies but rather from the politically motivated weakening and destruction of the rational principles that were necessary to operate a large enterprise with a demanding structure of equipment and facilities. The lack of discipline and respect for technical expertise and experience led to horrific accidents, from boiler explosions and fires in warehouses to trains running signals, resulting in huge losses of life and equipment.[29] The amount of rolling stock and equipment that was out of commission was so great that the vice ministers of Railways and Transport brought the problem to the attention of the party leadership at the second Lushan conference in the summer of 1961 when, in a bleak assessment of the economy, human error and lack of responsibility were discussed.[30]

Many ambitious projects, such as tunnels, bridges, and new stations, were also abandoned during construction because of depletion of funds. The political focus of the Great Leap Forward rested on the mobilization of human labor and agricultural production targets; in an interesting contrast, technological modernity was also celebrated in the media as a domestic achievement. Almost daily, newspaper articles reported on the building of new railroads, bridges, and tunnels, hailing the technical aspects of these projects as great examples of the technological progress of China's "democratic dictatorship."[31] According to official railroad sources, however, approximately 63 percent of the investment in railroad construction projects during the Great Leap Forward did not yield any economic returns.[32]

Another failed operational and managerial decision directly connected to the Great Leap Forward was the directive of the Ministry of Railways that railroad repair shops should begin producing railroad cars. Similar to the idea of agricultural collectives producing steel in so-called backyard furnaces, rail shops attached to the railroad bureaus were deemed to be ideal places for industrial production. Of course, maintenance and repair require material and human resources that are quite different from those required for the complex process of manufacturing engines and carriages. Many of the engines that were produced, several hundred according to an official railroad gazetteer, were completely unusable. Attempting to fulfill the demands of the authorities also meant that the maintenance and repair of engines and trains on shop floors were neglected to increase new production figures. Unusable industrial products and neglected maintenance of rolling stock came at a high cost to passenger and worker safety.[33] For example, the quality of the steel rails produced at Anshan Iron and Steel Works deteriorated to such an extent that by 1960 only one-third of the output complied with quality and safety standards.[34]

Although railroads supported the Great Leap Forward by supplying raw materials for industrialization and moving grain from the countryside to the cities, their role in passenger transport was less crucial because of the fiercely restricted mobility, especially from the countryside to the cities. Of course, the most prominent passenger at the time, Mao Zedong, had his own private train, consisting of eleven luxuriously equipped cars.[35] As is well known, Mao often traveled, and he was keen to keep his departures and destinations as secret as possible, so his train was stored in separate facilities at a special station in Fengtai district southwest of Beijing. Mao's train was a physical expression of his ultimate power because it brought rail traffic along the lines to a complete halt during the course of his journeys and disturbed national train schedules for days on end. All the stations along the line would be closed and the platforms would be cleared of travelers and the usual hawkers. Thousands of guards secured his train route, thus incurring considerable cost for the provincial authorities in charge of the routes. To add a touch of reality to the lonely platform scenes, Mao's staff arranged for security officers to pose as food vendors at the stations.[36]

Mao undertook a number of trips during the Great Leap Forward to see for himself how the people's commune experiment was working in reality.[37] As revealed in documentary film clips, during his famous 1958 "nationwide inspection tour," Mao's train would stop in the countryside right next to the fields, where he would disembark and inspect the grain.[38] Although Mao wanted to overcome his isolation and interact with the people and see his experiments for himself, the train as a physical, moving entity provided a protective bubble that allowed eager officials and cadres to set the stage for the observer from the train window. For example, when Mao visited Hubei province during the Great Leap Forward in 1958, the provincial party secretary, Wang Renzhong, ordered local farmers to take rice plants from distant fields and transplant them next to the train tracks in order to convey the impression of a bountiful harvest instead of the reality of the bitter famine.[39] The same staging maneuver was used with regard to the backyard furnaces for steel production. Local party officials ordered furnaces to be built along the rail tracks at regular intervals and peasant women dressed in colorful clothing to work on the furnaces so as to give the impression of a happy and productive environment.[40]

Although it was illegal for farmers to attempt to avoid the famine by moving to the cities, many nevertheless succeeded in escaping the countryside. According to internal documents from 1960, a large number of farmers from Shandong, Hebei, and Henan provinces made their way onto the trains without tickets, trying to reach the better-off areas in the northeast, northwest, or the larger cities.[41] The border areas in particular—such as southern prefectures in Yunnan and in Shenzhen, across the border from Hong Kong, and the northern Ili Kazakh Autonomous Prefecture in Xinjiang, along the border with the Soviet Union—saw substantial "illegal migration" of desperate people.[42]

Railroads felt these developments through the loss of revenue from passenger transport and destroyed freight. Sheer hunger led farmers to take violent action and raid freight trains in search of food. According to an investigation by journalist-turned-historian Yang Jisheng, grain transported along rail lines as well as stored at depots was looted by "bands of farmers."[43] At the same time, drastic steps were taken to prevent farmers from leaving the famine-ridden areas by any form of transportation and escaping to cities where they might receive help and, of even more concern to party leaders, where they would likely spread the news about the catastrophe developing in the countryside. As a result, rail depots, such as the one at Xinyang, a prefectural city in southern Henan province where famine death rates were extraordinarily high, were strictly controlled by the railroad public security bureaus.[44]

Events such as riots at the Wuwei train station in Gansu province in 1961 indicate that security at train stations and train depots became a huge problem for the local and regional railroad administrations. Several hundred looters in Wuwei raided barley and coal from depots as well as waiting trains in both broad daylight and at night. The looters far outnumbered the railroad guards and police, who were unable to halt the plunder. According to an official report from 1961, approximately half of all trains experienced robberies and looting, which increasingly took place in the larger towns. As a result, public order along the railroad lines in Gansu province came to a halt.[45] In some cases, the massive breakdown of public order along railroad lines led to equally massive countermeasures by the government in attempts to reestablish social and political order.

Cases are also known of entire factories and work units systematically stealing material, such as steel, cement, or timber, from stations and railroad depots for their own benefit, often with the approval of their party leaders in the factory and sometimes even in collaboration with the station managers.[46] For example, in late 1961 provincial authorities in Jilin province established a huge joint task force, involving twenty thousand party cadres, to investigate 12,487 locations along the rail network. The operation identified almost ten thousand suspect workers, who were arrested and punished for crimes such as theft, profiteering, smuggling, and the formation of criminal gangs.[47]

Although railroads succeeded in providing an important source of freight transportation for the government by moving grain from the countryside to the cities, not all the ambitious new megaconstruction railroad projects as part of the iron and steel campaign of the Great Leap Forward succeeded. Construction of a line between Chengdu, the capital of Sichuan province, and Dujiangyan, also in Sichuan, moved thousands of farmworkers from the fields to the construction site, which was rigorously controlled by party cadres. The project was a failure in two respects: the massive reduction of farm laborers led to declining agricultural productivity, and the project's technical and construction challenges could not be overcome by the agricultural workers. The line was abandoned before completion.[48]

Finally, the demands by the central government on the rail network to transport grain from the countryside to the cities completely ignored the realities of existing freight and operation capacities. By early 1959 a huge amount of grain was wasted because of the lack of freight cars, and much was left to rot on sidings at railroad stations or even next to the roads leading to the stations owing to the lack of gasoline.[49] As the railroad network became increasingly overwhelmed, even at the train stations of the major cities huge amounts of freight began to pile up, often leading to massive spoilage. For example, in 1960 the train station at Dalian had to deal with seventy thousand tons of unclaimed freight, and the Zhengzhou rail hub along the Tianjin-Pukou line discarded the mounting freight in a ditch.[50]

In light of these operational and logistical obstacles, the recovery of China's rail network, and the national economy in general, presented new challenges once the Great Leap Forward ended in 1961. Growth of the railroad sector was slow, however. According to official statistics, the ratio of investment in railroads as part of overall national investment actually decreased by more than one-half by 1965, making necessary line extensions and improvements to existing lines almost impossible.[51] When the Third Front program began in 1964 (lasting until 1971), railroads became part of a mostly secret development program designed to move China's industrial bases inland as strategic preparation in the event of war with the Soviet Union, which the Chinese leadership at the time perceived to be relatively likely.[52] Because the Third Front program required the mass mobilization of human labor, trains once again became a symbol for connecting the cities with the countryside through the organized movement of people. Urban youths, teens as well as students, were sent to work on rural communes or huge construction projects, and special trains loaded with hundreds of youths would take them to their assignments. The trains would sometimes drop them off at stations far out in the countryside where there was not even a platform.[53] In a way, the trains became the last outpost of civilization, demarcating the separation of the youths' fairly comfortable urban lives and the harsh rural lives awaiting them beyond the train tracks. Such experiences would be repeated by millions of young people when, during the Cultural Revolution, trains delivered sent-down youths to work assignments in the countryside.

## Serving the Cultural Revolution

Whatever recovery the railroad network experienced in the mid-1960s was only an interlude before even more of its operations faced serious challenges when the Cultural Revolution erupted in the summer of 1966. As part of the government administration, railroads were immediately drawn into the political movement as leading cadres at the Ministry of Railways and various regional railroad bureaus were criticized in big-character posters.[54] By August, every work unit within the rail system was following the orders of the party Central Committee, which outlined the goals of the Cultural Revolution, targeting "those within the party who are in authority and are taking the capitalist road."[55] As a result of such political endorsements from the very top of the party, cadres at all levels in the railroad institutional hierarchy were denounced as "black elements" or "capitalist roaders" and were subjected to abuse in the name of Chairman Mao and his movement.[56]

By September 1966, politics began to directly affect the operational side of the railroad network when the State Council announced that any Red Guards who wished to travel throughout the country for the purpose of "igniting the fires of revolution" would be granted free travel, board, and accommodations.[57] In August, when Mao Zedong began to hold mass rallies in Tiananmen Square in support of the Red Guards, railroads were already struggling with a daily increase of two hundred thousand to five hundred thousand passengers taking the train to Beijing.[58] This unrestrained and attractive offer to young people, especially Red Guards, to engage in "revolutionary networking" (chuanlian) throughout the country put extraordinary strains on railroad personnel, equipment, and operational management that almost completely interrupted the network. Passenger cars were destroyed by overuse and overloading, trains were delayed, and freight transport and repair schedules were disrupted with dire consequences.[59] In contrast to the Great Leap Forward, when railroads had to cope in response to the economic and social consequences of the political mayhem, the politics of the Cultural Revolution actively drew railroad operations into the chaos of the movement, especially during the first two years.

Autobiographical descriptions abound of the "revolutionary tourism" by the Red Guards and other youths. Let me here just note several representative examples. Almost all firsthand reports address the travelers' exhilaration and enthusiasm that stemmed from their excitement about the opportunity for revolutionary networking, to visit unfamiliar parts of the country for the first time, and to be able to travel on their own without parental or other supervision.[60] Red Guards heading for Beijing to see Chairman Mao were admitted at train stations merely by showing some papers, and they were whisked onto trains that became hopelessly overcrowded with travelers. Passengers piled on top of one another on seats and slept on newspapers in the aisles and even in the toilets. With the continued flow of Red Guards to Beijing, conditions at the major train stations became increasingly chaotic, often leading to violence. Desperate students who were unable to obtain free tickets for their journeys home did not hesitate to lie down on the tracks outside the cities, forcing the trains to halt and take them on. Inside the carriages, interactions among Red Guards from various provinces reflected their political and social behavior on the streets. Red Guards looked down on students pursuing revolutionary networking without the proper credentials, and Beijing Red Guards parading their political and cultural superiority bullied Red Guards from the south. United in boredom during long train journeys and brimming with revolutionary zeal, groups of Red Guards made revolution on the trains by subjecting passengers to interrogation about their class status and family backgrounds, and ultimately throwing all "class enemies" off the train.[61]

With increasing chaos on and off the tracks, the accident rate rose to an all-time high. Between 1965 and 1969 China's railroad network saw a sevenfold increase in heavy train accidents, with 964 accidents in 1969 alone.[62] Boiler explosions, fires in passenger carriages, runaway trains, and track derailments were the most frequent accidents. An additional operational complication not addressed in public documents was the suspension of train schedules during 1966 and 1967, making train travel for nonrevolutionary purposes extremely erratic and adding to the disorder at the stations throughout the network.[63] In light of the high accident rate we may also assume that the lack of unified schedules made operational management of passenger and freight movements on the tracks ever more difficult to oversee. For example, on the Jin-Pu line a collision between a freight train and a passenger train carrying Red Guards at Baimashan station in November 1966 killed ten people, wounded more than forty, damaged two platforms, and destroyed fifteen carriages.[64]

In many cases, revolutionary in-fighting crippled the day-to-day work in the railroad bureaus and at the stations, posing additional challenges to operational management of the network. Bengbu station on the Jin-Pu line is representative of the spread of the chaos of the Cultural Revolution throughout the rail system. In December 1966, rebel factions (*zaofanpai*) from the machine and carriage workshops took control of the train sheds and their feeder tracks, occupied the station's broadcast building, and immobilized the track system for several days. Trains were stalled for more than 80 hours as 177 trains clogged the tracks. Travelers on 33 passenger trains had no other choice but to disembark and camp out on the tracks. Of course, this bottleneck resulted in massive delays along the entire corridor and along the regional lines.[65]

The damage inflicted on the railroads as physical and operational entities, however, disgusted and disillusioned many railroad employees and workers. Similar to the military, the railroad administration as a work unit had held a high status since the early 1950s because of the many benefits and privileges it conferred on its employees and workers.[66] This changed during the political climate of the Cultural Revolution when "being red" was much more highly valued than "being expert," and technical skills and professional training carried little revolutionary merit. As a result of the political rectification campaigns, many highly educated railroad engineers and professionals were attacked during the Cultural Revolution and sent for reeducation in the countryside, where their knowledge and talents were wasted as they labored in the fields and the commune kitchens.[67]

Although railroad workers would not admit it in public at the time, they hated having to accommodate the Red Guard revolutionary tourism on orders from the party Central Committee, which interfered with their professional work.[68] Employees and workers in the railroad system thus experienced a challenge to their professional identities that was indirectly tied to a generational conflict with the young revolutionaries. In contrast, members of the PLA railroad construction corps fared much better during the Cultural Revolution. According to the recollections of former military construction team members, these *tiedaobing* actually appreciated being assigned to projects in the countryside instead of being posted in the more politicized urban environment. Although they were forced to attend political meetings and study sessions, construction work was regarded as a revolutionary priority, so their work was not interrupted as much as that of the railroad workers in the cities.[69]

With respect to the institutional development of Chinese railroads, the political directives emanating from by Mao Zedong and the party Central Committee had to be followed by the railroad administration at every hierarchical level during the early years of the Cultural Revolution. Paradoxically, the revolutionary activism and power seizures at the top led to the empowerment of local and regional railroad stations and work units via control by factional rebel groups. As we have seen, the engineered chaos at a regional station such as Bengbu caused ripple effects throughout the entire network and gave the rebels a local, workplace-specific status as fervent revolutionaries carrying out Mao's wishes. In fact, a document circulated by the Ministry of Railways in late December 1966 allowed each railroad bureau, construction bureau, and design school to take charge of pursuing the revolutionary movement as it saw fit and expressly stated that "permission from the party committee of the Ministry of Railways is no longer necessary."[70] The process of institutional decentralization was now officially sanctioned.

With the chaos in transport operations and the political and institutional constraints from Mao's drastic move to purge and downsize ministries in 1967, the Ministry of Railways was unable to control or coordinate the national network. Ministries with strategic significance in industry and defense, such as the railroads, were less hard hit than the cultural and education bureaucracies.[71] However, Minister of Railways Lü Zhengcao still "struggled against" and deposed in January 1967. Thereafter, all railroad bureaus, construction bureaus, design schools, factories, railroad branch bureaus, and railroad stations became embroiled in ongoing power struggles and denunciations of the so-called revisionists. This decentralization and revolutionary empowerment of individual institutional units in the railroad hierarchy began to have consequences for the economy, public safety, and defense. As a last resort to stem the chaos, in May 1967 Premier Zhou Enlai, with Mao's approval, called in the army to restore order and some level of operations to the strategically important ministries.[72] At a meeting with representatives of the railroad transportation network and the military in Beijing at the end of the year, Zhou expressed his concern about the unresolved chaos in the railroad bureaus, including Shanghai, Bengbu, and those in the Northeast, and sternly warned them "not to point the spearhead against the PLA which would be a colossal mistake."[73]

From an institutional perspective, the arrival of the PLA meant the replacement of party groups in charge of the ministry with a military control commission (*junshi guanzhi weiyuanhui*) charged with creating the "unified leadership" of the Ministry of Railways.[74] In pragmatic terms, the takeover by a commission of PLA officers set a new tone because every unit within the railroad bureaucracy had to strictly follow the orders of the military commission. In addition to this institutional recentralization, the commission also established new priorities for the operation and management of the railroad network, as confirmed in a public document issued by the central party leadership. According to this "command" (*mingling*), protecting unobstructed rail transport, strictly prohibiting destruction of railroad equipment and assets, ending free travel, and ensuring observance of all sorts of safety measures were to guide work within the railroad system, with severe punishment according to the law for those who ignored these orders.[75]

The military commission's operational guidelines in combination with the halt of unrestrained free revolutionary travel contributed to a general and surprisingly quick recovery of railroad productivity. One might question how this was possible in the context of dealing with so many personnel in such a large bureaucratic institution. The railroad military commission used the only viable approach—namely, extensive institutional reform. By the end of 1968 the military commission had reduced the existing twenty-six railroad units at all hierarchical levels. Only four units remained—in charge of political work, production, logistics, and office administration. The reduction of staff was even more dramatic. The number of staff working for the ministry was reduced from 1,960 employees to only 280, including the seventeen members of the military commission. Those cut were released to study at the ministry's cadre school or to participate in manual labor.[76]

On the one hand, the role of the military in the shaping of railroad administration during the Cultural Revolution can be seen as part of a move to undo the worst effects of the decentralization that had been carried out in the spirit of revolutionary politics. On the other hand, the massive recentralization under a purely military command had several immediate operational consequences. The draconian reforms certainly addressed those factors that were most important for restoring freight and passenger operations according to an economic rationale. The safety record of the railroads immediately improved and the resumption in the flow of freight contributed to a general recovery of industry and agriculture. By 1970 both agricultural and industrial output surpassed their previous peak levels before the Cultural Revolution, and they were headed on a long-term upward trend.[77] This important development validated the return to a more pragmatic approach to rail operations as well as to China's strategic interests related to foreign policy.

For example, railroad lines in the south were important for transporting armaments and supplies to North Vietnam. According to 1968 British Foreign Office files, the Chinese central leadership was anxious to end the rail disruptions so as to continue its support for the North Vietnamese war effort.[78] That the military became so ensconced in China's railroads, however, had deep implications for the railroad bureaus, which felt under siege and alienated as a professional and administrative elite. Continued internal political struggles ensued, resulting in the local railroads becoming stronger and more insular administrative and operational units.

### Railroad Bureau Strongholds

The Cultural Revolution did not wreak as much havoc on China's economic growth as the Great Leap Forward, despite the intensity and scope of the many political campaigns unfolding during the decade from 1966 to 1976 (see Map 8.1). In fact, economists such as Dwight Perkins have shown that China's economy did not slow down during this period, except for the two years of extreme political chaos, 1967 and 1968, and by 1970 industry and agriculture were again producing at pre–Cultural Revolution levels. As Perkins also points out, however, growth came at the cost of ever-increasing levels of investment and energy inputs that were used in ineffective ways as the Cultural Revolution continued that did not lead to an increase in the standard of living but instead to stagnant wages.[79]

Published figures for the railroad sector confirm this interpretation of the economic growth pattern. For example, the total transported freight volume decreased by 24 percent between 1966 and 1968, but it quickly recovered and in 1970 surpassed the 1966 volume by 23 percent. Unfortunately, official figures published under the aegis of the Ministry of Railways and local railroad bureaus do not give us any specific information about labor productivity or efficiency rates. The number of days needed for the turnover of freight cars increased steadily from 1966 to 1976, however, indicating inefficiencies. For example, in 1970 the average total turnover time (measured in days) was 12 percent longer than that in 1965, with a 10 percent increase in time spent on changing freight cars. By 1976 the turnover took 26 percent more time, with a 60 percent increase in changing freight cars compared with the 1965 base

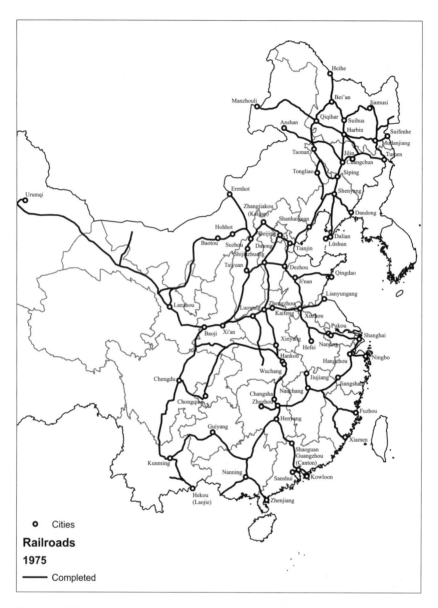

**Map 8.1**   Major railroads, 1975. Map © Elisabeth Köll (cartographic design Matthew Sisk).

line. Considering a fairly steady decline in the density of freight cars in use per day during the Cultural Revolution decade, it appears that increasingly more labor time was spent on switching and turning over freight cars for service.[80]

The greatest challenge came from the residual political factionalism taking place in local railroad bureaus in the mid-1970s after the heyday of the Cultural Revolution had subsided. Certain railroad bureaus and branch bureaus such as Xuzhou, at the intersection of the Long-Hai and Beijing-Shanghai lines, continued their revolutionary struggle, disrupting traffic flows at dangerous and economically damaging levels.[81] Even the limited information in the bureaus' yearbooks published more than a decade after the Cultural Revolution points to bureaus fully embroiled in political campaigns "under the influence of the Great Cultural Revolution," especially during the Criticize Lin Biao and Confucius campaign in from 1973 to 1976 (see Figure 8.1).[82] The withdrawal of the military control commission from the Xuzhou branch bureau in April of that year may have been a factor encouraging revolutionary factionalism and power politics, because it ended seven years of administration by the military. The ensuing chaos manifested itself with the establishment of a Criticize Lin Biao and Confucius Liaison Center for the Xuzhou section, involving both the bureau as an institution and the leading cadres from all related grassroots work units.[83] Several line accidents resulted in a heavy loss of life and equipment, and by late 1974 Xuzhou as a rail hub was defunct, rendering any rail movement to the south into the Yangzi area or north to Tianjin impossible. The Xuzhou Railroad Bureau became infamous for being the "old disastrous" (*lao da'nan*) work unit among the line networks.[84]

The Criticize Lin Biao and Confucius campaign also affected other railroad compounds, such as the machine works at Dalian and Datong.[85] But it was the role of the Xuzhou Railroad Bureau in paralyzing national freight and passenger transportation that finally led to intervention by the central government. For Deng Xiaoping in particular, who at Mao's orders returned from political exile in Jiangxi province to rejoin the government as vice premier in 1974, boosting China's economy was a priority, and smooth freight and coal transportation via the railroad network was an indispensable precondition.[86] To achieve his long-term goals, Deng Xiaoping first consolidated the military by restoring general discipline, reducing troop size, and increasing

Fig. 8.1 Train attendants organize passengers to participate in the Criticize Confucius and Lin Biao Campaign on a train from Qiqihar to Beijing, 1974. © Li Zhensheng / Contact Press Images from "Red Color News Soldier" (Phaidon, 2003).

its educational and technical levels.[87] Mirroring his approach to military reform, Deng used the Xuzhou Railroad Bureau as an example of "strategic civilian consolidation" to restore order in the rail sector.[88] In the interpretation of historical sociologist Ezra Vogel, because even Mao Zedong was inconvenienced by having to cancel a train trip during the chaos on the tracks and because Deng's political adversaries on the Shanghai Revolutionary Committee realized the importance of an open rail link for supplies to reach Shanghai, Deng was able to "move quickly and forcefully in Xuzhou."[89]

In addition to appointing the experienced organizer of large projects, Wan Li, as minister of railroads, Deng Xiaoping resorted to soliciting support via official documents directly issued by the party and approved by Mao Zedong. At the end of an extensive meeting with all provincial-level party secretaries in charge of industry in March 1975, Central Party Document (*Zhongfa*) No. 9, "The Decision of the Central Committee of the Chinese Communist Party on Improving Railroad Work," abolished all overlapping jurisdictions at the Xuzhou Railroad Bureau and placed the bureau under the authority of Wan Li and his ministry.[90] In addition, the document demanded the abolition of factions and threatened swift and serious punishment of those resisting organizational discipline and destroying property.

Deng Xiaoping emphasized the urgency of the problem and need for action in a speech to the assembled party secretaries on March 5, 1975, in which he skillfully used railroads as both real examples and metaphors for his ideas about creating economic stability and growth.[91] He blamed the lack of unified leadership for the decline in railroad transportation and promoted the Central Committee's decision to "reaffirm consolidation and centralization." He also recognized the importance of cooperation between local-level and ministry-level rail administration as a specific characteristic of railroads.[92] In his comments on the high accident rates and the lack of discipline, Deng used concrete examples of railroad operational problems due to the careless behavior of its workforce:

> The railroad accidents these days are alarming, and in comparison, the 755 massive and large train accidents that occurred last year are multiples of the 88 accidents in 1964 when we had an all-time low. Many of the recent accidents are due to negligence, including in maintenance and repair of engines and rail cars. This proves the lack of both regulations and discipline! Now we must reaffirm certain rules and regulations. Engine drivers should not leave their trains to eat their meals, and they need to bring lunch boxes to be eaten on the train—this is an old regulation that makes sense. Nowadays they willfully leave their engines to have meals, often resulting in the trains being late. Drinking alcohol on duty is prohibited, but this age-old rule is no longer strictly enforced! Being drunk and making a mistake with the railroad switch can cause massive collisions. For these reasons, rules and regulations must be restored and strengthened and their organizational and disciplinary nature must absolutely be enhanced. This problem exists not only in

various departments within the Ministry of Railways but also at other localities and in other departments.[93]

Deng Xiaoping went on to criticize the chaos created by two types of trouble-makers, those confused and led astray by political factionalism and those "bad persons" using the factional chaos to enrich themselves and sabotage national economic reconstruction. Deng placed the ringleader at the Xuzhou Railroad Bureau in the latter category and demanded that he be given until the end of the month to change his politics or receive harsh punishment.[94]

From an institutional perspective, the most interesting aspect of Deng's speech is his observation that troublemakers within the railroad system were aligning with local troublemakers and that their collaboration must be cut off before spreading to the capital. For example, the factional activities at Nan-chang Railroad Bureau were supported at the provincial level. Deng reaf-firmed the authority of the Ministry of Railways by announcing that this time "the transfer of personnel within the various railroad departments must happen under the unified control of the Ministry of Railways. The Ministry of Railways has this power [quan]. The problem of factionalism along the rail-roads cannot be solved by the localities but only by the Ministry of Rail-ways."[95] Backed by Central Party Document No. 9 and Deng Xiaoping's speech, Minister of Railways Wan Li met with party and government leaders in Xuzhou. After the immediate arrest of the factional troublemaker and leader of the Xuzhou Railroad Bureau, Wan Li went on to hold several mass meetings with employees, party officials from Xuzhou city, and maintenance workers, hoping to win wide support from the newly appointed leaders of the bureau and to return the bureau to economic and political stability.[96] Because this approach to reestablishing order and institutional discipline proved successful, it was also applied to other railroad bureaus suffering from operational chaos due to factionalism, such as those in Taiyuan, Nanchang, and Kunming. As a result, by the end of March 1975 the dispatch of trains and the loading of freight in Xuzhou began to normalize and the entire rail sector saw a recovery during the second quarter of the year.[97]

Deng Xiaoping's approach to the consolidation of the Xuzhou Railroad Bu-reau under the authority of the Ministry of Railways became a blueprint for restoring other economic sectors whose productivity had been seriously dam-aged by the disruptive factional infighting. Deng had announced in his early

March speech that "the experience gained in handling the problems in railway work will be useful to the other industrial units."[98] He later recommended the Xuzhou experience as a model (*dianxing*) and a case study for the iron and steel industry in dealing with similar problems.[99] In return, the successful changes in and consolidation of the railroad, iron and steel, and aerospace sectors became models for Deng Xiaoping's "all-round readjustment" of the Chinese economy in 1975.[100]

The selection of the railroad sector as the first strategic target for consolidation made sense because its functional operations, especially freight and coal transportation, were a basic requirement for the next step in consolidating heavy industry. The initial focus on the railroad sector, however, was necessary for other reasons as well. The case of Xuzhou exemplified the strong local autonomy of the railroad bureaus being exploited by factional rebels, the complicated geographical distribution of administrative authority over the bureaus, and the close ties between the railroad's work-specific communities and the local communities. That Deng Xiaoping suggested including the families of railroad workers and even farmers living along the railroad tracks in the rectification of the troubled bureaus indicates the close links between these communities.[101] The explicit reaffirmation of the power and centralized authority of the Ministry of Railways under Wan Li can be interpreted as a programmatic example of consolidating the administrative structure of the rail system and reestablishing the ministry's reach into the bureaus via top-down channels of command. For that purpose, the ministry also took direct control of Jiaotong University in Beijing, four major railroad academies, and the railroad medical schools in Nanjing and Shanghai by removing their provincial and municipal cadres.[102] From a political perspective, the elimination of political enemies and the replacement of incompetent and disloyal personnel with capable and loyal staff contributed to Deng's larger goal of political readjustment and accelerated economic growth.[103]

The railroad sector was also appropriate for promoting the restoration of regulations and work efficiency. Although these issues were mentioned in the context of other industries and enterprises that had to be straightened out, arguably no other industrial sector provided more vivid and dramatic examples of the causal connection between discipline, safety, and economic productivity.[104] Individual negligence and the lack of work discipline were directly responsible for damage to goods and rail facilities at freight yards, and errors in train operations led to catastrophic accidents. The loss of human life and damage to equipment, with its resulting blockage of rail routes, made apparent the high economic costs of insufficient discipline and professionalism and its undermining of socialism. The general point is exemplified by the propaganda poster in Figure 8.2 where railroad officials at Dandong station are admonishing the workers in the rail yard to handle goods and freight logistics with care and to avoid any risk of fire due to negligent behavior.[105]

Toward the end of the Cultural Revolution the rail sector began to recover, but not immediately. In fact, rail statistics show that total transported freight volume in 1976 dropped by 5 percent and accidents increased by 17 percent compared with the previous year.[106] Factional politics at the center were again responsible for this negative development. Under the increasing radical influence of the Gang of Four and Mao's withdrawal of support for Deng Xiaoping's readjustment policies, Deng eventually became the target of an antirevisionist campaign, ending with his political purge in April 1976.[107] Radical supporters of the Gang of Four gained the upper hand in railroad

**Fig. 8.2** Propaganda poster "Learning from the Freight Yard at Dandong Station," ca. 1974. Reproduced from the author's collection.

bureaus such as Zhengzhou, and they launched direct attacks on the readjustment achieved in the previous year, with slogans such as "Just as it went up, let productivity go down" and "Dragging down transportation productivity means victory."[108] Cadres previously charged with improving rail work and discipline were now criticized and attacked.

The political chaos erupting at major railroad bureaus, such as Zhengzhou, Lanzhou, Taiyuan, Nanchang, Chengdu, and Kunming, affected not only rail line productivity throughout the country but also the economic and industrial productivity in those provinces dependent on the supply of resources and materials. For example, the chaos at Zhengzhou resulted in the complete shutdown of the line's bureau system twelve times during 1976, with a massive loss of freight volume and no trains dispatched for one hundred days.[109] As a central rail hub for moving coal and grain between China's northeast and southwest, the disruption at Zhengzhou caused supply problems for a number of provinces and cities. Radical unrest and rail blockages at the Lanzhou Railroad Bureau forced almost half of the metallurgical and petrochemical enterprises in Gansu province to halt or halve production because of supply shortages.[110] Approximately 80 percent of the province's motor vehicles were left without gasoline because oil wells in Xinjiang and Gansu provinces had to shut down.[111]

Considering this setback in the economic and administrative consolidation of China's railroad system, the specific role and structural nature of the railroad bureaus might explain why radical factionalism regained power with such a vengeance. Despite impressive efforts to readjust the railroad sector according to Deng Xiaoping's policies, it is plausible that nine months in 1975 were insufficient to turn around all the railroad bureaus and to cement ideological and administrative changes within the workforce. Political radicalism based on the Gang of Four's "turn to the left" and attacks on Deng Xiaoping found support across the country, although spontaneous public protests in various provinces and cities also indicated increasing public dissatisfaction, especially after the death of Premier Zhou Enlai in January 1976.[112]

That railroad bureaus again became strongholds of radical politics with catastrophic economic consequences points to the institutional structure of the system; the nationally fragmented, locally entrenched railroad bureau system allowed a rapid return of the radicals who had been sidelined under the consolidation policies and who saw an opportunity to regain power and settle scores. With a strong institutional identity and disregard for the politically weakened ministry, the relatively small number of radicals in the railroad bureaus were able to inflict chaos and much economic damage. Fortunately, the death of Mao Zedong and the military coup against the Gang of Four brought the Cultural Revolution to an end in October 1976. Without losing any time, the Ministry of Railways held a meeting in Beijing for all work units and departments under its control to reaffirm the new directives of the party Central Committee and placed straightening out the troubled railroad bureaus at the top of its agenda.[113]

In the immediate post-Mao years, the rail sector renewed efforts to internally reorganize enterprise management (*qiye guanli*) along the 1975 guidelines and publicly placed the blame for the massive disruptions on the Gang of Four. Newspaper articles with headlines like "Evidence for the Gang of Four's Guilt in Destroying Railroad Transportation" in the party and government mouthpiece *People's Daily* (*Renmin ribao*) supported such efforts in no uncertain terms.[114] Blaming the members of the Gang of Four, already imprisoned, for all aspects of the chaos in the rail system seems to have been a strategic move to encourage the general railroad workforce to quickly embrace the return to normalized operations without fear of political retribution. At the top level, the Ministry of Railways ordered the full replacement of the leadership at the troubled Zhengzhou and Lanzhou Railroad Bureaus with newly dispatched cadres, and it reorganized the leadership groups in the work units under its direct command.[115] In contrast, the resilience of railroad workers on the job during the difficult times and their renewed dedication to the country's political and economic recovery led them to be publicly praised as new role models.[116] By the end of 1978 the success of the reorganization was obvious by the 30 percent increase in freight transportation since 1976 and the drop in the accident rate by almost 50 percent.[117] Railroads were preparing to enter China's reform era.

## Rail Reforms and High-Speed Trains

With the beginning of China's early economic reforms in 1978, my analysis leaves the more familiar ground of modern history and enters the realm of contemporary economics, politics, and society. As a historian I am aware of the danger of trying to integrate select current events and developments into a narrative that belongs to the rightful domain of interpretations by social scientists and journalists. I believe, however, that bringing the historical trajectory of railroads in China to an abrupt closure in 1978 would obscure the fact that the Chinese rail sector still continues to grapple with issues such as bureaucratic centralization, local rail bureau power, and specific patterns of passenger and freight transportation. Although I make no attempt to assess the efficiency and viability of traditional vis-à-vis high-speed rail development in the Chinese political economy, it is not inappropriate to address their different roles within the economy and society and to consider their institutional evolution from a historical perspective.

In the wake of the economic consolidation and reforms, China's railroad sector developed into a highly centralized bureaucracy controlled by the Ministry of Railways, which answered directly to the State Council (Guowuyuan), the highest central administrative organ of the Chinese state. The ministry oversaw management of the rail network via fourteen regional railroad bureaus and forty-one branch railroad bureaus (*tielu fenju*), which together constituted the managerial level of the system. The branch bureaus were in charge of the local railroad stations and the rail workshops and depots as the operational base of the system.[118] The ministry coordinated the national network train schedule, which was published by the ministry's own publishing house.[119] Another aspect of the ministry's recentralization involved incorporating the construction corps of PLA railroad soldiers. Per decree of the State Council and the party Central Committee, railroad soldiers and their units came under the full authority of the Ministry of Railways in January 1984, with their demilitarized units renamed railroad engineering headquarters.[120]

Before 1981 the government covered all the ministry's costs related to rail operations and investments in return for the ministry's net profits.[121] When the government's economic reforms in the mid-1980s allowed state-owned enterprises (SOEs) to produce at extra capacity and to sell those goods at market prices, the railroad sector, especially the railroad bureaus, began to diversify their business portfolios. Throughout the network, cadres at the railroad bureau level used their local business connections and relationships with the local governments to build businesses, ranging from logistic centers to travel services and property development.[122]

As part of the government's structural reforms targeting the SOE sector in the 1990s, the Ministry of Railways began to corporatize transport services, and even branch railroad bureaus, by turning them into limited liability companies. This development, however, was not evidence of any extensive privatization of the rail sector because only some railroad bureaus were turned into corporations, and even those that did become corporations did not experience any significant change in governance.[123] In line with the reform policies' demands for a reduction in the number of state employees in the SOEs, the ministry reduced the number of staff by streamlining its administrative structure and by spinning off related enterprises and institutions, such as colleges and schools, and putting them under the authority of the Ministry of Education.[124] As a result, the total number of people employed by the Ministry of Railways dropped from 3.4 million (including 2 million in transport operations) at the end of 1995 to 2.1 million people (including 1.5 million in transport operations) in 2009.[125]

Because the modernization of logistics and transportation was an important part of the government's economic agenda, structural changes were introduced to tackle efficiency problems in the rail system. In 2001 an experiment to separate freight and passenger transportation from railroad construction and management so as to improve management and market orientation ended in failure.[126] Another attempt at structural reform came in March 2005 with the complete abolition of the managerial level occupied by the branch railroad bureaus. According to the announcement by Minister of Railways Liu Zhijun, this step was intended to improve the railroad bureaus' direct control over station management, transportation capacity, and standards of technological equipment. Even more significant was Liu's comment that the dismantling of the forty-one branch rail bureaus would solve the structural problems of two separate legal entities (bureaus and branch bureaus) managing the same property and assets.[127]

In many ways, this drastic move addressed the old problem of competing rights and responsibilities between bureaus and their branches in the same geographical area. Apart from constant disputes about control over transportation, bureaus and branch bureaus struggled with separate accounts and petty cash reserves in the branch bureaus. In addition, branch bureaus competed with each other for the limited funds dispensed by the railroad bureau for rail repairs, investments as well as for rolling stock, thus affecting the entire train car transfer system.[128] Commentators on the reform, many of whom had professional railroad backgrounds, emphasized the enormous difficulties in separating government and market-driven railroad units (*tielu zhengqi fenkai*) because of their divergent interests in the railroad sector. Some even questioned whether the ministry should lead the reform because "under the current structure, the Ministry of Railways is to gain the greatest benefits. And for this very reason, the Ministry of Railways is the greatest obstacle to a separation of government and market-economy units in the railroad sector."[129]

During the following years, the ministry did not achieve greater transparency or efficiency due to the predicament of being an institution that "had both a commercial and a social service obligation and acted as a government agent as well as an enterprise."[130] Interviews I conducted in 2010 at the Ministry of Railways in Beijing confirmed other scholars' observations that, during Liu Zhijun's tenure, network expansions, equipment upgrades, and speed elevation programs, instead of genuine structural reforms, dominated the ministry's agenda.[131] As representatives of the ministry pointed out, the focus on developing high-speed rail for passenger transportation and heavy-axle loads for freight transport addressed the enormous gap between the high market demand for rail services and the shortcomings in rail transport capacity.[132] Although freight transportation was more profitable than passenger transport (with the exception of certain high-speed lines), the interviewees repeatedly stressed the ministry's responsibility to provide train services for the millions of migrants returning home for Chinese New Year as well as subsidized tickets for students attending colleges far from home. Driven by the goal to ensure social and by extension political stability, the state continued to regulate the fares for passenger services and did not allow the railroad administration to set ticket prices.[133]

The inability of the railroads to fulfill market demand for freight transportation was, and still is, a major concern in the ministry's development plans. In 2010 only a third of cargo owners wishing to use the railroads for shipments were actually able to do so, leaving a large part of the logistics business to the trucking and aviation industries.[134] Approximately half of all rail freight consisted of coal and coke cargo, and the lower speed of freight trains sharing the same rail network resulted in capacity bottlenecks and inefficiencies.[135] Even the development of China's high-speed railroad network should be evaluated in the context of freight capacity. As representatives of the ministry pointed out, the push for high-speed rail development would not only benefit China's spatial urbanization and population distribution but also move a substantial part of the conventional rail passenger traffic to exclusive high-speed lines, thus freeing up new freight capacities.[136]

Although the Ministry of Railways put forward the first proposal for a high-speed connection between Beijing and Shanghai as early as 1990, it was not until late in the first decade of the twenty-first century that high-speed rail development really began to take off. One of the reasons for the delay was the debate over the type of technology to use—whether magnetic levitation trains on special maglev tracks or high-speed trains running on conventional standard-gauge tracks.[137] In consideration of the high costs of a maglev train system and encouraged by the successful experiments with conventional high-speed technology on a test line from Shenyang to Qinhuangdao in China's Northeast, the State Council decided to adopt the latter as the standard for the future network.[138] The opening of the high-speed rail line from Wuhan to Guangzhou in December 2009 became a milestone because this dedicated passenger trunk line established a high-speed corridor connecting central China and the middle Yangzi region with south China and the Pearl River delta. At a maximum speed of 218 miles per hour, the train covers 660 miles in only three hours and fifteen minutes. In addition, elegant new railroad stations and impressive bridge projects give a physical presence to the ambitions of the Ministry of Railways with regard to the future of this new infrastructure (see Map 8.2).[139]

Ironically, the massive investment in high-speed rail services—motivated by the goal to build the world's largest network despite insufficient financial resources (and oversight)—indirectly led to the demise of the Ministry of Railways. As the ministry's debt spiraled out of control, corruption became rampant at all administrative levels, even involving the minister.[140] When in 2011 two high-speed trains crashed in a catastrophic accident due to neglect of safety standards and corrupt practices, the incident triggered national public outrage and government investigations into the rail administration and ended with the eventual trial and imprisonment of Minister Liu Zhijun.[141] In response to renewed calls for major rail reform, the government abolished the Ministry of Railways in March 2013. Attempting to address the problematic combination of administrative and commercial

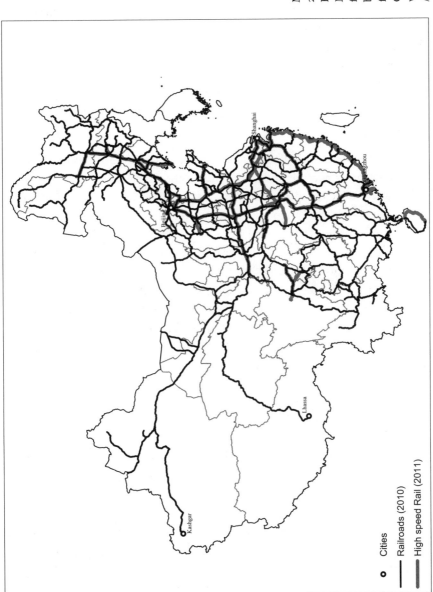

Map 8.2 Major railroads, 2010–2011. Map © Elisabeth Köll (cartographic design Matthew Sisk). Map following data compiled by Yifan Li and Lex Berman for the GIS project ChinaMap, 2010, at http://worldmap.harvard.edu/chinamap/.

Cities

Railroads (2010)

High speed Rail (2011)

Kashgar

Lhassa

Beijing

Shanghai

Guangzhou

responsibilities in the former ministry, a newly formed National Railway Administration (Guojia tieluju) took over its administrative functions, and the China Railway Corporation (Zhongguo tielu zong gongsi), a SOE, took over its commercial functions.[142] Both units are supervised by the Ministry of Transport, which was established in 2008. Marking the termination of sixty-three years of institutional survival, the State Council's restructuring plan ended with the cold sentence "The Ministry of Railways is not to be continued."[143]

## Conclusion

This chapter began with the survival and adaptation of China's railroads as transport infrastructure and an administrative system during the most politically challenging periods of the Great Leap Forward and the Cultural Revolution. Forced to align its operations and services with the political realities of the time, the railroad sector survived. As I have shown, the politically engineered disrespect for professional railroad expertise and the breakdown in normal transport conditions stretched the system to its limits and led to high accident rates and operational gridlocks. With historical hindsight, it seems miraculous that the railroads were able to maintain services even to the extent they did. During the period of China's economic reforms, the ministry's unbridled investment spending without accountability magnified the levels of corruption, which in turn resulted in negligence in safety and a lack of discipline. What does this tell us about the institutional development of the rail sector?

In many ways, the story of China's rail sector involves a constant tug of war between the central government, represented by the Ministry of Railways, and the local and regional railroad bureaus in charge of operations. From the late 1950s through the 2010s we have witnessed continual attempts by the ministry to centralize and restore power and a pushback from local and regional railroad bureaus with strong ties to local and regional governments and society. The dichotomy between centralization and decentralization represents a historical continuation of the fragmented institutional development that originated during the Republican period. After 1949, railroad bureaus managed to adapt operations to the needs of the political directives during crisis periods but also exploited their relative autonomy to sabotage the central government's normalization efforts.

The characterization of the Ministry of Railways as a "kingdom" or a "state within the state" in China simultaneously represents both envy and criticism.[144] The size of the rail sector, its huge workforce, and the self-sufficient rail compound communities with ample social services ranging from hospitals to schools strengthened the professional and institutional identity of railroad workers. The rail sector was inaccessible and opaque to outsiders because railroads had their own police force and their own court system, the railway transportation court.[145] Although all railroad courts were ultimately transferred to the localities and integrated into the national court system in late 2012, the long entanglement of the Ministry of Railways in the legal entities under its purview raised many questions about transparency and judicial fairness.[146]

Despite the many challenges of structural changes and market reforms, however, the railroad workforce did not lose its professional and institutional identity.[147] When the Ministry of Railways in Beijing was finally abolished, employees and retirees of the rail administration came out in their railroad uniforms to have their pictures taken in front of the entrance to the ministry, and many left comments expressing disappointment and shock on blogs that discussed the closure. Whether they will develop the same level of loyalty to the ministry's institutional successors remains to be seen.

# Conclusion: The Legacies of China's Railroad System

O nly a few months after the founding of the PRC, the *People's Daily* in January 1950 proudly announced the reopening of the rail line from Beijing to Hankou, with a travel time of fifty-three hours.[1] Today the trip takes five and a half hours via a high-speed train from the capital to Wuhan, where passengers alight at a station with a futuristic design and a roof resembling the wings of a crane, the symbol of the city. High-speed rail lines connect Shanghai and Beijing in less than five hours, moving along tracks parallel to the old Tianjin-Pukou rail corridor, which continues to be used for passenger and freight transportation. Railroad stations with ambitious ultramodern architecture celebrate the high-speed rail expansion to the western provinces, where they stand out in the vast and barren landscapes of Gansu and Xinjiang as symbols of China's quest for economic modernization through state-driven infrastructure investment.

Passenger transportation is still an important part of the service portfolio of China's railroad sector. The heavy air pollution disrupting flight schedules and the severe congestion immobilizing traffic on highways leading in and out of the cities have made high-speed railroads, with their easy access to urban infrastructure networks, serious competitors to air travel. According to the China Railway Corporation, 52 percent of all railroad trips in 2016, a total of 1.44 billion trips, were via the high-speed trains.[2] Regular trains remain indispensable for the mass transportation of migrant workers in the cities who return to their hometowns and villages during the holiday season. Approximately 145 million migrants took the train for Spring Festival travel (*chunyun*) in 2015, and the number of those opting for high-speed trains instead of regular trains is increasing.[3] The question of whether the continuous construction and operation of high-speed rails in the long run will prove to be cost-effective and deliver high returns to the government's considerable investment, which is beyond the scope of this study, is still hotly debated by economists.

Transportation of seasonal agricultural migrant labor is one service area in which, for economic, geographic, and logistical reasons, the provision of cheap rail transportation remains absolutely necessary. In the 1980s and 1990s tens of thousands of seasonal wheat harvesters (*maike*) from surrounding counties and provinces took trains to central and northwestern Shaanxi province to earn cash wages for working in the fields. During peak season, open freight and box cars transported the workers in less-than-orderly fashion as the train stations were transformed into de facto camping and distribution stations for the migrant workers.[4] Harvesting cotton in Xinjiang province also depends on a constant supply of rural migrant labor and hence on rail transportation. Every year special trains bring in hundreds of thousands of laborers from neighboring Gansu, Qinghai, and Ningxia provinces to earn cash wages for their seasonal farm work.[5]

In light of the impressive expansion of domestic networks and advances in high-speed rail, does the history of China's railroad matter at all for our understanding of current rail developments in the early twenty-first century? The legacy of the Chinese railroad system, which began to take off in the early twentieth century, can be identified most prominently via the institutional organization of today's railroad administration. As I have shown, the railroad bureau system has survived from the early Republic through occupation, war, and numerous politically driven reorganizations and crises into the twenty-first century. In fact, as an institution the railroad bureau system even survived the abolition of the Ministry of Railways in 2013 and continues under its successor, the China Railway Corporation. This solely state-owned enterprise controls eighteen railroad bureaus, each with its own specific geographically defined administrative reach. The bureaus are still officially classified as *tieluju*, although the China Railway Corporation also refers to them as companies (*gongsi*) to indicate their subordinate status vis-à-vis the controlling company.[6]

The majority of the bureaus trace their institutional roots to the early Republic, and many of them have not experienced major changes in their administrative responsibilities since then. For example, the portfolio of railroad administration for the Ji'nan Railroad Bureau today is fairly similar to that during the Republican period. The Ji'nan Railroad Bureau is in charge of all lines within Shandong province, including the Shandong section of the Beijing-Shanghai high-speed line, and it still maintains its headquarters and other physical assets in the old rail district of Ji'nan.[7] Urban growth now surrounds the rail district, and it no longer occupies the western outskirts of the city; rather, it has become part of the city center. New additions to the bureau system, such as the Chengdu, Kunming, Urumqi, and Qinghai-Tibet Railroad Bureaus, reflect the post-1949 and reform-era network expansion into the southern, western, and central regions of the country.[8]

From a financial perspective, the Chinese railroad sector today performs little better than it did during the pre-1949 period. As I have shown, the financial performance of individual lines has always depended on their business portfolio, and those that have been profitable are mainly transporting freight, such as the Jin-Pu Railroad, or providing crucial city and interregional connections, such as the Shanghai-Nanjing line. During the early Republic in particular, those lines, affected by warlord troops and military campaigns, saw their profits dwindle and rolling stock destroyed. Despite the damage from the various lengthy military and political campaigns and hence the need to seek supplementary railway equipment loans from foreign markets, the government never opened up the railroad sector to private ownership. Instead, throughout the Republican period the Nationalist government continued to rely on the railroads to provide services without compensation, so it is questionable whether the government ever would have wanted to give up state control and easy subsidies in exchange for private ownership and stricter governance. Even more importantly, as historians have noted, China's financial environment in the early twentieth century was not conducive to establishing a bond market to raise the substantial capital necessary for large infrastructure projects.[9]

The lack of private and foreign investment has remained an important issue for the Chinese government. The 2013 abolition of the Ministry of Railways reflects not only administrative but also economic considerations—namely, to make the Chinese rail sector more attractive to foreign investment.[10] As a fully state-owned entity, the China Railway Corporation has not had much success in attracting foreign capital, especially as it continues to face massive annual net losses and piling mountains of debt.[11]

The institutional structure of China's railroad administration can be traced back to foreign influence, resulting in the railroads' managerial, spatial, and linguistic separation; their relative lack of interconnectivity; and a post-1949 network expansion that began from a core of existing lines in the eastern and northeastern provinces. After the Communist revolution the state loomed large in the rebuilding and expansion of the railroad network. The enormous technological and engineering feats of railroad construction in mountains, deserts, and other inhospitable areas would not have been possible without centralized state efforts to provide administrative, financial, and especially human resources. The PRC government immediately recognized the importance of railroads to building the new nation-state, to distribute economic goods, and to supply military, political, and technical personnel. However, the party-driven political campaigns and their disruption of railroad operations not only negatively affected transport productivity and efficiency but also sabotaged proper managerial and operational processes, leading to high accident rates and network blockages and thereby frustrating professionals and exacerbating factional politics.

Even today, railroads in China are still part of nation-building efforts to integrate the ethnic minority areas and to reduce economic and social inequalities between coastal and central China and the western regions. In the wake of the economic reforms of the early 1990s, which focused on developing an export-oriented economy, railroads played an important role in government plans for economic growth. For example, bringing large-scale rail infrastructure to Tibet was on the government's political agenda for integrating this poor, ethnically diverse region with the core of the Chinese economy, and, by extension, creating a greater Han Chinese presence there. Premier Zhu Rongji expressed this vision in 2001 when he stated, "Poor infrastructure is the main constraint to Tibet's economic growth. You must speed up infrastructure construction in railways, roads, airports, power, communications, and waterworks. After ample validation and preparations, work is about to start on the Qinghai-Tibet railroad. The building of this great rail artery across the Qinghai-Tibet plateau will not only have a great impact on Tibet's development but will also play a major role in the strategy of the great development of western China. It must be meticulously designed, meticulously organized, and meticulously constructed. You should do your best to have the entire line open to traffic within six years."[12] The speed of construction for this ambitious project did not disappoint, and the line from Xining in Qinghai province to Lhasa in Tibet was opened in 2006. Of course, there also exists severe criticism of rail and infrastructure building in Tibet with respect to its negative impact on Tibetan culture and language and the natural environment.

A major point emphasized in this study is the agency of the Chinese people who worked for and traveled on Chinese railroads and the land owners and local residents who interacted with the railroads' physical presence and technology. As I have shown, the practical embrace of rail technology and transportation services occurred both rapidly and early, thus contradicting the pervasive image of technophobic Chinese viewing the railroad as a disturbance to the feng shui of their land and grave sites. Channeled into party propaganda throughout the Maoist years, the agency of Chinese citizens with regard to railroad construction has now resurfaced with new vigor. Most remarkable is that Chinese citizens are once again protesting both railroad construction and the lack thereof. For example, in 2008 Shanghai residents, due to fear of electromagnetic radiation and other concerns, protested against the planned extension of the high-speed magnetic levitation train.[13] Because of publicity as well as the high profile of Shanghai urban residents, the government accommodated the protests and abandoned the expansion plans. By contrast, when residents in Linshui county in rural Sichuan province demonstrated against the government's decision not to build a railroad line through the county and instead to route it through the birthplace of Deng Xiaoping in a neighboring county, violent encounters with the police ensued.[14] In this case, the particularistic political interests at the central level won out over the economic interests of the rural residents, who are still waiting for their county to be connected to the railroad network.

Historians exploring the role of railroads in other national contexts have noted that "more than any other technical design or social institution, the railway stands for modernity."[15] The Chinese railroad system is no exception. Despite its evolution from a rather messy, uncoordinated line network in the last decades of the Qing empire, Chinese railroads have become widely publicized metaphors of economic and social modernity, even though the nationalization of the railroads after 1911 did not translate into a straightforward story of state building based on railway construction. Nevertheless, as visual and literary metaphors, railroads have made their mark in the public realms of advertising, literature, poetry, and film, adding new dimensions to the concepts of class, status, gender roles, and urban and rural identities as they were transformed by interactions within train carriages, on stations platforms, and along the tracks. Representing the process of simultaneous continuity and transformation, after 1949 the PRC government cleverly adjusted the railroad metaphor to a new interpretation of socialist progress, technological independence, and political conquest. As a visual representation of these goals, the emblem of China's railroad administration features the Chinese character for "people" (*ren*) embracing a steel rail, symbolizing the people's railroad.[16] It is telling that this sign is still one of the most ubiquitous and enduring official emblems in China's public space, having survived the numerous institutional transformations and reorganizations, and today it is still used as the company emblem for the China Railway Corporation.

The introduction of disciplinary regulations for railroad work and railway passengers presents another aspect of modernity that constitutes part of the historical development of all national railroad regimes. High-speed trains in China have created demand for passenger education regarding proper treatment of the technical equipment and safety measures at the seats and in the carriages. Similar to passenger education during the Republican period, these days informational pamphlets and trained staff instruct passengers regarding correct behavior in the carriages and note the large fines in cases of violations, such as smoking in the carriages.[17] The use of the railroad as a metaphor for discipline and urban modernity has had enduring appeal, especially after the political upheavals of the 1960s and 1970s when millions of young people from the cities were sent to work in the countryside. It is not a coincidence that many films and television dramas focus on this traumatic period in Chinese history. The popular 2012 television series *Zhiqing* (Sent-down youth) begins with the emotional arrival of sent-down youth at a bleak train stop in the countryside. The last installment of the series features the elated return of select protagonists to the cities and urban modernity by train from that same stop.[18]

The aspirational goals behind the railroad as a tool of operational efficiency and professionally administered technology have filtered into the workforce. Chinese railroad bureaus and compounds were one of the country's first institutions to employ large numbers of white-collar workers in managerial and administrative positions as well as skilled workers with on-the-job and professional training. Railroad engineers trained at Jiaotong University and other technical institutes were the backbone of China's administrative and technocratic elites throughout the twentieth century. As in railroad yards throughout the world, staff and workers have developed a strong sense of loyalty to their respective companies that provide a socioeconomic welfare infrastructure, ranging from hospitals and housing to clubs and schools. After 1927 the combination of social services for employees, their strong professional identity and involvement in railroad culture, and the insertion of the Guomindang via party branches into the railroad administration and compounds helped foster administrative centralization and in the 1930s the firm alignment of the Ministry of Railways with the Guomindang's political agenda.

This issue leads us to the question of whether the history of Chinese railroads represents a case of a strong institution in a weak state, a concept scholars have previously discussed in their assessments of the strength or weakness of the Chinese state and its institutions during the Republican period.[19] In his revisionist approach, historian Stephen Halsey argues that the threat of European imperialism, as it developed in the second half of the nineteenth century, led to a new phase of innovative state-making in China. Although I am hesitant to support this broad statement in its entirety, I agree that Chinese officials tried to compete with their political and economic rivals by "conscious imitation as well as independent trial and error."[20] Halsey does not discuss railroads, but one can argue that the evolution of Chinese railroads from the late Qing to the Republican period represents a case of institution building using both imitation and trial-and-error approaches, eventually leading to an institutional combination of Western railroad organization with Chinese administrative and labor practices. In terms of personnel management and company structure, Western-style discipline and modern technology were combined with traditional forms of accounting, hiring systems, and labor processes, creating a mix of modern, Western-style railroad companies with the traditional characteristics of Chinese firms.

After 1911, and particularly under the Guomindang government, the Chinese railroad system at all levels experienced rational bureaucratization and centralization, but its administrative field units, the regional railroad bureaus, were left with sufficient autonomy to run their own geographically defined rail sections. The Ministry of Railways, although integrated into the state-building efforts of the Republic, was able to maintain some autonomy at the lower administrative levels of the bureaus more successfully than other national administrative bodies such as the Ministry of Finance.[21] I argue that the institutional development of China's railroads in many ways exemplifies a general theme in the historical trajectory of the Republic, namely, the social, political, and economic realms became both more *and* less regional (or provincial) at the same time. Although the railroad administration became more aligned with the Nationalist government and its agenda by introducing bureaucratic centralization and professional and technological standardization, it simultaneously also became more regional through the presence of local railroad bureaus and their role in influencing the local economy and society.

Identifying the symbiotic relationship between railroads and the state throughout the twentieth century, this study has shown that railroads needed the support of a stable, although not necessarily strong, state for their successful development as business and administrative institutions. In return, the state relied on a well-managed railroad system and transportation service to reach its political and economic goals. My discussion of rail disruptions during the radical campaigns of the 1950s and 1960s shows that the state tolerated damage to the rail network only up to a certain limit before it stepped in. As a theme of continuity from the late 1930s throughout the PRC, railroads supported the state through their services but they also symbolized the power of the state. Therefore, dysfunctional rail service was also considered to be a sign of dysfunctional political power and unbalanced social order that would not be tolerated.

The history of China's railroad development is as much a global story as it is a Chinese story. This book reveals how China adopted railroads from the West as technological and infrastructural concepts but retained Chinese agency as operators, managers, builders, and consumers of their services. From a global perspective, China's railroad network was financed and built under semicolonial conditions, and even after nationalization, Western advisers and a mix of European and North American methods shaped the emergence of Chinese railroad management, training, and administration. As I document, until the end of World War II hardware equipment and technical progress remained completely dependent on imports from Great Britain and the United States. From 1949 to the political rift in 1961, engines, rail equipment, and technical advisers all hailed from the Soviet Union. China's rail development today, especially its high-speed sector, depends on technology imports, keeping alive political debates about indigenous innovation and perceived dependency on foreign technology.[22]

The global dimension of China's railroad development has now reached a new phase as the government has announced its One Belt, One Road initiative, with the aim of placing China at the center of global economic affairs.[23] Railroads, as part of a newly envisioned Silk Road, will complement a Maritime Silk Road in a quest to connect China with markets and products in Europe, the Middle East, South Asia, and Africa. Although China built railroads on the African continent as early as the 1960s, it is now assuming a new role, not only providing Africa's first electrified railroad from Ethiopia to Djibouti but also establishing standards in technology, engineering quality, and speed.[24] After being on the receiving end of equipment and technology for much of the late nineteenth and twentieth centuries, by imposing its own railroad standards in Africa, China is now on the giving side and ensuring its control over future supply chains on the continent.

In light of President Xi Jinping's grand vision for the One Belt, One Road initiative and China's integration into the global economy, it makes sense to return to Sun Yat-sen's bold program for China's railroad development, first proposed in 1921.[25] Sun considered railroads absolutely necessary for the development of the Chinese economy and recommended that the U.S. railroad network serve as a model. He hoped to finance his ambitious plans through foreign investment, but such investment never materialized and his plans never came to fruition. Sun Yat-sen's vision for China's rail expansion and its direction through state control, thus also justifying railroad nationalization, was very much based on his desire to unify China politically. China's global railroad visions, as expressed in the One Belt, One Road initiative, have now merged with Sun's vision of domestic political stability and state-led growth to claim China's economic and political leadership on the global stage. That railroads continue to occupy a central role in the realization of visions promoting national unity and economic development, as voiced by Sun Yat-sen and now by Xi Jinping, points to one of the major continuities in modern Chinese history.

# Jin-Pu Railroad Organization Chart, Circa 1929

## Jin-Pu Railroad Management Bureau

### 1. *Administrative Office in Tianjin*

- First Suboffice
- Second Suboffice

### 2. *Mechanical Works Department*

- Tianjin Mechanical Works
- Ji'nan Mechanical Works
- Puzhen Mechanical Works
- Works Suboffice
- First Central Division
- Xuzhou Section
- Bengbu Section
- Pukou Section
- Second Central Division
- Ji'nan Section
- Yanzhou Section
- Tai'an Section
- Lincheng Section
- Third Central Division
- Tianjin Section
- Cangzhou Section
- Dezhou Section
- Pukou Electric Power Plant
- Inspections / Controlling

Adapted from Nie Zhaoling, *Tielu tonglun* [Introduction to railways] (Shanghai: Shangwu, 1930), 58–66. Asterisks indicate departments that supervise between three and six additional units.

### 3. Engineering Department

- First Central Division*
- Second Central Division*
- Third Central Division*
- Land Office
- Ji'nan Gardens
- Puzhen Timber Yard
- Ji'nan-Tianjin Suboffice
- Hanzhuang-Ji'nan Suboffice
- Pukou-Hanzhuang Suboffice
- Engineering Suboffice
- Inspections / Controlling

### 4. General Affairs Department

- Tianjin-Chentangzhang Materials Storage
- Ji'nan Materials Yard
- Pukou Materials Yard
- Supported Schools
- Central Medical Office
- Pukou Medical Station
- Puzhen Hospital
- Bengbu Hospital
- Xuzhou Hospital
- Ji'nan Hospital
- Cangzhou Hospital
- Tianjin Hospital
- First Security Corps*
- Second Security Corps*
- First Central Police Division*
- Puzhen Yard Force
- Second Central Police Division*
- Third Central Police Division*
- Ji'nan Yard Force

### 5. Accounting Department

- Ticket Printing Office (Tianjin)
- Audit Office
- Tianjin Cashier's Office
- Accounts Settlement
- Cashier
- Documents

## 6. Operations Department

- First Main Section*
- Second Main Section*
- Third Main Section*
- Telegraph Office
- Ji'nan-Tianjin Telegraph Suboffice
- Hanzhuang-Ji'nan Telegraph Suboffice
- Pukou-Hanzhuang Telegraph Suboffice
- Harbor Affairs

## 7. Secretariat

# Revenue of Major Chinese Government Railroad Lines (thousand yuan per mile of line), 1915–1935

| Line | 1915 | | | 1918 | | | 1923 | | |
|---|---|---|---|---|---|---|---|---|---|
| | Passengers | Goods | Total | Passengers | Goods | Total | Passengers | Goods | Total |
| Peking-Mukden | 9,064 | 14,692 | 25,757 | 12,614 | 18,937 | 34,448 | 22,216 | 37,298 | 63,382 |
| Shanghai-Nanjing | 11,538 | 4,027 | 16,828 | 14,010 | 7,451 | 21,279 | 25,072 | 11,944 | 41,947 |
| Peking-Hankou | 4,762 | 14,961 | 20,969 | 6,498 | 20,155 | 29,219 | 7,428 | 26,472 | 38,965 |
| Tianjin-Pukou | 4,813 | 5,676 | 12,403 | 7,242 | 8,654 | 18,335 | 11,089 | 13,449 | 27,717 |
| Shanghai-Hangzhou-Ningbo | 7,572 | 3,200 | 11,419 | 8,868 | 3,808 | 13,424 | 15,145 | 7,026 | 24,351 |
| Canton-Kowloon | 7,655 | 834 | 9,055 | 8,322 | 1,470 | 10,024 | 9,771 | 2,176 | 8,813 |
| Peking-Suiyuan | 3,253 | 7,031 | 13,525 | 2,815 | 10,127 | 14,295 | 2,874 | 11,322 | 15,124 |
| Canton-Hankou* | | | | | | | 2,087 | | |
| Ji'nan-Qingdao† | | | | | | | 8,293 | 22,053 | 31,251 |

| Line | 1927 | | | 1930 | | | 1935 | | |
|---|---|---|---|---|---|---|---|---|---|
| | Passengers | Goods | Total | Passengers | Goods | Total | Passengers | Goods | Total |
| Peking-Mukden | 18,994 | 27,784 | 51,386 | 19,003 | 22,327 | 46,130 | 23,770 | 49,454 | 88,172 |
| Shanghai-Nanjing | 25,335 | 5,543 | 40,040 | 41,006 | 10,762 | 61,192 | 45,767 | 18,931 | 76,567 |
| Peking-Hankou | NA | NA | 14,006 | NA | NA | 24,543 | 9,520 | 29,427 | 41,908 |

| | | | | | | | | | |
|---|---|---|---|---|---|---|---|---|---|
| Tianjin-Pukou | NA | NA | 9,216 | 8,855 | 7,601 | 19,491 | 13,316 | 19,283 | 37,776 |
| Shanghai-Hangzhou-Ningbo | 13,952 | 5,388 | 26,113 | 21,992 | 9,990 | 35,945 | 23,543 | 12,084 | 39,213 |
| Canton-Kowloon | 9,744 | 2,035 | 12,177 | 15,193 | 2,340 | 18,282 | 19,654 | 2,496 | 23,133 |
| Peking-Suiyuan | 2,911 | 6,056 | 9,910 | 3,188 | 6,126 | 10,486 | 3,393 | 14,462 | 20,201 |
| Canton-Hankou* | | | | | | | | | |
| Ji'nan-Qingdao† | 12,752 | 24,868 | 39,225 | 14,092 | 29,477 | 45,411 | 10,443 | 38,039 | 52,243 |

*Source*: Ministry of Communications (subsequently the Ministry of Railways), *Statistics of Government Railways* [Zhongguo tielu tongji] (Peking (subsequently Nanking): Tiedaobu tongjichu, 1915–1936). The series covers the railroads' fiscal years until 1935/1936. Because of the impact of the civil war years on railroad operations, reports were published with long delays. The volume with 1925 data was published in 1929, and the volume with 1928 appeared in 1933. From 1926 onward each volume contained English and Chinese versions. Beginning in 1930 the name of the series changed slightly to *Statistics of Chinese National Railways* [Zhonghua guoyou tielu kuaiji tongi huibian].

*Notes*: A small percentage of revenue—never more than 15 percent, and typically less than 5 percent—came from activities unrelated to traffic: ferry and telegraph services, hotels, interchange of rolling stock, and rentals of equipment and the physical plant.

Data on freight tonnage are not available for 1926–1931, due to military disturbances. Until 1933, the years surveyed are calendar years; from 1934 on, they are fiscal years running from July to June.

*Data for the Canton-Hankou line, completed in 1936, are taken from the Hupeh (Hubei)–Hunan section, which opened in 1922.

†The Ji'nan-Qingdao line became a Chinese government railroad in 1922.

# Freight Transported by Major Chinese Government Railroad Lines (yuan per ton), 1915–1935

|  | 1915 | | | | | 1918 | | | | |
| Line | Agriculture | Animals | Minerals | Manufactures | Total | Agriculture | Animals | Minerals | Manufactures | Total |
|---|---|---|---|---|---|---|---|---|---|---|
| Peking-Mukden | 319,793 | 43,944 | 1,720,564 | 282,823 | 2,807,120 | 851,040 | 90,108 | 3,578,370 | 713,478 | 6,013,682 |
| Shanghai-Nanjing | 382,826 | 7,240 | 31,863 | 46,751 | 506,291 | 794,972 | 40,293 | 56,588 | 136,884 | 1,131,302 |
| Peking-Hankou | 250,501 | 41,432 | 748,157 | 197,407 | 1,749,958 | 597,598 | 97,520 | 2,082,063 | 450,518 | 3,932,303 |
| Tianjin-Pukou | 358,148 | 10,491 | 190,096 | 116,371 | 1,322,970 | 886,155 | 58,424 | 542,392 | 239,454 | 2,315,832 |
| Shanghai-Hangzhou-Ningbo | 102,541 | 2,598 | 13,863 | 55,120 | 225,528 | 170,769 | 20,523 | 35,714 | 139,046 | 464,787 |
| Canton-Kowloon | 12,218 | 5,935 | 862 | 6,449 | 36,608 | 18,664 | 6,712 | 1,685 | 45,591 | 95,308 |
| Peking-Suiyuan | 124,937 | 37,439 | 208,987 | 52,477 | 539,366 | 297,536 | 89,333 | 427,232 | 129,079 | 1,305,378 |
| Canton-Hankou* | | | | | | | | | | |
| Ji'nan-Qingdao† | | | | | | | | | | |

|  | 1923 | | | | | 1935 | | | | |
| Line | Agriculture | Animals | Minerals | Manufactures | Total | Agriculture | Animals | Minerals | Manufactures | Total |
|---|---|---|---|---|---|---|---|---|---|---|
| Peking-Mukden | 785,227 | 109,951 | 5,374,147 | 839,127 | 8,012,656 | 544,259 | 77,037 | 5,260,815 | 894,002 | 8,006,350 |
| Shanghai-Nanjing | 796,341 | 53,146 | 354,512 | 239,917 | 1,613,773 | 908,278 | 62,166 | 297,578 | 387,963 | 2,061,645 |

| | | | | | | | | | |
|---|---|---|---|---|---|---|---|---|---|
| Peking-Hankou | 802,999 | 102,583 | 3,678,713 | 588,438 | 5,757,889 | 864,579 | 34,982 | 2,666,076 | 398,923 | 4,899,830 |
| Tianjin-Pukou | 999,043 | 65,958 | 1,129,668 | 403,581 | 3,036,091 | 1,077,436 | 51,901 | 1,673,187 | 443,895 | 3,921,460 |
| Shanghai-Hangzhou-Ningbo | 310,009 | 31,287 | 92,831 | 231,900 | 870,728 | 497,893 | 43,453 | 96,781 | 1,036,697 | 1,226,807 |
| Canton-Kowloon | 71,221 | 12,362 | 9,169 | 32,437 | 147,914 | 35,279 | 24,017 | 1,314 | 29,690 | 119,928 |
| Peking-Suiyuan | 408,154 | 144,955 | 722,359 | 161,183 | 1,961,604 | 455,999 | 83,894 | 1,188,153 | 73,572 | 2,354,405 |
| Canton-Hankou* | 42,121 | 17,171 | 157,552 | 39,341 | 336,131 | 35,358 | 23,315 | 169,593 | 65,613 | 484,405 |
| Ji'nan-Qingdao† | 284,907 | 54,490 | 1,181,598 | 343,999 | 2,012,499 | 495,052 | 46,188 | 1,998,764 | 312,211 | 3,554,311 |

*Source:* Ministry of Communications (subsequently the Ministry of Railways), *Statistics of Government Railways* [Zhongguo tielu tongji] (Peking (subsequently Nanking): Tiedaobu tongjichu, 1915–1936). The series covers the railroads' fiscal years until 1935 / 1936. Because of the impact of the civil war years on railroad operations, reports were published with long delays. The volume with 1925 data was published in 1929, and the volume with 1928 appeared in 1933. From 1926 onward each volume contained English and Chinese versions. Beginning in 1930 the name of the series changed slightly to *Statistics of Chinese National Railways* [Zhonghua guoyou tielu kuaiji tongi huibian].

*Data for the Canton-Hankou line, completed in 1936, are taken from the Hubei-Hunan section, which opened in 1922.

†The Ji'nan-Qingdao line became a Chinese government railway in 1922.

# Number of Passengers by Ticket Class, Major Chinese Government Railroad Lines, 1918–1935

**1918 and 1923**

| Line | 1918 | | | | | | 1923 | | | | | |
|---|---|---|---|---|---|---|---|---|---|---|---|---|
| | First | Second | Third | Fourth | Excursion | Total | First | Second | Third | Fourth | Excursion | Total |
| Peking-Mukden | 73,023 | 111,794 | 3,165,095 | — | 10,238 | 3,360,150 | 82,255 | 93,570 | 3,370,313 | 49,578 | 17,289 | 3,678,774 |
| Shanghai-Nanjing | 36,415 | 207,713 | 4,897,533 | 1,125,695 | 21,854 | 6,289,210 | 60,720 | 425,143 | 8,017,389 | 2,155,411 | 56,472 | 10,852,064 |
| Peking-Hankou | 12,516 | 48,669 | 3,486,545 | — | 17,126 | 3,564,856 | 4,338 | 26,042 | 4,033,646 | — | 4,403 | 4,233,170 |
| Tianjin-Pukou | 15,876 | 25,670 | 2,254,193 | 46,848 | 14,859 | 2,357,446 | 9,490 | 42,743 | 3,500,026 | 108,135 | 9,630 | 3,776,827 |
| Shanghai-Hangzhou-Ningbo | 11,311 | 241,624 | 4,242,767 | 538,136 | 10,947 | 5,944,785 | 20,191 | 229,425 | 4,939,331 | 881,798 | 18,871 | 6,112,391 |
| Canton-Kowloon | 7,292 | 35,638 | 1,460,226 | — | 671 | 1,503,827 | 3,753 | 4,815 | 602,814 | — | 1,115 | 968,434 |
| Peking-Suiyuan | 9,154 | 17,801 | 826,267 | — | 5,375 | 858,597 | 10,153 | 9,292 | 1,242,716 | — | 1,152 | 1,277,130 |
| Canton-Hankou | — | — | — | — | — | — | 870 | 630 | 349,630 | 212,911 | 1,534 | 597,332 |
| Ji'nan-Qingdao | — | — | — | — | — | — | 6,744 | 68,074 | 3,541,764 | — | 10,209 | 3,631,812 |
| Total including government privileges† | 173,333 | 723,630 | 21,949,033 | 1,710,679 | 86,286 | 24,642,961 | 204,929 | 961,515 | 32,757,184 | 3,916,996 | 135,410 | 39,226,997 |

**1932 and 1935**

| Line | 1932 | | | | | | 1935 | | | | | |
|---|---|---|---|---|---|---|---|---|---|---|---|---|
| | First | Second | Third | Fourth | Excursion | Total | First | Second | Third | Fourth | Excursion | Total |
| Peking-Mukden | 116,646 | 118,976 | 4,473,869 | — | 18,013 | 4,792,918 | 84,940 | 145,186 | 4,249,586 | — | 3,188 | 4,598,262 |
| Shanghai-Nanjing | 37,534 | 232,048 | 5,176,194 | 1,990,886 | 14,636 | 7,819,420 | 48,027 | 328,127 | 5,779,792 | 4,524,207 | 86,706 | 11,141,784 |
| Peking-Hankou | 5,571 | 23,476 | 2,639,055 | — | 955 | 2,990,534 | 3,777 | 18,529 | 2,834,115 | — | 5,537 | 3,434,319 |
| Tianjin-Pukou | 8,102 | 39,021 | 2,643,020 | — | 6,327 | 2,867,483 | 4,952 | 20,705 | 2,595,675 | — | 44,233 | 2,854,057 |
| Shanghai-Hangzhou-Ningbo | 13,797 | 194,196 | 3,846,148 | 982,641 | 15,784 | 5,116,602 | 16,215 | 162,644 | 3,539,117 | 1,172,172 | 31,083 | 5,053,666 |

| | | | | | | | | | | | | |
|---|---|---|---|---|---|---|---|---|---|---|---|---|
| Canton-Kowloon | 17,718 | 86,229 | 1,499,262 | — | 6,403 | 1,674,892 | 17,171 | 77,887 | 1,215,564 | — | 8,171 | 1,351,195 |
| Peking-Suiyuan | 2,872 | 3,066 | 912,145 | — | 905 | 956,408 | 3,286 | 4,429 | 1,123,164 | — | 10,569 | 1,213,268 |
| Canton-Hankou* | 2,905 | 9,650 | 882,955 | — | 958 | 972,521 | 2,487 | 8,221 | 824,708 | — | 1,078 | 1,012,012 |
| Ji'nan-Qingdao | 5,128 | 34,953 | 2,964,502 | 24,327 | 11,834 | 3,068,133 | 3,634 | 30,139 | 2,468,259 | — | 21,053 | 2,540,141 |
| Total including government privileges† | 214,033 | 772,553 | 18,016,350 | 2,997,854 | 83,482 | 33,971,740 | 245,424 | 1,366,285 | 33,527,743 | 5,777,046 | 283,805 | 43,683,126 |

*Source:* Ministry of Communications (subsequently the Ministry of Railways), *Statistics of Government Railways* [Zhongguo tielu tongji] (Peking [subsequently Nanking]: Tiedaobu tongjichu, 1915–1936). The series covers the railroads' fiscal years until 1935 / 1936. Because of the impact of the civil war years on railroad operations, reports were published with long delays. The volume with 1925 data was published in 1929, and the volume with 1928 appeared in 1933. From 1926 onward each volume contained English and Chinese versions. Beginning in 1930 the name of the series changed slightly to *Statistics of Chinese National Railways* [Zhonghua guoyou tielu kuaiji tongi huibian].

*Data for the Canton-Hankou line, completed in 1936, are taken from the Hubei-Hunan section, which opened in 1922.

†Beginning in 1920, the annual statistics include "government privilege" (predominantly military, but also some civil passengers), in addition to the four classes and excursion tickets. The reports suggest that these were not new categories of tickets but merely new categories of analysis.

# Average Miles per Passenger Journey by Ticket Class, Major Chinese Government Railroad Lines, 1918–1935

## 1918

| Line | First | Second | Third | Fourth | Excursion | Total average |
|---|---|---|---|---|---|---|
| Peking-Mukden | 116 | 102 | 106 | — | 169 | 106 |
| Shanghai-Nanjing | 87 | 58 | 35 | 59 | 76 | 40 |
| Peking-Hankou | 261 | 163 | 70 | — | 72 | 72 |
| Tianjin-Pukou | 382 | 209 | 91 | 190 | 236 | 99 |
| Shanghai-Hangzhou-Ningbo | 74 | 37 | 21 | 45 | 62 | 24 |
| Canton-Kowloon | 71 | 78 | 32 | — | 53 | 34 |
| Peking-Suiyuan | 41 | 43 | 42 | — | 11 | 42 |
| Canton-Hankou* | — | — | — | — | — | — |
| Ji'nan-Qingdao | — | — | — | — | — | — |

## 1923

| Line | First | Second | Third | Fourth | Excursion | Total average |
|---|---|---|---|---|---|---|
| Peking-Mukden | 109 | 91 | 69 | 176 | 127 | 78 |
| Shanghai-Nanjing | 83 | 48 | 30 | 69 | 48 | 39 |
| Peking-Hankou | 295 | 208 | 68 | — | 294 | 75 |
| Tianjin-Pukou | 445 | 257 | 81 | 209 | 196 | 99 |
| Shanghai-Hangzhou-Ningbo | 90 | 48 | 22 | 54 | 84 | 28 |
| Canton-Kowloon | 43 | 80 | 37 | — | 30 | 37 |
| Peking-Suiyuan | 60 | 60 | 49 | — | 33 | 50 |
| Canton-Hankou* | 209 | 183 | 51 | 45 | 127 | 50 |
| Ji'nan-Qingdao | 141 | 80 | 40 | — | 179 | 41 |

## 1932

| Line | First | Second | Third | Fourth | Excursion | Total average |
|---|---|---|---|---|---|---|
| Peking-Mukden | 79 | 76 | 48 | — | 86 | 51 |
| Shanghai-Nanjing | 109 | 84 | 41 | 68 | 77 | 54 |
| Peking-Hankou | 286 | 243 | 73 | — | 94 | 85 |

## 1935

| Line | First | Second | Third | Fourth | Excursion | Total average |
|---|---|---|---|---|---|---|
| Peking-Mukden | 88 | 77 | 55 | — | 91 | 57 |
| Shanghai-Nanjing | 147 | 91 | 38 | 66 | 102 | 55 |
| Peking-Hankou | 307 | 243 | 65 | — | 263 | 98 |

| Tianjin-Pukou | 420 | 291 | 88 | — | 203 | 98 | 453 | 293 | 88 | — | 324 | 106 |
| Shanghai-Hangzhou-Ningbo | 86 | 57 | 31 | 62 | 85 | 39 | 99 | 71 | 32 | 64 | 90 | 42 |
| Canton-Kowloon | 82 | 83 | 47 | — | 52 | 50 | 82 | 81 | 55 | — | 62 | 58 |
| Peking-Suiyuan | 83 | 181 | 52 | — | 41 | 55 | 73 | 145 | 51 | — | 85 | 59 |
| Canton-Hankou* | 206 | 203 | 60 | — | 217 | 64 | 214 | 209 | 56 | — | 150 | 69 |
| Ji'nan-Qingdao | 186 | 103 | 50 | 206 | 150 | 53 | 151 | 112 | 52 | — | 149 | 54 |

*Source:* Ministry of Communications (subsequently the Ministry of Railways), *Statistics of Government Railways* [Zhongguo tielu tongji] (Peking (subsequently Nanking): Tiedaobu tongjichu, 1915–1936). The series covers the railroads' fiscal years until 1935/1936. Because of the impact of the civil war years on railroad operations, reports were published with long delays. The volume with 1925 data was published in 1929, and the volume with 1928 appeared in 1933. From 1926 onward, each volume contained English and Chinese versions. Beginning in 1930 the name of the series changed slightly to *Statistics of Chinese National Railways* [Zhonghua guoyou tielu kuaiji tongi huibian].

*Data for the Canton-Hankou line, completed in 1936, are taken from the completed Hupeh (Hubei)-Hunan section, which opened in 1922.

# Freight Designated for Export (tons), Shipped from Hankou to Guangzhou and onward to Hong Kong by Train, October 18–December 31, 1937

| Product | Registered with railroad for shipment | Shipped | Still awaiting shipment |
|---|---|---|---|
| Wood oil | 5,910 | 1,984 | 3,926 |
| Antimony | 6,000 | 4,700 | 1,300 |
| Tea | 107 | 89 | 18 |
| China glass | 267 | 110 | 157 |
| Pig casings | 126 | 117 | 9 |
| Bristles | 126 | 117 | 9 |
| Egg products | 157 | 77 | 80 |
| Gallnuts | 30 | 30 | 0 |
| Skins | 65 | 19 | 46 |

*Source:* Arthur N. Young, Exporters Association, January 17, 1938, cited in Translation of Chinese telegram, May 13, 1939, from Dr. T. V. Soong in Hong Kong to Generalissimo Chiang Kai-shek and Dr. H. H. Kung in Chungking (Chongqing), marked confidential, box 4, folder "Special telegrams and letters," XPF Papers, BLHBS.

# Abbreviations

| | |
|---|---|
| BAT | British-American Tobacco Company |
| BLHBS | Baker Library, Harvard Business School |
| BNA | British National Archives |
| CCP | Chinese Communist Party |
| CES | Chinese Engineering Society |
| CIS | Chinese Institute of Engineers |
| GDSDAG | Guangdong Provincial Archives |
| GMD | Guomindang |
| JMDAG | Ji'nan Municipal Archives |
| MAN | Maschinenfabrik Augsburg-Nürnberg |
| PLA | People's Liberation Army |
| PRC | People's Republic of China |
| SDDAG | Shandong Provincial Archives |
| SMA | Shanghai Municipal Archives |
| SMR | South Manchurian Railway |
| SOE | state-owned enterprise |
| TJDAG | Tianjin Municipal Archives |
| XPF Papers | Hsia Pin-fang Papers, 1930–1951 |

# Glossary

*anquan* security

*ban* squad

*bang* group

*banghui* gang association

*baogong* contract-labor system

*Beijing shijian* Beijing time

*bendi ren* locals

*bu pa ku, bu pa si* fearing neither
hardship nor death

*cache* wash the engines

*cha bu duo* at around

*chuanlian* revolutionary networking

*chunyun* Spring Festival travel

*dagai* roughly

*dang zhibu* party branch

*dangzong zhibu* general party branches

*danwei* work unit

*dianchang* power plant

*dianxing* model

*difang mingong* local, temporary
unskilled worker

*difangzhi* local gazetteer

*diquxing* regionalism

*duan* section

*dufa* reading method

*erdeng* second class

*fabi* currency introduced by the GMD
in 1935

*fan geming fenzi* counterrevolutionary

*fei* fliers

*fenduan* subsection

*fengshou* bumper harvest

*fu zeren* take responsibility

*geming lieshi* revolutionary martyr

*gong* wage labor

*gonghui* labor union

*gongli* kilometer

*gongren* worker

*gongsi* company

*gongtou* foreman

*gongwusi* Operations Department

*guan* government (versus merchant)

*guanliju* administration bureau, or line
management office

**Guojia tieluju** National Railroad
Administration

**Guowuyuan** State Council

*guo you* government-owned

*guwen* adviser

*guyuan* hired laborer

*hei maozi* black hat

*hei shehui* underworld society

*hukou* household registration permit

*jianduju* supervisory office

**Jianshebu** Ministry of Construction

*jiaofu* porter

**Jiaotongbu** Ministry of Communications and Transportation

**Ji'nan jichang** Ji'nan Machine Works

**Jin-Pu tielu bingguan** Jin-Pu Railroad Hotel

**Jin-Pu tieluju** Jin-Pu Railroad Bureau

**Jin-Pu tielu yiyuan** Jin-Pu Railroad Hospital

*jishu zhuanjia* technical expert

*jixing huowu lieche* express goods train

*ju* bureau

*junren* soldier

*junshi guanzhi weiyuanhui* military control commission

*kaigong* opening ceremony

*ke* administrative division

**Kong miao** Temple of Confucius

**Kongzi lin** Forest of Confucius

**Kuangwuju** Bureau of Mining

*kuangwu tielu zongju* mining and railroad bureau

*lao da'nan* old disaster

*lian* company (military)

*lijin* commercial transit tax

**Luzheng si** Bureau of Public Roads

*maike* wheat harvester

*meiyun wei gang* coal transportation as the core

*mingling* command

*nianhua* New Year's paper print

**Nongshangbu** Ministry of Agriculture and Commerce

*pa* crawlers

*pai* platoon

*pao dan bang* black-market small traders

*qiye guanli* enterprise management

*qu* region

*quan* power

*quandang, quanmin, quanlu* one party, one people, one line

*ren gongshe* person, people's commune

*renmin tielu* people's railroad

**Ruifuchang jiqi gongsi** Ruifuchang Machine Company

*sandeng* third class

*shang* merchant (vs. government)

**Shangbu** Ministry of Commerce

*shang you* commercial / private

*shenjing* nerve

*shi* division

*shixi* apprenticeship

**Shuili weiyuanhui** Water Resources Commission

*shunzi* in due sequence

*shuyu* idiom

*siji* engine driver

*silu* fireman

*tiedaobing* militarized construction team, railroad army corps, railroad soldier

*tiedao bingtuan* railroad corps

**Tiedaobu** Ministry of Railways

**Tiedao guanli xueyuan** Railroad Management College

*tiedao silingbu* railroad headquarters

*tiedao youjidui* guerrilla squad

*tiedao zongdui* railroad columns

*tielu fenju* branch railroad bureau

**Tielu guanliju** Railroad Management Bureau

*tieluju* railroad bureau

*tielu xueyuan* railroad academy

*tielu zhengqi fenkai* separating government- and market-driven railroad units

*tongche* connecting the final two rails

*toudeng* first class

*tuan* group

*tuanti lüxing* group travel

*waidi ren* outsiders

**Waiwubu** Ministry of Foreign Affairs

*wei renmin er si* die for the people

*wending* stability

*wenming* enlightenment

*xiao shehui* small society

*xibu fazhan* "Developing the Western Region"

*xinhao* signal

*xuexisheng* apprentice

*yamen* magistrate's office

*yiding shijian* firm (i.e., definite) time

*ying* camp

*yongyuan* hired laborer

**Youchuanbu** Ministry of Posts and Communications

*youjidui* guerrilla

*yuan* employee

*yunshu zhihuibu* transportation command center

*yunzhuan gongsi* transportation company

*zaofanpai* rebel faction

*zhanchang guanli banfa* "Station Management Method"

*zhanshi* ordinary soldier

*zhejiu* depreciation

*zhengchang* order and regularity

*zhiyuan* full employee

*zhixia* under supervision

*zhongfa* central party document

**Zhongguo gongchengshi xuehui** Chinese Engineering Institute

**Zhongguo lüxingshe** China Travel Service

**Zhongguo renmin jiefangjun tiedaobing** People's Liberation Army railroad soldiers

**Zhongguo tielu xiehui** Chinese Railroad Association

**Zhongguo tielu zong gongsi** China Railway Corporation

**Zhonghua quanguo tielu xiehui** China National Railroad Association

**ZhongMei gongchengshi xiehui** Association of Chinese and American Engineers

*zhuce* register

*zhun zhiyuan* employee-in-training

**Ziyuan weiyuanhui** National Resources Commission

*zongju* head office

**Zongli yamen** Foreign Affairs Office (Qing dynasty)

**Zongwusi** General Office Department

*zongzhang* minister

*zuo huoche* play train

*zuo xiao maimai* small trader

# Notes

## Introduction

1. "Tientsin-Pukou Railway," *Peking and Tientsin Times,* December 3, 1912.

2. Zhang Yue, "China Sets Plan to Boost Rail Network," State Council, People's Republic of China, June 29, 2016, at http://english.gov.cn/premier/news /2016/06/29/content_281475382711365.htm, accessed October 15, 2016.

3. Sun Yat-sen, *The International Development of China* (New York: G. P. Putnam's Sons, 1929 [1st ed., 1922]); Howard L. Boorman, ed., *Biographical Dictionary of Republican China,* 4 vols. (New York: Columbia University Press, 1967–1971), 3:170–189.

4. For example, the neighborhood surrounding the Shanghai railroad station and the former North Station, or Beizhan along Tianmu Road, is still a good example of an area dominated by railroad-related offices, locomotive depots, housing, hotels, and now even parking garages under the Shanghai Railroad Bureau's administration.

5. Adding the rail mileage in northern Taiwan, the Chinese total came to 255 miles. Lee En-han, *China's Quest for Railway Autonomy, 1904–1911: A Study of the Chinese Railway Rights Recovery Movement* (Singapore: National University of Singapore Press, 1977), 13; Jack Simmons, *The Railway in England and Wales, 1830–1914* (Leicester, UK: Leicester University Press, 1978), 276–277; Ralph William Huenemann, *The Dragon and the Iron Horse: The Economics of Railroads in China* (Cambridge, MA: Harvard University Press, 1984), 76–77.

6. See, for example, the following classics: Robert Fogel, *Railroads and American Economic Growth: Essays in Econometric History* (Baltimore: Johns Hopkins University Press, 1964); H. J. Habakkuk, *American and British Technology in the Nineteenth Century* (Cambridge: Cambridge University Press, 1962); John F. Stover, *Iron Road to the West: American Railroads in the 1850s* (New York: Columbia University Press, 1978); Patrick O'Brien, *The New Economic History of the Railways* (New York: St. Martin's, 1977); Ralf Roth and Marie-Noëlle Polino, eds., *The City*

*and the Railway in Europe* (Burlington, VT: Ashgate, 2003); T. R. Gourvish, *Railways and the British Economy, 1830–1914* (London: Macmillan, 1980); Jacob Metzer, *Some Economic Aspects of Railroad Development in Tsarist Russia* (New York: Arno Press, 1977); Steven J. Ericson, *The Sound of the Whistle: Railroads and the State in Meiji Japan* (Cambridge, MA: Council on East Asian Studies, Harvard University, 1996); Ian J. Kerr, ed., *Railways in Modern India* (New Delhi: Oxford University Press, 2001); Walter Licht, *Working for the Railroad: The Organization of Work in the Nineteenth Century* (Princeton, NJ: Princeton University Press, 1983).

7. I use the American term "railroad" instead of the British term "railway" throughout the book. Ministry of Railways, however, is the official English translation used by the ministry itself during both the Republican period and the PRC.

8. Max Weber, *Economy and Society: An Outline of Interpretive Sociology*, ed. Guenther Roth and Claus Wittich, 2 vols. (Berkeley: University of California Press, 1978), 2:956–1005; Alfred Chandler Jr., *The Visible Hand: The Managerial Revolution in American Business* (Cambridge, MA: Harvard University Press, 1977).

9. See, for example, David Faure, *China and Capitalism: A History of Modern Business Enterprise in China* (Hong Kong: Hong Kong University Press, 2006); Madeleine Zelin, *The Merchants of Zigong: Industrial Entrepreneurship in Early Modern China* (New York: Columbia University Press, 2006); Sherman Cochran, *Encountering Chinese Networks: Western, Japanese, and Chinese Corporations in China, 1880–1937* (Berkeley: University of California Press, 2000); Brett Sheehan, *Industrial Eden: A Chinese Capitalist Vision* (Cambridge, MA: Harvard University Press, 2015); Elisabeth Köll, *From Cotton Mill to Business Empire: The Emergence of Regional Enterprises in Modern China* (Cambridge, MA: Harvard University Asia Center, 2003).

10. Richard White, *Railroaded: The Transcontinentals and the Making of Modern America* (New York: W. W. Norton, 2012).

11. Ghassan Moazzin, "Networks of Capital: German Bankers and the Financial Internationalisation of China (1885–1919)" (PhD diss., University of Cambridge, 2017); Elisabeth Kaske, "Sichuan as Pivot: Provincial Politics and Gentry Power in Late Qing Railway Projects in Southwestern China," in *Southwest China in a Regional and Global Perspective* (c. 1600–1911), ed. Ulrich Theobald and Cao Jin (Boston: Brill, 2018), 379–423; Thomas Kampen, *Revolutionäre Eisenbahnplanungen: Die Aufstände in der Provinz Sichuan und das Ende des chinesischen Kaiserreiches (1911)* [Revolutionary railroad planning: The uprisings in Sichuan province and the end of the Chinese empire (1911)] (Berlin: Wissenschaft und Technik Verlag, 2002); Joseph W. Esherick, *Reform and Revolution in China: The 1911 Revolution in Hunan and Hubei* (Berkeley: University of California Press, 1977).

12. Huenemann, *The Dragon and the Iron Horse*. Thomas Rawski devotes a chapter to transportation and communication infrastructure in his comprehensive macroeconomic analysis of economic growth during the Republic. See Thomas G. Rawski, *Economic Growth in Prewar China* (Berkeley: University of

California Press, 1989), 181–238; Leung Chi-Keung, *China, Railway Patterns and National Goals* (Chicago: University of Chicago Press, 1980); Ernest P. Liang, *China, Railways and Agricultural Development, 1875–1935* (Chicago: University of Chicago Press, 1982); Chang Jui-te (Zhang Ruide), *Ping-Han tielu yu huabei de jingji fazhan (1905–1937)* [The Beijing-Hankou Railroad and the economic development of North China, 1905–1937] (Taibei: Zhongyang yanjiuyuan jindaishi yanjiusuo, 1987); Chang Jui-te (Zhang Ruide), *Zhongguo jindai tielu shiye guanli de yanjiu: Zhengzhi cengmian de fenxi (1876–1937)* [A study of the industrial management of modern Chinese railroads: A political-level analysis, 1876–1937] (Taibei: Zhongyang yanjiuyuan jindaishi yanjiusuo, 1991); Ding Xianyong, *Xinshi jiaotong yu shehui bianqian: Yu Minguo Zhejiang wei zhongxin* [New communications and social transformation: Focusing on Zhejiang province during the Republican period] (Beijing: Zhongguo shehui kexue chubanshe, 2007).

13. For railroad infrastructure in Manchuria see, for example, Joshua Fogel, *Life along the South Manchurian Railway: The Memoirs of Ito Takeo* (London: Routledge, 1988); Prasenjit Duara, *Sovereignty and Authenticity: Manchukuo and the East Asian Modern* (Lanham, MD: Rowman and Littlefield, 2003); Jie Xueshi, ed., *Mantie yu Zhongguo laogong* [The South Manchurian Railway and Chinese labor] (Beijing: Shehui kexue wenxian chubanshe, 2003); Yoshihisa Tak Matsusaka, *The Making of Japanese Manchuria, 1904–1932* (Cambridge, MA: Harvard University Press, 2001); Bruce A. Elleman and Stephen Kotkin, eds., *Manchurian Railways and the Opening of China: An International History* (Armonk, NY: M.E. Sharpe, 2010); Ayumu Yasutomi, *Manshukoku no kinyu* [The financial system of Manchukuo] (Tokyo: Sobunsha, 1997). As for the SMR representing the only railroad system on the Chinese mainland, see Minoru Sawai, ed., *The Development of Railway Technology in East Asia in Comparative Perspective* (Singapore: Springer Nature Singapore, 2017).

14. Rawski, *Economic Growth in Prewar China*.


## 1. Technology and Semicolonial Ventures

1. Fung Yee, "A Chinese View of Railways in China," *The Nineteenth Century: A Monthly Review* 27, no. 156 (February 1890): 225–226.

2. William Barclay Parsons, *An American Engineer in China* (New York: McClure, Phillips, 1900), 261.

3. For the debate on semicolonialism and business systems, see Jürgen Osterhammel, "Semi-colonialism and Informal Empire in Twentieth Century China: Towards a Framework of Analysis," in *Imperialism and After: Continuities and Discontinuities*, ed. Wolfgang J. Mommsen and Jürgen Osterhammel (London: Allen and Unwin, 1986), 290–314. See also Jürgen Osterhammel, "British Business in China, 1860s–1950s," in *British Business in Asia since 1860*, ed. Rupert Davenport-Hines and Geoffrey Jones (Cambridge: Cambridge University

Press, 1989), 189–216; Jürgen Osterhammel, *Colonialism: A Theoretical Overview,* trans. Shelley Frisch (Princeton, NJ: Wiener, 1997); Yen-p'ing Hao, *The Comprador in Nineteenth Century China: Bridge between East and West* (Cambridge: Cambridge University Press, 1979).

4. Lloyd E. Eastman, *Family, Fields and Ancestors: Constancy and Change in China's Social and Economic History, 1550–1949* (Oxford: Oxford University Press, 1988), 167; see also Diana Lary, *China's Republic* (Cambridge: Cambridge University Press, 2007), 25–26; Christian Wolmar, *Blood, Iron and Gold: How the Railways Transformed the World* (New York: Public Affairs, 2009).

5. On the Self-Strengthening Movement, see, for example, David Pong, *Shen Pao-chen and China's Modernization in the Nineteenth Century* (Cambridge: Cambridge University Press, 1994); Wang Ermin, *Qing ji bing gongye de xingqi* [The rise of the military industry in the Qing dynasty] (Taibei: Zhongyang yanjiuyuan jindaishi yanjiusuo, 1978); Stephen R. Halsey, *Quest for Power: European Imperialism and the Making of Chinese Statecraft* (Cambridge, MA: Harvard University Press, 2015), 113–145.

6. Benjamin Elman, *On Their Own Terms: Science in China, 1550–1990* (Cambridge, MA: Harvard University Press, 2005), 362.

7. Ibid., 310–319. As Xiong Yuezhi and Wang Ermin show, a considerable number of textbooks and treatises on military and natural sciences, authored in the mid-nineteenth century, became available to a sophisticated Chinese readership in translation or as original texts. Xiong Yuezhi, *Xi xue dong zhe yu wan Qing shehui* [The dissemination of Western learning and late Qing society] (Shanghai: Renmin chubanshe, 1989); Wang Ermin, *Qing ji bing gongye de xingqi,* 205–222, app. 2.

8. See "Huoche yu tielu lüelun" [A brief account of engines and railroads], *Gezhi huibian,* Summer 1877, 1B–11B.

9. Ibid., 6A–7A.

10. Ibid., 1B–11B.

11. "Huolunche lu" [Report about railroads], *Xiaohai xuebao,* June 1876, 4. Many thanks to Maybo Ching for drawing my attention to this source.

12. For images in an article on travels in Great Britain, see "Lüyou biji" [Travel diary], *Xiaohai xuebao,* August 1877, 2. For British images, see *Illustrated London News,* May 1842; and Michael Freeman, *Railways and the Victorian Imagination* (New Haven, CT: Yale University Press, 1999), first endpaper, 99, 109.

13. See Wolfgang Schivelbusch, *Geschichte der Eisenbahnreise: Zur Industrialisierung von Raum und Zeit im 19. Jahrhundert* [History of the train journey: Industrialization of space and time in the 19th century] (Munich: Hanser, 1977).

14. James A. Flath, "The Chinese Railroad View: Transportation Themes in Popular Print, 1873–1915," *Cultural Critique* 58 (Fall 2004): 168–190, quote 168–169.

15. Ibid., 176. The print can be found in *Dianshizhai huabao* [Dianshizhai pictorial], no. 12, (1884). For an introduction to the pictorial see Xiaoqing Ye, *The Dianshizhai Pictorial: Shanghai Urban Life, 1884–1898* (Ann Arbor: Center for Chinese Studies, University of Michigan, 2003).

16. Flath, "Chinese Railroad View," 178.

17. Elman, *On Their Own Terms.*

18. Ibid., 54; see also Hsien-chun Wang, "Discovering Steam Power in China, 1840s–1860s," *Technology and Culture* 51, no. 1 (January 2010): 31–54, in particular 45–53.

19. Elman, *On Their Own Terms,* 82.

20. On the Taiping Rebellion see Stephen R. Platt, *Autumn in the Heavenly Kingdom: China, the West, and the Epic Story of the Taiping Civil War* (New York: Knopf, 2012); Philip A. Kuhn, "The Taiping Rebellion," in *The Cambridge History of China*, vol. 10, part 1, ed. John K. Fairbank (Cambridge: Cambridge University Press, 1970), 264–350.

21. On the abortive fate of the Wusong Railroad, see Hsien-chun Wang, "Merchants, Mandarins, and the Railway: Institutional Failure and the Wusong Railway, 1874–1877," *International Journal of Asian Studies* 12, no. 1 (January 2015): 31–53.

22. Erik Baark, *Lightning Wires: The Telegraph and China's Technological Modernization, 1860–1890* (Westport, CT: Greenwood Press, 1997), 166.

23. Mongton Chih Hsu, *Railway Problems in China* (New York: Columbia University, 1915), 15–24.

24. Elisabeth Köll, *From Cotton Mill to Business Empire: The Emergence of Regional Enterprises in Modern China* (Cambridge, MA: Harvard University Asia Center, 2003). For the role of government in promoting industrial enterprises after 1895, see ibid., 31–51.

25. Zhang Jian, *Zhang Jizi jiulu* [The nine records of Zhang Jizhi], ed. Zhang Xiaoruo, 7 vols., *Shiyelun*, vol. 2 (1931; repr., Taibei: Wenhai chubanshe, 1980); see also Ssu-yü Teng and John K. Fairbank, *China's Response to the West: A Documentary Survey, 1869–1923* (Cambridge, MA: Harvard University Press, 1977), 108–119.

26. Mi Rucheng, *Zhonghua Minguo tielushi ziliao (1912–1949)* [A history of railroads in Republican China (1912–1949)] (Beijing: Zhongguo shehui wenxian chubanshe, 2002).

27. See, for example, Lin Cheng, *The Chinese Railways: A Historical Survey* (Shanghai: China United Press, 1935); Jin Jiafeng, ed., *Zhongguo jiaotong zhi fazhan jiqi quxiang* [Developments and trends in Chinese transportation] (Nanjing; Zhongzhong shuju, 1937).

28. Lü Weijun et al., *Shandong quyu xiandaihua yanjiu (1840–1949)* [Research on the regional modernization of Shandong (1840–1949)] (Ji'nan: Qilu shushe, 2002), 54–59.

29. Ian J. Kerr, *Engines of Change: The Railroads That Made India* (Westport, CT: Praeger, 2007), 24.

30. Cheng, *Chinese Railways,* 82; P. H. B. Kent, *Railway Enterprise in China: An Account of Its Origin and Development* (London: E. Arnold, 1907), 152–153. Ralph William Huenemann quotes a 5.85 percent true interest rate on the 1908 loan. Huenemann, *The Dragon and the Iron Horse: The Economics of Railroads in China* (Cambridge, MA: Harvard University Press, 1984), 120.

31. *Investment Values of Chinese Railway Bonds* (Paris: La Librairie fran-çaise, 1923), 45 and table 1.

32. Lee En-han, *China's Quest for Railway Autonomy 1904–1911* (Singapore: Singapore University Press, 1977), table 4; *Santo tetsudo kaisha ni kansuru chosa hokoku: furoku hoshin tetsudo shakkan keiyaku* [Survey report on the Shandong Railway Company: Appendix with the Loan Agreement of the Pukou railway terms] (Dairen: Manshu Nichinichi Shinbunsha, taisho 4 [1915]); Ghassan Moazzin, "Networks of Capital: German Bankers and the Financial Interna-tionalisation of China (1885–1919)" (PhD diss., University of Cambridge, 2017).

33. *Santo tetsudo kaisha ni kansuru chosa hokoku*, appendix on Pukou terms in 1915.

34. David Faure, *China and Capitalism: A History of Modern Business Enter-prise in China* (Hong Kong: Hong Kong University Press, 2006). One notable excep-tion to rather restrained domestic railroad investment was overseas Chinese Chen Yixi who returned from the United States to his hometown Taishan in Guangdong province to build the Xinning Railroad, which was completed in 1909. In the wake of the Japanese occupation of Guangzhou in 1938, the government ordered the dismantling of all local railroads, including the 85 miles of the Xinning Railroad. The line was never rebuilt. See Madeleine Y. Hsu, *Dreaming of Gold, Dreaming of Home: Transnationalism and Migration between the United States and South China, 1882–1943* (Stanford, CA: Stanford University Press, 2000), 156–173.

35. *Investment Values of Chinese Railway Bonds*; Ghassan Moazzin, "Net-works of Capital."

36. "Records relating to German railroad construction in China, 1898–1916," Business Manuscripts MSS:705, 1898–1916, 15 vols., Baker Library, Harvard Business School (hereafter BLHBS); ibid., annotated draft of "Final Agreement," vol. 5 (1903 / 1904), pp. 1–8 (separate pagination). The term "engineer" in the document refers to civil engineers with specific professional training and expertise relevant to railroad construction and operation. In American English, the term "railroad engi-neer" refers to the person operating the train (known as the engine driver in British terminology). See Walter Licht, *Working for the Railroad: The Organization of Work in the Nineteenth Century* (Princeton, NJ: Princeton University Press, 1983).

37. BLHBS, 1904, annotated draft of "Final Agreement," vol. 5, pp. 1–8 (sepa-rate pagination); BLHBS, vol. 11 (1908 / 1909), "Stand der Bauarbeiten am 15. Feb-ruar 1909" [State of the construction work on February 15, 1909], February 16, 1909, no pagination.

38. Cheng, *Chinese Railways*, 60.

39. "Vertraulich: Im Anschluss an den Bericht vom 17. Juni 1909" [Confiden-tial: Following the report from June 17, 1909], BLHBS, vol. 11, 1908–1909, June 22, 1909, no pagination.

40. Cheng, *Chinese Railways*, 33–35.

41. Köll, *From Cotton Mill to Business Empire*, 176.

42. John Earl Baker, *Chinese Railway Accounts* (n.p.: Jiaotongbu, 1923), 87.

43. "Im Anschluss an den Bericht No. 215 vom 3. Dezember 1908" [Following up on the report no. 215 from December 3, 1908], BLHBS, vol. 11, 1908–1909, no pagination.

44. Köll, *From Cotton Mill to Business Empire.*

45. 1914–16, No. 5551 Annual Series, Diplomatic and Consular Reports, China, Report for the Year 1914 on the Trade of Hankow, 3–5, FO 228/2594, British National Archives (BNA).

46. See, e.g., Peter C. Perdue, *China Marches West: The Qing Conquest of Central Eurasia* (Cambridge, MA: Belknap Press of Harvard University Press, 2005), 442–461.

47. Tientsin-Pukow Railway relief map, inserted into BLHBS, vol. 8, 1907.

48. Graf Verri, "Notizen zu Bericht ueber Erkundung einer Bahntrasse im Abschnitt Tsi-nan-fu and Yen-tschou-fu" [Notes for the report on the exploration of the tracks in the section between Ji'nan and Yanzhou], BLHBS, vol. 3, March 30, 1902.

49. J. G. H. Glass, *Report on the Concessions of the Pekin Syndicate, Limited, in the Provinces of Shansi and Honan, China, with Estimates of Cost of Railways and Other Works Necessary for Their Development* (n.p., 1899), 3–4. For the history of the syndicates, see Frank H. H. King, "Joint Venture in China: The Experience of the Pekin Syndicate, 1897–1961," *Business and Economic History* 19 (1990): 113–122.

50. Glass, *Report on the Concessions of the Pekin Syndicate,* 3–5; for railroad engineers working in India, see Kerr, *Engines of Change.*

51. Glass, *Report on the Concessions of the Pekin Syndicate,* 43–47.

52. Ibid., 43.

53. Ibid., 46.

54. Ibid., 39–40.

55. Ibid., 47.

56. For an excellent analysis of the challenges to land surveying and map-making, see Sui-wai Cheung, "Trigonometrical Survey and the Land Maps in China, 1368–1950," in *Colonial Administration and Land Reform in East Asia,* ed. Sui-wai Cheung (London: Routledge, 2017), 117–141.

57. For more on maps, see Iwo Amelung, "New Maps for the Modernizing State: Western Cartographic Knowledge and Its Application in 19th and 20th Century China," in *Graphics and Text in the Production of Technical Knowledge in China: The Warp and the Weft,* ed. Francesca Bray, Vera Lichtman, and Georges Metailie (Leiden: Brill, 2007), 685–726; Hilde De Weerdt, "Maps and Memory: Readings of Cartography in Twelfth- and Thirteenth-Century Song China," in *Imago Mundi* 61, no. 2 (2007): 145–167. For property rights and contract culture, see Madeleine Zelin, Jonathan K. Ocko, and Robert Gardella, eds., *Contract and Property in Early Modern China* (Stanford, CA: Stanford University Press, 2004).

58. "Cangzhou cheng" [The city of Cangzhou], hand-drawn map, inserted in BLHBS, vol. 5, 1904, no pagination.

59. Ibid.

60. BLHBS, vol. 1, 1898; Klaus Mühlhahn, *Herrschaft und Widerstand in der "Musterkolonie" Kiautschou: Interaktionen zwischen China und Deutschland, 1897– 1914* [Rule and resistance in the "model colony" Kiautschou: Interactions between China and Germany, 1897–1914] (Munich: Oldenbourg, 2000), 472.

61. *Ji'nan tieluju zhi, 1899–1985* [Gazetteer of the Ji'nan Railroad Bureau, 1899– 1985] (Ji'nan: Ji'nan tieluju shi zhi bianzuan lingdao xiaozu, 1993), 68.

62. Fear of railroads in the West, even among the urban elite, was not unknown. For example, Pope Gregory XVI feared the "infernal machines" that might transport revolutionary ideas and unwanted economic competition. See Eamon Duffy, *Saints and Sinners: A History of the Popes* (New Haven, CT: Yale University Press, 2006), 281; Owen Chadwick, *A History of the Popes, 1830–1914* (Oxford: Clarendon Press, 1998), 50–51.

63. *(Shandong sheng) Dezhou xianzhi* [Gazetteer of Dezhou county (in Shandong province)] (1935; repr., Taibei: Chengwen chubanshe, 1968); *(Shandong sheng) Jihe xianzhi* [Gazetteer of Jihe county (in Shandong province)] (1933; repr., Taibei: Chengwen chubanshe, 1968); *(Shandong sheng) Jining xianzhi* [Gazetteer of Jining county (in Shandong province)] (1927; repr., Taibei: Chengwen chubanshe, 1968).

64. For more on the incidents, see Paul Cohen, *History in Three Keys: The Boxers as Event, Experience, and Myth* (New York: Columbia University Press, 1997), 47.

65. Ibid.; Susan Naquin, *Peking: Temples and City Life, 1400–1900* (Berkeley: University of California Press, 2000), 681.

66. Cohen, *History in Three Keys*, 86.

67. Ibid., 272.

68. Ibid., 288.

69. Ibid., 42.

70. See Mühlhahn, *Herrschaft und Widerstand in der "Musterkolonie" Kiautschou.*

71. Wang Shouzhong, *Deguo qinlüe Shandong shi* [A history of the German invasion of Shandong province] (Beijing: Renmin chubanshe, 1988), 152–153.

72. Both Wang Shouzhong and Klaus Mühlhahn use this diary as their only primary source, which gives one average price for land in Gaomi village. *Choubi oucun: Yihetuan shi liao* [Occasional writings: Historical materials on the Boxer Uprising] (1900; repr., Beijing: Zhongguo shehui kexue chubanshe, 1983), 173.

73. Jeff Hornibrook, *A Great Undertaking: Mechanization and Social Change in a Late Imperial Chinese Coalmining Community* (Albany: State University of New York Press, 2015), chap. 4. With regard to the land acquisition for a proposed railroad line through Pingxiang near the Anyuan mines, Hornibrook confirms that estimating a true price for particular fields and land assets in the late Qing and Republican periods is virtually impossible.

74. Statement by chief engineer Dorpmüller, BLHBS, vol. 13, February 1913. On the career of Dorpmüller after his return to Germany and service as Reichs-

verkehrsminister (minister of transportation) in Hitler's government, see Alfred Gottwald, *Dorpmüller 1920–1945* (Freiburg: EK-Verlag, 2009).

75. William Barclay Parsons, *Report on the Survey and Prospects of a Railway between Hankow and Canton* (New York, 1899), 40. For a similar statement by Dorpmüller in 1913, see BLHBS, vol. 13, February 1913.

76. Parsons, *An American Engineer in China*, 265.

77. Glass, *Report on the Concessions of the Pekin Syndicate*, app. 84A.

78. Ibid.

79. Ibid., 159–160, app. S1.

80. Ibid., 60, 63.

81. "Chinese government railways Tientsin-Pukow Line, northern section," BLHBS, vol. 14, December 31, 1912, 2.

82. "Rechenschaftsbericht betreffend der Kosten der Nordstrecke der Tientsin-Pukow-Eisenbahn" [Accountability report concerning the cost of the northern section of the Tientsin-Pukow Railroad], BLHBS, vol. 15, January 24, 1914, 11.

83. Ibid., 6–8.

84. BLHBS, vol. 3, January 1–May 31, 1902.

85. BLHBS, vol. 12, 1909.

86. None of the provincial or county archives in Shandong have land sale records related to the Jin-Pu Railroad, and they are not included in the records from the English and German sections kept in the Foreign Office files at the National Archives in London or in the Baker Library Historical Collections, Harvard Business School.

87. BLHBS, vol. 12, June 1909.

88. Ibid., 7. I also was unable to find any documentation in Chinese local archives.

89. Inserted draft map, BLHBS, vol. 3, 1900.

90. *Shandong shengzhi: Kongzi gulizhi* [Shandong provincial gazetteer: Gazetteer of the former Kong estate] (Beijing: Zhonghua shuju, 1994); Kong Demao and Kong Kelan, *The House of Confucius*, trans. Rosemary Roberts, ed. Frances Wood (London: Hodder and Stoughton, 1988); Ke Lan, *Qiannian Kong fu de zuihou yidai* [The last generation of the thousand-year-old Kong mansion] (Tianjin: Tianjin jiaoyu chubanshe, 1999); Luo Chenglie, *Qufu shiji baiti* [100 topics on Qufu's historical sites] (Ji'nan: Qilu shushe, 1987).

91. Kong Demao and Kong Kelan, *House of Confucius*, 122.

92. Ke Lan, *Qiannian Kong fu de zuihou yidai*.

93. Qufu became one of the main tourist attractions during the Republican period, and together with Mount Tai (Taishan) was actively promoted by the Jin-Pu Railroad as a travel destination. See Jin-Pu tielu guanliju zongwuchu bianchake, *Jin-Pu tielu lüxing zhinan* [Travel guide for the Jin-Pu Railroad], 1921; BLHBS, vol. 12, 1909.

94. John Grant Birch, *Travels in North and Central China* (London: Hurst and Blackett, 1902), 73.

95. Anthony Northey, *Kafka's Mischpoche* [Kafka's family] (Berlin: Verlag Klaus Wagenbach, 1988), 22–28. His uncle's work and railroad experience found its way into Franz Kafka's work, particularly the fragmentary fiction "Erinnerung an die Kaldabahn" [Remembering the Kalda line] from 1914; ibid., 39–45.

96. BLHBS, vol. 12, no. 1443, July 1909.

97. BLHBS, vols. 1–3, 1898–1901.

98. BLHBS, vol. 12, 1909.

99. Han Suyin, *Destination Chungking* (Boston: Little Brown, 1942), 10.

100. "Vertraulich: Im Anschluss an den Bericht vom 17. Juni 1909" [Confidential: following the report from June 17, 1909], BLHBS, vol. 11, 1908–1909, June 22, 1909, no pagination.

101. BLHBS, vol. 12, 1909, report from August 13, 1909, no pagination.

102. "Hankow" *North-China Herald*, May 9, 1900, 822.

103. A Mr. Petri's criminal misbehavior caused great anguish to Dorpmüller and the management. BLHBS, vol. 12, report from August 13, 1909, no pagination.

104. For photographs of Chinese railroad laborers, see the Shandong Provincial Archives (SDDAG), unmarked photo collection, 1920s. On the *gongtou* system, see Köll, *From Cotton Mill to Business Empire;* Elizabeth J. Perry, *Shanghai on Strike: The Politics of Chinese Labor* (Stanford, CA: Stanford University Press, 1993); Emily Hong, *Sisters and Strangers: Women in the Shanghai Cotton Mills, 1919–1949* (Stanford, CA: Stanford University Press, 1986).

105. "Die Missstaende an der Tientsin-Pukow Bahn," [Irregularities on the Tientsin-Pukow line], BLHBS, vol. 12, 1909, 1–8 (separate pagination).

106. *Shandong shengzhi: Tielu zhi* [Gazetteer of Shandong province: Railroad gazetteer] (Ji'nan: Shandong renmin chubanshe, 1993), 236; *Ji'nan tieluju zhi,* 226–227.

107. "Chinese government railways Tientsin-Pukow Line, northern section," December 31, 1912, BLHBS, vol. 14, p. 5.

108. BLHBS, vol. 15, June 20, 1914.

109. Shanghai Municipal Archives (SMA), Q55-2-493, Jiaotong yinhang zonghang: Yewulei [Bank of Communications head office: Business affairs], 1936–1938.

110. *Ji'nan tieluju zhi,* 68–69.

111. BLHBS, vol. 12, "J. no. 1443," July 1909, report by Dr. Betz.

112. Wolmar, *Blood, Iron, and Gold,* at 329, and see 324–329.

113. Faure, *China and Capitalism;* Hsien-chun Wang, "Merchants, Mandarins, and the Railway," 50–51.

114. Steven W. Usselman, *Regulating Railroad Innovation: Business, Technology, and Politics in America, 1840–1920* (Cambridge: Cambridge University Press, 2002).

115. Richard White, *Railroaded: The Transcontinentals and the Making of Modern America* (New York: Norton, 2012).

## 2. Managing Transitions in the Early Republic

1. For a detailed narrative of the 1911 revolution, see, for example, Joseph Esherick, *Reform and Revolution in China: The 1911 Revolution in Hunan and Hubei* (Berkeley: University of California Press, 1976). On the political, social, and financial aspects of the Railway Rights Recovery Movement, see Lee En-han, *China's Quest for Railway Autonomy, 1904–1911: A Study of the Chinese Railway-Rights Recovery Movement* (Singapore: Singapore University Press, 1977); Elisabeth Kaske, "Sichuan as Pivot: Provincial Politics and Gentry Power in Late Qing Railway Projects in Southwestern China" in *Southwest China in a Regional and Global Perspective (c. 1600–1911)*, ed. Ulrich Theobald and Cao Jin (Leiden: Brill, 2018), 379–423; Thomas Kampen, *Revolutionäre Eisenbahnplanungen in China: Die Aufstände in der Provinz Sichuan und das Ende des Chinesischen Kaiserreiches (1911)* [Revolutionary railroad planning in China: The uprisings in Sichuan province and the end of the Chinese empire (1911)] (Berlin: Wissenschaft und Technik Verlag, 2002); Mary Backus Rankin, "Nationalistic Contestation and Mobilization Politics: Practice and Rhetoric of Railway-Rights Recovery at the End of the Qing," *Modern China* 28, no. 3 (July 2002): 315–361; *Investment Values of Chinese Railway Bonds* (Paris, 1923), 6–7.

2. On the late Qing reforms see, for example, Peter Zarrow, *After Empire: The Conceptual Transformation of the Chinese State, 1885–1924* (Stanford, CA: Stanford University Press, 2012), and Joan Judge, *Print and Politics: 'Shibao' and the Culture of Reform in Late Qing China* (Stanford, CA: Stanford University Press, 1996).

3. Thomas Rawski, *Economic Growth in Prewar China* (Berkeley: University of California Press, 1989), 208–212; Ernest P. Liang, *China, Railways and Agricultural Development 1875–1935* (Chicago: Department of Geography, University of Chicago, 1982), 10–11.

4. "Railroad Finances," *Journal of the Association of Chinese and American Engineers* 3, no. 5 (June 1922): 22–23.

5. For the post-1911 period I refer to the nationalized government-owned railroads as railroad companies, which includes their administrative role managing a specific line within the rail network.

6. Kampen, *Revolutionäre Eisenbahnplanungen*, 126.

7. Zhang Ruide, *Zhongguo jindai tielu shiye guanli de yanjiu: Zhengzhi cengmian de fenxi (1876–1937)* [A study of the industrial management of modern Chinese railroads: A political-level analysis (1870–1937)] (Taibei: Zhongyang yanjiuyuan jindaishi yanjiusuo, 1991), 134.

8. "The Railroads of China," *Journal of the Association of Chinese and American Engineers* 3, no. 5 (June 1922): 17–19.

9. "Chinese Government Railway Operations for 1920, from the Annual Report of the Ministry of Communications," *Journal of the Association of Chinese and American Engineers* 3, no. 6 (July 1922): 29–34.

10. Lin, *Chinese Railways*, 63–65.

11. For a brief period between February and September 1919, mining and railroad matters were administratively united under the Mining and Railroad Bureau (Kuangwu tielu zongju). Wang Xiaohua and Li Zhancai, *Jiannan yanshen de Minguo tielu* [Difficulties extending the railroads in the Republic of China] (Zhengzhou: Henan renmin chubanshe, 1993), 75–76.

12. Ibid., 44–74.

13. Wei Qingyuan, ed., *Zhongguo zhengzhi zhidu shi* [A history of the Chinese political system] (Beijing: Zhongguo renmin daxue chubanshe, 1989), 646–647.

14. Wang Xiaohua and Li Zhancai, *Jiannan yanshen de Minguo tielu*, 75–77; Kong Qingtai et al., eds., *Guomindang zhengfu zhengzhi zhidushi cidian* [A dictionary of the political system of the Guomindang government] (Hefei: Anhui jiaoyu chubanshe, 2000), 165–167.

15. Liu Shoulin et al., eds., *Minguo zhiguan nianbiao* [Chronology of the Republic of China] (Beijing: Zhonghua shuju, 1995), 50–53.

16. Ibid.; Wang Xiaohua and Li Zhancai, *Jiannan yanshen de Minguo tielu*, 75–77; the original six departments were increased to nine in 1917.

17. *Shandong shengzhi: Tielu zhi* [Gazetteer of railroads in Shandong province] (Ji'nan: Shandong renmin chubanshe, 1993), 547.

18. For continuously updated information on all railroad bureaus, see the official website *Tielu gang* (Railroad network), under the section *Tieluju zhuanji* (Special topics on railroad bureaus), http://www.tielu.cn/tieluju/, accessed May 21, 2018.

19. Tielu xiehui bianjibu, ed., *Minguo tielu yinian shi* [One year of railroads in the Republic] (Beijing tielu xiehui bianjibu, 1914 [compiled 1913]) (Beijing, 1914), inserted table, no pagination; *Ji'nan tieluju zhi, 1899–1985* [Ji'nan Railroad Bureau, 1899–1985] (Ji'nan: Ji'nan tieluju shizhi bianzuan lingdao xiaozu, 1993), 10, 13.

20. Even Chang Jui-te's (Zhang Ruide) otherwise detailed studies on prewar rail development in China give the railroad bureau system short shrift. See Chang Jui-te, *Zhongguo jindai tielu shiye guanli de yanjiu;* and Chang Jui-te, "Technology Transfer in Modern China: The Case of Railway Enterprise (1987–1937)," *Modern Asian Studies* 27, no. 2 (1993): 291–296.

21. Yang Yonggang, *Zhongguo jindai tielushi* [A history of modern Chinese railroads] (Shanghai: Shanghai shudian chubanshe, 1997), 154.

22. Wang Xiaohua and Li Zhancai, *Jiannan yanshen de Minguo tielu*, 76–77.

23. Zhonghua quanguo tielu xiehui bianjibu, eds., *Zhonghua quanguo tielu xiehui diyici baogao* [First report of the China National Railroad Association] (Beijing: Zhonghua quanguo tielu xiehui bianjibu, 1912), 5.

24. Sun Zhongshan [Sun Yat-sen], *Guofu quanji* [Collected writings of the father of the nation], 6 vols. (Taibei: Zhongyang wenwu gongyingshe, 1957), 3:65–66.

25. Zhonghua quanguo tielu xiehui bianjibu, ed., *Zhonghua quanguo tielu xiehui diyici baogao*, 33–75.

26. Liu Shoulin et al., *Minguo zhiguan nianbiao*, 50–53, 591–593; *Who's Who in China*, 1919 ed. (Shanghai: Millard's Review, 1925 repr., Hong Kong: Chinese Materials Center, 1982), 34–35.

27. *Who's Who in China,* 1919 ed., 42–44; Howard Boorman, ed., *Biographical Dictionary of Republican China,* 4 vols. (New York: Columbia University Press, 1967–1971), 3:362–364.

28. See, for example, Tielu xiehui bianjibu, ed., *Tielu xiehui huibao bacui* [Best selection from the journal of the railroad association] (Beijing: Tielu xiehui bianjibu, 1913), vols. 1 and 2.

29. Ching-Chun Wang, "Why the Chinese Oppose Foreign Railroad Loans," *American Political Science Review* 4, no. 3 (August 1910): 365–373; Ching-Chun Wang, "The Hankow-Szechuan Railway Loan," *American Journal of International Law* 5, no. 4 (July 1911): 653.

30. Wang, "The Hankow-Szechuan Railway Loan"; Ching-Chun Wang, "The New China Will Be a New United States," *New York Times,* November 10, 1912.

31. Hu Dongchao, *Zhongguo tielu zhinan* [Guide to China's railroads] (Shanghai: Guangzhi shuju, 1905).

32. Ibid., at 9. For the debate over the term *wenming,* see Kristin Stapleton, *Civilizing Chengdu: Chinese Urban Reform, 1895–1937* (Cambridge, MA: Harvard University Asia Center, 2000).

33. Hu Dongchao, *Zhongguo tielu zhinan,* 43–50. Later in his career, Hu Dongchao assumed the position of chief engineer on the Sichuan-Hankou line, but he purportedly was charged with incompetence and negligence in the engineering projects under his supervision. See Lee, *China's Quest for Railway Autonomy,* 135.

34. Report by K. Luxburg, July 3, 1911, vol. 13, Baker Library, Harvard Business School (BLHBS).

35. Ibid., July 9, 1909, vol. 12, BLHBS.

36. Georg Baur, *China um 1900: Aufzeichungen eines Krupp-Direktors* [China around 1900: Writings of a director working for Krupp], ed. Elisabeth Kaske (Cologne: Böhlau, 2005), diary entry February 19, 1892.

37. Report by K. Luxburg July 9, 1909, vol. 12, BLHBS.

38. Ibid. For a similar complaint about the absence of German from Chinese railroad school curricula in 1914, see Julius Dorpmüller "Stellung der deutschen Sprache in der Verwaltung der Tientsin-Pukow Eisenbahn (Nordstrecke)" [The position of the German language in the management of the Tientsin-Pukow Railroad (northern section)], 1914, vol. 15, 1–8 (separate pagination), BLHBS.

39. Tielu xiehui bianjibu, ed., *Tielu xiehui huibao bacui* (Beijing: Tielu xiehui bianjibu, 1914), 444.

40. Baur, *China um 1900,* diary entry May 18, 1892, 362–363. Baur admitted that his conviction fell on deaf ears and that his argument for English was regarded by his superiors as "damaging to German interests."

41. On the issues of textbooks and print culture in the Republic, see, for example, Robert Culp, *Articulating Citizenship: Civic Education and Student Politics in Southeastern China, 1912–1940* (Cambridge, MA: Harvard University Asia Center, 2007).

42. "Tielu yingyong Zhongguo wenzi shou" [Railroads should use Chinese characters], in Tielu xiehui bianjibu, *Tielu xiehui huibao bacui* (Beijing: Tielu xiehui bianjibu, 1913), 585–587.

43. Huang Yifeng, *Tielu zhiye zhidao* [Guide to railroad employment] (Shanghai: Shangwu, 1936), 85–91.

44. Stuart Woolf, "Statistics and the Modern State," *Comparative Studies in Society and History* 31, no. 3 (July 1989): 588–604; Silvana Patriarca, *Numbers and Nationhood: Writing Statistics in Nineteenth-Century Italy* (Cambridge: Cambridge University Press, 1996).

45. J. Adam Tooze, *Statistics and the German State, 1900–1945: The Making of Modern Economic Knowledge* (Cambridge: Cambridge University Press, 2001), 7.

46. Ching-chun Wang, "The Administration of Chinese Government Railways," *Chinese Social and Political Science Review* 1, no. 1 (1916): 68–85, at 81.

47. S. F. Mayers (British & Chinese Corp.) to Sir Beilby Alston (His Britannic Majesty's Minister), Peking, August 22, 1922, FO 228/2803, British National Archives (BNA).

48. British Legation, Peking to the Wai Chiao Pu, November 4, 1926, and W. F. Ker (Consul General), Tientsin, December 14, 1926, to Wm. Forbes & Co., Tientsin, FO 228/2803, BNA.

49. Boorman, *Biographical Dictionary of Republican China*, 4:366–369.

50. A. W. Coats, "Henry Carter Adams: A Case Study in the Emergence of the Social Sciences in the United States, 1850–1900," *Journal of American Studies* 2, no. 2 (October 1968): 195.

51. H. C. Adams to Carter, January 27, 1914, H. C. Adams Papers, Box 13, Bentley Historical Library, University of Michigan. Quoted in Paul B. Trescott, "Western Economic Advisers in China, 1900–1949," *Research in the History of Economic Thought and Methodology* 28A (2010): 6.

52. H. C. Adams, *Manual of Railway Accounts* (Peking, 1926), 12.

53. H. C. Adams to Teddy and Carter, Peking, November 28, 1913, H. C. Adams Papers, Box 13. Quoted in Trescott, "Western Economic Advisers in China," 7.

54. H. C. Adams to Carter, Shanghai, December 21, 1913, H. C. Adams Papers, Box 13. Quoted in ibid.

55. H. C. Adams to Teddy and Carter, Peking, November 28, 1913, H. C. Adams Papers, Box 13. Quoted in ibid., 6.

56. Wang, "The Administration of Chinese Government Railways," 81.

57. Ralph William Huenemann, *The Dragon and the Iron Horse: The Economics of Railroads in China* (Cambridge, MA: Harvard University Press, 1984).

58. For assessments of the statistical record of Republican China, see John K. Fairbank, "Bibliographical Essay," in *Cambridge History of China*, vol. 12, *Republican China, 1912–1949*, part 1 (Cambridge: Cambridge University Press, 1983), 831; William C. Kirby, James Chin Shih, Man-houng Lin, and David A. Pietz, eds.,

*State and Economy in Republican China: A Handbook for Scholars*, 2 vols. (Cambridge, MA: Harvard University Asia Center, 2001), 1:10.

59. See, for example, Zhang Kaiyuan, *Xinhai geming yu Zhongguo zhengzhi fazhan* [The Xinhai (1911) Revolution and China's political development] (Wuhan: Huazhong shifan daxue chubanshe, 2005); Li Chien-nung, *The Political History of China, 1840–1928*, trans. Ssu-yu Teng and Jeremy Ingalls (Princeton, NJ: D. Van Nostrand, 1956); James E. Sheridan, *China in Disintegration: The Republican Era in Chinese History, 1912–1949* (New York: Free Press, 1975); Lloyd E. Eastman, *The Abortive Revolution: China under Nationalist Rule, 1927–1937* (Cambridge, MA: Council on East Asian Studies, Harvard University, 1990).

60. "Journal of Thomas Johnston Bourne (of Winfarthing, China, and Wimborne), Written at the Request of His Children at Odd Times from 1939 to 1940" (unpublished manuscript), 32. I thank Dr. Tao Tao Liu for drawing this source to my attention.

61. C. P. Fitzgerald, *Why China? Recollections of China, 1923–1950* (Portland, OR: ISBS, 1985), 57–58.

62. Ibid., 58–59.

63. John Earl Baker, *Explaining China* (London: A. M. Philpot, 1927), 71. "Engine driver" refers to the engineer in the operational sense as the person who drives the train, in contrast to the term engineer in the general professional sense.

64. Ibid.

65. Ibid., esp. 77.

66. Fitzgerald, *Why China?*, 64–65.

67. R. H. Tawney, *Land and Labour in China* (London: Allen and Unwin, 1932), 86.

68. Tielu xiehui bianjibu, *Minguo tielu yinian shi*, table in appendix, no pagination.

69. Ibid. For example, the Dao-Qing Railroad from Qinghua to Sanliwan in Shanxi was a short line for coal transportation in Shanxi province, operating under a supervisory office (*jianduju*); the Zheng-Ding Railroad from Shijiazhuang to Taiyuan, originally a French concession, operated under a supervisory office and became a branch line of the Peking-Hankou line after it was officially nationalized in 1932. See Lin Cheng, *The Chinese Railways: A Historical Survey* (Shanghai: China United Press, 1935), 70.

70. Alfred D. Chandler Jr., *The Visible Hand: The Managerial Revolution of American Business* (Cambridge, MA: Belknap Press of Harvard University Press, 1977), 106.

71. Ibid., 107.

72. Memo prepared by managing director, May 17, 1909, FO 233/132/71, BNA, archived at 112.

73. Ibid., 113.

74. Ibid., 114.

75. Tielu xiehui bianjibu, *Minguo tielu yinian shi,* table in appendix, no pagination. For numbers on industrial labor, see Rawski, *Economic Growth in Prewar China.*

76. Qingdao shubi gummin seibu tetsudo, *Qingdao shubi gummin seibu tetsudobu chosa shiryo* [Survey material from the political branch of the railroad department of the Qingdao occupation forces], vol. 25, *JinPu tetsudo chosa hokokusho* (Research report on the *Jin-Pu* railroad) (n.p.: Taisho 8, 1919), 27–28, chart from January 1915.

77. Ibid., 29–34, chart from June 1916.

78. Ibid., 34–37, chart from June 1917.

79. Ibid., 37–48, chart from July 1918.

80. This was the case for the Beijing-Hankou line and the Shanghai-Nanjing line.

81. Dossier 5c, Tientsin-Pukow and Shantung Railways, June 1918–April 1927, FO 228 / 280, BNA.

82. *Zhonghua guoyou tielu HuNing HuHangSong xian zhiyuanlu* [Employee record of the national HuNing HuHangSong railroad] (n.p: 1920), 1–6, Shanghai Municipal Archives (SMA), Y 2–1–1097.

83. Memorandum of S. F. M. (S. F. Mayers), British & Chinese Corporation, Peking, January 30, 1919, FO 228 / 2803, BNA; S. F. Mayers to under secretary of state, Foreign Office, March 12, 1919; draft memorandum, April 22, 1919, ibid. On the German and Japanese presence in China and changes in railroad control on the Shandong peninsula in the wake of World War I, see Elisabeth Köll, "Chinese Railroads, Local Society, and Foreign Presence: The Tianjin-Pukou Line in pre-1949 Shandong," in *Manchurian Railways and the Opening of China: An International History,* ed. Bruce A. Elleman and Stephen Kotkin (Armonk, NY: M. E. Sharpe, 2010), 123–148, esp. 124–127.

84. Memorandum of S. F. M. (S. F. Mayers), British and Chinese Corporation, Peking, January 30, 1919, FO 228 / 2803, BNA; S. F. Mayers to under secretary of state, Foreign Office, March 12, 1919, FO 228 / 2803, BNA.

85. Dechamfils (Consul-General in Nanking) to Sir Donald Macleay (HM's Minister), Peking. November 12, 1925, FO 228 / 2803, BNA.

86. Mr. A. C. Clear to Mr. S. F. Mayers (British & Chinese Corporation, Ltd, Peking), December 9, 1918, FO 228 / 2803, BNA; quote from Mr. C. L. G. Wayne (Traffic Department, Shanghai-Nanking Railroad) to Mr. A. C. Clear (engineer in chief and general manager, Shanghai-Nanking Railroad), December 6, 1918, FO 228 / 2803, BNA.

87. "Telegramabschriften: Tientsin-Pukow Bahn" [Telegram transcripts: Tientsin-Pukow line], vol. 15, 1914, BLHBS.

88. Nie Zhaoling, *Tielu tonglun* [Introduction to railroads] (Shanghai: Shangwu, 1930), 58–66.

89. For a detailed discussion of Ji'nan's urban history, see David D. Buck, *Urban Change in China: Politics and Development in Tsinan, Shandong, 1890–1949* (Madison: University of Wisconsin Press, 1978).

90. Zhuang Weimin, *Jindai Shandong shichang jingji de bianqian* [The transformation of the market economy in modern Shandong] (Beijing: Zhonghua shuju, 2000).

91. Zhang Runwu and Li Xue, *Tushuo Ji'nan lao jianzhu: Jindai shi juan* [Old buildings in Ji'nan: Modern history volume] (Ji'nan: Ji'nan chubanshe, 2001), 6–11; Luo Tengxiao and Li Houji, eds., *Ji'nan daguan* [A grand view of Ji'nan] (Ji'nan: Ji'nan daguan chubanshe, 1934); Ji'nan shi shizhi bianzuan weiyuanhui, ed., *Ji'nan shizhi* [Ji'nan city gazetteer] (n.p.: Ji'nan shi shizhi bianzuan weiyuanhui, 1999), vol. 2.

92. Zhang Runwu and Li Xue, *Tushuo Jinan lao jianzhu*, 126–128; Toa Dobunkai, *Shina shobetsu zenshi: Santosho* [Complete gazetteers of China's provinces: Shandong province] (Tokyo: Toa Dobunkai, Taisho 6, 1918), 4:436–476.

93. Maps in Zhang Runwu and Li Xue, *Tushuo Ji'nan lao jianzhu*, 2–11; Buck, *Urban Change in China*, 100.

94. Zhang Runwu and Li Xue, *Tushuo Ji'nan lao jianzhu*, 107–116; *Shandong dizhi* (Local gazetteer of Shandong) (n.p.: Zhonghua shuju, [1930s?]; Ji'nan tieluju shizhi bianzuan lingdao xiaozu, *Ji'nan tieluju zhi, 1899–1985* [Gazetteer of the Ji'nan Railroad Bureau, 1899–1985] (Ji'nan, 1993), 72–73.

95. *Tielu zhigong jiaoyu xungan* [Magazine for the education of railroad employees], vol. 9, (1925), 23.

96. Interviews at Ji'nan Machine Works, June 19, 2005.

97. A blacksmith is a classic occupation for men seeking employment on railroads. My great-grandfather trained as a blacksmith before joining the railroad system of the Habsburg Empire and becoming an engine driver in southern Tyrol.

98. Walter Licht, *Working for the Railroad: The Organization of Work in the Nineteenth Century* (Princeton, NJ: Princeton University Press, 1983); Lothar Gall and Manfred Pohl, eds., *Die Eisenbahn in Deutschland: von den Anfängen bis zur Gegenwart* (Munich: Beck, 1999); interviews at the Ji'nan Machine Works, July 30, 2003, and July 10 and 15, 2005.

99. In preparation for his work as consultant and agent, Krupp sent Baur to study Chinese in Berlin in the Friedrich Wilhelm University's Department for Oriental Languages. Baur developed extremely good relations with the Chinese government bureaucracy, and in 1892 he was appointed adviser on railroad issues by Li Hongzhang and in 1913 he was appointed by President Yuan Shikai as technical adviser on steelworks construction. Baur, *China um 1900*.

100. Ibid., diary entry September 29, 1893, 531.

101. O. J. Todd, *Two Decades in China* (Peking: Association of Chinese and American Engineers, 1938), 400.

102. Baur, *China um 1900*, diary entries December 5–11, 1892, 467–472.

103. I am grateful to the comments of a preliminary reader of this book for Harvard University Press on this point. Finding the most effective combination of academic education and practical training was a challenge even in countries

with a longer tradition in science education such as Germany. In the 1880s young German engineers were accused of lacking powers of "observation" and "appreciation of the importance of individual details" because of the heavy academic orientation of the faculty and the absence of required practical training. Kees Gispen, *New Profession, Old Order: Engineers and German Society, 1815–1914* (Cambridge: Cambridge University Press, 1989), 151.

104. Ling Hongxun, *Zhan Tianyou xiansheng nianpu* [A chronology of the life of Mr. Zhan Tianyou] (Taibei: Zhongguo gongchengshi xuehui, 1961); Xie Fang, *Zhongguo tielu zhi fu: Zhan Tianyou* [Zhan Tianyou, the father of Chinese railroads] (Guangzhou: Guangdong renmin chubanshe, 2008).

105. "Jin-Pu beiduan zongban de ren" [The northern section of the Jin-Pu line gets an employee], *Guo bao*, August 7, 1909, newspaper article inserted in vol. 12, 1909, BLHBS.

106. Baur, *China um 1900*, diary entry September 21, 1893, 527.

107. Ling Hongxun, *Qishi zishu* [Autobiography at seventy] (Taibei: Sanmin shuju, 1968), 17–18.

108. Arthur Judson Brown, *The Chinese Revolution* (New York: Student Volunteer Movement, 1912), 76.

109. Chandler, *The Visible Hand*, 79–205; Thomas C. Cochran, *Railroad Leaders, 1845–1890: The Business Mind in Action* (Cambridge MA: Harvard University Press, 1953); Licht, *Working for the Railroad*, 269.

110. A. Viola Smith and Anselm Chuh, comps., *Motor Highways in China* (Shanghai, 1929), 211.


## 3. Moving Goods in the Marketplace

1. Kevin H. O'Rourke and Jeffrey Williamson, *Globalization and History: The Evolution of a Nineteenth-Century Atlantic Economy* (Cambridge, MA: MIT Press, 1999), 2.

2. See, for example, Albert Fishlow, *American Railroads and the Transformation of the Ante-bellum Economy* (Cambridge, MA: Harvard University Press, 1965); George Rogers Taylor, *The Transportation Revolution, 1815–1860* (New York: Rinehart, 1951); Albert Fishlow, "Internal Transportation in the Nineteenth and Early Twentieth Centuries," in *The Cambridge Economic History of the United States*, vol. 2, *The Long Nineteenth Century*, ed. Stanley L. Engerman and Robert E. Gallman (Cambridge: Cambridge University Press, 2008), 543–642; Dan Bogart and Latika Chaudhary, "Engines of Growth: The Productivity Advance of Indian Railways, 1874–1912," *Journal of Economic History* 73, no. 2 (June 2013): 339–370.

3. Ernest P. Liang, *China, Railways and Agricultural Development, 1875–1935* (Chicago: University of Chicago Press, 1982); Thomas G. Rawski, *Economic Growth in Prewar China* (Berkeley: University of California Press, 1989).

4. Rawski, *Economic Growth in Prewar China;* see also Ralph William Huenemann, *The Dragon and the Iron Horse: The Economics of Railroads in China, 1876–1937* (Cambridge, MA: Council on East Asian Studies, Harvard University, 1984).

5. Figures extrapolated from the Ministry of Communications (subsequently the Ministry of Railways), *Statistics of Government Railways* [Zhongguo tielu tongji] (Peking [subsequently Nanking]: Tiedaobu tongjichu, 1915–1936). The series covers the railroads' fiscal years until 1935 / 1936. Because of the impact of the civil war on railroad operations, reports were published with long delays. The volume with 1925 data was published in 1929, and the volume with 1928 data appeared in 1933. From 1926 onward each volume contained English and Chinese versions. Beginning in 1930, the name of the series changed slightly to *Statistics of Chinese National Railways* [Zhonghua guoyou tielu kuaiji tongi huibian].

6. Ministry of Communications, *Statistics of Government Railways.*

7. "The Shanghai-Nanking Railway," *North-China Herald,* January 14, 1910, 67; ibid., July 1, 1910, 71.

8. Liang, *China, Railways and Agricultural Development, 1875–1935;* Rawski, *Economic Growth in Prewar China.*

9. "In Praise of the Peanut," *North-China Herald,* January 13, 1911, 85; "Taianfu [Shantung]," *North-China Herald,* May 20, 1911, 484.

10. Amano Motonosuke, *Shandong sho keizai chosa shiryo* [Research materials on the economy of Shandong province], vol. 3, *Shandong nogyo keizai ron* [Report on Shandong's agricultural economy] (Dairen: Minami Manshu tetsudo kabushiki kaisha, 1936), 125.

11. Qingdao shi gangwuju, ed., *Zhonghua Minguo 20 nian gangwu tongji nianbao* [Yearbook of port statistics for 1931] (Qingdao, 1931), 286–289.

12. Ibid., 292–295.

13. Ibid.

14. "Trade in South China: The Crisis during 1920," *North-China Herald,* July 30, 1921, 354.

15. Qingdao shi gangwuju, *Zhonghua Minguo,* 282–295.

16. Ibid.

17. Sherman Cochran, *Encountering Chinese Networks: Western, Japanese and Chinese Corporations in China, 1880–1937* (Berkeley: University of California Press, 2000), 64–65; Liang, *China, Railways and Agricultural Development,* 116–117.

18. Cochran, *Encountering Chinese Networks,* 66–68.

19. "China's Railway Ambitions: Expansive Views of Mr. C. C. Wang," *North-China Herald,* August 16, 1919, 412.

20. Ibid.

21. "The Cocoon Season," *North-China Herald,* June 24, 1910, 761.

22. Ibid.

23. "Build China's Railways," *Far Eastern Review* 19 (September 1923): 588–589.

24. Ibid.

25. "Shanghai shangye chuxu yinhang: Zonghang, 1923–27" [Shanghai Commercial and Savings Bank: Headquarters, 1923–27], Q275-1-772, Shanghai Municipal Archives (SMA); "Jingmu cheze yinhangtuan daibao jiaotongbu zhixia Hu-HangYong tielu guanliju" [Financial records with the banking consortium of the Shanghai-Hangzhou-Ningbo Railroad Management Bureau], 1921, pp. 126–131, SMA, Q275-1-772.

26. "Jingmu cheze yinhangtuan daibiao jiaotongbu zhixia Jin-Pu tielu guanliju" [Train car loan bank consortium representing the Jin-Pu Railroad under the Ministry of Communications], 1921, pp. 119–124, SMA Q275-1-772, Shanghai shangye chuxu yinhang: Zonghang.

27. Gouvernement de la République Chinoise, *Railway Equipment Loan, 1922.* From the author's collection.

28. See Huenemann's negative assessment of the railroads' financials in *The Dragon and the Iron Horse,* 182–185.

29. Dr. Wendschuh, "Bericht ueber eine Informationsreise entlang der Suedstrecke der Tsientsin-Pukou Bahn, Anfang Oktober 1912" [Report on an informational journey along the southern section of the Tsientsin-Pukou line, early October 1912], vol. 14, 1912, Baker Library, Harvard Business School (BLHBS).

30. Ibid., 5.

31. Ibid., 6.

32. J. F. Baker, "Comparison of Chinese and American Railway Practices," in Julean Herbert Arnold, *Commercial Handbook of China* (Washington, DC: Government Printing Office, 1926), 127–128.

33. Ministry of Railways, *Statistics of Government Railways* [Zhongguo tielu tongji] (Nanjing: Tiedaobu tongjichu, 1936), 69–78, and table 22.

34. Shandong sheng difang shizhi bianzuan weiyuanhui, *Shandong shengzhi: Tielu zhi* [Gazetteer of railroads in Shandong province] (Ji'nan: Shandong renmin chubanshe, 1993), 152.

35. "Shanghai and the Railways," *North-China Herald,* August 5, 1911, 327.

36. "The Canton Railway Loop," *North-China Herald,* March 17, 1928, 425.

37. "Hongkong-Canton Entente: Kowloon and Hankow Railway All but Linked," *North-China Herald,* March 24, 1928, 472.

38. See Lin Cheng, *The Chinese Railways: A Historical Survey* (Shanghai: China United Press, 1935), 65–68.

39. "A Railway Disaster," *North-China Herald,* February 18, 1910, 358.

40. Ibid.

41. "Translation. First enclosure, of a translated agreement from March 20, 1914, signed by Chao Ching Hua (managing director of the Tianjin-Pukou Railroad) and Lin Tsoo Tsin (general manager, Wai Tung Transporting Company)," British National Archives (BNA), FO 228/2803, pp. 1–5 (separate archival pagination).

42. Ibid.

43. Ibid., 2.

44. Ibid.

45. Ibid., 2–4.

46. Ibid.; letter from Dechamfils (British consul, Nanjing) to Sir John Jordan, January 17, 1919, FO 228 / 2803, BNA, p. 2.

47. Ibid., 4.

48. See E. T. Williams, trans., *Recent Chinese Legislation Relating to Commercial, Railway, and Mining Enterprises, with Regulations for Registration of Trade Marks, and for the Registration of Companies* (Shanghai, 1904).

49. Dechamfils to Sir John Jordan, January 17, 1919, BNA, FO 228 / 2803.

50. "Shanghai-Nanking Railway. Commission on Goods Traffic," signed by A. C. Clear, second enclosure, translated agreement, July 1, 1917, 1, FO 228 / 2803, BNA. By 1919 the commission rate had been raised to 5 percent for freight of 50,000 yuan or more and to 10 percent for 100,000 yuan or more. Dechamfils to Sir John Jordan, January 17, 1919, FO 228 / 2803, BNA.

51. Ibid.

52. Ibid., 1.

53. "Jin-Pu tielu ge zhuanyun gongsi shoutie," January 1918, Tianjin Municipal Archives (TJDAG), 128-2-3-2010. The petition was signed by ten transportation companies (*zhuanyun gongsi*): Tongyuan, Xingcheng, Minyuan, Lihui, Kangyun, Duanchunyi, Lixing, Yuancheng, Huitong, and Yuetai.

54. Ibid., 12.

55. Ibid., 8–9.

56. Ibid., 9.

57. Ibid., 9–10.

58. Ibid., 10–11.

59. Wendschuh, "Bericht," vol. 14, 1912, BLHBS.

60. Dechamfils to Sir John Jordan, FO 228 / 2803, BNA, January 17, 1919; see also Huenemann, *The Dragon and the Iron Horse*, 204–205.

61. This suspicion was expressed by the consul at the end of his letter. Dechamfils to Sir John Jordan, January 17, 1919, FO 228 / 2803, BNA.

62. Enclosure in E. N. Ensor (Hankow) to Sir Frederick Maze (Inspector General of Customs, Shanghai), May 17, 1937, China Maritime Customs (CMC), reel 277 679 (1) 28314. "Investigations Outside Railway Premises into Alleged Malpractices by Shippers of Specified Goods by Rail in a Treaty Port Where There Is a CIB [Customs Inspection Bureau] Inspection Post."

63. Dechamfils to Sir John Jordan, January 17, 1919, FO 228 / 2803, BNA.

64. Julean Herbert Arnold, *Commercial Handbook of China* (Washington, DC: Government Printing Office, 1926), 126.

65. On the contract-labor system in the early Republican period, see Elisabeth Köll, *From Cotton Mill to Business Empire* (Cambridge, MA: Harvard University Asia Center, 2003), 95.

66. Arnold, *Commercial Handbook of China,* 126.

67. V. T. [?] Pratt to Sir Beilby Alston, HM Minister, Peking, April 20, 1922, FO 228 / 2803, BNA.

68. Ibid.

69. "Soochow: A New Line to Hangchow," *North-China Herald,* June 10, 1910, 618.

70. "The Tientsin-Pukou Railway," *North-China Herald,* November 4, 1910, 271; see also Figure 1.3 in Chapter 1.

71. "Shiuchow [Kwangtung]: Railway Matters," *North-China Herald,* May 20, 1911, 483–484.

72. "The Provincial Railways: Hangchow," *North-China Herald,* September 9, 1911, 660; "The Trade of Shanghai," *North-China Herald,* August 31, 1918, 532–534.

73. "Soochow: A New Line to Hangchow," *North-China Herald,* June 10, 1910, 618; "The Trade of Shanghai," *North-China Herald,* August 31, 1918, 532–534.

74. "The Coal Deposits of Kiangsi," *North-China Herald,* February 1, 1919, 263.

75. See Li Yan, *Dao-Qing tielu lüxing zhinan* [Dao-Qing railroad travel guide] (Jiaozuo: Dao-Qing tielu jianduju, 1918), 2–5, 17–18.

76. *Ji'nan tieluju zhi, 1899–1985* [Ji'nan Railroad Bureau, 1899–1985] (Ji'nan: Ji'nan tieluju shizhi bianzuan lingdao xiaozu, 1993), 16; Jennifer Ning Chang, "Vertical Integration: Business Diversification, and Firm Architecture: The Case of the China Egg Produce Company in Shanghai, 1923–1950," *Enterprise and Society* 6, no. 3 (2005): 419–451.

77. *Ji'nan tieluju zhi,* 169.

78. Ibid., 178.

79. Shandong sheng difang shizhi bianzuan weiyuanhui, *Shandong shengzhi: Tielu zhi,* 183; *Ji'nan tieluju zhi,* 168.

80. Zhongguo tielu shi bianji yanjiu zhongxin, ed., *Zhongguo tielu dashiji (1876–1995)* [Chronology of Chinese railroads (1876–1995)] (Beijing: Zhongguo tiedao chubanshe, 1996), 131.

81. Elizabeth J. Remick, *Building Local States: China during the Republican and Post-Mao Eras* (Cambridge, MA: Harvard University Asia Center, 2004), 37.

82. For a comprehensive treatment of the tariff issue, see Felix Boecking, *No Great Wall: Trade, Tariffs, and Nationalism in Republican China, 1927–1945* (Cambridge, MA: Harvard University Asia Center, 2017).

83. Albert Feuerwerker, "Economic Trends in the Late Ch'ing Empire, 1870–1911," in *The Cambridge History of China,* vol. 11, *Late Ch'ing 1800–1911,* part 2, ed. John King Fairbank and Kwang-Ching Liu, 61–62 (Cambridge: Cambridge University Press, 1980).

84. "The Shanghai-Nanking Railway," *North-China Herald,* January 14, 1910, 67. Rawski also cites similar incidents in *Economic Growth in Prewar China,* 232–233.

85. "The Provincial Railways: Hangchow," *North-China Herald*, September 9, 1911, 660.

86. "The Likin Barriers," *North-China Herald*, February 10, 1911, 314 and March 30, 1912, 841; "Abolition of Likin," *North-China Herald*, January 31, 1920, 280; "Proposed Abolition of Likin: China Willing If Import Duties Increased," *North-China Herald*, March 13, 1920, 682; "Dr. C. C. Wu on the Nationalist Party Outlook," *North-China Herald*, July 16, 1927, 94.

87. Remick, *Building Local States*, 38.

88. "Opium on Railways," *North-China Herald*, January 11, 1919, 70. For a comprehensive treatment of smuggling, see Philip Thai, *China's War on Smuggling: Law, Economic Life, and the Making of the Modern State, 1842–1965* (New York: Columbia University Press, 2018). For railroad workers' opium consumption, see Stephen L. Morgan, "Personnel Discipline and Industrial Relations on the Railways of Republican China," *Australian Journal of Politics and History* 47, no. 1 (March 2001): 24–38.

89. "The Peking Railway Conference: List of Reforms Necessary for Efficiency," *North-China Herald*, August 13, 1927, 272.

90. Ibid.

91. Ibid.

92. "Unifying China's Railways: Through Passage of Goods and Travellers," *North-China Herald*, November 20, 1920, 549.

93. "The Peking Railway Conference," *North-China Herald*, August 13, 1927, 272.

94. "The Awakening of Taianfu," *North-China Herald*, July 29, 1911, 274.

95. "Currency and Railways," *North-China Herald*, October 9, 1920, 83.

96. David D. Buck, "Railway City and National Capital: Two Faces of the Modern in Changchun," in *Remaking the Chinese City: Modernity and National Identity, 1900–1950*, ed. Joseph W. Esherick (Honolulu: University of Hawai'i Press, 2001), 65–89.

97. Liu Haiyan, *Kongjian yu shehui: Jindai Tianjin chengshi de yanbian* [Space and society: The transformation of modern Tianjin, city] (Tianjin: Tianjin shehui kexueyuan chubanshe, 2003).

98. Zhuang Weimin, *Jindai Shandong shichang jingji de bianqian* [The evolution of the market economy in modern Shandong] (Beijing: Zhonghua shuju, 2000).

99. "Tsinanfu," *North-China Herald*, October 14, 1911, 92.

100. For a detailed discussion of Ji'nan's urban history, see David D. Buck, *Urban Change in China: Politics and Development in Tsinan, Shandong, 1890–1949* (Madison: University of Wisconsin Press, 1978).

101. Zhang Runwu and Li Xue, *Tushuo Ji'nan lao jianzhu: Jindai shi juan* [Old buildings in Ji'nan: Modern history volume] (Ji'nan: Ji'nan chubanshe, 2001), 6–11; *Ji'nan daguan* [A grand view of Ji'nan] (Ji'nan: Ji'nan daguan chubanshe, 1934); *Ji'nan shizhi* [Ji'nan city gazetteer] (Ji'nan: Ji'nan shi shizhi bianzuan weiyuanhui, 1999), vol. 2.

102. Zhang Runwu and Li Xue, *Tushuo Ji'nan lao jianzhu,* 26–28; Toa Dobunkai, *Shina shobetsu zenshi: Shantosho* [Complete gazetteers of China's provinces: Shandong province] (Tokyo: Toa Dobunkai, Taisho 6, 1918), 4:436–476.

103. For a photograph of the station, see Zhang Runwu and Li Xue, *Tushuo Ji'nan lao jianzhu,* 121.

104. *Shandong dizhi* [Local gazetteer of Shandong] (n.p.: Zhonghua shuju?, 1930s?); *Ji'nan shizhi ziliao* [Information on Ji'nan City] (Ji'nan: Ji'nan shizhi bianzuan weiyuanhui, 1982), vol. 3.

105. Zhuang Weimin, *Jindai Shandong shichang jingji de bianqian.*

106. Lü Weijun et al., *Shandong quyu xiandaihua yanjiu: 1840–1949* [Research on the Shandong region and modernization: 1840–1949] (Ji'nan: Qilu shushe, 2002).

107. "Hsuchowfu: The Northern Central Supply Station," *North-China Herald,* November 5, 1927, 228; see also "How Sun Chuan-Fang Saved Hsuchowfu," *North-China Herald,* December 17, 1927, 475.

108. Juanjuan Yuan, "Yudahua: The Growth of an Industrial Enterprise in Modern China, 1890–1957" (PhD diss., Johns Hopkins University, 2007), 60–61. I thank Linda Grove for encouraging me to think about Shijiazhuang. For the development of rural industrial production in northern China and its commercial integration, see Linda Grove, *A Chinese Economic Revolution: Rural Entrepreneurship in the Twentieth Century* (Lanham, MD: Rowman and Littlefield, 2006).

109. Zhuang Weimin, *Jindai Shandong shichang jingji de bianqian,* 144.

110. Ma Yinchu, *Zhonghua yinhang lun* [Essays on banking in China] (Shanghai: Shangwu yinshuguan, 1934), 150–157 and 158–174. As a method of short-term financing, promissory notes addressed the problem of a low or a lack of cash flow because merchants selling agricultural commodities via rail transport were not able to collect payment until their consignments arrived at the destination station and were accepted by the buyer.

111. Ibid., 105.

112. "Pukou and the Railway: Possibilities of the Future," *North-China Herald,* July 13, 1912, 95.

113. "The Port of Pukow," *Far Eastern Review,* January 1917, 306.

114. "Pukou and the Railway," *North-China Herald,* July 13, 1912, 95. The remains of the power plant (*dianchang*) in Pukou today sit between the ferry wharf and the railroad station.

115. The sadly dilapidated former Jin-Pu railroad station and station compound are closed to the public and in 2018 were still awaiting renovation to reemerge as a railroad museum.

116. "Chefoo-Weihsien Railway," *North-China Herald,* February 8, 1919, 331; see also "The Chefoo Railway Question," *North-China Herald,* March 22, 1919, 767.

117. "Chefoo-Weihsien Railway," *North-China Herald,* December 27, 1919, 827.

118. "The Port of Chefoo," *North-China Herald,* March 20, 1920, 743.

119. *Guide to China* (Tokyo: Imperial Japanese Government Railways, 1924), 240.

120. "Unhappy Isolation of Tsingkiangpu," *North-China Herald*, January 12, 1929, 60.

121. *Guide to China*, 78.

122. Ibid., 133.

123. R. H. Tawney, *Land and Labour in China* (London: Allen and Unwin, 1932), 17, 55.

124. Ibid., 127.

125. Liang, *China, Railways and Agricultural Development*, esp. chaps. 4 and 5.

126. Rawski, *Economic Growth in Prewar China*.

127. Zhuang Weimin, *Jindai Shandong shichang jingji de bianqian*.

128. Kenneth Pomeranz, *The Making of a Hinterland: State, Society, and Economy in Inland North China, 1853 to 1937* (Berkeley: University of California Press, 1993), 268.

## 4. Moving People, Transmitting Ideas

1. See Henrietta Harrison, *The Making of the Republican Citizen: Political Ceremonies and Symbols in China, 1911–1929* (Oxford: Oxford University Press, 2000); Sherman Cochran, *Encountering Chinese Networks: Western, Japanese and Chinese Corporations in China, 1880–1937* (Berkeley: University of California Press, 2000); Wen-hsin Yeh, *Shanghai Splendor: Economic Sentiments and the Making of Modern China, 1843–1949* (Berkeley: University of California Press, 2008); Joan Judge, *Republican Lens: Gender, Visuality, and Experience in the Early Chinese Periodical Press* (Berkeley: University of California Press, 2015); Karl Gerth, *China Made: Consumer Culture and the Creation of the Nation* (Cambridge, MA: Harvard University Asia Center, 2003).

2. Unless otherwise indicated, statistical data in this chapter come from the annual reports of the Ministry of Communications (subsequently the Ministry of Railways), *Statistics of Government Railways* [Zhongguo tielu tongji] (Peking [subsequently Nanking]: Tiedaobu tongjichu, 1915–1936). The series covers the railroads' fiscal years until 1935/1936. Because of the impact of the civil war on railroad operations, reports were published with long delays. The volume with 1925 data was published in 1929, and the volume with 1928 data appeared in 1933. From 1926 onward each volume contained English and Chinese versions. Beginning in 1930 the name of the series changed slightly to *Statistics of Chinese National Railways* [Zhonghua guoyou tielu kuaiji tongi huibian].

3. For UK data, see J. Armstrong, "The Role of Coastal Shipping in UK Transport: An Estimate of Comparative Shipping Movements in 1910," *Journal of Transport History* 8 (1987): 158–174. Chinese population data are taken from Dwight H. Perkins, *Agricultural Development in China, 1368–1968* (Chicago: Aldine, 1969), 192–216.

4. See, for example, Steven J. Ericson, *The Sound of the Whistle: Railroads and the State in Meiji Japan* (Cambridge, MA: Harvard University Asia Center, 1996); Ian J. Kerr, *Building the Railroads of the Raj, 1850–1900* (Oxford: Oxford University Press, 1995); John R. Stilgoe, *Metropolitan Corridor: Railroads and the American Scene* (New Haven, CT: Yale University Press, 1983); Michael Freeman, *Railways and the Victorian Imagination* (New Haven, CT: Yale University Press, 1999).

5. Figures extrapolated from Ministry of Communications, *Zhongguo tielu tongji.*

6. See Anne Reinhardt, *Navigating Semi-colonialism: Shipping, Sovereignty, and Nation-Building in China, 1860–1937* (Cambridge, MA: Harvard University Asia Center, 2018).

7. The Shanghai-Nanjing Railroad's shares of revenue derived from freight were 25 percent in 1915, 29 percent in 1923, 18 percent in 1930, and 25 percent in 1935. The percentages do not add up to 100 percent because a small but non-trivial percentage of the revenue—never more than 15 percent, and typically less than 5 percent—came from activities unrelated to traffic: ferry and telegraph services, hotels, interchange of rolling stock, and rentals of equipment and physical plants.

8. Ministry of Communications, *Zhongguo tielu tongji,* various years. Passenger journey data were based on tickets sold and included repeat journeys.

9. *Zengding shisi ban Xihu youlan zhinan* [Revised fourteenth edition of the travel guide for West Lake] (1913; repr., Shanghai: Shangwu yinshuguan, 1922), 129–130, 122.

10. Frank Rhea, comp., *Far Eastern Markets for Railway Materials* (Washington, DC: Government Printing Office, 1919), 79.

11. "The Tramways: Two New Train Cars," *North-China Herald,* January 7, 1910, 30; "The Shanghai-Nanking Railway: A Trial Trip," *North-China Herald,* June 3, 1910, 549.

12. "Canton: The Canton-Hankow Railway," *North-China Herald,* October 25, 1910, 470.

13. "The Tientsin-Pukow Railway," *North-China Herald,* November 30, 1912, 582.

14. Ibid.

15. Harry Alverson Franck, *Roving through Southern China* (New York: Century, 1925), 411–412.

16. Rhea, *Far Eastern Markets for Railway Materials,* 79.

17. William Barclay Parsons, *An American Engineer in China* (New York: McClure, Phillips, 1900), 277–279; Isaac Taylor Headland, *A Tourist's Guide to Peking* (Tientsin: China Times, 1907), 1.

18. Ministry of Communications, *Zhongguo tielu tongji,* various years.

19. Ministry of Communications, *Zhongguo tielu tongji* (for 1924) (Peking, 1925), 15. The rolling-stock inventories in the annual statistical reports suggest that on some lines third- and fourth-class travelers used the same cars; on others,

they were separate. Ministry of Communications, *Zhongguo tielu tongji* (for 1925) (Peking, 1926), 16.

20. Ministry of Communications, *Zhongguo tielu tongji* (for 1923) (Peking, 1924).

21. On migration to Manchuria, see Jie Xueshi and Matsumura Takao, eds., *Mantie yu Zhongguo laogong* [The South Manchurian Railway and Chinese labor] (Beijing: Shehui kexue wenxian chubanshe, 2003); Thomas R. Gottschang and Diana Lary, *Swallows and Settlers: The Great Migration from North China to Manchuria* (Ann Arbor: Center for Chinese Studies, University of Michigan, 2000); Sören Urbansky, *Kolonialer Wettstreit: Russland, China, Japan und die Ostchinesische Eisenbahn* [Colonial competition: Russia, China, Japan, and the China Eastern Railroad] (Frankfurt: Campus Verlag, 2008), chap. 3.

22. Ministry of Communications, *Zhongguo tielu tongji* (for 1919) (Peking, 1920), 15.

23. Rhea, *Far Eastern Markets for Railway Materials*, 79.

24. Chu-Kê Ling, *China's Railway Rolling Stock: A Study of Postwar Purchases* (Seattle: College of Economics and Business, University of Washington Press, 1946), 43.

25. Emily Georgina Kemp, *Chinese Mettle* (London: Hodder and Stoughton, 1921), 37.

26. "Railway Eccentricities in Hupeh," *North-China Herald*, October 21, 1911, 175.

27. "Tientsin-Pukou Railway: Tientsin to Shanghai in 32 Hours: Account of a Journey," *Peking and Tientsin Times*, December 1912.

28. Ibid.

29. Passenger tickets were sold for first class (*toudeng*), second class (*erdeng*), and third class (*sandeng*) on regular trains, with supplementary tickets required for bulky luggage and personal goods.

30. Ministry of Communications, *Zhongguo tielu tongji*, various years.

31. Wu Xiangxiang and Liu Shaotang, *Lu an shanhou yuebao tekan: Tielu* [Special issue of the monthly magazine on the reconstruction of the Shandong case: Railroads] (1923; repr., Taibei: Zhuanji wenxue chubanshe, 1971), prices calculated from table on p. 37.

32. Chen Mingyuan, *Wenhuaren de jingji shenghuo* [Economic life of cultural people] (Shanghai: Wenhui chubanshe, 2005), 105.

33. Ibid.

34. Ibid., 123.

35. Ministry of Communications, *Zhongguo tielu tongji*, see figures for years 1932 and 1935.

36. Naofumi Nakamura, "Railway Systems and Time Consciousness in Modern Japan," *Japan Review* 14 (2002): 13–38; Dallas Finn, *Meiji Revisited: The Sites of Victorian Japan* (New York: Weatherhill, 1995).

37. *Xin Tianjin zhinan* [Guide to new Tianjin] (n.p., 1927); *Zhongguo lüxing zhinan* [China travel guide] (Shanghai: Shangwu yinshuguan, 1926).

38. *Xin Tianjin zhinan*, 230–235.

39. *Jin-Pu tielu lüxing zhinan* [Travel guide to the Jin-Pu Railroad] (n.p., 1933), app., no pagination.

40. *Bei-Ning tielu zhinan*, [Travel guide of the Bei-Ning Railroad] (n.p., 1907); *Zhonghua guoyou zhinan* (China national guide] (n.p., 1910).

41. Edward R. Tufte, *Envisioning Information* (Cheshire, CT: Graphics Press, 1990), 54. I thank Michael Szonyi for bringing this study to my attention.

42. Ibid.; *Zhongguo lüxing zhinan.*

43. Harrison, *The Making of the Republican Citizen*, 67.

44. Nakamura, "Railway Systems and Time Consciousness in Modern Japan"; Vanessa Ogle, *The Global Transformation of Time, 1870 to 1950* (Cambridge, MA: Harvard University Press, 2005).

45. *Suzhou tielu dalunche gongsi kaiwang Wusong* [A train of the Suzhou Railroad Company to Wusong], woodblock print, no date, circa 1880s, author's collection.

46. Dr. Wendschuh, "Bericht ueber eine Informationsreise entlang der Suedstrecke der Tsientsin-Pukou Bahn, Anfang Oktober 1912" [Report on an informational journey along the southern section of the Tsientsin-Pukou line, early October 1912], vol. 14, 1912, BLHBS.

47. See Elisabeth Köll, *From Cotton Mill to Business Empire* (Cambridge, MA: Harvard University Asia Center, 2003), chap. 5; Kristin Stapleton, *Civilizing Chengdu: Chinese Urban Reform, 1895–1937* (Cambridge, MA: Harvard University Asia Center, 2000).

48. Wen-hsin Yeh, "Corporate Space, Communal Time: Every Day Life in Shanghai's Bank of China," *American Historical Review* 100, no. 1 (February 1995): 97–122.

49. In *North-China Herald*, see for example "Soldiers at Play," March 30, 1912, 847; "Foreigners Warned," August 2, 1913, 359; "The War in Shantung," October 31, 1914, 331; "Hupeh-Szechuan Railway," January 8, 1916, 70.

50. "The Peking-Hankow Line: The Old Order and the New," *North-China Herald*, March 25, 1910, 697–698.

51. "Shanghai-Nanking Railway Sleeping Cars," *North-China Herald*, June 17, 1910, 699.

52. P. T. Carey, "Control of Train Traffic by Telephone," *Journal of the Association of Chinese and American Engineers* 4, no. 5 (1920): 1–14.

53. Wang Tongling, *JiangZhe lüxing ji* [Record of travels in Jiangsu and Zhejiang] (Beijing: Wenhua xueshe, 1928); Wang Tongling, *Shaanxi lüxing ji* [Record of travels in Shaanxi] (Beijing: Wenhua xueshe, 1928).

54. Yan Changhong, *Xisu dongjian ji: Zhongguo jindai shehui fengsu de yanbian* [Western customs moving east: The evolution of modern Chinese customs] (Changsha: Hunan chubanshe, 1991), 178.

55. Köll, *From Cotton Mill to Business Empire*, chap. 4.

56. Letter from Dorpmüller to Cordes, December 4, 1912, vol. 14, BLHBS.

57. Ibid.

58. See David S. Landes, *Revolution in Time: Clocks and the Making of the Modern World* (Cambridge, MA: Belknap Press of Harvard University Press, 1983); Ian R. Bartky, *Selling the True Time: Nineteenth-Century Timekeeping in America* (Stanford, CA: Stanford University Press, 2000); Michael O'Malley, *Keeping Watch: A History of American Time* (New York: Viking, 1990).

59. Ian R. Bartky, *One Time Fits All: The Campaigns for Global Uniformity* (Stanford, CA: Stanford University Press, 2007).

60. See Hui-yu Caroline Ts'ai, *Taiwan in Japan's Empire Building: An Institutional Approach to Colonial Engineering* (London: Routledge, 2009), 98. Regarding standard time as a tool of discipline, Ts'ai quotes Lü Shao-li, *Shuiluo xiangqi: Rizhi shiqi Taiwan shehui de shenghuo zuoxi* [Whistles from the sugarcane factory: Ways of life in Taiwanese society under Japanese rule] (Taibei: Yuanliu chubanshe, 1998). For railroads in India and the Middle East, see Ritika Prasad, "Tracking Modernity: The Experience of Railways in Colonial India, 1853–1947" (PhD diss., University of California, Los Angeles, 2009); Ogle, *The Global Transformation of Time, 1870 to 1950.*

61. Elizabeth R. VanderVen, *A School in Every Village: Educational Reform in a Northeast China County, 1904–31* (Vancouver: University of British Columbia Press, 2012), 142.

62. Guo Qingsheng, "Zhongguo biaozhun shizhi kao" [Examination of China's standard time system], *Zhongguo keji shiliao* [Chinese materials on science and technology] 22, no. 3 (2001): 271.

63. Ibid., 273.

64. Ibid.

65. Li Zhanzai, "Tielu yu Zhongguo jindai minsu shanbian" [Railroads and the transmutation of modern Chinese customs], *Shixue yuekan*, no. 1 (1996): 57.

66. *Jin-Pu tielu lüxing zhinan* [Travel guide of the Jin-Pu Railroad] (n.p., 1921).

67. Ye Shengtao et al., *Kaiming guoyu keben* [Chinese textbook of the Kaiming Company], 2 vols. (1932; repr., Shanghai: Shanghai kexue jishu wenxian chubanshe, 2005), 1:103–105, 189–190.

68. Ibid., 1:189.

69. Ibid., 1:103–105.

70. Michael Nylan, "Highway Networks in China's Classical Era," in *Highways, Byways and Road Systems in the Pre-modern World*, ed. Susan E. Alcock, John Bodel, and Richard J. A. Talbert (Chichester, UK: Wiley Blackwell, 2012), 33–65, esp. 48–49.

71. See, for example, Richard E. Strassberg, trans., *Inscribed Landscapes: Travel Writing from Imperial China* (Berkeley: University of California Press, 1994); Susan Naquin, *Peking: Temples and City Life, 1400–1900* (Berkeley: University of California Press, 2000).

72. J. M. Hargett, *On the Road in Twelfth-Century China: The Travel Diaries of Fan Chengda (1126–93)* (Wiesbaden: Franz Steiner Verlag, 1989).

73. Xi He and David Faure, *The Fisher Folk of Late Imperial and Modern China: An Historical Anthropolgy of Boat-and-Shed Living* (London: Routledge, 2016). For a detailed description of the temple festival, its participants, and the role of the railroad, see *North-China Herald*, May 19, 1877, 183–185, app. 1.

74. Naquin, *Peking;* Timothy Brook, *The Confusions of Pleasure: Commerce and Culture in Ming China* (Berkeley: University of California Press, 1999).

75. Eric Teichman, *Travels of a Consular Officer in Eastern Tibet: Together with a History of the Relations between China, Tibet and India* (Cambridge: Cambridge University Press, 1922), 13.

76. *JinPu tielu lüxing zhinan* (1933); *JinPu canche, xiaoying, shitang, binguan yingye baogao ji jinhou jihua yijianshu* [Report on the business of the dining car, petty sales, dining hall, and hotel of the JinPu Railroad and suggestions for further plans in the future] (n.p., 1936).

77. JiaoJi tielu guanliju [Management office of the Qingdao Railroad], student travel passes (1926), Shandong Provincial Archives (SDDAG), J 110-01-315; see also JiaoJi tielu guanliju, letter to National Qingdao University, 1932, SDDAG, J 110-01-413.

78. Yajun Mo, "Itineraries for a Republic: Itineraries for a Republic, Travel Culture and Tourism in Modern China, 1866–1954" (PhD diss., University of California, Santa Cruz, 2011), 178–185; Xing Jianrong and Li Peide, eds., *Chen Guangfu riji* [Diary of Chen Guangfu] (Shanghai: Shanghai shudian chubanshe, 2002); Linsun Cheng, *Banking in Modern China: Entrepreneurs, Professional Managers and the Development of Chinese Banks, 1897–1937* (Cambridge: Cambridge University Press, 2003).

79. Hanqin Qiu Zhang, Ray Pine, and Terry Lam, eds., *Tourism and Hotel Development in China: From Political to Economic Success* (Binghamton, NY: Haworth Press, 2005), 14.

80. Carl Crow, *The Travelers' Handbook for China* (New York: Dodd, Mead, 1913), 158; "Astor House Hotel Co., Ltd.," *North-China Herald,* October 3, 1914.

81. Japanese Government Railways, *Guide to China* (Tokyo: Imperial Japanese Government Railways, 1924).

82. Ibid., 271.

83. Ibid.

84. Crow, *The Travelers' Handbook for China,* 208–209.

85. Mo, "Itineraries for a Republic," 177.

86. "Two Railway Hotels Planned for Chufu," *Journal of the Association of Chinese and American Engineers* 1, no. 3 (November 1920): 46. On Tai'an as a sightseeing venue, see also Paul Hutchinson, ed., *A Guide to Important Mission Stations in Eastern China (Lying Along the Main Routes of Travel)* (Shanghai: Mission Book, 1920), 49–57.

87. "New Hotels on Chinese Railways," *North-China Herald,* May 21, 1921, 512.

88. See Japanese Government Railways, *Guide to China* and "The Awful Journey to Tientsin," *North-China Herald,* August 25, 1928, 442.

89. GuangJiu tielu guanliju, *GuangJiu tielu lüxing zhinan* [Travel guide of the Canton-Kowloon Railroad] (n.p., 1922).

90. For the use of local gazetteers by travelers in imperial China, see Joseph Dennis, *Writing, Publishing, and Reading Local Gazetteers in Imperial China, 1100–1700* (Cambridge, MA: Harvard University Asia Center, 2015), 300–309.

91. Long Haitielu zonggongsuo, *LongQinYuHai tielu lüxing zhinan,* 1918; *DaoQing tielu lüxing zhinan,* 1918; *Jin-Pu tielu lüxing zhinan,* 1921; *HuNingHuHangYong tielu disanqi lüxing zhinan* [Travel guide for third section of the Hu NingHuHangYong Railroad] (n.p., 1922); *JiuLong tielu lüxing zhinan* [Guide for travel on the Jiu-Long Railroad] (n.p., 1922).

92. GuangJiu tielu guanliju, *GuangJiu tielu lüxing zhinan.*

93. Ibid., 14–19.

94. Ibid.

95. Ibid., 20–23, 25, 31–32, 47–48.

96. Ibid., 56–57.

97. David Faure and Elisabeth Köll, "China: The Indigenisation of Insurance," in *World Insurance: The Evolution of a Global Risk Network,* ed. Peter Borscheid and Niels Viggo Haueter (Oxford: Oxford University Press, 2012), chap. 20.

98. Advertisement in *Lüxing zazhi* [China traveler], September 1928, no pagination.

99. Yu Dafu, "HangJiang xiaoli jicheng" [Trip on the Hangzhou Railroad], in *Dafu youji* [The travel diary of (Yu) Dafu] (Shanghai: Wenxue chuangzao chubanshe, 1936; facsimile repr., Tianjin: Baihua chubanshe, 2004), 1–30.

100. *Xin youji huikan* [Series of new travel reports] (n.p., 1924 [1921]).

101. *HuNing HuHangYong tielu lüxing zhinan* [Travel guide for the Shanghai-Nanjing and Shanghai-Hangzhou-Ningbo Railroads] (n.p., 1919); LongHai tielu conggongsuo, *LongQinYuHai tielu lüxing zhinan*; *DaoQing tielu lüxing zhinan* [Guide for travel on the DaoQing Railroad (of the JingHan line)], 1918.

102. Guangyi shuju bianji, comp., *Quanguo tielu lüxing zhinan* [National Railroad travel guide] (Shanghai: Guangyi shuju, 1921), 60–61.

103. Tetsudo Sho [Ministry of Railways], *Tetsudo ryoko annai* [Guide to railroad travel] (Tokyo: Taisho 10, 1922).

104. Ibid.

105. Constantine N. Vaporis, "The Gokaido Highway in Early Modern Japan," in Alcock, Bodel, and Talbert, *Highways, Byways and Road Systems in the Pre-modern World,* 95–105.

106. Strassberg, *Inscribed Landscape;* see also Emma Jinhua Teng, *Taiwan's Imagined Geography: Chinese Colonial Travel Writing and Pictures, 1683–1895* (Cambridge, MA: Harvard University Asia Center, 2004).

107. *Jin-Pu tielu lüxing zhinan* [Travel guide for the Tianjin-Pukou Railroad], 1933; *YueHan tielu xunkan* [Magazine for the YueHan Railroad], 1932 and 1933.

108. Tiedaobu lian yunchu, *Zhonghua minguo quanguo tielu lüxing zhinan* [Travel guide for all railroads in Republican China] (Nanjing [?]: Tiedaobu lian yunchu, 1934).

109. Ye Shengtao et al., *Kaiming guoyu keben.*

110. Ibid., 1:78.

111. Wolfgang Schivelbusch, *The Railway Journey: Trains and Travel in the 19th Century,* trans. Anselm Hollo (New York: Urizen Books, 1979), 84.

112. Ibid.

113. Feng Zikai, "Chexiang shehui" [Rail carriage society], in Lu Xun, *Zhongguo xiandai sanwen mingjia mingzuo yuanbanku,* ed. Wang Bin (Beijing: Zhongguo wenlian chuban gongsi, 1997), 1–6.

114. Zhang Henshui, "Ping-Hu tongche," serialized in *Lüxing zazhi* in 1935.

115. Sun Fuyuan, *Fuyuan youji* [Travels of Fuyuan] (Shanghai: Beixin shuju, 1926), 15–18.

116. Gu Yongdi, comp., *Xu Zhimo shi quanji* [The complete poems of Xu Zhimo], 2nd ed. (Shanghai: Xuelin chubanshe, 1997).

117. Zhang Henshui, "Ping-Hu tongche."

118. Gerth, *China Made,* 188.

119. Sherman Cochran, ed., *Inventing Nanjing Road: Commercial Culture in Shanghai, 1900–1945* (Ithaca, NY: East Asia Program, Cornell University, 1999); Gerth, *China Made;* newspaper ads for Klim milk and BAT cigarettes in *Shenbao* (Shanghai), November 4 and 15, 1924.


## 5. Professionalizing and Politicizing the Railroads

1. "How War Ruins the Railways: Detailed Damage to Tsin-Pu Line Due to Recent Campaign," *North-China Herald,* August 25, 1928, 310.

2. C. P. Fitzgerald, *Why China? Recollections of China, 1923–1950* (Portland, OR: ISBS, 1985); Zhang Ruide, *Zhongguo jindai tielu shiye guanli de yanjiu: Zhengzhi cengmian de fenxi (1876–1937)* [A study of the industrial management of modern Chinese railroads: A political-level analysis (1876–1937)] (Taibei: Zhongyang yanjiuyuan jindaishi yanjiusuo, 1991).

3. "China's Railways," *North-China Herald,* December 22, 1928, 472–473.

4. Margherita Zanasi, *Saving the Nation: Economic Modernity in Republican China* (Chicago: University of Chicago Press, 2006); Lloyd E. Eastman, Jerome Ch'en, Suzanne Pepper, and Lyman P. Van Slyke, *The Nationalist Era in*

*China, 1927–1949* (Cambridge: Cambridge University Press, 1991); Elizabeth J. Remick, *Building Local States: China during the Republican and Post-Mao Eras* (Cambridge, MA: Harvard University Asia Center, 2004); Julia C. Strauss, *Strong Institutions in Weak Polities: State Building in Republican China, 1927–1940* (Oxford: Clarendon Press, 1998); Zwia Lipkin, *Useless to the State: "Social Problems" and Social Engineering in China, 1927–1937* (Cambridge, MA: Harvard University Asia Center, 2006).

5. Strauss, *Strong Institutions in Weak Polities*; William C. Kirby, "Engineering China: The Origins of the Chinese Developmental State," in *Becoming Chinese*, ed. Wen-hsin Yeh (Berkeley: University of California Press, 2000), 137–160.

6. Strauss, *Strong Institutions in Weak Polities*. The Sino-Foreign Salt Inspectorate was created as a tax collecting agency in 1913, ibid., 63–66

7. Arthur Judson Brown, *The Chinese Revolution* (New York: Student Volunteer Movement, 1912), 76.

8. On the development of higher education in the wake of the May Fourth Movement in Republican China, see Wen-Hsin Yeh, *The Alienated Academy: Culture and Politics in Republican China, 1919–1937* (Cambridge: Council on East Asian Studies, Harvard University, 1990), esp. chap. 3; H. G. W. Woodhead, ed., *The China Yearbook, 1912–1930* (Tianjin: North-China Daily News and Herald, 1931), 530.

9. *Tiedao nianjian, di'erjuan* [Railroad yearbook, part 2] (Shanghai: Tiedaobu mishuting tushushi, 1935), 1031–1035. On Shanghai Jiaotong University's architectural evolution, especially its engineering buildings, see Cao Yongkang et al., *Nanyang zhujun: Shanghai jiaotong daxue lishi jianzhu pin* [Nanyang's architectural charm: The historical buildings of Shanghai Jiaotong Unversity] (Shanghai: Shanghai Jiaotong daxue chubanshe, 2016), 136–158.

10. *Tiedao nianjian, di'erjuan*, 1031. Between 1928 and 1949 the Nationalist government referred to Beijing as Beiping to confirm the status of Nanjing as the new capital of the Republic of China. I continue to refer to the Beijing campus for reasons of clarity.

11. This number excludes the students from the Science College at Shanghai Jiaotong University.

12. *Tiedao nianjian, di'er juan*, 1032–1034.

13. Ibid., 1035.

14. *Zhonghua guoyou tielu HuNingHuHangYong xian zhiyuanlu* [Employee directory of the Chinese national Shanghai-Nanjing and Shanghai-Hangzhou-Ningbo lines], 1920, 1–6, Shanghai Municipal Archives (SMA), Y2-1-1097.

15. Ibid.; Minami Manshu Tetsudo Kabushiki Kaisha, *A Brief Survey of the Manchoukuo State Railways* (Mukden: General Direction, 1936).

16. *HuNingHuHangYong liang lu shencha weiyuan baogao* [Investigative report on the two lines of Shanghai-Nanjing and Shanghai-Hangzhou-Ningbo] (n.p., 1929); *JinPu tielu zhiyuanlu* [Record of employees on the Jin-Pu railroad] (n.p., 1929).

17. "Notice," advertisement by the Ministry of Communications appearing in several issues of *Journal of the Association of Chinese and American Engineers* 4, no. 6 (June 1923), no consecutive pagination; 4, no. 5 (May 1923): 2; 1, no. 3 (November 1920), advertising section, no pagination.

18. "China's Railways: Tasks of the Foreign Advisor," *North-China Herald*, April 20, 1929.

19. Huei-min Sun, "From Literati to Legal Professions: The First Generation of Chinese Law School Graduates and Their Career Patterns," in *Knowledge Acts in Modern China: Ideas, Institutions, and Identities,* ed. Robert Culp, Eddy U, and Wen-hsin Yeh (Berkeley: Institute of East Asian Studies, University of California, 2016), 89–113.

20. Tiedaobu zongwusi wenshuke, *Tiedaobu zhiyuanlu* [Employee directory of the Ministry of Railways] (Beijing: Ministry of Railways, 1929), see General Office Department (*zongwusi,*), 9A–20B, and Operations Department (*gongwusi*), 26A–32B.

21. Ibid., *gongwusi,* 26A–28B.

22. Ibid.; for career backgrounds in 1911, see Zhonghua quanguo tielu xiehui bianjibu, *Zhonghua quanguo tielu xiehui diyici baogao* [First report of the China National Railroad Association] (Beijing: Zhonghua quanguo tielu xiehui shiwusuo, 1911).

23. Douglas R. Reynolds, *China, 1898–1912: The Xinzheng Revolution and Japan* (Cambridge, MA: Council on East Asian Studies, Harvard University, 1993); Vera Schwarcz, *The Chinese Enlightenment: Intellectuals and the Legacy of the May Fourth Movement of 1919* (Berkeley: University of California Press, 1986).

24. Tiedaobu zongwusi wenshuke, *Tiedaobu zhiyuanlu, gongwusi,* 29B–31A.

25. Ibid., 27B.

26. Ziyuan weiyuanhui, *Zhongguo gongcheng renminglu* [Who's who among Chinese engineers] (Changsha: Shangwu yinshuguan, 1941), foreword, no pagination.

27. Benjamin A. Elman, *On Their Own Terms: Science in China, 1550–1900* (Cambridge, MA: Harvard University Press, 2005), 434. According to Elman, the Chinese Engineering Society had 254 members in 1923, 304 members in 1924, and more than 700 members in 1927.

28. *Journal of the Association of Chinese and American Engineers* 1, no. 3 (November 1920), title page.

29. Ibid., masthead.

30. P. H. Chen, "A Comparison of the American and European Bridge Standards," *Journal of the Association of Chinese and American Engineers* 4, no. 6 (June 1923): 5 (italics added).

31. Ibid., 8.

32. O. J. Todd, *Two Decades in China: Comprising Technical Papers, Magazine Articles, Newspaper Stories and Official Reports Connected with Work under His Own Observation* (Taibei: Ch'eng Wen, 1971), 396.

33. Ibid., 203.

34. Ibid., 203–204, 214.

35. See Culp, U, and Yeh, *Knowledge Acts in Modern China.*

36. Kees Gispen, *New Profession, Old Order: Engineers and German Society, 1815–1914* (Cambridge: Cambridge University Press, 1989), 45–46.

37. Ziyuan weiyuanhui, *Zhongguo gongcheng renminglu* (Changsha: Shangwu yinshuguan, 1941), app., no pagination.

38. Ibid.

39. Chiao-Tung University [Nanyang College], *Special Bulletin*, 1933, 1–2.

40. Ibid., 6.

41. "Zhonghua xian you lianghao gonglu—Wang jun Yinhuai xian you lianghao jiankang" [China now has good roads—Wang Yinhuai now has good health], *Lüxing zazhi* [China traveler] (Shanghai: Zhongguo lüxingshe) 10, no. 3 (1936), no pagination.

42. Interviews at Ji'nan Machine Works, June 19, 2005.

43. Tiedaobu yewusi laogongke, *Gongren renshu ji gongzi tongji* [Statistics on numbers of workers and wages], 1931, 12–13. For an informed description of the training of firemen and engine drivers in the Kenya Colony before World War II, see Pheroze Nowrojee, *A Kenyan Journey* (Nairobi: Transafrica Press, 2014), 34–47.

44. YueHan tielu yuansi zilibiao [Employee records of the Yue-Han Railroad], 1940–1949, Guangdong Provincial Archives (GDSDAG), 40-1-722, pp. 123, 130; Odoric Y. K. Wou, *Mobilizing the Masses: Building Revolution in Henan* (Stanford, CA: Stanford University Press, 1994) presents relatively similar wage patterns for workers on the railroads in Henan province during the early 1920s.

45. *JinPu tielu guanliju zhiyuanlu* (n.p., 1937).

46. Interviews at Ji'nan Machine Works, June 19, 2005.

47. Ibid.

48. "Jingwuchu jinzhi jiaru banghui lianjie" [Office for police affairs forbidden to join secret societies], 1948, GDSDAG, 40-1-174. The file contains over one hundred of such documents.

49. "JinPu lu gonghui gaikuang" [Profile of the unions on the Jin-Pu Railroad], *Tielu zhigong banyuekan* 99 (1934): 8–13.

50. For this practice, see Elizabeth J. Perry, *Shanghai on Strike: The Politics of Chinese Labor* (Stanford, CA: Stanford University Press, 1993); Elisabeth Köll, *From Cotton Mill to Business Empire* (Cambridge, MA: Harvard University Asia Center, 2003); Gail Hershatter, *The Workers of Tianjin, 1900–1949* (Stanford, CA: Stanford University Press, 1986).

51. "JinPu lu gonghui gaikuang," *Tielu zhigong banyuekan* 99 (1934); in *JinPu zhi sheng* [The T. P. R. echo], for example "JinPu tielu guanli ju banshi guize" [Work regulations for the Jin-Pu Railroad management bureau], 1(1928): 9–13 (separate pagination); and "Guowai lujie xinwen [Foreign transportation news]: Trans-Continent Air and Railway Service Planned," 7(1928):5 (separate pagination).

52. Perry, *Shanghai on Strike.*

53. Elizabeth J. Perry, *Anyuan: Mining China's Revolutionary Tradition* (Berkeley: University of California Press, 2012), 76.

54. Ibid., 76–77.

55. Wou, *Mobilizing the Masses*; Yang Hongjian, *Xuzhou tielu gongren yundong shihua* [Historical narratives of the railroad workers' movement in Xuzhou] (Xuzhou: Xuzhou tielu fenju gonghui, 1994), 612–613.

56. Interviews at the Ji'nan Machine Works, July 2005.

57. Sun Yat-sen, *The International Development of China* (New York: G. P. Putnam's Sons, 1929), "The Northwestern railway system," 7.

58. On Sun Yat-sen's economic program, see Michael R. Godley, "Socialism with Chinese Characteristics: Sun Yat-sen and the International Development of China," *Australian Journal of Chinese Affairs*, no. 18 (July 1987): 109–125.

59. Chiang Kai-shek, *China's Destiny and Chinese Economic Theory* (New York: Roy Publisher, 1947), 180, 287.

60. The China Handbook Editorial Board, *China Handbook, 1950* (New York: Rockport, 1950), 609.

61. Chi-Keung Leung, *China: Railway Patterns and National Goals* (Chicago: Department of Geography, University of Chicago, 1980), 80–81.

62. C. C. Wong, "Some Dangers of Railway Development in China," in *Readings in Economics for China*, ed. C. F. Remer (Shanghai: Commercial Press, 1922), 603–644, 618.

63. Ling Hongxun, *Qishi zishu* [Autobiography at seventy] (Taibei: Sanmin shuju, 1968), 126–127.

64. See, for example, Zhen Ni, "Jiu yi ba san zhou nian" [The third anniversary of Japan's invasion of Manchuria], *Yuelu dangsheng* [The party's voice of the Yue-Han Railroad], no. 206 (September 1934): 14–15; *Tielu yuekan: JinPu xian* [Railroads monthly: The JinPu line] 2, no. 1 (1932) to 4, no. 1 (1934). A white sun on a blue background (symbolizing the blue sky) was the Guomindang party emblem. Knowledge of China's national boundaries and the railroad network was tested in geography exams at Shanghai Jiaotong University in 1931 where students were asked to "locate the Chinese Eastern and the South Manchurian Railways and point out their connections with other lines" (Yeh, *The Alienated Academy*, 95).

65. Rudolf G. Wagner, "Ritual, Architecture, Politics, and Publicity during the Republic: Enshrining Sun Yat-sen," in *Chinese Architecture and the Beaux-Arts,* ed. Jeffrey W. Cody, Nancy S. Steinhardt, and Tony Atkin (Hong Kong: Hong Kong

University Press, 2011), 236–278; Henrietta Harrison, *The Making of the Republican Citizen: Political Ceremonies and Symbols in China, 1911–1929* (Oxford: Clarendon Press, 2000), 207–239; Wang Liping, "Creating a National Symbol: The Sun Yatsen Memorial in Nanjing," *Republican China* 21, no. 2 (2013): 23–63.

66. Ye Shengtao et al., *Kaiming guoyu keben* [Chinese textbook of Kaiming Company], 2 vols. (1932; repr., Shanghai: Shanghai kexue jishu wenxian chubanshe, 2005), 2:17–18, at 18.

67. Ibid., 2:76–78. The text book stated that "Because this is a famous historic site of our nation, people traveling on the Tianjin-Pukou line often want to get off at Qufu to sightsee there" (175–176). Travel by plane did not yet widely feature in textbooks and was primarily associated with business travel, such as to the capital Nanjing for urgent government affairs (151–153).

68. Arif Dirlik, "The Ideological Foundations of the New Life Movement: A Study in Counterrevolution," *Journal of Asian Studies* 34, no. 4 (August 1975): 945–980, at 945.

69. Walter Hanming Chen, "The New Life Movement," *Information Bulletin* (Nanking: Council of International Affairs) 2, no. 11 (December 1936): 189–229, esp. 206–207, 212.

70. The National Resources Commission functioned as a quasi "technocratic civil service" in the early 1930s, but it later became aligned with the military and political goals of the Nationalist government, especially during the war period. See William C. Kirby, "Technocratic Organization and Technological Development in China: The Nationalist Experience and Legacy, 1928–1953," in *Science and Technology in Post-Mao China,* ed. Denis Fred Simon and Merle Goldman (Cambridge, MA: Council on East Asian Studies, Harvard University, 1989), 41; see also Kirby, "Engineering China."

71. James Reardon-Anderson, *The Study of Change: Chemistry in China, 1840–1949* (Cambridge: Cambridge University Press, 1991), 230–257, at 255.

72. Chinese Ministry of Information, *China Handbook, 1937–1943* (New York: Macmillan, 1943), list of national holidays, no pagination, front section facing preface.

73. Gerald Friedman, *State-Making and Labor Movements: France and the United States, 1876–1914* (Ithaca, NY: Cornell University Press, 1998), 94.

74. Sheldon M. Garon, *The State and Labor in Modern Japan* (Berkeley: University of California Press, 1989), 17.

75. Yang Hongjian, *Xuzhou tielu gongren yundong shihua*, 487.

76. Zhang Dezhou, "Wo duiyu zhigong jiaoyu de jianglai guan" [My future perspective on the education of workers], *Tielu zhigong jiaoyu xunkan* (Magazine for the education of railroad workers), no. 1 (1922): 15–16. The author was a teacher at the Tianjin Railroad Workers School.

## 6. Crisis Management

1. *China Handbook, 1937–43* (New York: 1943), 240–241.

2. Willy Kraus, *Private Business in China* (Honolulu: University of Hawai'i Press, 1991), 51.

3. For the battle of Xuzhou, see Diana Lary, "Defending China: The Battles of the Xuzhou Campaign," in *Warfare in Chinese History*, ed. Hans van de Ven (Leiden: Brill, 2000), esp. 410.

4. Peter Merker, "The Guomindang Regions of Jiangxi," in *China at War: Regions of China, 1937–1945*, ed. Stephen R. MacKinnon, Diana Lary, and Ezra F. Vogel (Stanford, CA: Stanford University Press, 2007), 288–313.

5. Ibid., 293–294.

6. Micah S. Muscolino, *The Ecology of War in China: Henan Province, the Yellow River, and Beyond, 1938–1950* (Cambridge: Cambridge University Press, 2015), at 16.

7. Ibid., 58.

8. Ibid., 72.

9. Lü Weijun et al., *Shandong quyu xiandaihua yanjiu, 1840–1949* [Research on the Shandong region and modernization, 1840–1949] (Ji'nan: Qilu shushe, 2002); David D. Buck, *Urban Change in China: Politics and Development in Tsinan, Shandong, 1890–1949* (Madison: University of Wisconsin Press, 1978), 139.

10. Junshi weiyuanhui junlingbu diyiting disanchu, *Pohuai gong (tie) lu banfa* [Methods of sabotaging the railroads] (n.p., Junshi weiyuanhui junlingbu diyiting disanchu, 1939).

11. Interview with Yang Baoqing, Hefei, Anhui, October 2005.

12. Junshi weiyuanhui junlingbu diyiting disanchu, *Pohuai gong (tie) lu banfa.*

13. Shandong sheng zonggonghui, *Shandong gongren yundongshi* [History of the workers' movement in Shandong] (Ji'nan: Shandong renmin chubanshe, 1988), 232–250.

14. Ibid., 233–235.

15. Shandong province and counties' announcements on the local situation (railroad, water, farming etc.) during war, 1940, Shandong Provincial Archives (SDDAG), J 102-14-22.

16. Zhi Xia, *Tiedao youjidui* [The railroad guerrilla squad] (Shanghai: Shanghai renmin chubanshe, 1977), see the author's postscript on 605.

17. Shandong sheng zonggonghui, *Shandong gongren yundongshi,* 250.

18. Ju Zhifen, "Labor Conscription in North China: 1941–45," in MacKinnon, Lary, and Vogel, *China at War,* 207–226, esp. 220.

19. Ibid., 220–221.

20. Ibid.

21. Diana Lary, "The Context of the War" in MacKinnon, Lary, and Vogel, *China at War,* 8–9.

22. Stephen J. Zaloga, *Armored Trains* (Botley, UK: Osprey, 2008). I thank Robert Gardella for sharing his insights on the use of armored trains.

23. "Translation from a Chinese Memorandum: Situation in the Interior of North China," Hong Kong, January 18, 1939, box 4, folder "Puppet activities," 1930–1951, MS 781, Hsia Pin-fang (XPF) Papers, Baker Library, Harvard Business School (BLHBS).

24. Frederic Wakeman, *The Shanghai Badlands: Wartime Terrorism and Urban Crime, 1937–1941* (Cambridge: Cambridge University Press, 1996), 128–129.

25. Liu Shoulin et al., eds., *Minguo zhiguan nianbiao* [Chronology of the Republic of China] (Beijing: Zhonghua shuju, 1995).

26. Wei Qingyuan and Bai Hua, eds., *Zhongguo zhengzhi zhidu shi* [A history of the Chinese political system], 2nd ed. (Beijing: Zhongguo renmin daxue chubanshe, 2005).

27. Interviews, former workers of the Jin-Pu Railroad Company, Ji'nan Machine Works, Ji'nan, July 15, 2005.

28. See Frederic Wakeman, "Occupied Shanghai: The Struggle between Chinese and Western Medicine," in MacKinnon, Lary, and Vogel, *China at War,* 272.

29. Interviews with former workers of the Jin-Pu Railroad Company, Ji'nan Machine Works, Ji'nan, July 15, 2005.

30. Interviews with Yao Hongsheng and Ma Minsheng at Ji'nan Machine Works, Ji'nan, July 15 and 19, 2005.

31. Ibid.

32. According to Morris Bian's thorough analysis, the term *zhiyuan* became an entirely new category of factory workers and was introduced because of the rapid expansion of the administrative bureaucracy in state-owned enterprises during the early 1940s. Morris Bian, *The Making of the State Enterprise System in Modern China* (Cambridge, MA: Harvard University Press, 2005), 84–85.

33. Ibid.

34. Parks Coble, *Chinese Capitalists in Japan's New Order: The Occupied Lower Yangzi, 1937–1945* (Berkeley: University of California Press, 2003). For shop-floor conditions and the interactions between workers and management during the Japanese occupation, see Elisabeth Köll, *From Cotton Mill to Business Empire* (Cambridge, MA: Harvard University Asia Center, 2003), 264–274.

35. Interviews, Yao Hongsheng, Hou Jiakun, Shang Linxiang, and Chen Fupeng at Ji'nan Machine Works, Ji'nan, July 14, 2005.

36. Ibid.

37. A rich photographic record exists showing the refugee situation on trains and at railroad stations in China during the war. For moving photographs by Frank Capa and Jack Birns, see, for example, Stephen R. MacKinnon, *Wuhan 1938: War, Refugees, and the Making of Modern China* (Berkeley: University of California Press, 2008); Jack Birns, Carolyn Wakeman, and Ken Light, eds., *As-*

*signment Shanghai: Photographs on the Eve of Revolution* (Berkeley: University of California Press, 2003).

38. Translation of Chinese telegram, May 13, 1939, XPF Papers, BLHBS.

39. Translation of Chinese telegram, May 13, 1939, from Dr. T. V. Soong in Hong Kong to Generalissimo Chiang Kai-shek and Dr. H. H. Kung in Chungking, marked confidential, box 4, folder "Special telegrams and letters," XPF Papers, BLHBS.

40. See Coble, *Chinese Capitalists in Japan's New Order.*

41. "The Translation from a Chinese Memorandum," January 18, 1939, XPF Papers, BLHBS.

42. Ibid.

43. Ibid.

44. Ibid.

45. Ibid.

46. Philip Thai, *China's War on Smuggling: Law, Economic Life, and the Making of the Modern State* (New York: Columbia University Press, 2018).

47. Ibid.

48. Memorandum No. 2509, Hebei youzheng guanliju (Postal administration office of Hebei province), July 11, 1918, Tianjin Municipal Archives (TJDAG), W 2-152, 425–426.

49. Wakeman, "Occupied Shanghai," 272.

50. Yue-Han tielu guanliju [Management Office of the Guangzhou-Hankou Railroad] (1946–1949), Guangdong Provincial Archives (GDSDAG), 40-1-508. For reports documenting smuggling activities along the Canton-Kowloon line in the early postwar years and after the closing of the border between Hong Kong and China in 1949, see Hong Kong Public Records Office, HK RS 48-1-254, "On smuggling," 1946–1953.

51. Interview records Yue-Han tielu guanliju (1947–1949), GDSDAG, 40-1-6.

52. Jian Shenghuang, *YueHan tielu quanxian tongche yu kangzhan de guanxi* [The relationship between transport services along the entire Guangzhou-Hankou Railroad line and the war of resistance] (Taibei: Taiwan shangwu yinshuguan, 1980), 111.

53. See, for example, newspaper reports in *North-China Daily News, China Weekly Review,* and other foreign publications on the first three years of the Japanese occupation compiled in 1940 by Shuhsi Hsü, *A New Digest of Japanese War Conduct* (Shanghai: Kelly and Walsh, 1941).

54. Parks M. Coble, *China's War Reporters: The Legacy of Resistance against Japan* (Cambridge, MA: Harvard University Press, 2015).

55. R. Keith Schoppa, *In a Sea of Bitterness: Refugees during the Sino-Japanese War* (Cambridge, MA: Harvard University Press, 2011).

56. Wilma Fairbank, *Liang and Lin: Partners in Exploring China's Architectural Past* (Philadelphia: University of Pennsylvania Press, 1994), 101.

57. Ibid., 103–105.

58. W. H. Auden and Christopher Isherwood, *Journey to a War* (London: Faber and Faber, 1939).

59. See, for example, Qing Yin, *Zhanshi ba sheng lüxingji* [Diary of travel through eight provinces during wartime] (n.p.: Dahua tushu zazhishe, 1940[?]); for excellent photographic documentation, see Zhongguo tiedao bowuguan, *KangRi fenghuo zhong de Zhongguo tielu* [Chinese railroads in the raging flames of the anti-Japanese war) (n.p., 2016).

60. Xiao Hong, "Flight from Danger," in *The Dyer's Daughter: Selected Stories of Xiao Hong,* trans. Howard Goldblatt (Hong Kong: Chinese University Press, 2005), 251–271.

61. Chen Baichen, "Men and Women in Wild Times," in *Twentieth-Century Chinese Drama: An Anthology,* ed. Edward M. Gunn (Bloomington: Indiana University Press, 1983), 126–173.

62. Interview with Chen Xinsheng, Shanghai, September 2005. I thank Daqing Yang for the introduction to Chen.

63. Ibid.

64. Ibid.

65. Ibid.

66. Ibid.

67. Li Ziming, *Huocheshang de Minguo* (The Republic on the rails) (Beijing: Zhongguo tiedao chubanshe, 2014), 192; see also the photographs in Zhongguo tiedao bowuguan, *KangRi fenghuo zhong de Zhongguo tielu.*

68. Interview, Chen Xinsheng, Shanghai, September 2005.

69. Ibid.

70. Lary, "The Context of the War," 8–9.

71. See Leung Chi-Keung, *China, Railway Patterns and National Goals* (Chicago: Department of Geography, University of Chicago, 1980); Ralph William Huenemann, *The Dragon and the Iron Horse: The Economics of Railroads in China* (Cambridge, MA: Harvard University Press, 1984); Zhang Ruide, *Zhongguo jindai tielu shiye guanli de yanjiu: Zhengzhi cengmian de fenxi (1876–1937)* [A study of the industrial management of modern Chinese railroads: A political-level analysis (1876–1937)] (Taibei: Zhongyang yanjiuyuan jindaishi yanjiusuo, 1991); Zhang Ruide, *Ping-Han tielu yu Huabei de jingji fazhan (1905–1937)* [The Beijing-Hankou railroad and the economic development of North China (1905–1937)] (Taibei: Zhongyang yanjiuyuan jindaishi yanjiusuo, 1987).

## 7. Postwar Reorganization and Expansion

1. J. N. Westwood, "Soviet Railway Development," *Soviet Studies* 11, no. 1 (July 1959): 33; Iván Wiesel, "Cuban Economy after the Revolution," *Acta Oeconomica* 3, no. 2 (1968): 203–220.

2. See, for example, Jeremy Brown and Paul G. Pickowicz, eds., *Dilemmas of Victory: The Early Years of the People's Republic of China* (Cambridge, MA: Harvard University Press, 2007); Sherman Cochran, ed., *The Capitalist Dilemma in China's Communist Revolution* (Ithaca, NY: East Asia Program, Cornell University, 2014); Zhang Jishun, *Yuanqu de dushi: 1950 niandai de Shanghai* [A city displaced: Shanghai in the 1950s] (Beijing: Shehui kexue wenxian chubanshe, 2015); William C. Kirby, "Continuity and Change in Modern China: Economic Planning on the Mainland and in Taiwan, 1943–1958," *Australian Journal of Chinese Affairs,* no. 24 (July 1990): 121–141.

3. "Rehabilitation of Railways," in *China Handbook 1950* (New York: Rockport Press, 1950), 610–619.

4. Ibid., 610.

5. Ibid., 614.

6. Ibid., 615.

7. Ibid., 615–617.

8. Larry M. Worztel, "The Beijing-Tianjin Campaign of 1948–1949," in *Chinese Warfighting: The PLA Experience since 1949,* ed. Mark A. Ryan, David M. Finkelstein, and Michael A. McDevitt (Armonk, NY: M. E. Sharpe, 2003), 69.

9. Ibid., 57–59. For a thorough analysis of the battle over Manchuria between the Nationalists and Communists and their strategic military decisions, see Odd Arne Westad, *Decisive Encounters: The Chinese Civil War, 1946–1950* (Stanford, CA: Stanford University Press, 2003), 172–179.

10. Ibid., 60–62.

11. Jack Birns, Carolyn Wakeman, and Ken Light, eds., *Assignment Shanghai: Photographs on the Eve of Revolution* (Berkeley: University of California Press, 2003).

12. For a full list of the regions and their lines, see Lu Yangyuan and Fang Qingqiu, eds., *Minguo shehui jingji shi* [Socioeconomic history of Republican China] (Beijing: Zhongguo jingji chubanshe, 1991), 738–740; see also *China Handbook 1950,* 610.

13. Lu Yangyuan and Fang Qingqiu, *Minguo shehui jingji shi,* 740.

14. Dalian jiche cheliang gongchang chanzhi bianzuan weiyuanhui, ed., *Tiedaobu Dalian jiche cheliang gongchang zhi, 1899–1987* [Dalian locomotive and rolling stock factory of the Ministry of Railways, 1899–1987] (Dalian: Dalian chubanshe, 1993), 28.

15. Ibid., 29.

16. Ibid., 28.

17. Rowena Ward, "Delaying Repatriation: Japanese Technicians in Early Postwar China," *Japan Forum* 23, no. 4 (2011): 477–478. See also Daqing Yang, "Resurrecting the Empire? Japanese Technicians in Postwar China, 1945–49," in *The Japanese Empire in East Asia and Its Postwar Legacy,* ed. Harald Fuess (Munich: Iudicium, 1998), 185–205.

18. *Ji'nan tieluju zhi, 1899–1985* [Gazetter of the Ji'nan Railroad Bureau, 1899–1985] (Ji'nan: Ji'nan tieluju shi zhi bianzuan lingdao xiaozu, 1993), 16.

19. Interviews with former workers at the Ji'nan Machine Works, June 2005.

20. Ibid.

21. For a discussion of the *fabi* during the war and the hyperinflation, see Parks M. Coble, *Chinese Capitalists in Japan's New Order: The Occupied Lower Yangzi, 1937–1945* (Berkeley: University of California Press, 2003), 91–96.

22. Interviews with former workers at the Ji'nan Machine Works, June 2005.

23. Ji'nan shi zonggonghui, *Ji'nan gongren yundong shi, 1840–1949* [A history of the Ji'nan workers' movement, 1840–1949] (Beijing: Zhongguo gongren chubanshe, 1992), 307.

24. Ibid., 308.

25. *Jiaotong bu Jin-Pu qu tielu guanliju ribao*, 1947, Shanghai Municipal Archives (SMA), Y12-1-256. The revenue figures from November 1947 appear in the December 23, 1947, issue.

26. Interviews with former workers at the Ji'nan Machine Works, June 2005.

27. Interview with Yao Hongsheng, Ji'nan Machine Works, June 2005.

28. Ji'nan tieluju shizhi bianzuan lingdao xiaozu, *Ji'nan tieluju zhi, 1899–1985*, 548–549.

29. Ibid., 549.

30. Ibid., 549–550.

31. Li Fuchun, *Report on the First Five-Year Plan for Development of the National Economy of the People's Republic of China in 1953–1957* (Peking: Foreign Languages Press, 1955), 8.

32. Ibid., 22–23.

33. Ibid., 24.

34. Zhongguo tiedao xuehui, *Zhongguo tielu, 1949–2001* [Chinese Railroads, 1949–2001] (Beijing: Zhongguo tiedao chubanshe, 2003), 32. Total operating mileage was 13,160 miles in 1949, 14,200 miles in 1952, and 16,600 miles in 1957. Total mileage of double- and multitrack sections was 540 miles in 1949, 880 miles in 1952, and 1,400 miles in 1957.

35. Ibid.

36. Ibid., 27.

37. Zhongguo tielu shi bianji yanjiu zhongxin, ed., *Zhongguo tielu dashiji (1876–1995)* [Chronology of Chinese railroads (1876–1995)] (Beijing: Zhongguo tiedao chubanshe, 1996), 155.

38. H. J. von Lochow, *China's National Railways: Historical Survey and Postwar Planning* (Peiping: [published by the author], 1948). The book contains a map of China's 1948 rail network based on a 1928 map by Julius Dorpmüller, the former chief engineer of the Tianjin-Pukou Railroad (app., facing p. 162).

39. Eldon Griffin, *China's Railways as a Market for Pacific Northwest Products: A Study of a Phase of the External Relations of a Region* (Seattle: Bureau of

Business Research, College of Economics and Business, University of Washington, 1946), 40–41.

40. Ibid., 41.

41. Li Fuchun, *Report on the First Five-Year Plan,* 29. The Yingtan-Xiamen Railroad was completed in 1957, Baoji-Chengdu in 1958, and Lanzhou-Urumqi in 1966.

42. Chang Kia-Ngau, *China's Struggle for Railroad Development* (New York: John Day, 1943), 120.

43. Ibid., 122, 148–149.

44. Deborah Kaple, "Agents of Change: Soviet Advisers and High Stalinist Management in China, 1949–1960," *Journal of Cold War Studies* 18, no. 1 (Winter 2016): 11.

45. Westwood, "Soviet Railway Development," 26.

46. Ibid., 29.

47. Ibid., 30.

48. Ibid.

49. Shen Zhihua, *Sulian zhuanjia zai Zhongguo, 1948–1960* [Soviet experts in China, 1948–1960] (Beijing: Xinhua chubanshe, 2009), 59–60.

50. Ibid., 62. In his careful comparison of data from different national archives, historian Shen Zhihua does not validate one particular number, but he confirms that in the 1950s the overwhelming majority of Soviet experts were military experts.

51. Ibid., 74.

52. Kaple, "Agents of Change," 14–15.

53. Shen Zhihua, *Sulian zhuanjia zai Zhongguo,* 83.

54. Ibid., 91.

55. Ibid., 232.

56. Articles and photographs, *Renmin ribao* (*People's Daily*), October 16, 1957, 1.

57. Shen Zhihua, *Sulian zhuanjia zai Zhongguo,* 144–145, 232–233; Kaple, "Agents of Change," 14–15.

58. Interview with Ma Minsheng, Ji'nan Machine Works, August 2005.

59. Ibid.

60. Ibid.

61. Chen Ji, "Zhandou zai guofang xianshang de tielu gongren" [Railroad workers in battle at the frontline of national defense], *Renmin ribao,* November 29, 1950, 2.

62. Ibid.

63. Ibid.

64. Ji'nan tieluju shizhi bianzuan lingdao xiaozu, *Ji'nan tieluju zhi, 1899–1985,* 20.

65. Ibid.

66. Gao Guangwen, *Tiedaobing* [Railroad army corps] (Beijing: Zhongguo qingnian chubanshe, 1972), 29.

67. Ibid.

68. Ibid. The military structure for the *tiedaobing* comprised approximately eleven divisions (*shi*). Each division contained three-to-five groups (*tuan*), three-to-five camps (*ying*), three-to-five companies (*lian*), platoons (*pai*), and squads (*ban*).

69. Chen Yuanmou, *Zuori tiedaobing* [Yesterday's railroad soldiers] (Beijing: Zhongguo shuji chubanshe, 1994).

70. Annual report on China, 1952, British National Archives (BNA), FO 371/99229.

71. Several extensive interviews with Yang Baoqing and his wife, Hefei, Anhui, September 2005. I thank Professor Yang Jian for the introduction and invaluable help in organizing and conducting the interviews.

72. Ibid.

73. Ibid.

74. Ibid.

75. Ibid.

76. Ibid.

77. Ibid.

78. Ibid.

79. Ibid.

80. Ibid.

81. *Tiedaobing huace* [Pictorial volume on railroad soldiers] (Beijing: Zhongguo renmin jiefangjun tiedaobing shanhou gongzuo lingdao xiaozu, 1984).

82. Several long interviews with Yang Baoqing, Hefei, Anhui, September 2005.

83. Ibid.

84. Ibid.; see also the photographs in *Tiedaobing huace*, 25–29.

85. Several long interviews with Yang Baoqing, Hefei, Anhui, September 2005.

86. Ibid.

87. See, for example, Quanguo tiedaobing lishi wenhua yanjiuhui [National research association on the history and culture of the railroad army corps], at http://www.tdblyxh.com, sections "Tiedaobing: Tiebing houdai" [Railroad corps: The descendants of railroad soldiers] and "Tiedaobing: Tiebing licheng" [The history of railroad soldiers], accessed May 26, 2018; Chen Yuanmou, *Zuori tiedaobing*.

88. Several long interviews with Yang Baoqing, Hefei, Anhui, September 2005.

89. Ibid.

90. In 2003 the China Railways Material Group assumed the tasks of the China Railroad Construction Corporation. "Company Profile," China Railways Material Group, accessed February 15, 2017, at http://www.cccme.org.cn/shop/cccme12475/introduction.aspx, accessed May 26, 2018.

91. See photographs in Martin Parr and Gu Zheng, *The Chinese Photobook: From the 1900s to the Present* (New York: Aperture, 2015), 228–231. I am grateful to the late Raymond Lum for drawing my attention to this source.

92. "Yingxiong xiujian cheng kunlu: Wanshui qianshan zhi dengxian" [Heroes built along Kunming Road: Busy but lonely for thousands of miles], *Renmin ribao*, March 24, 1974, 3.

93. Ibid. The stone stele near Xintiecun railroad station on the Chengdu-Kunming line is an example.

94. For photographs and inscriptions of the monument, see http://blog.sina .com.cn/s/blog_8812919f0101fryo.html, accessed May 30, 2018. Liu Hong, "Kunming xianshang de tie'erju lieshi lingyuan" [Martyr cemetery of the second railroad bureau on the Kunming line] (2014). Liu Hong's father was a railroad soldier whose death is commemorated by the monument.

95. Michael Nylan, "The Power of Highway Networks during China's Classical Era (323 BCE–316 CE): Regulations, Rituals, Metaphors, and Deities," in *Highways, Byways, and Road Systems in the Pre-modern World*, ed. Susan E. Alcock, John Bodel, and Richard J. A. Talbert (Malden, MA: Wiley-Blackwell, 2012), 52–54.

96. Ibid., 54–55.

97. For photographs and inscriptions, see http://blog.sina.com.cn/s/blog _8812919f0101fryo.html, accessed May 30, 2018. Liu Hong, "Kunming xianshang de tie'erju lieshi lingyuan."

98. Guo Qingsheng, "Jianguo chuqi de Beijing shijian" [Beijing time in the early construction of the PRC], *Zhongguo keji shiliao* [Historical materials on Chinese science and technology) 24, no. 1 (2003): 1–5.

99. Ibid., 2.

100. Ibid., 4.

101. *Nü siji* (Female engine driver), film directed by Xian Qun (Shanghai dianying zhipianchang, 1951).

102. Ibid.; for further discussion of representation of the relationship between humans and machines during China's socialist industrialization, see Emma Yu Zhang, "Socialist Builders on the Rails and the Road: Industrialization, Social Engineering, and National Imagination in Chinese Socialist Films, 1949–1965," *Twentieth-Century China* 42, no. 3 (October 2017): 255–273.

103. Ibid.

104. *Tekuai lieche* (Express train), film directed by Zhao Xinshui (Ji'nan: Qi Lu yinxiang chubanshe, 1965), scene at 21:36.

105. YueHan tielu guanliju zongwuchu, *YueHan tielu guanliju zhiyuanlu* [Employee record of the Guangzhou-Hankou Railroad] (n.p., 1939); *JinPu tielu zhiyuanlu* [Record of employees of the JinPu Railroad] (n.p., 1929); Zhonghua guoyou tielu, *JingHu HuHangSong xian zhiyuanlu* [Employee record of the JingHu HuHangSong line] (n.p., 1931).

106. Ji'nan tieluju shizhi bianzuan lingdao xiaozu, *Ji'nan tieluju zhi, 1899–1985*, 21; see also "Xin Zhongguo de diyipi huoche nü chengwuyuan" [New China's first female train attendants], *Renmin ribao*, March 18, 1950, 5.

107. Zhongguo tielu shi bianji yanjiu zhongxin, *Zhongguo tielu dashiji (1876–1995)*, 185.

108. I am grateful to Reylon Yount for pointing me to the text and music of this song. For the song's text, see http://baike.baidu.com/item/%E7%81%AB%E8%BD%A6%E5%90%91%E7%9D%80%E9%9F%B6%E5%B1%B1%E8%B7%91/7170530, accessed May 26, 2018, "Shuji: huoche xiangzhe Shaoshan pao" [Lyrics: The train to Shaoshan].

## 8. Permanent Revolution and Continuous Reform

1. See Yang Jisheng, *Tombstone: The Great Chinese Famine, 1958–1962*, trans. Stacy Mosher and Guo Jian (New York: Farrar, Straus and Giroux, 2012). In his authoritative study Yang puts the number of famine victims at approximately 36 million. See also Cao Shuji, *Da jihuang* [The great famine] (Hong Kong: Shidai guoji chuban youxian gongsi, 2005); Frank Dikötter, *Mao's Great Famine: The History of China's Most Devastating Catastrophe, 1958–1962* (New York: Walker, 2010); Zhou Xun, *The Great Famine in China, 1958–1962: A Documentary History* (New Haven, CT: Yale University Press, 2012); Kimberley Ens Manning and Felix Wemheuer, eds., *Eating Bitterness: New Perspectives on China's Great Leap Forward and Famine* (Vancouver: University of British Columbia Press, 2011).

2. Yang, *Tombstone*, 326; Loren Brandt and Thomas Rawski, eds., *China's Great Economic Transformation* (Cambridge: Cambridge University Press, 2008).

3. Roderick MacFarquhar and Michael Schoenhals, *Mao's Last Revolution* (Cambridge, MA: Belknap Press of Harvard University Press, 2006); Kenneth Lieberthal, *Governing China: From Revolution through Reform*, 2nd ed. (New York: W. W. Norton, 2004).

4. See Rana Mitter, *A Bitter Revolution: China's Struggle with the Modern World* (Oxford: Oxford University Press, 2004), 194–196.

5. Nara Dillon, "The Politics of Philanthropy: Social Networks and Refugee Relief in Shanghai, 1932–1949," in *At the Crossroads of Empires: Middlemen, Social Networks and State-Building in Republican Shanghai*, ed. Nara Dillon and Jean C. Oi (Stanford, CA: Stanford University Press, 2008), 179–205.

6. Jeremy Brown, *City versus Countryside in Mao's China: Negotiating the Divide* (Cambridge: Cambridge University Press, 2012), 29.

7. "Tianjin shi qiansong nanmin wuqian ren huanxiang shengchan" [The city of Tianjin sends back five thousand refugees to return home to engage in production], *Renmin ribao* [*People's Daily*], March 2, 1949.

8. Brown, *City versus Countryside in Mao's China*, 32.

9. Ibid.

10. Kenneth Lieberthal, *Revolution and Tradition in Tientsin, 1949–1952* (Stanford, CA: Stanford University Press, 1980); Dwight H. Perkins, *Market Control and Planning in Communist China* (Cambridge, MA: Harvard University Press, 1966); Kenneth R. Walker, *Planning in Chinese Agriculture: Socialization and the Private Sector, 1956–1962* (Chicago: Aldine, 1965).

11. Brown, *City versus Countryside in Mao's China*, 36, 41.

12. For the *hukou* policy, see Lieberhal, *Revolution and Tradition in Tientsin;* Dorothy J. Solinger, *Contesting Citizenship in Urban China: Peasant Migrants, the State, and the Logic of the Market* (Berkeley: University of California Press, 1999); Mark W. Frazier, *The Making of the Chinese Industrial Workplace: State, Revolution, and Labor Management* (Cambridge: Cambridge University Press, 2002).

13. Brown, *City versus Countryside in Mao's China*, 45.

14. Ibid., 45–46.

15. For discussions, see Yang, *Tombstone;* Cao Shuji, *Da jihuang;* Dikötter, *Mao's Great Famine;* Felix Wemheuer, *Famine Politics in Maoist China and the Soviet Union* (New Haven, CT: Yale University Press, 2014); Brown, *City versus Countryside in Mao's China.*

16. Thus far, the archives of the Ministry of Railways and of individual regional railroad bureaus remain closed to both Chinese and foreign scholars because the railroad sector is classified as strategically important for national defense.

17. Miao Qiulin, *Zhongguo tielu yunshu* [China's rail transportation] (Beijing: Zhongguo tiedao chubanshe, 1994), 43. The original figures given by Miao are 7,000 km, 8,000 km, and 70,000 km.

18. Ibid., 44.

19. Miao Qiulin, *Zhongguo tielu yunshu*, 44–45.

20. Ibid., 45. See also Zhongguo tielu shi bianji yanjiu zhongxin, ed., *Zhongguo tielu dashiji (1876–1995)* [Chronology of Chinese railroads (1876–1995)] (Beijing: Zhongguo tiedao chubanshe, 1996).

21. Miao Qiulin, *Zhongguo tielu yunshu*, 45.

22. Ibid.

23. Ibid., 44–45.

24. For the ideological course of the Great Leap Forward, see Michael Schoenhals, *Saltationist Socialism: Mao Zedong and the Great Leap Forward, 1958* (Stockholm: Föreningen för orientaliska studier, 1987).

25. Miao Qiulin, *Zhongguo tielu yunshu*, 45. See also Zhongguo tielu shi bianji yanjiu zhongxin, *Zhongguo tielu dashiji.*

26. Miao Qiulin, *Zhongguo tielu yunshu*, 45.

27. Ibid.; see also Zhongguo tielu shi bianji yanjiu zhongxin, *Zhongguo tielu dashiji.*

28. Miao Qiulin, *Zhongguo tielu yunshu*, 451–455, esp. 453; see also *Tielu anquan zhidao* [Guide to railroad safety] (Beijing: Tiedaobu chubanshe, 1986).

29. Miao Qiulin, *Zhongguo tielu yunshu,* 48. See also *Tielu anquan zhidao;* Shanghai tieluju zhi bianweihui, ed., *Shanghai tieluju zhi* [Gazetteer of the Shanghai Railroad Bureau] (Beijing: Zhongguo tiedao chubanshe, 2004). For examples of gruesome train accidents, see Dikötter, *Mao's Great Famine.* For discussion, see Yang, *Tombstone;* Dikötter, *Mao's Great Famine,* 272–273.

30. Dikötter, *Mao's Great Famine,* 122. For the content of the 1961 Lushan conference, see Kenneth Lieberthal and Bruce J. Dickson, *A Research Guide to Central Party and Government Meetings in China, 1949–1986* (Armonk, NY: M. E. Sharpe, 1989), 121–122.

31. *Renmin ribao,* see, for example, "1956 nian: Wei dajuejin de yinian" [1956: One big year in the Great Leap Forward], June 27, 1957; "Jishu gexin bixu jianchi zhengzhi guashuai" [Technical innovation must support the leadership of politics], June 11, 1958; "Huoche feichi guo changjiang: Qiannian lixiang cheng xianshi, wanzhong huangteng qing tongche" [Trains speed across the Yangzi River: A thousand-year-old ideal has become reality, millions of people rejoice in celebrating the opening to traffic], October 16, 1957.

32. Miao Qiulin, *Zhongguo tielu yunshu,* 48. See also *Tielu anquan zhidao;* Zhongguo tielu shi bianji yanjiu zhongxin, *Zhongguo tielu dashiji.*

33. Miao Qiulin, *Zhongguo tielu yunshu,* 48–49. See also *Tielu anquan zhidao;* Shanghai tieluju zhi bianweihui, *Shanghai tieluju zhi.*

34. Dikötter, *Mao's Great Famine,* 147.

35. Premier Zhou Enlai and PLA General Zhu De also had their own private train carriages. The carriages are now on display on the outskirts of Beijing in Eastern District Hall of the Chinese Railroad Museum (Zhongguo Tielu Bowuguan Dongjiaoguan), which showcases the history of Chinese engines and trains.

36. Li Zhisui, *The Private Life of Chairman Mao: The Memoirs of Mao's Personal Physician Dr. Li Zhisui* (New York: Random House, 1994), 128–130. In the 1960s Mao received a new East German train equipped with air-conditioning, recessed lighting, and modern appliances (ibid., 129–130, 344–345).

37. Ibid., 267.

38. "Mao's Bloody Revolution Revealed," BBC Five documentary, 2007, hosted by Philip Short, at min. 38:46–39:09.

39. Li, *The Private Life of Chairman Mao,* 278.

40. Ibid.

41. Information from *neibu cankao* [Internal Reference] material, distributed only to high-ranking officials, is quoted by Brown, *City versus Countryside in Mao's China,* 59.

42. Yang, *Tombstone,* 473.

43. Ibid.; see also *neibu cankao,* quoted by Brown, *City versus Countryside in Mao's China,* 59.

44. Yang, *Tombstone*, 50. Yang refers to official party statistics citing the death of 436,882 people in Xinyang prefecture between October 1959 and April 1960. Ibid., 42.

45. Ibid., 473–474.

46. Dikötter, *Mao's Great Famine*, 200–201, 210.

47. Yang, *Tombstone*, 478.

48. Ibid., 202. Similar deployment of thousands of workers for railroad and highway work occurred in Fengyang county, Anhui province (ibid., 275). In Yunnan province, ten thousand rural workers were sent to construct railroads. Dikötter, *Mao's Great Famine*, 62.

49. Dikötter, *Mao's Great Famine*, 138.

50. Ibid., 156.

51. Miao Qiulin, *Zhongguo tielu yunshu*, 52–53.

52. Barry Naughton, "The Third Front: Defence Industrialization in the Chinese Interior," *China Quarterly*, no. 115 (September 1988): 351–386; Covell Meyskens, "Third Front Railroads and Industrial Modernity in Late Maoist China," *Twentieth-Century China* 40, no. 3 (October 2015): 238–260.

53. See Brown, *City versus Countryside in Mao's China*, 179.

54. Zhongguo tielu shi bianji yanjiu zhongxin, *Zhongguo tielu dashiji*, 293–294.

55. MacFarquhar and Schoenhals, *Mao's Last Revolution*, 93.

56. Zhongguo tielu shi bianji yanjiu zhongxin, *Zhongguo tielu dashiji*, 294. The literature on the development of the Cultural Revolution is vast. See especially Roderick MacFarquhar, *The Origins of the Cultural Revolution*, 3 vols. (New York: Columbia University Press, 1974–1997); MacFarquhar and Schoenhals, *Mao's Last Revolution;* Andrew G. Walder, *China under Mao: A Revolution Derailed* (Cambridge, MA: Harvard University Press, 2015).

57. MacFarquhar and Schoenhals, *Mao's Last Revolution*, 110.

58. Zhongguo tielu shi bianji yanjiu zhongxin, *Zhongguo tielu dashiji*, 294.

59. Ibid.; Miao Qiulin, *Zhongguo tielu yunshu*, 53–54.

60. For extensive descriptions, see, for example, Song Bolin, *Hongweibing xing shuai lu: Qinghua fuzhong lao hongweibing shouji* [The rise and fall of the Red Guards: Written notes by the Old Red Guards at Qinghua Middle School] (Hong Kong: Desai chuban youxian gongsi, 2006); Xu Youyu, *1966: Women na yidai de huiyi* [1966: The memories of our generation] (Beijing: Zhongguo wenlian chubanshe, 1998); Gordon A. Bennett and Ronald N. Montaperto, *Red Guard: The Political Biography of Dai Hsiao-Ai* (Garden City, NY: Doubleday, 1971); Rae Yang, *Spider Eaters: A Memoir* (Berkeley: University of California Press, 1997).

61. Yang, *Spider Eaters*, 132–133.

62. Miao Qiulin, *Zhongguo tielu yunshu*, 451–452.

63. Interview, Chen Xinsheng, Shanghai, September 2005.

64. Zhongguo tielu shi bianji yanjiu zhongxin, *Zhongguo tielu dashiji*, 296.

65. Ibid., 297.

66. Martin King Whyte, "Urban Life in the People's Republic, in *The Cambridge History of China*, vol. 15, *The People's Republic of China*, part 2, *Revolutions within the Chinese Revolution, 1966–1982*, ed. Roderick MacFarquhar and John K. Fairbank (Cambridge: Cambridge University Press, 1991), 699.

67. For the fate of the railroad engineer, see Feng Jicai, *Voices from the Whirlwind: An Oral History of the Chinese Cultural Revolution* (New York: Pantheon Books, 1991), 128–145.

68. Interviews with retired workers at Ji'nan Machine Works, May 2005.

69. Interview with Yang Baoqing, Hefei, Anhui, September 2005.

70. Zhongguo tielu shi bianji yanjiu zhongxin, *Zhongguo tielu dashiji*, 297.

71. MacFarquhar and Schoenhals, *Mao's Last Revolution*, 156–161.

72. Ibid., 159–160.

73. "Zhou zongli, Li Fuchun, Li Xiannian zongli jiejian tielu yunshu xitong zaofanpai he junguan hui daibiaoshi de jianghua" [Talks by Premier Zhou, Vice Premiers Li Fuchun and Li Xiannian at the meeting with representatives of the rail transportation network factions and military control], December 28, 1967, Beijing (n.p.: Zhongguo renmin jiefangjun, 6307 budui, 1968), 4. I thank Matthew Lowenstein for making this document available to me.

74. Zhongguo tielu shi bianji yanjiu zhongxin, *Zhongguo tielu dashiji*, 298.

75. Ibid., 298–299.

76. Ibid., 303.

77. Dwight H. Perkins, "China's Economic Policy and Performance," in *The Cambridge History of China*, vol. 15, part 2, 482.

78. Restricted letter from L. V. Appleyard, British Chargé d'Affaires, Peking, to J. D. I. Boyd, Far Eastern Department, August 20, 1968, British National Archives (BNA), FO 21 / 8.

79. Perkins, "China's Economic Policy and Performance," esp. 482–483, 535–536.

80. Miao Qiulin, *Zhongguo tielu yunshu*, 60. According to table 2-4-2, freight car density in 1976 was 8 percent lower than that in 1965.

81. Zhongguo tielu shi bianji yanjiu zhongxin, *Zhongguo tielu dashiji*, 325.

82. *Xuzhou tielu fenjuzhi, 1908–1985* [Gazetteer of the branch railroad bureau in Xuzhou, 1908–1985] (Xuzhou: Xuzhou tielu fenju shizhi bianshen weiyuanhui, 1989), 52.

83. Ibid.

84. Ibid.

85. Dalian jiche cheliang gongchang chanzhi bianzuan weiyuanhui, ed., *Tiedaobu Dalian jiche cheliang gongchang zhi, 1899–1987* [Dalian locomotive and rolling stock factory of the Ministry of Railways, 1899–1987] (Dalian: Dalian chubanshe, 1993), 44; Tiedaobu Datong jiche gongchang zhi bianzuan weiyuanhui, *Datong jiche gongchang zhi, 1954–1985* [Gazetter of the Datong locomotive factory, 1954–1985] (Shanxi sheng: Tiedaobu Datong jiche gongchang, 1987), 30.

86. See MacFarquhar and Schoenhals, *Mao's Last Revolution*, 381–383.

87. Ezra F. Vogel, *Deng Xiaoping and the Transformation of China* (Cambridge, MA: Belknap Press of Harvard University Press, 2011), 97–103.

88. Ibid., 103, and 104–109.

89. Ibid., 104.

90. Ibid., 105.

91. For the full text of Deng's speech, see Deng Xiaoping, "Quan dang jiang daju, ba guomin jingji gao shang qu" [The whole party should take the overall interest into account and push the economy forward], in *Deng Xiaoping wenxuan* [Selected works of Deng Xiaoping], vol. 2, *1975–1982* (Beijing: Renmin chubanshe, 1983). Ibid., 2:4–7.

92. Ibid., 2:5.

93. Ibid.

94. Ibid., 2:6.

95. Ibid.

96. Vogel, *Deng Xiaoping,* 107–108.

97. Ibid., 108–109; MacFarquhar and Schoenhals, *Mao's Last Revolution,* 384.

98. Deng Xiaoping, "Quan dang," 7.

99. Deng Xiaoping, "Dangqian gangtie gongye bixu jiejue de jige wenti" [Some problems outstanding in the iron and steel industry], in *Deng Xiaoping wenxuan,* 2:8–11, at 8.

100. MacFarquhar and Schoenhals, *Mao's Last Revolution,* 386.

101. Deng Xiaoping, "Quan dang," 7.

102. Zhongguo tielu shi bianji yanjiu zhongxin, *Zhongguo tielu dashiji,* 327. The railroad academies were located in Lanzhou, Changsha, Shanghai, and Dalian.

103. Barry Naughton, "Deng Xiaoping: The Economist," in *Deng Xiaoping: Portrait of a Chinese Statesman,* ed. David Shambaugh (Oxford: Clarendon Press, 1995), 83–106.

104. See, for example, Deng Xiaoping, "Dangqian gangtie gongye bixu jiejue de jige wenti," 11.

105. Deng Xiaoping, "Quan dang," 4, 7. Dandong is located in the Northeast along the border with North Korea.

106. Miao Qiulin, *Zhongguo tielu yunshu,* 60, tables 2-4-1, 2-4-2, and 452–453.

107. For a detailed discussion of the political developments, see MacFarquhar and Schoenhals, *Mao's Last Revolution,* 404–412, 416–430.

108. Zhongguo tielu shi bianji yanjiu zhongxin, *Zhongguo tielu dashiji,* 328.

109. Ibid.; Miao Qiulin, *Zhongguo tielu yunshu,* 58–59.

110. Zhongguo tielu shi bianji yanjiu zhongxin, *Zhongguo tielu dashiji,* 329. Out of 156 key enterprises, 40 had to halt production and 33 had to cut it by one-half.

111. Miao Qiulin, *Zhongguo tielu yunshu,* 59.

112. MacFarquhar and Schoenhals, *Mao's Last Revolution,* 420–422.

113. Zhongguo tielu shi bianji yanjiu zhongxin, *Zhongguo tielu dashiji,* 330–331.

114. "'Sirenbang' pohuai tielu yunshu de yige zuizheng" [Destroying railroad transport is one crime of the "Gang of Four"], *Renmin ribao* [People's daily], April 1, 1977.

115. Miao Qiulin, *Zhongguo tielu yunshu*, 61–62.

116. "Liecheshang de tieren" [The iron man on the train], *Renmin ribao*, December 14, 1977; "Cong jieyue zhong duolaile zengchan de zhudongquan" [Taking the initiative to increase production from savings], *Renmin ribao*, November 4, 1977.

117. Miao Qiulin, *Zhongguo tielu yunshu*, 62, 452–453.

118. Zhonghua renmin gongheguo tiedaobu guoji hezuosi, *Zhongguo tielu 2010* [Chinese railroads 2010] (Beijing: Tiedaobu chubanshe, 2009), 4–5; Katrin Luger, *Chinese Railways: Reform and Efficiency Improvement Opportunities* (Heidelberg: Physica Verlag, 2008), 73–75.

119. Zhonghua renmin gongheguo tiedaobu, *Quanguo tielu shike biao: 1985* [National rail schedule: 1985] (Beijing: Tiedao chubanshe, 1985). I thank Nancy Hearst for obtaining a copy of this timetable for me.

120. Zhongguo tielu shi bianji yanjiu zhongxin, *Zhongguo tielu dashiji*, 378.

121. Linda Yin-nor Tjia, *Explaining Railway Reform in China: A Train of Property Rights Rearrangements* (London: Routledge, 2016), 50–51.

122. Ibid., 51.

123. Ibid., 53.

124. Ibid., 53–54.

125. Zhongguo tielu shi bianji yanjiu zhongxin, *Zhongguo tielu dashiji*, 501; Zhonghua renmin gongheguo tiedaobu guoji hezuosi, *Zhongguo tielu 2010*, 8.

126. Tjia, *Explaining Railway Reform in China*, 54.

127. "Zhongguo tielu da guimo gaige lakai xumu," *Zhongguo qingnian bao* [China youth daily], March 19, 2005.

128. "Tielu gaige: Qizhi zhongju, nanti daijie," *Nanfang zhoumo* [Southern weekly], April 21, 2005.

129. Wen Li, "Shei ying shi tielu gaige de zhudao zhe," *Shehui kexue bao* [Social sciences weekly], November 24, 2005.

130. Luger, *Chinese Railways*, 85.

131. See the comparative assessment in ibid., 78.

132. Interview with Liu Ya and Lin Jing, International Department, Ministry of Railways, Beijing, October 19, 2010.

133. Ibid.

134. Ibid. In 2004 only 28 percent of all cargo in China was transported by rail. Luger, *Chinese Railways*, 37.

135. Luger, *Chinese Railways*, 37.

136. Interview with Liu Ya and Lin Jing, International Department, Ministry of Railways, Beijing, October 19, 2010.

137. OSEC Business Network, *China Railway Market Study* (Zurich: OSEC, January 2011), 14.

138. Ibid.

139. See Zhonghua renmin gongheguo tiedaobu guoji hezuosi, *Zhongguo tielu 2010,* 16–18.

140. Wang Xiaobing et al., *Da dao wu xing* [No road to a brighter future] (Guangzhou: Nanfang ribao chubanshe, 2013).

141. For an excellent essay on the rise and fall of Liu Zhijun, see Evan Osnos, "Boss Rail: The Disaster That Exposed the Underside of the Boom," *New Yorker,* October 22, 2012, 44–53.

142. Laney Zhang, "China: Ministry of Railways Dismantled," Global Legal Monitor, Library of Congress, April 4, 2013, at http://www.loc.gov/law/foreign -news/article/china-ministry-of-railways-dismantled/, accessed July 19, 2018.

143. "Guowuyuan jigou gaige he zhineng zhuanbian fang'an" [The plan for reform of State Council organs and the evolution of functions], report presented at the Twelfth National People's Congress, Beijing, March 10, 2013; the report can be accessed at the official government news outlet for the 2013 meeting, at http://www.gapp.gov.cn/ztzzd/rdztl/2013lhzt/contents/3793/144924.shtml, accessed May 27, 2018.

144. Celia Hutton, "Demise of China's Unloved Railways Ministry," BBC News, Beijing, March 13, 2013, at http://www.bbc.com/news/world-asia-china-21756726, accessed May 29, 2018.

145. The rail transportation court for the Ji'nan Railroad Bureau began to operate in 1955. Ji'nan tieluju shizhi bianzuan lingdao xiaozu, *Jinan tieluju zhi 1899–1985,* 661–663. Together with the military tribunal and the maritime court, the railway transportation court was one of three special people's courts under the direct supervision of the Supreme People's Court. See June Dreyer Teufel, *China's Political System: Modernization and Tradition,* 8th ed. (Boston: Pearson Longman, 2012), 178.

146. Laney Zhang, "China: Railway Courts Integrated into National Court System," Global Legal Monitor, Library of Congress, September 12, 2012, at http://www.loc.gov/law/foreign-news/article/china-railway-courts-integrated -into-national-court-system/, accessed July 19, 2018.

147. On railroad workers coping with changing housing arrangements and social identities in the wake of the market reforms in Shanghai, see Lida Junghans, "Railway Workers between Plan and Market," 183–200, in *China Urban: Ethnographies of Contemporary Culture,* ed. Nancy N. Chen et al. (Durham, NC: Duke University Press, 2001), 192–193.

## Conclusion

1. Chen Ji, "Cong Beijing dao Hankou" [From Beijing to Hankou], *Renmin ribao (People's Daily),* January 29, 1950.

2. Luo Wangshu, "Railroads Forecast to Top 3 Billion Trips in 2017," *China Daily*, January 4, 2017, at http://usa.chinadaily.com.cn/china/2017-01/04/content _27855389.htm, accessed July 19, 2018.

3. Lucy Hornby, "Chinese Hit the Road for New Year Migration," *Financial Times*, February 17, 2015.

4. See the description and photographs by the famous photographer Hou Dengke, who worked for the Xi'an Railroad Bureau during his youth. Hou Dengke, *Maike* [Wheat hands] (Shanghai: Shanghai jinxiu wenzhang chubanshe, 2010), esp. 13, 19–25, 186–196.

5. "First Batch of Cotton Pickers Arrive in Xinjiang," *China Daily*, August 21, 2009, at http://www.china.org.cn/china/news/2009-08/21/content_18373410.htm, accessed May 28, 2018.

6. For official information on the Ji'nan Railroad Bureau, see "Zhongguo tielu zong gongsi suoshu qiye" [Affiliated companies under China Railway Corporation], at http://www.tielu.cn/jinan/, accessed May 28, 2018.

7. Ibid.

8. For the organizational structure and a list of railway bureaus under the China Railway Corporation, see the company's website, "Zhongguo tielu zong gongsi (China Railway)," at http://www.china-railway.com.cn/zgsgk/zzjg/201403 /t20140313_42265.html, accessed May 28, 2018.

9. David Faure, *China and Capitalism: A History of Modern Business Enterprise in China* (Hong Kong: Hong Kong University Press, 2006).

10. "Chinese Railways: Chariots of Fire—Will Anyone Take Up Li Keqiang's Offer to Invest?" *Financial Times*, September 18, 2014.

11. Lu Bingyang and Chen Na, "China Rail Corp. Loses 7.3. Billion Yuan in First Half," *Caixin*, September 2, 2016, at http://www.caixinglobal.com/2016-09-02 /100992389.html, accessed July 19, 2018.

12. Zhu Rongji, "Further Speed Up Tibet's Economic Development," in *Zhu Rongji on the Record: The Road to Reform, 1998–2003* (Washington, DC: Brookings Institution Press, 2015), 263–272, at 265–266.

13. Jeffrey Wasserstrom, "NIMBY Comes to China," *Nation*, January 18, 2008, at https://www.thenation.com/article/nimby-comes-china/, accessed July 19, 2018.

14. Jamil Anderlini, "China Sends in Security Forces after Clashes over Rail Plan," *Financial Times*, May 18, 2015.

15. Tony Judt, "The Glory of the Rails," *New York Review of Books*, December 23, 2010, at http://www.nybooks.com/articles/2010/12/23/glory-rails/, accessed July 19, 2018.

16. Zhongguo tielu shi bianji yanjiu zhongxin, ed., *Zhongguo tielu dashiji (1876–1995)* [Chronology of Chinese railroads, 1876–1995] (Beijing: Zhongguo tiedao chubanshe, 1996), 185.

17. Lanzhou tieluju xuanchuanbu, *Fuwu zhinan* [Service guide] (Lanzhou: Lanzhou tieluju, May 2016), pamphlet on board train D2707.

18. *Zhiqing* (Sent-down youth), TV series directed by Zhang Xinjian, 45 parts, first aired on China Central Television, May 29, 2012.

19. Julia Strauss, *Strong Institutions in Weak Polities: State Building in Republican China, 1927–1940* (Oxford: Clarendon Press, 1998); William C. Kirby, "Engineering China: The Origins of the Chinese Developmental State," *Becoming Chinese*, ed. Wen-hsin Yeh (Berkeley: University of California Press, 2000), 137–160; Stephen Halsey, *Quest for Power: European Imperialism and the Making of Chinese Statecraft* (Cambridge, MA: Harvard University Press, 2015).

20. Halsey, *Quest for Power*, 239.

21. Strauss, *Strong Institutions in Weak Polities*.

22. Nathaniel Ahrens, "Innovation and the Invisible Hand: China, Indigenous Innovation, and the Role of Government Procurement," *Carnegie Papers*, Asia Program, no. 114 (Washington, DC: Carnegie Endowment for International Peace, 2010).

23. Robbie Gramer, "All Aboard China's 'New Silk Road' Express," *Foreign Policy*, January 4, 2017, at http://foreignpolicy.com/2017/01/04/all-aboard-chinas -new-silk-road-express-yiwu-to-london-train-geopolitics-one-belt-one-road/, accessed June 1, 2018.

24. On Chinese railroad construction in Africa during the Cold War, see Jamie Monson, *Africa's Freedom Railway: How a Chinese Development Project Changed Lives and Livelihoods in Tanzania* (Bloomington: Indiana University Press, 2009); Wang Xiangjiang, Yao Yuan, and Liang Shanggang, "Spotlight: Africa's First Electrified Railway Embraces Full Chinese Standards," Xinhua, October 6, 2016, at http://news.xinhuanet.com/english/2016-10/06/c_135733876.htm, accessed June 1, 2018.

25. Sun Yat-sen, *The International Development of China* (New York: G. P. Putnam's Sons, 1929 [1st ed., 1922]). Sun Yat-sen's foreword and introduction date from 1921.

# Acknowledgments

This book has been in the making for a long time. I am deeply grateful for all the support and help that I received in researching and writing this study. Because this is the first comprehensive survey of the development of Chinese railroads during the last 120 years in any language, I experimented with how best to approach the topic. Fascinated by studies such as Michael J. Freeman's *Railways in the Victorian Imagination,* I first considered focusing on the cultural and social role of railroads but gave that up when I recognized its limits for discussing railroads from the ground up in different regional contexts. I then pondered for a while writing an economic history to contribute to the literature of assessing and quantifying the economic impact of railroads on China's development during the twentieth century. However, I came to realize that the necessary geographical and chronological coverage and depth made it too challenging for a comprehensive analysis covering the entire twentieth century. I finally decided on an institutional approach to railroad development because it offered the most flexibility and made the project manageable. Although sorting through all these options slowed the project, I am grateful for having had the chance to dive into different lines of research with exciting primary-source material and engage with scholars in different disciplines.

Without a doubt, there are important aspects of Chinese railroad development that this book does not cover at all or addresses only at a superficial level, such as the railroads' role in public finance and the larger political economy or their contributions to the history of technology in China. This book presents an attempt to explore the history of China's long twentieth century through the prism of institutional railroad development by integrating different methodological approaches and literatures into a comprehensive narrative. I hope that in the future historians will rise to the challenge of the existing gaps in our knowledge and continue to research railroads and their development in the larger context of China's historiography.

While researching, writing, and revising this book I have amassed an enormous number of intellectual debts. First of all, I thank Parks Coble, Sui-wai Cheung, Henrietta Harrison, Bill Kirby, Zhang Wei, David Faure, Kubo Toru, Maybo Ching, Madeleine Zelin, Linda Grove, Sherman Cochran, He Xi, Robert Culp, Wen-hsin Yeh, John Wong, Michael Szonyi, Brett Sheehan, Sue Thornton, Alan Rocke, Elisabeth Kaske, Nancy Hearst, Victor Seow, Charlotte Ikels, Nara Dillon, Helen Siu, Walter Friedman, Xavier Duran, Espen Storli, Micah Muscolino, Ezra Vogel, Caitlin Anderson, Maura Dykstra, Rudolf Wagner, Tang Fangcheng, Robert Bickers, Ye Bin, Warren McFarlan, Margherita Zanasi, Robert Gardella, Annie Reinhardt, Philip Thai, Fred Grant, Sun Huei-min, Elchi Nowrojee, Seung-Joon Lee, Matthew Lowenstein, and Ghassan Moazzin for their unflagging support and friendship over the years. They were kind enough to discuss and give guidance on the project at various stages and offered insightful comments on parts of the manuscript that I presented as papers at many conferences, workshops, and seminars. Philip Thai and Ghassan Moazzin generously shared their unpublished research. Elizabeth Perry and Emma Rothschild encouraged me to think about railroads from different perspectives and were most supportive in many other ways as well.

Alan Rocke read the entire manuscript and offered valuable comments from his perspective as a historian of science. Parks Coble, Bob Sullivan, and Ted Beatty read the manuscript at various stages and each time offered excellent feedback. I am also grateful to two anonymous readers for Harvard University Press whose detailed and thoughtful comments helped improve the quality of the manuscript. At Harvard Business School, Walter Friedman was a patient listener and great help to rethink the structure of the book, and Bill Kirby and Warren McFarlan reminded me of the importance of railroads in contemporary China. Mukti Khaire was a wonderful colleague, friend, and ally in research, with whom I discussed this project on our daily walk home across Weeks Bridge in Cambridge. Laura Linard, Mary Lee Kennedy, and Deborah Wallace not only took an interest in my project but, with the rest of the wonderful staff at Baker Library, including Kathleen Fox and Melissa Murphy, offered terrific support and accommodated my many requests with great efficiency and patience. Lin Poping's help was crucial in dealing with the Chinese databases. Caitlin Anderson provided superb research assistance and always stimulating insights as a historian of the British empire. Finally, I am grateful to Jeffrey Williams and Marc Szepan for keeping me up to date on new business and political developments in China's railroad sector.

At Harvard-Yenching Library, the late Ray Lum inspired exciting conversations about the material culture of railroads and their presentation in photography. Annie Xi Wang made work in the special collections a joy and offered much support. At the Fairbank Center's Fung Library, Nancy Hearst was not only an important resource for advice on post-1949 materials but also a wonderful friend, mentor, and a source of constant encouragement when I was stuck with my work. Nancy Hearst, Parks Coble, Bob Sullivan, and Alan Rocke were instrumental in helping the manuscript reach the finish line. At the University of Notre Dame, my colleagues in the History Department, especially Ted Beatty and Bob Sullivan, offered helpful comments and advice, and Karrie Koesel generously shared her insights on contemporary Chinese society and politics. Matt Sisk at the Hesburgh Libraries' Center for Digital Scholarship created the railroad maps with great expertise, patience, and a good sense of humor. I am grateful to Hye-jin Juhn for her superb assistance with library materials; I also want to thank my wonderful colleagues in the Dean's office who cheered me on (and up) during my year as an administrator. Megan Snyder made sure to keep me on track with my deadlines and looked after me in many other ways.

I am grateful to Rob Jennings, head of the group archives at John Swire & Sons Ltd., and to Jeffrey D. Smith at Contact Press Images, for permission to use their photographic images. Portions of Chapters 2 and 5 were first published in "The Making of the Civil Engineer in China: Knowledge Transfer, Institution Building, and the Rise of a Profession," in Robert Culp, Eddy U, and Wen-hsin Yeh, eds., *Knowledge Acts in Modern China: Ideas, Institutions, and Identities*, China Research Monograph 73 (Berkeley, CA: Institute of East Asian Studies, University of California, Berkeley, 2016) and are reprinted here with permission.

This research was assisted by an American Research in the Humanities in China Fellowship from the American Council of Learned Societies, made possible by funding from the National Endowment of the Humanities and the Starr Foundation, allowing me to spend a year in China in 2005 for the collection of archival materials and primary resources. Case Western Reserve University, Harvard Business School, and the University of Notre Dame supported my research with additional funding, for which I am extremely grateful. During 2005 the Shanghai Academy of Social Sciences was an ideal host institution, and I thank Zhao Nianguo, Yang Jian, Li Yihai, Li Li, Xiong Yuezhi, and Zhang Zhongmin for their support and patient willingness to help with research access. In Ji'nan, Yao Dongfang and Liu Yang at the Shandong Academy of Social Sciences were extremely helpful in arranging interviews with former railroad workers and facilitating access to archives and libraries. In Tianjin, Song Meiyun and Jiang Pei kindly introduced me to the archives and libraries at Nankai University and shared their research. In Guangzhou, Maybo Ching, Liu Zhiwei, and Chen Chunsheng were generous hosts during my research visit at Zhongshan University, and this project benefited greatly from their insights as historians and field researchers. Sun Huei-min and Jennifer Ning Chang looked after me as a colleague and friend during visits to Academia Sinica in Taibei. In Tokyo, Kubo Toru, Linda Grove, Takeshi Hamashita, and Tomoko Shiroyama shared their insights and helped with access to research institutions. In Hong Kong, David Faure, Sui-wai Cheung, He Xi, Helen Siu, Angela Leung, and John Wong discussed this research and offered thoughtful feedback. Of course, I am responsible for all remaining errors in the book.

Finally, at Harvard University Press I would like to thank Thomas LeBien for his enthusiasm and professionalism as editor and Kathi Drummy for her patience with me in meeting deadlines. I am also grateful to Simone Fink for her generous friendship and support, which allowed me to pursue my work far away from my family in Germany. From the beginning, my parents took great interest in this project and never wavered in their loving support throughout the years. It is sad that my mother did not live to see the publication of the book, especially as she shared my first unforgettable encounter, as a six-year-old, with the spectacle of trains and passenger crowds in the noisy platform hall of Frankfurt's beautiful nineteenth-century railroad station. Catherine Scallen, Cris Rom, and Alan Rocke have been family to me since I came to the United States, and I cannot thank them enough for their love, understanding, and encouragement. Sui-wai Cheung deserves special thanks as the greatest champion and supporter of my work—I am always grateful for his friendship, sound judgment, and loyalty. Finally, Michael Quirin initiated my interest in railroad studies when he gave me Wolfgang Schivelbusch's *Geschichte der Eisenbahnreise* (*The Railway Journey*) as a send-off gift before I began graduate school. With his premature death, the field lost a gifted intellectual historian of China and a formidable teacher. I know that he would have had many critical comments and astute insights. This book is dedicated to him.

# Index